# HAWTHORN HILL JOURNAL:

## Selected Essays

by
Richard deRosa

Sunnyside Press
Saint Johnsville, New York

Hawthorn Hill Journal: Selected Essays


Library of Congress Cataloging-in-Publication Data

deRosa, Richard, 1944-
Hawthorn Hill journal : selected essays / by Richard de Rosa.
p. cm.
ISBN 978-0-9717214-6-3
I. Title.
AC8.D553 2011
081--dc23
2011035413

Printed and bound in the USA

Sunnyside Press
Saint Johnsville, New York

*for* Sandy

*Contents*


| | | |
|---|---|---|
| | INTRODUCTION | 11 |
| | PREFACE | 15 |
| 1 | One Potato, Two Potato, Three Potato<br>*Mid-winter garden catalogue angst* | 19 |
| 2 | Poetry<br>*Poetry conforms to life's recurring patterns* | 23 |
| 3 | On Being Peculiar<br>*A personal homage to peculiarity* | 27 |
| 4 | Treasuring the Meaning of Things<br>*Investing things with enduring meaning* | 33 |
| 5 | Gentian: Not Sought but Found<br>*An Adirondack walk with my stepdaughter Lisa* | 37 |
| 6 | Here's Looking at You, Butterfly<br>*A chance encounter of a spiritual kind* | 41 |
| 7 | Folding in, Tilling Under<br>*Seasonal transitions* | 45 |
| 8 | Fragments<br>*Making sense of fragmented experience* | 49 |
| 9 | Reflection<br>*Thoughts on past essays* | 53 |
| 10 | Ravens<br>*On Ravens, poetry readings, and time* | 57 |
| 11 | Loss and Gain<br>*On letting go, holding on, and moving on* | 61 |
| 12 | Rain<br>*On the soothing, even spiritual properties of rain* | 65 |
| 13 | Garlic's Up !<br>*Garlic growing pains* | 69 |
| 14 | Chairs and Chekhov<br>*Is an empty chair really empty ?* | 73 |
| 15 | Charity<br>*On taking care of the home ground first* | 79 |

| | | |
|---|---|---|
| 16 | Bach and Butterflies<br>*A butterfly concerto— of sorts* | 83 |
| 17 | Asters, Goldenrod, and Space<br>*A Fall flowerscape and winter reading* | 87 |
| 18 | Transparency<br>*Getting away from oneself for a brief moment in time* | 91 |
| 19 | Reading<br>*Reader's blues and making choices* | 95 |
| 20 | Odds and Ends at Year's End<br>*Taking stock* | 99 |
| 21 | Rules to Live By, or Not !<br>*Who rules the roost?* | 103 |
| 22 | Shifting Gears<br>*Slipping into Spring's groove* | 109 |
| 23 | Compost: Metaphor or Meal ?<br>*In compost is the preservation of the earth* | 113 |
| 24 | Knocking Out Juxtipositions<br>*Meaningful coincidences* | 117 |
| 25 | It's all about Rivets !<br>*Keeping busy helps keeping it together* | 121 |
| 26 | Out Walking<br>*A walk through Nature's gallery* | 127 |
| 27 | Uncertainty's Allure<br>*Beware of hidebound ideologues* | 131 |
| 28 | Rites and Rituals<br>*On the necessity of ritual* | 137 |
| 29 | Of Swallows and Bluebirds<br>*The small stuff matters most* | 141 |
| 30 | Staying Home<br>*Charity does begin at home* | 145 |
| 31 | Beech Leaves<br>*Why is not always the question to ask* | 149 |
| 32 | Images<br>*Enduring imprints of experience* | 153 |
| 33 | Move Them Gooseberries<br>*Nothing in a garden is forever* | 157 |

*CONTENTS*


| | | |
|---|---|---|
| 34 | Contemplation<br>*Thought precedes action* | 161 |
| 35 | Solstice Thoughts<br>*Feeling rather than fact* | 165 |
| 36 | Of Orioles, Swallows, and Time<br>*Pattern and predictability are comforting* | 169 |
| 37 | Of Absence and Presence<br>*She's with me even when she's not* | 173 |
| 38 | Birth Tree<br>*Planting granddaughter Isadora's birth tree* | 177 |
| 39 | Hope is on the Wing<br>*Birdfeeder etiquette as a source of hope* | 181 |
| 40 | More Than Just a Walk<br>*No walk is ever the same* | 185 |
| 41 | The Teaching Life<br>*Teachers do make a difference* | 189 |
| 42 | Idealism<br>*Idealism should trump ideology* | 195 |
| 43 | Of Time and a Grandson's Birth<br>*Planting Grant's birth tree* | 199 |
| 44 | Katie<br>*Katie's birth is a reason not to give up on hope* | 203 |

# INTRODUCTION

Why do we so enjoy reading the observations and reflections of a gifted writer? Perhaps, in part, because it strikes a chord within us and gives voice to something we have witnessed ourselves and have been unable — or unwilling— to articulate. Perhaps, in part, because it provides a fresh perspective on a piece of the world that we have ignored or interpreted differently. Or perhaps, as the author suggests and attributes to C.S. Lewis, we read these reflections and observations because we so desperately want to know that we are not alone.

You are in for a treat as you launch into this selection of essays by Dick deRosa. Whether you are new to his work or one of his loyal fans, these essays will entice and stimulate you to look at the world around you with a different— and a more penetrating—eye. The subject matter for the pieces is broad, indeed—the joy of finding an unexpected stand of cinnamon ferns in the woods; the boyish anticipation of the return of his wife —the love of his life, after a few days' trip out of town; making sense of the world in the wake of September 11, 2001; the simple dignity of two Adirondack chairs sitting unoccupied; the planting of a "birth tree" on the occasion of the arrival of a new grandchild. Whatever his subject, Dick is keenly aware of the natural world around him and the creatures—animate and inanimate—with whom he cohabits that world. He deftly pays homage to his literary and scientific forbears in a way that makes us want to go back to their writings, as well.

I am fortunate to have Dick deRosa as my friend. Since his retirement from teaching, we have shared twice weekly walks around our "neighborhoods" in Otsego County. On these walks, we discuss all manner of things — the joys and anxieties of our lives; the beauty and ugliness in the world; the triumphs and disappointments in ourselves and our families. Stripping it to its essentials, we discuss what it means to be human. On our walks, Dick has been many things for me. He has been a Muse for my mid-life re-introduction to the natural world. He has been a brilliant student of the sounds and shapes and colors that surround us every day. He has been an attentive and active listener and confidant and a marvelous observer of me and his other fellow creatures on the planet. These walks— and talks — have made my life journey richer, indeed.

These essays have that same character. They are honest and unflinching. They give us insight into a man who cares very deeply about the world in which he lives and the people and things he loves. In so doing, I believe we get insight into ourselves and what it means to be human. Reading these essays enables us, for a while, to share that passion —and to know that we are not alone.

— Jim Dalton
Cooperstown, New York

HAWTHORN HILL JOURNAL

# Preface

THIRTEEN YEARS AGO I submitted my first essay to our local weekly newspaper fully expecting a thanks but no thanks response. After peeking at the mid section of the paper for several weeks and not finding my essay I got up my courage and called. The editor listened to my nervous query, and then asked if I had checked out the most recent edition. I had not. She suggested that I look, since they had published the essay and asked that I continue to do so on a bi-weekly basis. Thus began a thirteen-year odyssey that continues to this day, although I now write for a different paper and only intermittently.

They say that English teachers teach because they do not write—or can not. I suspect that in some cases that is true. I started writing essays because I have always wanted to but never could muster the courage to face public scrutiny. I still must push myself through a wall of fear whenever I send in an essay. Publishing this book makes me nervous as hell. It has been a life-long dream, one that I am unwilling to ignore any longer. Readers' responses over the years have been wonderful and the encouragement I have received from family and friends has given me the push that I needed.

We write, I think, because we feel a strong desire to share ourselves with others. I have quoted a line from C.S. Lewis more than once in my own essays. He writes of a young student who asks his country schoolteacher father why people read. His father's response is: we read to know that we are not alone. I also believe that we write for the very same reason. Nothing pleases me more than bumping into a reader on the street who tells me that she had just finished reading my essay and the minute she put it down she thought to herself, "Yeah, I feel that way too." Or, "I have been there, done that." One of my basic convictions is that as individuals we have far more in common with one another than we often realize. And that our salvation depends upon our nurturing this common ground together. It is a theme that often crops up in my writing.

When I started writing I did not give much thought to my writing or thought patterns. After I had published four or five essays, my wife looked up from reading the latest (she is my editor) and said, "You did not end by saying anything about Gabby." Actually, I had not realized that each of the previous essays did end with my commenting on some aspect of our relationship. Thus began a pattern that I have pretty much stuck to. Gabby is my almost fifteen-year-old Sheltie. We have been through a lot together. Readers often ask me how she is getting on. In fact, once while stopping for gas downtown a woman jumped out of her car, asked if I were the guy who wrote those essays, and then asked, " But where is Gabby?" Her disappointment at not meeting Gabby trumped meeting the guy who wrote those essays. Gabby, of course, reacted with indifference.

The road to Hawthorn Hill has been windy, but every turn in the road has brought, for the most part, great joy — and certainly a sense of having lived, to paraphrase Thoreau, well and deliberately. I started writing these essays while we lived in the village of Cooperstown long before we moved up to the hill. I started clearing the land in 1997, the year I completed my doctoral studies, built a small writing shed, put in some gardens, built a small barn, and then convinced Sandy that since the kids had all moved on it was time for us to do so as well. I retired from high school teaching in June of 2005, worked with the contractor building our home for eight months, and in February of 2006 we moved in for good. It has been a labor of love ever since. We have lived in several places, each unique in its own right, and developed lifelong, profoundly inspiriting friendships that endure to this day. But Hawthorn Hill is the home I have always been journeying to. The odyssey ended the day we moved in. These essays chronicle an evolving relationship with this lovely hillside we now call home. Everything I write, everything I think, everything I believe in is in some way connected to and nourished by this place.

I mention several animals in these essays besides Gabby. We buried two much beloved cats, Barney and Beulah, up here on the hill at the base of a lilac bush. I stop at their gravesite from time to time, say something silently to them, and then move on hoping no one is watching. My family figures prominently in several of these essays. They are identified within each.

CHAPTER ONE

# One Potato, Two Potato, Three Potato

*Mid-winter garden catalogue angst*

HAVING SETTLED ON a filing system it looks like I'm ready to make some gardening decisions over the next several weeks; it's crunch time. Catalogues arrive every day and are quickly placed in brightly labeled boxes which include notes, lists, unfiled magazine article, e-mails to and from potential suppliers, loose-leafs updated with current helpful hints, how-to-and-how-not-to bulletins, etc. Doesn't take long for these boxes to fill up. Getting around the study these days is pretty tricky —boxes here, piles there, a wrought-iron dictionary stand to my left, the American Horticultural Society's bulky encyclopedia of garden plants to my right. I've decided that this is the year to master some of those confounding Latin names. Having picked up Latin piecemeal over the years I'm pretty handy with cocktail party and literary Latinisms, but that's about as far as it goes. Actually, I prefer using common names, but since the 'better' catalogues prefer Latin, I'm determined to bone up a bit this year. Professional gardeners claim that using Latin names makes species identification more certain, less prone to error. That may be true, but when I envision a ribbon of blue poppies mingling with crimson sweet peas along the north fence of the vegetable garden it strikes me that *Meconopsis betonicifolia* and *Lathyrus odoratus* just don't hack it. Nope, give me a good common name any day! I'll impress myself with my botanical Latin in private.

This mid-winter gardening stuff is awfully debilitating. In an effort to manage my infamous dilettantism more efficiently I've devoted a portion of each day to reading up a bit on meditation. I figure some Zen focusing might just help me sort through each day's chores a bit more efficiently. It might be worth noting that I've done battle with the Demon of Disorder for years; he always outflanks me. He's just too much for me to handle. There's too much to do, so little time to do it. On the gardening front, my need to have at least one of everything is tempered only by my wife's exercise of her veto power over incursions into the family purse (I've given serious thought to a private gardening slush fund for next year. Another use for my empty coffee can collection.) She's a gadfly, a voice of reason in a wilderness of gorgeous irrationality. I want almost everything in these ostentatiously literary catalogues. They're filled with folk wisdom, warnings about the widening hole in the Ozone layer, tidbits of philosophy, and some pretty dandy phrasings reminiscent of those that used to fascinate me when I read the wine and dance columns in the New York Times. Wine might be described as quietly robust, or a new ballet as passively energetic. One catalogue from a famous grower in Connecticut, whose prices are anything but 'quietly robust,' reminds us that "Plants are as different as people, and like people, they almost always thrive when their basic needs are met." Absolutely! So why doesn't my wife just back off and let me tend to my needs? One potato catalogue from Maine makes me want to chuck village life once and for all, 'lite out for the territories,' and devote my life to potatoes—red ones, white ones, yellow ones, even blue ones! I'm trying to maintain a bit of balance; it's getting hard. One of my favorite mottoes appears in Russell Graham's perennial catalog: "Always treat the earth, our plants, our teeth and our customers with respect." How can I resist a plant purveyor who's concerned about my teeth? My order's in the mail.

Even worse, I'm getting a bit worried about the catalogues that haven't arrived yet! They should have been here by now. It doesn't matter that I have enough catalogues to start a library, especially if I add those of last year's whose replacements have yet to arrive. In deference to an embarrassing attack of angst yesterday, I called a Tennessee daylily grower's 800 number knowing full well I'd get a recorded message. A cowardly act? Absolutely. But it paid off. A 'voice' assured me that the new catalogue would be mailed in March and that if I happened not to be on the mailing list all I need do is leave my name and address and they will send me one. I'm delighted to report that I resisted the temptation to order a catalogue using my daughter's name—just to be safe. I do have a bit of willpower, even though it's seemingly in short supply.

Well, the last of the daylilies are ordered, the potato order went in this morning, the perennial orders are close to completion, and the vegetable order awaits the family comptroller's final review and approval. After all, we're cutting back this year and there must be some sort of reliable system of checks and balances in place. Now, if I could just decide about those peonies, sweet peas, dahlias, and ...

*"I'm particularly fond of birch trees."*

CHAPTER TWO

# Poetry

*Poetry conforms to life's recurring patterns*

I'VE BEEN THINKING ABOUT POETRY a lot lately. While driving home from work this week more attuned to what birds I might spot than anything else, I listened to a wonderful interview on PBS with Jay Parini, the author of a recently published study of Robert Frost. It coincides with my own rather piecemeal rereading of Frost, as well as a decision to spend some time this semester acquainting my students with the work of some of America's great poets. I've been wrestling with some poems of my own of late, so poetry has been on my mind, night and day, at a heightened level of intensity. These wrestling matches with language that poetry requires, whether writing it or reading it, are both exhilarating and often downright depressing. Which is why I ate several pieces of toast topped with marmalade a while ago, checked out daffodil up-pushings in the garden, and decided to tackle this essay while letting the poem I can't quite get a handle simmer on low a while. Maybe it will even go away and leave me alone! Call it a productive form of procrastination, a diversionary tactic I've mastered over the years. I eat when I can't write. And when I write I have to be well fed anyway. Can't win !

My interest this rainy day is the extent to which poetry is a part of our lives. It is a fact that poetry sections in bookstores are treated as if they were mushroom incubators. They're usually tucked away in some dark corner where they won't take up too much space, are infrequently visited, and require little attention by store clerks because few books, if any, are ever removed from the shelves—pretty low maintenance fare! One of the most interesting cultural ironies in this country is that while many claim to love poetry, few ever really read it, or even write it, unless it's in connection with a course, usually required. I'm sure that those of you reading this column who read, and even write poetry, find this hard to believe. But it is true. There are reasons, of course. As Marianne Moore so sagely puts it in her wonderful poem *Poetry*, "poetry should not be so derivative as to be unintelligible." Sad to say, but there is lots of self-serving verse out there. Is now and always will be. To continue with Moore, however, there are also lots of "imaginary gardens with real toads in them." One doesn't have to do much thumbing to stumble on the real.

Getting back to that drive home. While listening to Parini talk about Frost and taking in the sights, I thought about what Guy Davenport calls the "geometry of the imagination," about the topography of the mind, the patterns and rhythms of everyday life, the harmonies of form that constitute Nature. I'm particularly fond of birch trees. Many years ago while working as a freelance photographer I made hundreds of photographs of birch trees. There is something human about them that fascinates me. Look at a lone tree, or a clump for that matter, and you can't fail to notice its unique individuality. Given a clump of three, each will angle upwards towards the light in its own way. Each displays a distinct persona. It is uncanny. On that ride home I saw birch trees forging singular identities, geometry playing itself out in angles, squares, and cones shaped by a thousand-million tree branches, art in the slant of light on clapboards and parked cars, and figures and discernible shapes in cottony clouds tacking along darkening skies. Life, renewed by warmer suns and lengthened days, seemed more awake, more willing and anxious to restart its motors, to call the ancient rhythms into play. I saw people raking lawns, clearing brush, or just standing there out in the light of day looking the world over, opening themselves to Spring's soothing balms. I envisioned myself doing the same things, thinking the same thoughts I've thought every spring and will think every spring of my time on this earth. Life is patterns, rhythms, and replays. We shut things down only to open them up again.

So, when T.S. Eliot suggests that April is the cruelest month, he may have a point. But I'd rather shift with Whitman who in *When Lilacs Last in the Dooryard Bloom'd* reminds us of the loveliness of the lilac, the uplifting deep-woods song of the hermit thrush, and Venus, that ever-bright sky beacon whose light leads us everywhere always. Given the tilt and rotation of the planet, this trinity appears and disappears. But the pattern is there. It is part of the eternal rhythm of things, of what Willa Cather describes as the "immense design of things." Poetry reflects this design. Its patterns are life' s recurring rhythms. Poetry, which all too often is seen as alien to our lives, is in fact life itself. It distils being down to its most musical essences. Time for me to get the taste of marmalade out of my mouth, let the garden alone and get back to work on that poem !

CHAPTER THREE

# On Being Peculiar

*A personal homage to peculiarity*

I'VE NEVER THOUGHT OF MYSELF as particularly peculiar. But several things have happened lately that have caused me pause, made me take a look at myself and think this peculiarity thing through a bit. It started several weeks ago in the gym locker room, of all places. A friend, whose locker is just behind mine, happened to be there. We don't see one another much. When we do bump into one another we catch up a bit. We've chatted about books before, often sharing new titles and recent reading experiences. When he asked me what I've been reading lately I told him of my far-from-completed winter project of reading naturalist John Burroughs's complete works, all twenty-five volumes. Now that I think of it, and spring is here, and I'm quite a few volumes away from finishing that project, it does seem silly to have thought I would be able to tackle such a monumental task over the short space of a mere winter.

Not the first time I've scheduled impossible goals, however. And I'm sure it won't be the last. Keeps life interesting, gives me agendas brimming with impossible possibilities to choose from.

What struck me that morning had to do with my friend's reaction to my reading of Burroughs. As a playfully quizzical smile stretched across his face, he looked up at me and said, "Burroughs, that's pretty peculiar." He could tell from my reaction that I found it pretty peculiar that he found my reading Burroughs 'peculiar.' Thinking he might have touched a cord, he backtracked and said, "Well maybe not peculiar, but certainly different." When I explained that I'd always wanted to read Burroughs in his eccentric entirety and that such a goal complemented my avid interest in American nature writing and natural philosophy, it cleared things up a bit. But I left the gym wondering about his reaction—and about peculiarity in general. I've concluded, to paraphrase Whitman, if I am peculiar, well then, I'm peculiar. But then we all are, aren't we ?

It is probably accurate to suggest that each of us is different, even a bit eccentric. But I suspect that characterizing such differences as peculiarities stretches things a bit. Let's just say that each of us 'gets through time' differently. I've taken quite a bit of ribbing around this house over the years because of some of my 'eccentricities.' I suspect that it's the same in every house and that what we refer to around here as 'family sports' reflects the inner lives of most households. For instance, I'm constantly reminded of what a wonderfully matched pair my dog Gabby and I are. As my wife puts it, we're "two peas in a pod." Gabby's been described as "weird," "strange," and "a pain in the *****? "

On occasion it's difficult to know which one of us is being referred to, man or dog. That gives one an idea of our status around here. But we cope, as they say. Is it odd that a dog will go the other way when called ? Is it equally odd that her owner expects that she'll head over to the neighbor's house instead of heeding his command? Not really. I say come here, and she blithely goes there. It's a ritual we've grown quite accustomed to. Since a reprimand seems silly to me, I just fool her into thinking we're going twenty minutes before I really intend to leave. She disobeys, executes her good-neighbor policy, and gallops back home though the meadow at full speed clearly quite delighted with herself. I give her a big hug, open the car door, and off we go. Dog gurus would scold me for allowing such canine shenanigans. Gabby and I are happy. It works for us, so what difference does it make. Besides, I like a thinking dog, one that exercises a bit of free will! For Emerson it's Man thinking; for me it's Dog thinking.

This is too small a space to catalogue all of my peculiarities, but there is room enough for a few highlights. For instance, I remember coming home from a 'road trip ' several years ago. I'd gone to a famous botanical garden. As is my wont I came away from the gift shop laden with all manner of up-scale, over-priced garden stuff I had absolutely no use for, but had to have. I remember being most proud of the varied gardening sundries I'd gotten my wife. Wouldn't you be excited about having your own Dibble (A sleek bulb-planting tool), as well as some pretty fancy dirt manipulation implements and designer hand cream? Take my advice, guys. Next time, leave the Dibble on the shelf next to the orchid food and cactus juice. That went over about as handsomely as the kitchen 'theme' for my wife's last birthday. Wouldn't you be delighted to receive a heavyduty, state-of-the-art Bundt pan for your birthday from your loving husband and an equally impressive shiny metal colander from your son? Like father, like son! Train 'em early I say. Reaction? I knew your father was peculiar, don't tell me it's catching !

There are other things I do that might seem peculiar, like getting to airports hours before check in time. It's not that I'm afraid of missing the plane. Nope. There's all that traffic and the possibility of jams, flat tires, accidents, etc. As I always put it, one must "allow for the unpredictable." Then there's Gabby's apricot. I have the same very healthy cereal mix every morning, topped with several dried apricots. She dutifully waits at my feet for her apricot, always followed by a medium-sized dog biscuit. When we're away and she stays with a friend, her travel pack always includes her morning apricot and biscuit. We are two peas, since I do the same for myself. I don't have an American Express card, but I never leave home without an ample supply of breakfast rations. If l can't start my day with my own apricot-raison-cereal-flax seed mix I'm in existential trouble right off the bat. Gabby does not like being off her feed, and neither do I !

If these sorts of behaviors remind you of someone, I'll be quite pleased. I justify my peculiarities by assuming we all have them. I hope that is the case. If not, then I really am a bit off-kilter. Meanwhile, I'll continue giving my kids books they probably won't read, will hunt for birds and wildflowers that I probably won't find, will find joy in the year's first sighting of a White-throated sparrow, and will generally be on the lookout for anything just plain interesting or new. When it comes to gifts I'll stay clear of garden and kitchen themes. But when it comes to reading I'll stick with Burroughs. Reading him makes me peculiarly happy !

CHAPTER FOUR

# Treasuring the Meaning of Things

*Investing things with enduring meaning*

THE POET WILLIAM CARLOS WILLIAMS repeated this phrase often when theorizing about poetry: "No ideas but in things." It has been on my mind a lot lately. Not because it seems to be an accurate observation about poetry, but because it helps me to understand myself a bit more clearly. For whatever reason, and who knows why mind and memory work the way they do, I've been quite preoccupied with some of the stuff that clutters my study and barn. I'm the son of a pack rat and if the acorn really doesn't fall far from the tree, then I'm doomed. The problem is where to put it all. I solve it by stacking, tacking, shoving, pushing, and generally making room where I can. Above my desk are four rather long shelves filled with books. Trouble is, I can't see or get at any of them because they are hidden behind pictures, mementos, birthday and father's day cards that go back more than twenty years, empty honey jars from around the globe, stones from beaches from here to Thailand—and on it goes. And that just accounts for a few shelves. Try and picture the whole study, which isn't all that spacious to begin with. I've waged an unsuccessful campaign to be allocated a larger space. But, "she who must be obeyed"—at all costs—has consistently vetoed even the most thoughtful of my plans for taking over another, larger room. So I'm stuck. I have to make do.

If the shelves are cluttered, well then, there are the windows. One hasn't been open in at least five years, because the three plants that have lived there are so thickly interwoven and splayed against the window that only a machete could do the job. It's just not in me to do that. Watering them, by the way, is a real challenge. It's impossible to see where the pots are, so I just stick the nozzle of the watering can in the general area, tilt, pour, and hope for the best. When water trickles along the floor I ignore it and hope the cat will wake up thirsty. It's too tight a spot for Gabby. The other window is open, but getting it closed when it rains or is windy or cold is a real chore. A plant hangs on either side of the sash, but each has spread so much that the entire window is framed in green. The sill is cluttered with old bottles, driftwood, brass cans, and miniature wooden bowling pins I found beneath our barn last summer. Frankly, if l hadn't pulled up the barn floor last summer and started digging around I'd not be in as quite the fix I am now.

I suspect that most of us live atop piles of buried artifacts and don't even know it. In the old days people had personal landfills; now they have personal trainers and pizzas. Trash was either burned or buried under new construction sites. My barn, as is probably the case with scores of structures in the village, sits on an archaeological site of significant import, especially to this junk man. My mother may have been right when she suggested that I seemed ideally suited for either lobster fishing or junk collecting. Most of the treasures I pulled out of the dirt last summer (bottles, pots, pans, hinges, tin boxes of all sizes and shapes, petrified animal carcasses, rusted coils of wire, etc.) are still piled up in the barn awaiting cataloguing. But a lot has found its way into the house and some is starting to make its way to the hill. For instance, an old rusted hand pump will soon inaugurate our 'found sculpture' collection. As soon as I've got the generator going I'll drill a hole in a large Locust stump and stick the pump in it, pipe first, and there it will sit. It may not be a Calder or Smith, but the price is sure right.

What is it about all these things? Why do we cherish them? I think my father's pipe holds the answer. I never knew my father; he died when I was two and a half years old. I have a few pictures, some of his books, even several letters he wrote to my mother when courting her. And because be was an architect of some note, I have architectural drawings, plans, company records, etc. I have lots of his 'things,' but the pipe is special. I'm told that he carried it with him everywhere. He filled it, emptied it, perhaps even puffed on it while sitting there in our living room watching me crawl towards him across the Persian rug in his study that is now mine. When I touch the pipe I feel as if I'm touching him. When

I look at it I feel as if he is close by, almost within reach. Clearly, it has a meaning beyond itself. When I look at the honey jar my stepdaughter sent home from New Zealand and I think of her thinking of me. So, we keep and cherish these tangible objects because they animate our minds and our memories and give us meaning. Meanwhile, there's plenty of room for the pipe. It is one thing I will never part with.

CHAPTER FIVE

# Gentian: Not Sought but Found

*An Adirondack walk with my stepdaughter Lisa*

SOME PEOPLE SEARCH for that pot of gold at the end of a rainbow. I'll take a gentian over a pot of gold any day of the week. For that matter, a stand of Cinnamon ferns, a blanket of ground cedar dappled by early morning sunlight, or the chitter-chatter of red squirrels will do the trick just as well. Several days ago my stepdaughter and I hiked a lovely trail in the southern Adirondacks. The trail parallels three small lakes, ending at Murphy Lake, approximately 3.6 miles in from the trailhead. It is a pleasant walk over softly undulating terrain. The forest floor is covered with ferns, horsetails, ground cedar, and fall wildflowers.

I was especially pleased to see so many young Beech trees pushing their way up into the sunlight. It augurs well for the deer that love to browse on their succulent tips, and for the trees themselves. They've had a rough go of it as a result of a rather devastating beech blight that took a pretty heavy toll some years back. One of the most reassuring aspects of nature's personality is its resilience, its uncanny way of overcoming so many uninvited incursions into its space.

We walked in silence most of the time. Conversation gets in the way. We shared a thought or observation now and then. But walking requires concentration. It requires solitude. It requires that it be quiet enough to hear one's inner voice as well as one's footfalls and the forest's lovely voices. The kek-kek-kek of a raven is not an intrusion; it is just one instrument playing its part in that most natural of all symphonies. In its element it is beautiful. So we walked.

And as we walked my mind led me on quite a chase. In one of his books, *Light in August* I believe, William Faulkner reminds us that memory is so powerful because it never lets us forget what we think we've forgotten. He is so right. Sit and meditate for a spell or take a long walk and you'll discover how vast a universe the mind is. There are times when I'm walking or sitting that I am so overwhelmed by my mind's storage and recall capacities that I have to get up and dig a hole or hammer something together just to clear the air. But most of the time it is pretty darn pleasant and as you walk you discover yourself making sense of seemingly disparate experiences or finally understanding something that has eluded your cognitive grasp for some time. What's best is when you make sense of something you'd forgotten about. There you are rounding another curve in the trail or mounting the summit of a steep hill and suddenly the solution or answer pops into your head, clear as day. It's a wonderful feeling, one made more so because it has snuck up on you out of nowhere. The mind works at its own mysterious pace. We never know when it is going to break its silence to allow us the luxury of fitting a missing piece or two together. It is best to keep walking.

While walking the other day I thought of Thomas Jefferson, who advised a young ward to grab a musket and take a brisk two or three hour walk every day. I thought also of my friend 'Walkin' John' from Cherry Valley who died several years ago. John walked everywhere. When his legs gave out on him in his later years he'd accept a ride to town or the hospital, but always begrudgingly. He hated the cramped feeling of a car. He loved the outdoors. Because he walked everywhere he knew the woods and fields and hills of Cherry Valley better than anyone. He taught me a great deal and while we did not see a lot of one another, I valued his considerable wisdom. Not a formally educated man, John always struck me as a true philosopher. He walked, kept his eyes and ears open, and let his mind do the rest. Emerson is correct when he suggests that books are for a scholar's idle times. John's book was nature and he read her with a keen, discerning eye. I thought about a great deal more that day. I've forgotten most of it, but the few fragments that remain have given me a great deal to toy with.

As we walked the last few feet of the trail to Murphy Lake I looked to my left and saw a stand of blue gentians. I hadn't been looking for them. I hadn't been looking for anything in particular. In a sense, they found me. Their sky-blue color is spectacular. I'm miles away now, but I feel as close to them as if I were there. As we sat down on a boulder to eat lunch, I said to Lisa, wouldn't it be great if we saw a loon. Not five minutes later the dark velvet head of a loon pops quietly through the still black waters of the lake. It doesn't get any better. I have good walking shoes and a stout walking stick. I'm going to make them work a bit harder from now on.

CHAPTER SIX

## Here's Looking at You, Butterfly

*A chance encounter of a spiritual kind*

THERE IS CERTAIN CRISPNESS to the morning light as it slants through the trees these days. It is sharper, colder. The way it settled on a bluebird box this morning caught my eye. The box, a weathered gray, sits atop a cedar post at the low end of the meadow. The bluebirds that nested in it earlier this summer are long gone. Their little ones grew up, flew about the place quite noisily for several weeks, and then took off for parts unknown. The house, unoccupied since then, seems to enjoy the solitude, seems to stretch its tightened, weatherworn skin a bit more freely now. In fact, watching it as I did this morning, it seemed as if it were smiling. It had an unnatural buoyancy about it. Walking in the woods with Gabby a short time later, oddly enough thinking about Emerson's notion of correspondences, Andrew Wyeth popped into mind. It occurred to me that the close correspondence between the sun-drenched box and the light that animates so many of Wyeth's weathered surfaces acted as an unconscious catalyst for my reaction to the bluebird box. So many of his worn and textured surfaces shimmer in the same kind of animating cold light that bathed the bluebird box.

Such shifts in the nature of things occur with predictable frequency all year long. But there is a slice of time between seasons where Nature frets a bit uncertainly as the transition gets underway. We feel it too. One morning it is chilly enough for a sweater; the next morning summer is still in the air. It is tough to know just how to react. It is like packing for a vacation. If you are like me you pack for imagined contingencies, hope for the best. But butterflies don't pack. They just up and head for Mexico when our northern nights are a bit too chilly. Take the Monarch butterfly I stumbled on while rummaging through a squash vine laden trellis yesterday morning. At first I thought he might be dead and somehow stuck to the winter squash blossom he appeared glued to. I touched his tightly folded wings softly with the tip of my forefinger. He shivered ever so slightly. Alive! I touched him several more times, even stroked the soft downy surface of his wings between my thumb and forefinger. No movement at all. In the past when I have tried to get close to a butterfly, it's always, as Emily Dickinson so deftly puts it, been able to "off Banks of Noon/Leap plashless ... " into thin air and escape my grasp. This guy, wings folded like a jet plane parked on the hangar deck of an aircraft carrier, had no immediate travel plans. It had been a cold night, one where the mercury dipped pretty close to freezing. My guess is he had spent a pretty uncomfortable night and didn't plan on any swimming through air, plashless or otherwise, until his frail little body thawed out a bit. I can't imagine what he thought when I took off my glasses, bent down, and peered at him at eye level, our eyes not three inches apart. Ever looked a butterfly in the eye? I don't know what he thought, but no one will ever convince me that at whatever levels each of us operates, we didn't connect. Gabby and I returned later, after the sun had come up. Gone.

The signs of shifting seasons are everywhere. Maples are topping off; leaves flutter singly and in bunches. The forest floor, for a short time, is a magic carpet of lively colors. Nights get gradually colder, squirrels start storing acorns and hickory nuts in the damnedest of places, hawks and geese start migrating southward, and up on the hill the chickadees start hanging around their winter feeding station just to let me know that it's time for me to hang out the feeders. They'll have to wait for a while. Indian summer is just ahead and there is still plenty of natural food around to fill their bellies. They know I won't let them down.

It is the quality of light, though, that signals the shift for me. It fills the air differently. It is as bracing as the night air. It sculpts and hardens things; its warming, softening days are on the wane. It quickens the pace, awakens the soul to winter's sleep. It feels right.

*Getting the hill farm ready for winter sleep*

CHAPTER SEVEN

# Folding in, Tilling Under

*Seasonal transitions*

SUMMER IS OVER. It is not a bad thing. There is a chilly lilt to the air, mornings are nippy, and slipping on a light sweater every morning feels right and good. Just as the narrator in Robert Frost's poem *After Apple-Picking* is "overtired of the harvest I myself desired," I too am pleasantly overtired, anxious to make the transition to another season and another state of mind. Bringing home a tub of sunflower heads this morning made me sharply aware of my own inner shiftings. It seems to come out of thin air, not unlike the knife-like precision with which understanding, often elusive, slices its way into consciousness.

We've been spending a great deal of time recently getting the hill farm ready for its winter sleep. It is a pleasurable time of year. Perhaps one of my greatest joys is cleaning up the vegetable garden. There are stakes to be pulled out of the ground, pole bean teepees to dismantle, temporary fences to be removed. A jungle awash in plenty just several short weeks ago now takes on an eerily barren look. No sooner have I cleared the place out, lugged piles of tangled pole bean and tomato vines and thick sunflower and broccoli stems to the compost heap, than I stand there, leaning on my pitchfork, envisioning next year's garden. As usual, mistakes of placement and quantity have characterized this year's layout. Some people design their gardens. I've never been able to do that. I start with a vague preconception that takes shape as I work. By the time I start digging in the dirt a creative force akin to a juggernought storms in and takes over. Sandy is right. I've put things too close together again. There have been times this summer when we really needed a machete, not picking fingers and clippers. So, I stand there planning a garden open and accessible in the middle, with larger things, especially tomatoes and pole beans, planted along the perimeter fence where they can be attacked from both sides. If only I weren't so spatially challenged! Things look so far apart when planted as seeds and seedlings in early spring.

In addition to cleaning up, we've done a lot of tilling. We've put in some new perennial beds, split the rhubarb and moved it to a sunnier, more spacious location, and generally spruced things up a bit. Most of the woodland paths have been cleared and stand ready for next spring's plantings of ferns, wildflowers, and medicinal herbs. We still have to take some trees down, but we assuage our guilt by planting several more in their stead. The thirty-foot tall maple that shades the lower vegetable garden and new herb bed has to go, but just below it we'll be starting a new apple orchard, so its ghost will be able to savor the scent of apple blossoms and ripe apples for some time to come.

Gabby loves all these end of season chores. She especially loves snuggling down into freshly tilled dirt. At times I just stop whatever I'm doing and watch her lie prostrate in the rich, brown earth, happy as can be. For a dog, life doesn't get any better. I've often been tempted to join her, but since I have as well-programmed a super-ego as anyone, I've never been able to completely let go and slap myself down alongside her. Someone may be watching! One of these days. The older I get, the less I care about propriety anyway.

One chilly day will fold into the next, the trees will lose their multi-colored tresses, the resident bird population will reduce down to the normal flocks of chickadees and juncoes, and Gabby and I will be plodding through knee-deep snow just to get to the house so we can feed the birds and enjoy it all for a spell. There will come a time, along about January's inevitable thaw, when we'll be fooled by warm days and unseasonably cheery birdsong. We'll taste spring. Our juices will start to flow. We'll have to pack it in again for a while, but we'll know that another season of gardening mistakes and miscalculations is around the corner. As the poet Gary Snyder puts it, we'll have to get our deskwork done. Come spring and summer there's just too much farm work to do. Staying indoors is downright heretical !

CHAPTER EIGHT

# Fragments

*Making sense of fragmented experience*

IT HAS BEEN A WEEK of reflecting on fragments, what the poet William Wordsworth refers to as "spots of time." I suspect that what they have in common is a collective calling to thought. An art critic, whose name escapes me at the moment, wrote in an interesting discussion of Cézanne's painting that "art is the formal ordering of a private excitement." It has always struck me as being an enticingly concise characterization. So I guess what I've got here are several private excitements not yet willing to be shaped into some sort of form. They are too actively alive in my mind, a bit too immediate. It is as if in each case the private excitement continues to have some sort of inner resonance that effectively prohibits any sort of formal ordering process. Here they are:

Last week while driving north on County Route 31, I stopped at a small pond that always harbors large flocks of migrating geese. They seem to love this idyllic dent in the landscape. Who knows how many flocks, often numbering into the hundreds, alight there for a brief respite before taking wing and heading to warmer southern climes. Every few years they share the pond with snow geese. White birds with ink-dipped wing feathers, they fill one with a sense of awe, a kind of aesthetic excitement. This year several large flocks have lingered on the pond, often mixing with their Canada geese brethren. In the right morning light the gradations of tone from white to gray are marvelous. A beautiful sight as the early morning winter sun slips curtly across the horizon. As the sun lofts itself skyward, it seems a canvas splattered with gilded specks of white and gray. This morning, just after stopping the truck and turning off the engine, the entire flock of snow geese uplifted into thin cool air, seeming to hover motionlessly over the sun-glinted waters. It was as if they were suspended in space, as if a well-wisher at a wedding had thrown a handful of white confetti into the air that just sat there in space, suspended for several moments in time, countless motes of unearthly brilliance riding the invisible winds. I too felt frozen in time. And just as quickly as they launched themselves into flight, they disappeared over the adjacent hillside. Out of sight, but not out of memory. They've been flying in and about the deepest reaches of my mind ever since. They still light up the darkest corners of my mind.

The hill farm is abed now. There isn't much to do. Which is good. It is time to appreciate the place in a different way, to feel its contours and shapes from a slightly altered slant of mind. Several days ago Gabby and I did our loop walk, passing our beloved cats' grave site, then walking down the hill towards the new perennial beds, now covered with a thick blanket of hay mulch, themselves enshrouded in white. The hay is spread unevenly, a tuft sticking up here, a depression there. I can see that the moles are already at their winter work. As my eyes slid down the hill I felt as if I were looking at human shapes covered in thin mantles of white silk—asleep, motionless, otherworldly. I felt a strange sense of ease, of peacefulness. Gabby too felt something. She sat motionless too, looking off into the distance with a knowing, prescient look in her eye. I suspect we both felt a sense of awe, a sense that we'd shared a rather mystical experience. I sit here writing looking for words while seeing those shapes and wondering how it might be possible to do justice to both. At this point, when the private excitement is still so very much alive within I just have to ride it out for a while. Meaning will come in time. I am a patient waiter.

Yesterday when we did our loop walk I noticed scuff marks on the path. Clearly, some sort of primal battle had taken place—and quite recently. Feathers were strewn about. Who knows what happened. It is clear that some feathered creature, probably minding its own business and caught unawares, bit the dust. I suspect there are owls on the prowl and I've seen tracks often enough, especially during the winter, that indicate the presence of coyotes, foxes and dogs of various sizes.

We're neighbors. The predator's job of work is predation; I've no quarrel with that. It is the way things are. Nature has its ways; it protects itself and keeps its balance according to its own laws. No, what sticks with me is the image of the fight. Of the screams and squeals the dying animal must have uttered—as best it could. I think of life and death; of justice and injustice. I think of the cascading rush of oppositions that characterize human and natural life, of the ways in which nature maintains its often very terrifying balancing act. I guess what bothers me most is that this battle played itself on my homeground. The irony is that as helpless as I feel, I feel equally comforted by the fact that Nature has all well in hand. A part of me wants to feel good about that. It's just the pain , the suffering, and the invisibility of it all that tears me up.

We took a walk today and all was well. The chickadees were noisy as ever. Blue Jays darted here and there uttering their winter calls. Gabby feasted on the deer viscera left by a hunter in a neat pile atop the back hill. I dreamed of next year's gardens. But the images of the spectral white geese, the slumbering shades, and the invisible combatants remain. Still excited.

CHAPTER NINE

# Reflection

*Thoughts on past essays*

A WEEK INTO THE new century things look pretty good. The truck is running fine, Gabby and Buckley passed their annual physicals with flying colors, Sandy and I still have a lot to talk, argue, and laugh about at the breakfast table, our children seem to be ensconcing themselves comfortably in their varied lives, and the weather hasn't been bad at all. In fact, we find ourselves lamenting the absence of just a little bit of snow, since we love X-country skiing and wouldn't mind getting a bit in before heading to Canada for a more ambitious bit of trekking in mid-February. Normally when I put off servicing the snow blower I pay dearly; not so this year. I got it out to the shop late, picked it up last week, and now it sits there patiently awaiting its first call to winter duty. A large broom and light shovel have sufficed thus far. I know it can't last. Because of the mild weather of late we've taken a lot of walks along backcountry roads. While walking with Gabby yesterday I reflected a bit on what I've written in these columns this year and what I've learned from it all. A lot, actually.

It turns out that my *I Need a Truck* column elicited quite a bit of sympathy. One person stopped me and asked me why I didn't just go out and buy one. She seemed to think it was that simple. I started feeling a bit guilty after several people suggested that my wife Sandy was just downright mean to deprive me of something so apparently necessary to my spiritual well-being. Several months later, after *A Truck at Last* appeared, I'd hear about it in the strangest of places. While taking a shower at the gym several weeks ago, an acquaintance walked in, spotted me through the mist, and said, "Got a truck I see." I responded in my usually chatty way with "yup." It also happened while in the sauna several days later. I'm not a sauna talker. I like to sit there and mind my own business. And, I must confess, grumble to myself about the dolts who douse the electrical elements with wintergreen scented water in clear violation of the rules. Besides, I'm not much of a talker anyway, certainly not in such a place where far too much is, so to speak, 'out there.' I also don't wear my glasses in the hot house, so all I've got to go by is voice recognition. Anyway, well into one of my pseudo-Yoga meditations that day a friend came in, sat down, and said, "finally got a truck; how'd you wangle that?" I took on my uncharacteristic macho persona and said, " Well, a man's gotta do what a man's gotta do." He nodded in agreement and we went our separate sauna ways.

By the way, thank God Sandy's around to keep me in check. One of the reasons we get on so well is that we're so different— and have a great time kidding one another about it. I want it on the record that she never prevented me from getting a truck. She simply exhibited superior wisdom and self-control when it came to dealing with the reality that we just couldn't afford one no matter how much I wanted one. If I went out and got all the toys I'd like to have we'd be in deep ***. No, it is just a question of good sense winning out over nonsense. Which is why despite it all we still have a good credit rating. We do get into curious discussions about the nature of reality. I'm the type who sees debts as interesting, rather abstract and existentially questionable phenomena. Sandy sees them in rather concrete terms. I often don't see them because I just choose not to look at them. I'm not in charge of paying bills and haven't been for some time now. It is the only reason we've remained solvent over the years.

Perhaps one of the most interesting column-related things that happened this year occurred one late fall afternoon when a truck pulled up the hill driveway and stopped not far from where I happened to be planting an heirloom apple tree. A young woman got out, shielded her eyes from the sun, and said, "Are you the guy who writes those columns for *The Freeman's Journal*?" Well, it happened to be fellow columnist Mary Ashwood. We'd never met and she happened to be driving by, saw the sign, and thought she'd say hi. We had a nice chat, I showed her around, and she said some very nice things about the column. The funniest thing though is that she admitted she had this picture of what I looked like and I didn't fit the image at all! She had envisoned a short, wiry little guy. Instead, she got me—anything but wiry. I'd like to think I'm taller than I am. I'm not. And I'm certainly not wiry. I hated it when my mother used to take me shopping and head right for the 'husky' section. What damage mothers do. Anyway, Mary and I had a nice chat and I've thought about it a lot since. When I read her excellent columns I can see the real her behind them.

It continues to be a great deal of fun writing these essays. I've written about cats, dogs, gardening, kids, poetry, peculiarity, fences, things, and walks in the woods. I'm interested in what I've referred to elsewhere as the "existential aspects of everyday life." The little things interest me most because they are what tie our lives together. An English schoolmaster once told his son that "we read to know that we are not alone." I guess I write just looking for some company as I travel through time.

CHAPTER TEN

# Ravens

*On Ravens, poetry readings, and time*

I'VE ALWAYS BEEN INTRIGUED by time and black birds. With respect to the former, it's really Reynolds Price's fault. In his very fine novel *The Surface of the Earth,* the narrator finally tracks down the father who had abandoned him many years earlier. He asks his father what he's been up to all those years. His terse answer is intriguing: "Just getting through time son, just getting through time." Those words have haunted me ever since. Not in a scary way, but in the way that an interesting idea or concept captures the imagination and doesn't let go. It is a kind of tender gripping of the intellect. We undergo personal paradigm shifts all the time. And it usually has little to do with big things or ideas. Something just happens that gets us to thinking. The father's response in the Price novel has changed the way I think about time and, ultimately, life. It is not depressing, this notion of time. Rather, it reminds me that it is the individual's responsibility to get through time in as interesting a fashion as possible. In other words, the way that one gets through time is one's own fault.

I spend a great deal of time with teenagers. The one thing that they do that I've never gotten used to is complain about having nothing to do. Anybody who has taught high school as long as I have certainly must have developed a healthy aversion to all forms of the noun 'boredom.' I know I have. It is one of the few complaints that I have little patience with. My wife Sandy tells me that I don't understand because I probably skipped over those years, at least existentially. Perhaps.I do remember being less than intrigued by a teacher or a course now and then, but boredom never entered into the equation. There always seemed to be something to do. A book to read, a thought to think, a walk to take. I was never much for formal productions of any kind, so I lived my own theater and still do. As odd as it might sound, I love poetry but hate poetry readings. I love Shakespeare, but I'd rather read Hamlet sitting on the porch up on the hill than see it performed anywhere. As a friend says, there's no accounting. Guess not. At any rate, there is nothing more boring than hearing about how miserably bored someone is. My stock response is always the same; boredom is a self-inflicted disease. It requires some effort to get off one's dull duff !

Which leads me to ravens, via black birds. I blame it all on Wallace Stevens, whose poem *Thirteen Ways of*

*Looking at a Black Bird* not only altered my perception of any black bird that I might bump into, but effectively shattered my preconceptions of what it means to see and experience anything. For instance, when I see several crows clustered about winter-bare branches these days they transcend their mere crow-ness. They become analogies, metaphors, signs. Crows aloft overhead and dancing with the wind become emblems of a host of other things. So, when that lovely pair of ravens flew over our heads last week, Gabby and I were filled with an ineffable sense of awe.

We were just out walking through the snow. We never know what we're looking for. We just walk, look, think and do a bit more walking. I stopped to make a photograph of a dark evergreen woodfern whose fronds were spread fanlike against the white crystalline snow. I clicked the shutter and noticed Gabby looking up. Ferns don't excite her too much. I looked up too. There they were. A pair of ravens riding the high winds. They were having a great time up there in the ether, tumbling, wheeling about, a glancing ever so gentle touching of their wingtips from time to time. You had to be there.

I saw more than two black birds gliding along invisible wind currents. I saw the movement of time, the poetry of pure motion, and the loveliness of pure play. As Gabby and I make our dash through time we try to keep alert. It's about all we can do. You never know when you'll be standing foot deep in a snowy wood, look up, and see two winged blotches of black slicing effortlessly through time. I need to find a reliable wing maker.

CHAPTER ELEVEN

# Loss and Gain

*On letting go, holding on, and moving on*

LIFE'S UNCANNY WAY of achieving some sort of balance in the conduct of its daily affairs is astonishing. It calls little attention to itself. It simply gets up in the morning, if it ever sleeps, and gets things done. We are caught up in its alternating rhythms. We live our lives enshrouded in mystery, but that is one of life's wonders. Things happen. We think about them, feel them deeply, and at times try to describe what has happened to us. It is not easy. Language never quite measures up, even when it is beautiful. As Alexander Pope writes, "language is the dress of thought," but even when decked out in its Sunday best it never quite hits the mark. It is always an approximation, a working compromise. But it is all we have and we need be thankful for it. So, here I sit looking for ways to dress up an experience or two that I had recently, both unique and terribly common. A son's moving on, a father's recognition of the need to loosen the ties that bind while at the same time never spooling out the line completely. I'm a lousy fisherman, so you can imagine the trouble I'm having attending to two lines simultaneously.

Even though it is a bit out of my way, I always stop by the hill on the way to work just to check things out. It seems to give me the spiritual push I need. Sometimes I just sit quietly for a few minutes. When the driveway is clear I'll head up, park, and take a brief walk. Several days ago I just sat there. Too much snow on the ground anyway. I needed a few minutes to collect my thoughts and get around an event that made that day quite memorable. I had said my farewells the night before. It happened to be the morning of the day that my son would be leaving home to start a new life and job elsewhere. That very natural time had come. Time to move on. These rites of passage are natural, right, and true. But knowing that doesn't make it any easier. There is no language adequate to the task of describing how I felt sitting there at the bottom of the driveway that morning. A bit empty, a bit lost, a bit lonely. Pretty sad too. But you let go because you have to. It is the right thing to do. Even when you are shoving your kids along so that they can take wing with confidence and certainty about themselves you're at war with that selfish part of yourself that never ever wants to let go. So, you close your eyes, buck up, head for work and hope that somehow during the half hour that you are driving to work the pain will ease and you'll be fine.

I turned on the engine, eased the truck onto the road, and headed east. About a quarter of a mile from our place is a bog we call Beaver Pond. It is where we've watched Max and Myrna, a pair of Canada geese, raise their families each year for the past six. We always look forward to their spring arrival. I've checked my journals and discovered that they have pretty consistently returned about this time every March. I'm usually attuned to their arrival time and start looking for them days before they actually arrive. Tim's departure from home this week occupied my thoughts and Max and Myrna hadn't crossed my mind at all. But there they were, feeling their way rather cautiously across the ice. As is his wont, Max, looking a bit more portly this year, stuck his neck out at me, hissed, and did what he's always done: warned me to keep my distance. He'll never know just how much I appreciated that little hissyfit of his. Just for a few moments I stopped feeling sorry for myself. I thought of how lucky we are to have these wonderful birds in our lives. I thought about how terrific it is that we can count on their coming home about this time every year so that we can share in their lives and watch them raise their family. It also dawned on me that they too need to let go at some point and that life for all of us is always a process of finding a balance point between our gains and our losses.

At some point Max and Myrna will shove their little ones off into the windy blue. But only when they are ready. They will feel good about it because they have done their job, they have done their duty. They reminded me that morning that I have a great deal to feel good about and that while I lose something by Tim's going I gain so much more. And besides, he'll be coming home a lot and when he does they will be occasions of such indescribable joy. Gabby loves him too, but she doesn't waste time brooding. She just jumps all over him when he comes home. Dogs and geese can teach us a lot.

CHAPTER TWELVE

# Rain

*On the soothing, even spiritual properties of rain*

I'M WAITING FOR THOSE inevitable spring rains to wash the earth clean and set us about the business of rebirth and renewal that cleanses the soul and also gets those lilacs to blooming. Signs are everywhere. The tips of bulbs and early flowers are popping up here and there. Coltsfoot dapples our roadsides as if millions of miniature suns, shrouded by winter and cold, have suddenly emerged, signs of spring's imminent arrival. Little yellow faces stare up at me as I do my afternoon run. There are other signs as well. Birdsong permeates the air. Our winged friends, back from southern climes, are busy defining territory, finding mates, getting ready to raise their families, and generally getting things in shape. It's a pretty busy business. But despite all these wonderful signs, the one I look forward to most is perhaps several weeks away—April showers.

In *The South Country,* Edward Thomas writes this about rain: "It does work that will last as long as the earth. It is about eternal business. In its noise and myriad aspect I feel the mortal beauty of immortal things." In his poem, *Meditation in the Spring Rain,* Wendell Berry takes a walk in the rain-soaked woods bounding his Kentucky home and finds himself "lost, free and speechless." There is nothing I love to do more than take a walk in the woods in the rain. I've often been chided for that, as well as my habit of avoiding beaches when they are packed and strewn with prostrate bodies baking in the sun. Give me an empty beach enveloped in a soft misty rain and I'm as close to heaven as it is possible to be on this earth. It has always struck me odd that so many of us look upon rainy days as times to stay inside, to find lives within rather than without. Granted, we don't want rain every day. But it seems to me that beyond its capacity for waking a slumbering, almost stuporous earth, rain also has the miraculous capacity to awaken our souls as well. To walk through the woods during a gently falling April rain is to feel as if one is at the center of one's being. To paraphrase Thomas, it is a lovely fusing of the mortal and immortal, of the earthly with the heavenly. Rain's noise is nature's Mozart. Every walk is a different composition, a sonata one day, a thunderously percussive Beethoven symphony another.

The woods are a different place in the rain. Its musicality aside, every thing takes on a deeper, richer, bolder look and hue. The earth, enriched by years of decay, is a darker, lustier brown. Fern fronds, always lovely, become even lovelier. Is there anything more beautiful than a Maidenhair fern, perhaps a few violets or trout lilies peeping out here and there, swaying ever so softly in the wind as crystalline raindrops slither down its delicate leaves to the ground? Spider webs, woven under cover of night, sparkle and shine in the moist morning air. Heaven's night stars come down to earth for a spell. No, when the rains come I'm happy that things will start popping out of the ground, but I'm even happier for those long, lovely walks when meditation of the type Berry describes is made ever more possible by the accompanying music of the falling rain. Besides, as any woods walker knows, you don't really get all that wet out there. A hat and slicker and some waterproof boots keep one pretty dry. Trees are great, especially when they double as umbrellas.

One of our problems up on the hill is that we don't have a well or water source of any kind. Normally, we mulch everything that we can, which thus far has done the job pretty well. We also catch rainwater as it runs off the barn roof. I stick large barrels and old sheetrock buckets under the eaves and we usually have all the water we need. Once several summers ago during a drought we hauled water up daily in plastic apple juice containers. Not much fun, but it kept stuff alive. This year I'll have a pretty elegant cistern: an old clawfoot tub. We're renovating our bathroom in the village and because of the tight space the tub needs to fit into it won't do. Just what I've needed to collect rainwater up on the hill. I've already envisioned it sitting up there on a raised platform, perhaps swaddled by some sort of flowering vine, collecting all that glorious natural nectar.

Rain is good for walks, good for the soul, and good for the earth. It is also great for soothing a lonely boy's soul. Years ago I lay in a bunk bed in a cabin in the New Hampshire woods feeling lost, homesick, and pretty sorry for myself. It started to rain while I lay there. The tap-tap-tapping of the rain gradually deflected my attention away from my misery without my being at all conscious of its miraculously regenerative power. I just lay there listening to that beautiful music—and I've been doing so ever since. Wordsworth says that there are moments in our lives that have a "renovating virtue." That afternoon so long ago, mesmerized by a gently falling New Hampshire rain, has become for me one of those enduring, transcendent spots of time.

CHAPTER THIRTEEN

# Garlic's Up!

*Garlic growing pains*

I'M A HAPPY MAN. My garlic has come up. At last count sixty-five little green spears are sticking up out of the thick layer of hay mulch I lay down last fall. I can see braids of plump garlic festooning our kitchen walls. I can taste and feel myself biting into tender little garlic bits that appear in almost everything we cook. But such a vision has not come about easily. I take my gardening pretty seriously and over the years have enjoyed being described as a 'green thumb,' although I don't think anyone's thumb is necessarily any greener than anybody else's. It is really a matter of commitment, taking the time to learn a bit about each plant's idiosyncrasies and loving what you do with a passion that becomes a lovely obsession. Gardening failures are especially difficult to take when one has done everything right. Ironically, there are times when I do nothing right, just wing it, and things turn out decently well indeed.

For instance, last year we wanted to trim back several flowering shrubs. Sandy wanted me to check on pruning times and techniques in a book or two. For whatever reason, I had neither the interest nor the patience. I remembered what gardening writer Henry Mitchell once wrote: do it when you can, not necessarily when it is supposed to be done. I grabbed the lopping shears, headed for the back fence, and cut each shrub down to within six inches of its life. Guess what ? Within a month we had perfectly formed shrubs filling out with lusciously green new growth. And this year they look just fine. Have pruning shears, will travel !

I probably shouldn't have been so formal about my garlic project. I read several books, even built a raised bed replete with the finest organic matter scrounged this side of the Mississippi! I ordered the garlic so it would arrive in early fall, planted it according to 'Hoyle,' and waited expectantly through those long winter months, often interspersed with garlic dreams richly metaphorical enough to give Freud some late night interpretive nightmares. At times while walking the place during the winter I'd poke at the garlic bed through the snow just to let a bit of light and air through. Gabby would nose about looking not for garlic, but for moles. She had better luck than I. When spring rolled around and all the snow had melted I started a daily garlic vigil —day after day I looked, poked, waited—even prayed a bit. Along about mid-May when only one little spear had poked its way up through the loamy soil I started to fret and do what I do so splendidly well when I'm pretty sure I'm looking Failure square in the noggin. I started to question my ability to do anything well. I don't know if others get this way, which is pretty darn silly, but it is and has always been my way. Here I've been gardening pretty successfully for fully a quarter of a century suffering few mishaps of this sort and yet whenever it happens I start questioning and probing and looking for cracks in every corner of my being. I wish I could be like Gabby who probes one hole for a mole, sees one is not there, and simply shuffles off to look elsewhere without giving the empty hole a thought. My problem is that empty holes fill me with all sorts of dread and I have a hard time filling them up. So I've lived with the great garlic failure—until now. Perpetual scapegoat scrounge that I am, not only do I have a potentially fine garlic crop, I also think I'm pretty well within my rights in pinning the failure on someone else. And boy does that feel good.

When in doubt, and in a psychic tailspin, read a few more garlic growing manuals and ask around. I did. I consulted a few more books and talked to a whole bunch of people who knew people who had grown garlic for years and swore that it was the easiest thing in the world to grow. Imagine how I felt when I heard that. After all, I'm the guy who grows all sorts of stuff pretty successfully breaking or ignoring just about all the rules! A reliable source talked to her garlic growing friend who asked if I'd grown hard-necked or soft-necked garlic. Apparently, soft-necked garlic is better suited to warmer climes and often does not make it through cold northern winters. Hard-necked varieties are hardier. Well, I wasn't sure. I checked the order, but other than the variety's name, it didn't say anything about neck pliancy, or the lack thereof. I called the grower. Guess what ? They had sent me a soft-necked variety. Well, you can imagine the relief that I felt. First thought? It is their fault, not mine. And that's where it stands. As far as I'm concerned I'm exonerated! I feel a whole lot better about myself now

Gabby doesn't mind heading up the hill at any time for any reason. But I think she's a bit tired of going to the garlic patch first these days. It is not quite the starting place she's used to. I've messed around with our routine. Sandy has been up a few times, and while she's as excited as I am about our most recent success, she's not terribly interested in going up every day just to check out how much closer to heaven those little green shoots are. Tim's response to my e-mail announcing the garlic's arrival made loving reference to early forms of aging-related lunacy! Gabby tags along rather begrudgingly and just sits there watching me as I step gingerly between rows counting—and feeling pretty darn proud of myself. Come July I expect to harvest oodles of garlic. I plan on saving several of the choicest bulbs for next year's crop. And hey, I might even expand to several other varieties and become a garlic guy. Based on my projected garlic success, I've ordered a hundred strawberry plants. They'll be planted according to all the best organic methods available. If they fail I'll start looking for the real culprit right away. I wonder if when Gabby twitches at night she's dreaming garlic, strawberries, or moles!

CHAPTER FOURTEEN

# Chairs and Chekhov

*Is an empty chair really empty?*

FOR SOME TIME NOW I have been drawn to empty chairs. Perhaps 'empty' is not the right word. Rather, by 'empty' I mean anything but that. Certainly, a chair without someone sitting in it is, by most methods of rational reckoning, empty. I guess what I'm getting at is even though I often see chairs positioned and at the ready for sitting, more often than not they are unoccupied. I get a kick out of imagining their owners and thinking about what sitting in them might be like. I do a lot of snooping while driving and walking. The ways that we arrange chairs have always fascinated me — under trees, on porches, in public places, even in showrooms. One never sees the arranger, just the arrangement. Several weeks ago while on my way uptown in New York City I cut through Bryant Park. The park has been gentrified and in its midst is a massive green littered with matching dark green wrought iron chairs —hundreds of them. There seemed to be nothing random about their placement. Yet in the few moments I stood there marveling at the geometry of it all I saw quite vividly the occupant of each unoccupied chair. I made a quick sketch in my notebook and jotted down a few notes. The image has stuck with me and is as clear at this moment as it was that morning.

Much of this started quite a few years ago while visiting friends in Vermont. We shared a love of gardening and while touring their garden, I spotted three empty white Adirondack chairs underneath a birch tree. They were carefully angled towards one another in order to make conversation easier. The contrast between the stark whiteness of the chairs and the paper white birch of the tree startled me and that image is lodged in my mind for all time. For whatever bizarre reason, Chekhov's *The Cherry Orchard* came to mind. It just seemed to me that the three sisters who so enliven that wonderful play were sitting in those chairs. A photographer at the time, I made a number of photographs, picked one while processing the film in my darkroom, printed it, and titled it 'Three Sisters.' There is no doubt about it, those chairs are occupied. Three sisters sat in those chairs, perhaps every evening, as long as the weather permitted, and unraveled the secret passions of their lives to one another. In that way, they masked the stultifying ennui of their everyday lives.

Several years ago while visiting the Museum of Modern Art a painting by Ben Shahn caught my eye. I have looked for a print for years without any success. It is a pen and ink drawing of chairs and music stands on a stage. The chairs are empty, there is no music on the stands, and the spare black lines of the stands and chairs stand out sharply against the snow-white background. Yet, there is music in the air. There are people in those chairs playing beautiful music, perhaps a Beethoven sonata or a spirited Vivaldi flute concerto. The effect is extraordinary!

Up on the hill we have two sets of Adirondack chairs. Two are stained a dark, canyon green. Two are white. The green chairs call home a slightly shady spot just north of the garden and to the left of a Hawthorn tree. Odd as it might seem, we also have several folding chairs in the house, and most of the time I set one of those up so I don't have to sit in one of the green chairs. Sitting in one spoils the delight of looking at them and dreaming anyone into them that I please. Just below them are two white Adirondack chairs. Sandy and I often sit in them, as they command a spacious view of the perennial beds below. Truth is, I often feel a bit guilty when I settle myself into one of them. One never knows whose lap one might be sitting on. Lately the yellow and purple finches have used them as intermediate stops on their way to and from the finch feeder nearby. They look as if they belong. Gabby and I are content to sprawl on the grass or stick to the folding deck chairs.

Sandy's dad gave us two folding white metal chairs several years before his death. One of the chairs fell apart despite my inept repair attempts. The other remains and over the years has occupied several niches in our lives. My father-in-law's passing has left a void in our hearts that we will never fill. But we do have memories. Oh, do we have memories! There were times when he tested our patience and we wanted to kick him in the ***. Mostly, he made us laugh, kept us hopping, and we loved him deeply for it. In his own cantankerous way he was one of the most generous and loving people I have ever known. That is why that chair now sits at the intersection of two paths in the woods behind our upper meadow. Like those white chairs in my friend's Vermont garden, this chair is anything but empty. When Gabby and I walk back there and chance upon the chair, sometimes forgetting that it is there, a sense of sublime comfort settles in my soul. I think about Sud, and about the beautiful daughter he gave me to love. I also think about the lovely liveliness of empty white chairs.

*Sud's chair*

CHAPTER FIFTEEN

# Charity

*On taking care of the home ground first*

LAST WEEK WHILE Gabby and I were doing a bit of trail clearing we chanced upon a female ruffed grouse and her brood. I have heard the male, nature's resident percussionist, quite often, but I have never actually seen him. The rapid-fire beat of his wings has usually faded into a distant murmur long before I have had time enough to figure out exactly where he might be. Good for him. His fuss alerts the neighborhood, all creatures large and small head for cover, and all is well. It has always fascinated me how attuned to one another animals are. Species don't mingle much at all and stay tightly close to their territories. Each species has its distinct cultural practices and attitudes. But when the danger call goes out, in whatever form, all pay attention and there is often a quietly frenetic scattering about as all heed the alarm. Crows and blue jays are the most vociferous. Then again, an alarmed pileated woodpecker really stirs up quite a ruckus. There are some pretty interesting early warning systems out there, as well as some impressively selfless gestures that remind one quite poignantly that charity really does begin at home. That is what struck me when we startled the ruffed grouse last week.

Among animals there is a fascinating array of displays and maneuvers aimed at deflecting attention from the young. Killdeer are famous for their brokenwing display. If one chances anywhere close to their nest, often little more than a scratched out depression in an open, usually gravelly area, the female will feign a broken wing in a clever attempt to lure the predator away from her nest. It is a defensive mechanism that has worked well enough over time since there is no shortage of killdeer around. We know also what a female bear is capable of when she fears for her cubs' safety. Having never run into a female ruffed grouse with little ones in tow before, I came away impressed by her courage and willingness to sacrifice herself in defense of her young, who scattered about the woodland floor as if feathers flying from an exploded pillow. Gabby stood there transfixed, almost frozen, as she came right at us, darting here and there, every lateral or backward movement an attempt to get us as far away from her little ones as possible. Neither of us moved. After several minutes of this display she took off, keeping a low trajectory, landing amongst some honeysuckle about twenty-five yards way. By this time Gabby had thawed out and gathered her wits about her. She tore after the grouse, which led her in ever-widening circles, until she simply gave up. By this time, the little ones had scuttled up the hillside where mom eventually joined them and who knows where they headed after that.

The first thought I had: charity begins at home. Our language brims with such clichés, which through overuse become quite hackneyed. But even the worn and tired phrases that litter our conversations with one another, however unconsciously internalized, contain curious and quite durable specks and grains of truth. I think this encounter revitalized, at least for me, this timeworn notion of homespun charity. It also prompted me to think about some things that both Thoreau and Emerson wrote years ago about charity and philanthropy. For the grouse, charity necessarily began at home. It began at the moment that she feared for her brood's safety. Surely, her actions from that point on were instinctive. But that does not undermine or negate the beauty of her selfless gesture on behalf of her young. I've never been all that sure that instinct and instinctive behavior are as unthinking as many ethologists make them out to be. Humans adamantly believe that they alone act, at least most of the time, in response to rational thought processes. We flatter ourselves much of time by thinking of ourselves as quite reasonable characters. When we do something, of course it is a reasoned, rational act, even though prompted by some sort of ineffable 'feeling.' Frankly, I do not see myself as that much different from the grouse or any of the other animals that I have mentioned. And when Gabby gives me that look, or when she wakes me up in the middle of the night frightened by lightning I'm hard pressed to believe that thought and feeling are not in some wonderfully mysterious way connected and contingent upon one another.

Sandy and I have raised four children. As all parents know, there are many times when we act just as the grouse did. We do what we must to protect our young from imminent danger. We are willing to put ourselves in harm's way, activating whatever evolutionary or cultural gestures at our disposal, to protect our young. These are beautiful and genuinely charitable acts. It seems to me that authentic charitability is possible only when we have taken care of business at home. When we have reached out to members of our immediate and extended families. Only then is philanthropy possible. It is then that we can widen the circles of our lives to encompass others normally beyond our kith and kin. This sort of rippling out, one rooted in a stone first tossed close to home, makes the most moral sense.

I do not know what might be in store for Gabby and me when we resume our trail clearing chores later this afternoon. I am sure that something will happen to remind each of us that we are not alone. That is a very good feeling.

CHAPTER SIXTEEN

# Bach and Butterflies

*A butterfly concerto—of sorts*

ALL SUMMERS SEEM TO FLY BY. Despite the swiftness of their flight, however, each leaves something unique behind. We never remember whole experiences— summers, vacations, lectures, etc. What we remember are isolated moments that carry with them an ineffable flavor, call it significance, that lingers and over time seems to transcend itself. One of my favorite writers, to whom I turn often, is the philosopher Susanne Langer. She writes that "symbolization is the ultimate activity of the human mind," and that artists create significant forms that symbolize an infinite variety of meanings and possibilities for us. She writes eloquently about music, that wonderfully invisible form that has the capacity to raise us to amazing heights of ecstasy and equally astonishing depths of beautifully felt sadness and despair. Art helps us to see the transcendent significance of things because it elevates our awareness and moves us away from our normal perceptions of things. This is the summer that I will remember for those wonderful chamber music concerts at The Farmers' Museum, especially the night of the Brandenburg Concertos, and a butterfly on a bush in a garden far away in Delaware a week later that brought it all back in a hauntingly beautiful way.

I haven't bought a recorder yet, but I plan to. That was my first thought after leaving the concert several weeks ago. When I get to New York City for a few days soon I plan to look around for one. I don't want an inferior plastic one; I want a quality wooden one. I need all the help I can get. Years ago my mother insisted that I take violin lessons. I recall squeaking my way to *Mary Had A Little Lamb* and, if memory serves me well, when I parted ways with my teacher she breathed a very well earned, very deep, sigh of relief. I had known all along what my mother couldn't seem to accept; I am not a natural music maker. I love listening to it and up until several years ago could whistle just about anything with some degree of tonal accuracy and gusto — that is, until I grew a beard and lost my whistling genes completely. Sandy is suspicious of there being any coincidence, but I am convinced that there is a connection. If not genetic, then certainly psychic. I am sure that there is a therapist out there somewhere who specializes in this sort of thing, as they seem to specialize in just about everything, but I'm not ready to go that route quite yet. I figure I have other more pressing hang-ups than that. And since I am as committed to my beard as anything in my life, I will just have to get along without. That is one of the reasons for giving a recorder a try. I have visions of sitting on the deck up on the hill and twinkling dulcet tunes out over the meadow while Gabby lazes at my feet, every so often giving me one of those life couldn't be any better looks. Think of it.

Music offers us a lovely way to get through time, especially when weeding, digging up potatoes, framing rough openings for barn windows, or merely sauntering along some woodland trail. I usually split my time between the music that I have come to know and love over the years and compositions of my own that bristle with a brilliance that, luckily, an unsuspecting world will never know about. Every once in a while I try a measure or two out on a creature that happens to be nearby, even Gabby. None has ever seemed terribly moved! Years ago, like most sixties types, I dabbled with the guitar. Frankly, it served me best as a hitchhiking prop. After mastering some of the basic cords, which did not come too easily, I beefed up my repertoire with a somewhat predictable collection of Dylan; Peter, Paul, and Mary; and Joan Baez tunes. A one-night gig at a coffeehouse in Connecticut owned by a friend convinced me that my road to any kind of glory led elsewhere. I still have the guitar. I have picked it up a few times over the years—and put it down very quickly. I wish I had known then what I know now. Some of us are born to be music makers. For most of us, creative listening will have to do. I have learned that each is a rewarding activity in its own right. I have also learned the imprudence of coveting what is beyond one's reach. Besides, there is something inexplicably pleasurable about winging one's way to paradise while someone else flies the plane. This is the summer of beautiful music. Imagine driving a few hundred miles south several days after hearing those exquisite concertos played with such brilliance. Imagine stopping at a garden along the way. Imagine walking along lovely sylvan pathways and being stopped in your tracks by a butterfly whose weightless dartings from blossom to blossom seem the living embodiment of music heard just days before. Gabby and I both have a great deal of faith that Bach, butterflies, and a great deal more await us around the next of life's mysterious bends. I suspect she prefers squirrels.

CHAPTER SEVENTEEN

# Asters, Goldenrod, and Space

*A Fall flowerscape and winter reading*

SOME WEEKS ANNOUNCE themselves with a singular distinction. It seems that everything that follows is a sort of mental fugue, a variation on a dominant, almost pestering theme. Golden yellow and various shades and hues of lavender and purple have colored my mental landscape this week. It is perhaps my favorite time of year. Ever since spending summers on a farm not far away in the tiny hamlet of Quaker Street I have looked forward to summer's ebb. It is not because I have any wish that summer close its doors. In fact, there have been times this summer when I have wished for a time warp or rupture of some sort so that I might savor it just a little bit longer —and get some work done. I suspect it is a constant of human nature that one plans to get far more done than one ever does. Of late I have been working against rain, cold snaps, shorter days, and the return of the teaching year to frame, side, and finish off the exterior of a small barn that seems to defy completion. There is something quite enticing about listening to the opera while cutting lengths of siding on wobbly sawhorses as rain pelts the metal roof with its soft rhythms. Not quite so captivating is the pain in a shoulder whose resistance to overuse, especially after hours of drawing a handsaw back and forth over dimension lumber of varying widths and thicknesses, appears to be on the wane. As if the shoulder were not enough, there is the lower back, with all of its structural deficiencies despite exercises, hot baths, salves of all sorts, and ineffective chiropractic manipulations. So, while I mourn summer's passing there is something to be said for laying the tools aside and devoting one's energies to labors of a more abstract, cerebral nature. A time for reflection, for tooling up for next summer's inviting exigencies. Emerson reminds us that "books are for a scholar's idle times." It is not idleness characterized by inactivity. Rather, it is a notion that suggests the necessity of a delicate balance in the conduct of our daily lives. The one is enlivened by the other.

So, I begin the process of laying the land and barn to rest for a time and turning my mind to other tasks. Robert Frost says it so well when in *After Apple-Picking* the narrator writes that he is "over-tired of the task I myself desired." Come early spring I can hardly hold myself back. Come early fall I am ready to lay low for a while. Time to teach, start working through the stacks of books that have piled up, time to get some writing projects tackled. Time, that is, to start living in time differently. Which is why those fields of goldenrod and asters have been so profoundly affecting this week as I drive to and from work. They shimmer in the cold, early morning light that only late September knows. They seem to soften my being, bring on a feeling of supple repose. It is a drowsiness that awakens memory. I drive and drive and before I know it I am a young boy, back on the farm, walking through these very same fields as if time and place had stood still, lost in the whirl and swish of heavenly hues. I want to fly, I want to sprout wings, I want to be light as air. I feel what one writer describes as the 'incredible lightness of being.'

The fields of flowers will fade to varying hues of brown, their stalks will stiffen against the wind only to be tamped down by winter's snows. Billions of seeds will take wing on invisible winds to remerge next summer as celebrants of nature's timeless dance. I will take these thoughts and images with me through winter's whiteness. There will be times, probably deep in the dark of a winter night, when the many images that have shaped this summer will parade across the screen of my mind. They will come and go, resting back there in the mind's storage bins where so much of what constitutes our lives seems always so elusively close to the surface. I will relive the many hours spent in the barn, out in the perennial beds, or just sitting. There will come a time when I will take out some paper and start listing. I will also read my journals and garden notes, tracking progress here, noting chores undone there. I will read books like Gaston Bachelard's *The Poetics of Space* because in Michael Pollan's *A Place of My Own* he mentions

Bachelard's chapter on the house and "the significance of the hut."

I call what I am building a barn, but in essence, it is a glorified hut. I have always been intrigued by notions of space—how we use it, what we fill it with, etc. Perhaps that comes from being the son of an architect whose closest attachment to architecture is to build two fairly modest 'huts' with little more than a design of sorts in his head and a basic carpentry book at hand to make sure he is covering the basics.

Gabby loves to walk through the field adjacent to our place. We fit in a walk several days ago before a brush hog leveled it. I suspect she does not differentiate much between and among flowers; it is all smells and sniffings, at ground level, to her. I gloried in the purples and golds; she got her nose dirty pawing at suspected mole holes and then sticking her nose where it didn't belong. We walked back to the barn where she dozed and I messed around doing odds and ends. She probably had mole dreams. I dreamed endless fields of flowers. I dreamed myself into winter where I busied myself with memories, the passage of time, the poetics of space, time, and — huts.

CHAPTER EIGHTEEN

# Transparency

*Getting away from oneself for a brief moment in time*

IN ONE OF HIS MOST FAMOUS ESSAYS, *Nature,* Emerson describes the very mystical experience of achieving a oneness with nature wherein one loses complete touch with one's fleshy being. To use his words, he became a "transparent eyeball." Over the years, I have had some lively conversations with friends for whom such mysticism seems nonsensical. There is something a bit suspect about such claims, but I have always taken Emerson on faith, if not literally, then for the philosophical and figurative truth of what he writes. Truth can come at us in any manner of guises and while Emerson might engage in a fair measure of rhetorical bombast from time to time, he does get his point across. The same holds true for Thoreau, whose characteristically quirky pronouncements cause even the most die-hard of disciples to wink and blink a bit. For instance, in *Walden* he describes chancing upon a woodchuck one afternoon while on his customary saunter about the Concord countryside. He claims that at the very moment he spotted the furry beast he felt an irresistible urge to snatch it up and devour it right on the spot. Health food nut that he was, even Thoreau would have found raw woodchuck oddly indigestible! Even the staunchest of disciples knows better than to read such gestures literally. The point is that even the most civilized among us is capable of some rather primal urges. We should be thankful to Rousseau who so sagely reminds us that we are indeed quite noble savages. Thoreau thought better of eating uncooked woodchuck; his honesty is what we admire here, as well as his good diet sense. In short, each of us has a moment or two from time to time when the boundaries get a bit fuzzy and our feral instincts seem just a mite too pushy. My own sense is that we retain and sustain our humanity because we realize these things about ourselves. To ignore and deny them is to imperil our civility.

Thoreau claims to have had his fair share of mystical moments. Emerson's are what intrigue me at present. I had one myself several days ago while sitting alone atop a windswept rock face in Canada's Laurentian Mountains. We had hiked quite a few miles that day and returned to the inn for a late lunch. I have done quite a lot of walking lately. The more I do, the more I like it. I didn't feel at all walked out and actually experienced the strangest of sensations while sitting at our sun-drenched table savoring a bowl of simmering cream of broccoli soup. Sitting I might have been, but my feet were still walking. I can only liken it to a term I hate: hat-head.

You know, that ring around the head sensation a hatless head feels. I guess it is similar to what is described as phantom pain. As soon as we had finished lunch, I beat feet for the summit of a nearby hill. I felt great to be on the road again. There is no greater feeling than swishing through leaf-strewn mountain trails on a brisk fall afternoon as warm splashes of sun spill through a gradually disappearing canopy. The beauty of such transitions is nature's uncanny process of self-revelation. As each season's layers peel away, the world is born anew, again, and again, and again. Birch trees, obscured from view for most of late spring and summer, now stand out quite starkly against a seamless backdrop of greens and browns. Their sun-stained trunks and quirky branches call attention to themselves quietly, as if to say, we have waited rather long enough for our time in the sun. Our time has come; indeed it has. These images, coupled with an infinity of thoughts, most lost forever, coursed through my mind as I walked aimlessly up the hill. I often advise students to write without thinking. I walk the same way. Such writing gets out of the way of thought. Such walking makes clear, clean, unfettered thought possible. The time for synthesis and for making sense of things comes later.

Which is why I am writing this now. Much later. I walked to the summit, a craggy outcropping with a panoramic view of several small glacial lakes, picked a spot, sat down, and leaned back against my backpack. I woke up, as if out of a dream, some time later. I do not know what happened. The sun warmed me, the wind enfolded me, consciousness left me, yet I remained very much awake, aware of everything and nothing at all. It felt wonderfully strange, light, sweetly pleasant. If transparency of being is possible, then I have experienced it. It is hard to describe since it is so elusive, so much there and not there. I suspect that such moments are rare, as they should be. Such delights must ripen as memory over time. I can not say that I had metamorphosed into a transparent eyeball. There is something eerily uncomfortable about becoming an eyeball. I can say that I did feel disembodied. I did feel absent from myself while yet very present. It is a very sweet, very airy sensation. Gabby did not make the trip with me. Had she been there, I am sure that she would have sat quietly by my side. She would have sensed something. There are times when I look in her eyes and those dark pools filled with ancestral wisdom wonder what has taken me so long.

CHAPTER NINETEEN

# Reading

*Reader's blues and making choices*

THERE IS ONE QUESTION that I dread being asked. It is this: have you read .... ? Invariably, whenever someone asks me this question my answer is the same: no. Just as invariably, my well-meaning questioner follows up my no with: well, you must. My initial instinct is to offer this retort: why must I? I do not say this most of the time. It seems too combative a response, even condescending. Do I often feel ignorant, out of touch, even not very well read? Yes. All the time. Often, a pesky voice, eerily like my mother's (no Freudian analyses, please) says: Richard, you read all the time, what is your problem? I think I know what it is. Call it reader's blues. There is another more comforting way to approach this issue. If I were to turn the tables on my friend and ask if she had read one of 'my' (like most readers, I am controlling and possessive of *my* books!) books, the answer most likely will be: no. If my sense of self is accurate, while I infrequently suggest that a book must be read, I never hesitate to extol a book's virtues. There are enough books in the world to go around and there is no reason why anyone 'must' read any book. In fact, one of life's realities is that a universe of readers can read like hell over a lifetime and hardly ever cross reading paths. Several years ago, a friend asked me if I had read a book that seemed quite the rage at the time. I had not read it; I still have not. He seemed unhinged by my indifference. The grave look on his face hinted at a moral transgression on my part. I suggested that since I had not yet read the complete works of many classical writers, why in heaven's name should I feel the least bit guilty about not reading such an immature book. Actually, I feel that same way about books that I do about wine. In most cases, if not all, both taste better with age.

I feel those blues all the time, night and day, even in my dreams. Yet, I read all the time and always have. I suspect I always will. Each of us reads differently, at different paces, and with different intents in mind. Some of us even read several books at a time. A friend who teaches rhetoric at a major university claims that he reads approximately ten books a year. He reads each very carefully—several times. A friend, now deceased, who taught classics at several major universities, observed that one is very lucky indeed to read one good book well over the course of a month. In an intriguing essay that defines good readers and writers, Vladimir Nabokov avers that good readers are re-readers. The first read is merely a brushing up against a book's outer skin. Reading is excavating. The longer and more deliberately one digs, the more one is likely to find. Of course, digging through a good book's soil is a very subjective exercise indeed. One might say that a good book, a classic, if you will, holds up rather well after repeated digs.

My reading habits, and tastes, have changed over the years. I have some favorites that I come back to time and time again. Every reader does. Frankly, there are times when I wonder why I bother with new books when all reading roads seem to lead, inevitably, back to those few books that took possession of my soul years ago and just won't let go. There is still some space in the lot. I guess that is why I keep at it. One never knows what delights might be tucked away on some local bookseller's shelf. Some of my best reads have come about quite by chance. I used to read rather more deliberately than I do now. I would make reading decisions impossible to keep. For instance, I'd set myself up for failure by announcing, usually to Sandy, who always has the good sense to ignore such grand schemes, that this winter I would read all of so and so. Well, it never worked. I would read three or four of so and so's books and then abort the effort, not because I had not enjoyed the journey, but because three or four of anybody is quite enough—at least over the short haul. Variety is the spice of any reading life. These days my reading is much more eclectic and I am the happier for it. For instance, several months ago I read Michael Pollan's *A Place of My Own: The Education of an American Builder*. In the course of his discussion, he mentions quite a few books, several of which intrigued me. I am in the middle of one now and have started a new list comprised of titles in that book that seem equally inviting. The range of topics is as varied as it is zany. I would not have it any other way. My reading chair is surrounded by stacks of unread books begotten, not by reviews or friends' suggestions, but by other books. And so it goes. There is neither rhyme nor reason to my reading these days and I am a happier reader now than I have ever been.

Gabby usually lies alongside my chair while I read. Every once in a while she shifts positions, looks up, sighs deeply, and settles back down into herself. She likes it when I read, whatever it is that I am reading, and so do I.

CHAPTER TWENTY

# Odds and Ends at Year's End

*Taking stock*

IT IS TAKING STOCK TIME. One of the joys of writing these essays is discovering in the process of writing what it is that really wants to be written about. Perhaps the best definition of writing I know is this: writing is a process of discovering what you have to say. I always sit down with an informing notion in mind and, more often than not, once I get started, feel myself pulled towards a destination not listed in the original itinerary. One of writing's attractions is its uncanny capacity to chart its own course. For instance, I sat down this morning believing myself well outfitted to write about one thing. For whatever unaccountable reason, perhaps because the phrase 'taking stock' has been bouncing around in my head, I started thumbing through my 'column notes' folder. Among a ragtag collection of words, phrases, short and long lists, and even a doodle every now and then, I found several titles for future columns. Among them: 'Mulching, Slugs, and Warfare: A Reflection; 'In Search of a Schedule'; 'Footprints in the Snow'; 'Life as a Non-Linear Journey' and, oddly enough, 'Broccoli.' I resolve, in the coming year, to work these suggestive titles up into essays. The first refers to the battle every organic gardener wages against slugs, especially if he uses only the most environmentally sound methods. I do, which is why even in the dead of winter I hatch plans for another spring offensive against the enemy. Sandy thought I had lost it two springs ago when I kept a daily kill count! I am always scheduling myself in order to get things done; no schedule, however fortified by any method, has ever worked for long. I follow and step into my footprints day after day when walking the winter woods when no snow has fallen for days. Where those footprints will lead, I do not know. Stopping is not possible. Something there is about footprints in the snow. No life is linear and there is nothing about linearity that appeals to me. My life continues to be characterized by zigzags, backtracks, and missteps. I have every intention of keeping it that way. Broccoli? Lots of possibilities there and few have anything to do with picking it or eating it.

A January 1998 note reads as follows: why garden ? It is followed by some famous garden writers' names. It most likely had been my intent to get their books thinking that they might help me answer that question, since I had been wrestling with an essay entitled "What Is It About Owning Land?" It seemed to me then, and it still does now, that there is a close and crucial connection between the two. To own land and not work it in some way seems a sacrilege to me. I remember now that I had been reading Ken Nolling's very intriguing book *Why We Garden*. Nolling's notion is that no matter what we do on our land, at heart we are working the soil. A healthy crop of carrots is possible only when the soil is loamy and contains all the nutrients, drainage, and air flow necessary to good carrot growth. The same is true for all plants. Soil not only grows good root crops, it produces some mighty handy metaphors as well. I have not answered this question to any degree of satisfaction. About the most profound notion I have been able to come up with is I just love to do it and as I sit here typing while snow blankets the landscape I can't wait to get out there after the first frost and get those peas in and start getting the hill soil up to planting snuff.

A transcription from a December 1998 entry reads as follows: teacher and old guys, black terns, yellow - headed blackbirds, gin gimlet, heat, Palomino, Ross, Indian, dinner in Minimac, Seany. A seemingly random collection at first glance, yet collectively they are the defining moments of a road trip through Nebraska, North Dakota, Minnesota, and Michigan. I have written about images and memory often. I have always felt that each life is a mosaic of sorts, an ongoing work of art. Inside us there is this incomprehensible storage and sorting system that knows, at a deep, unconscious level, what all this stuff means. I have not written about the teacher in a convenience store in North Dakota who clearly loved being kidded by her old students, the joy of seeing black terns along route 2 in North Dakota, or the heat of a summer Nebraska day that almost did me in. I have not written about the eagles I didn't see but felt as I chased after their shadows on a cold, rainy day in Michigan's Seany Wildlife Preserve, a place where young Ernest Hemingway found a purity and lightness of being he never recaptured.

Taking stock. That is what it is all about. Asking questions that often have not one answer, but many. A lone Indian walking down a deserted road in Ross, North Dakota endures as the living animation of lost time and the eternal, very lonely search for self and meaning. Shadows of eagles sought but not seen slide as if breaths of fresh night air before memory's eyes. Terns, black as coal, hang from memory's rafters. Taking stock. Moving from one year to the next gathering the past into the present so that the future makes for a fuller present. Time moves and stands still. An interesting paradox. Gabby and I. Taking stock. Moving through time.

CHAPTER TWENTY ONE

# Rules to Live By, or Not!

*Who rules the roost?*

SIGNS OF SPRING ABOUND. This morning while on my first run since moving into our new house a small flock of chatty Canada geese flew low overhead aiming for the swamp down the road. It has been warm enough the last few days to melt the ice. They have the ability to fly aerial reconnaissance missions that enable them to scope things out long before we earthlings see and feel what they have known for weeks. A neighbor said to me when we chatted briefly yesterday that "spring is here." I am not pessimistic by nature, but I do know that these prematurely warm days can feel wonderfully inspiriting and at the same time be predictably misleading. My own approach is to take whatever good weather we get, knowing full well that even though spring is working its way slowly and subtly our way, its arrival is still weeks away. That is all right with me. My flagging, winter brittle spirit is always ready for a facelift. But like so many of us, I am never completely ready to heave to at the first signs of winter's turning. For instance, I usually have my seeds planted by now (according to my garden journal I normally plant on or about March 8). Things are all set up in the basement (There is always quite a lag time for me between set up and action!). The plan is to tackle that project this weekend, one already crowded with chores. Most likely it will be mid-week before I get to it. My seed packets sit on the floor beside me and just to my left on my landfill-like desk are the few catalogues that I have culled from the huge pile that we started with. I love garden catalogues, especially the more creatively designed ones. Some have excellent writing and it has crossed my mind from time to time to teach a class sometime using catalogues as the basic texts. If it were up to me, and it is not, I would have a whole shed devoted to garden catalogue storage. I am the lord of my study; the rest of the house is clearly under different management. I can clutter my place up all I want, but outside these walls a different set of rules comes into play.

One rule that I follow, but which befuddles me, is the hidden toaster rule. Now that we have all this storage space, Sandy has it in her head that the countertops ought to be forever clear—and clean. When I want to toast a few slices of bread I do not want to have to reach into a dark cabinet to retrieve what I consider to be a standard countertop appliance. Where I come from a toaster is always out, plugged in, and at the ready. It is not a mushroom; it needs light and air to survive and its survival depends on its being used. When I toast up some bread and then spread it all too thickly with butter and apricot preserve, I do not want to think about returning it to its dark, lonely redoubt. In some respects it seems a bit disrespectful. Plus, it is just one step too many for me to process.

An acquaintance stopped by the other day and I put the question to her: don't you think it is silly to store a toaster in a cabinet? Well, she looked at me in what can only be characterized as 'that way,' and said: "I hate having my toaster out when it is not being used. I always put it away when I am finished." I am not about to write a government grant to research this toaster storage thing, although given what I know about government grants and earmarks, I would probably stand a pretty good chance. I just do not get it.

My not getting it is not limited to toaster storage issues. I guess if I had participated a bit more actively in the initial nesting process I would have less to grouse about. For instance, we now have a coat closet just to the left of the door to the attached garage. I will not miss scraping ice and snow off my windshield—and Sandy's, for that matter. I am told that this closet is for our things and that the closet to the right of the main entry door is a guest closet. Theoretically, I am supposed to come in the garage door as often as practicable. My boots are to come off there and my coat, hat, and gloves are to go in that closet. Here is the rub: the only time I use the garage door is when I drive the car in or out. Most of the time, especially when working about the place, I use the main door. And if the main door is my preferred exit, why not keep my gear in the guest closet? Because, like it or not, it is the designated guest closet and that is all there is to it. One thing is certain: the rules will not change. One does the best that one can. I suspect that over time I will head for the main door, look down for my boots, see that they are not there, walk around the corner, put them on, and then trudge back to the main door and out. I could go out through the garage door at that point, but the chances are good that I had left my hat and gloves on the foyer table back where I started. These are not among life's toughest survival problems, but they do provide for moments of metaphysical complexity. Much as I try, I just do not get it.

Gabby and I have walked by the swamp almost daily this week and each day one can feel the gathering warmth. Soon it will be teeming with life. While huffing and puffing my way up hill this morning on the last leg of my run I heard several red-winged blackbirds chattering at one another in the brush alongside the road. It was my first sighting and certainly a sign that one season is about to give up the ghost. The chickadees have been spilling out their phoebe-like songs the last several days and every once in a while a bright crimson male cardinal shows up twanging its spring aria and that too means that spring is around the corner. We know that some corners are sharper than others and that when driving it always seems as if the place we are headed to is just around the next bend. Spring plays this game with us every year. It is an annual tease whose function is to brighten our spirits and to get us thinking spring thoughts.

Fortunately these transitions always take time. A spirit folded in during winter takes a while to unfold. It is good that the thawing process takes a bit of time. False starts are welcome tastes of what is to come.

Gabby too has new rules to follow. Among them is a willingness to be wiped when she comes in either door. She used to hate it. Now, the minute she crosses either threshold she swivels about and stands at the ready to be toweled. She now appears to relish a ritual she used to hate. I do not know what the resident rule maker did to effect this startling behavioral transformation. She clearly gets it!

*"... Spring is just around the corner."*

CHAPTER TWENTY TWO

## Shifting Gears

*Slipping into Spring's groove*

SPRING'S DEFT HANDIWORK is behind the eccentric weather patterns that have hounded us lately. Actually, come spring we're always so anxious for warmth and green, birdsong with a lively lilt, and all the other telltale signs that we forget spring always comes in fits and starts. One warm day and we assume that winter is on the wane and spring is just around the corner. After all, there are so many clear signs, it just has to be so. A bit of a thaw, a gentle rain or two, patches of bare earth dappling sunny roadside banks and, if you are at all like me, it feels as if it is time to set out the porch furniture. Trouble is, earth's clock runs on a different, more eccentric timetable. Our internal clocks, wound up by whatever power keeps each of our individual psyche's clunking along, start sounding false alarms that really mess us up. We get up one morning and see and feel spring in the air. Goose chatter filters down from above. Cardinals sit on bare power and telephone lines spilling out their inimitable spring songs. I drive to work, glance back at all the winter gear stuffed in the cramped space behind my seat and think, time for the annual spring gear shift. In my dreamiest of moments I feel myself swishing through the tall grass of an upland meadow or plunging into a roadside thicket in search of that Brown Thrasher nest that has eluded me all these years. Great thoughts! The very next day an ornery, inconsiderate nor'easter on its way to who knows where shatters my dreams by dumping six inches of uninvited white stuff all over the place. The wind has picked up, the beetle-browed crests of snowdrifts once again stare down at me, and poor Gabby can't even make it halfway up the driveway to the barn.

The internal thaw has started. We have begun to awaken from winter's long sleep. We want spring so badly that we forget it always arrives in this teasing, mercurial way. No sooner do we taste it than, bang, a stiff northern wind decides to stretch its legs south for another blow or two, just to remind us who is boss. The saving grace is that this annual ritual of rebirth is just around the corner. Its gait is unsteady; it needs time to get reacquainted with itself. It sure does try one's patience. I try to make the most of these tantalizing gaps. I think spring thoughts as much as possible. I do spring things. Such antics seem to help.

The pond down the road, after melting a bit, is now covered with snow. Every morning on the way to work I look for Max and Myrna, the nesting pair of geese we've been watching for six years now. There is no sign of life there yet. But there is hope, and in a not so dark recesses of my mind I see them there, waddling across the road, goslings in tow. Max stops right smack in the middle of the road, sticks out his tongue at me and hisses. The look in his eye means don't mess with me buddy. I don't. They plop into the pond and paddle off to feed along the far bank. It is a wonderful sight to see, either in actuality or as a recurring image in a mid-winter or early spring dream. External events and phenomena come and go. Images remain. Max and Myrna appear as if out of nowhere each spring. They disappear just as stealthily come late fall. But they have never left me, not since the first day that Sandy and I spotted them six years ago. Add all the images and memories of a lifetime up and, well, you have something.

Other ponds around have opened up and some spring arrivals have already set up shop. That is what gives me hope. It is what keeps me thinking that Max and Myrna will be here soon. One pond I visit is already alive with activity. Mallards, Canada geese, and Red-Winged Blackbirds are staking their territories, selecting nesting sites, and going about the business of establishing harmonious relations absent the disturbing acrimony that seems to plague humankind these days. Interesting!

Most of my seeds have arrived. I looked in my journal the other day and noticed that I started our first batch of vegetable seeds last year on March 19th. I sometimes start things a bit too early. I have waited a week. I can't wait any longer. At the very least, all my tomato and eggplant seeds will hit the soil running this afternoon. I need to feel soil sifting through my fingers. I need to see pots lined up on the shelves of the plant stand that sits against our patio doors. I need to see little wooden plant markers sticking out of the soil. And I need to peer into those pots every day looking for signs of life. I even look forward to that day eight weeks from now when despite my failsafe record keeping system I'll wonder whether a six-pack of tomatoes is Sungold, Brandywine, or Beefmaster. It always happens. I can never understand it. Maybe there is some truth to the notion that an evil garden genius lurks about just for that sole purpose. I can't blame it on the kids anymore; they've been gone for years. At any rate, there may be snow on the ground outside, but on the inside our own little Eden will start taking shape. I can feel my soul greening.

Gabby and I went for a short walk yesterday. She seemed different. She jumped up and down, rolled around in the snow, and seemed much more attuned to the lives taking care of business around her. She stared at several crows atop a tree for several minutes without moving a muscle or making a sound. A Red-winged Blackbird chirruped quite eloquently from the crotch of a bare elderberry bush. She didn't bark; she just listened. Her first spring concert. The signs and songs of spring are in the air. It is a lovely music heard by the souls of all living things.

CHAPTER TWENTY THREE

# Compost: Metaphor or Meal?

*In compost is the preservation of the earth*

I AM A VERY LUCKY MAN. How many wives, after putting in a hard day at the office, would be willing, even eager, to accept an invitation to drive five miles up into the hills just to see a husband's newly turned, neatly piled, ruggedly handsome compost piles? Not too many, I suspect. But after dinner off we went. I couldn't wait to see the look on Sandy's face. She didn't disappoint me. After a contemplative sweep of the four bins arrayed proudly in front of her, she smiled, nodded, looked at me, and said, 'nice, honey.' That is all I needed to hear; I was in heaven! And off we went on one of our 'perusals' of the grounds. Needless to say, I felt pretty good, even strutted a bit as we walked. I swelled with the kind of pride an artist must feel after having just finished a painting over which he has labored a very long time. There are all kinds of art and artistry out there. I read somewhere this past week, I think in Rebecca Solnit's very compelling history of walking, *Wanderlust*, that gardening is an artful enterprise and that as gardeners go about the business of creating their little paradises here on earth they confront the same issues that painters face. After all, a garden is a space reshaped by one's imagination, which is really what filling up a canvas is all about. Several contemporary nature writers have suggested that the world out there becomes a landscape when the viewer engages in a subjective act of recreation. Call my compost bins, comprised of easily moved wood pallets, a landscape within a landscape, one that needs tidying up now and then so as to conform to my aesthetic needs.

Actually, I do a lot of tidying up around the place, so much so that my son last week suggested that my penchant for moving things around all the time suggested a deeper malaise not necessarily aesthetic in nature. He didn't elaborate; I got the point. He'll get his comeuppance when he comes home in two weeks. Lots of reshaping to do that requires the strength and stamina of his younger body. Who knows, the compost bins might need some work by then. Right now they remind me of a cow —four bins, just like a cow's stomach, in a row. A cow's digestive system made visible. At the rate we are producing weeds these days this cow may have six stomachs by then!

Compost is neat stuff. I love it. So does Gabby. Hers is a lusty, gustatory love. She gets perfectly good dry food every night at home, yet she can't wait to snoot about a freshly dumped, sheet rock bucketful of sloshy organic matter. Heaven takes different forms for each of us, I guess. I scold her, she backs off, but as soon as I turn a corner and get involved in a chore she sneaks off and dines at will. I feel good about returning earth's bounty home, about not wasting anything, about farming organically and feeling good about myself for doing so. My annoying refrain is that I don't let a chemical within ten miles of the place. Sandy rightly chides such self-righteous pronouncements. But it is true. I do worry about airborne assaults that I can't do anything about. I do not see myself as any sort of crusader. I have my principles and convictions and I stick by them. I have always felt that ideology is essential and that Socratic self-examinations of life are equally essential. I am also convinced that individual actions borne out of conviction and conscience are the most powerful. Individual acts serve as exemplars. Individual acts are like flat stones skimmed along a pond's glossy surface. Effects ripple outward concentrically from a vital center. Three decades ago I read books by Scott Nearing and Ruth Stout. I have applied many of their methods. What stands out, however, is the ripple effect of their documented lives. Had I not valued them as individuals I probably would not have taken their notions so seriously. Effects do have curious causes!

I have read much of the *literature* of composting. Interesting, isn't it, that there is a *literature* of just about everything. I confess that my stomach tightens a bit when someone justifies a stance or action by stating that well, the literature says this or that. Surely there is much written that is informative and quite useful to society. It is also true there is a vast body of useless, unread stuff out there gathering dust that should be spared the agony of its vapid existence by being tossed out. I know from reading about compost what it is, how it becomes compost, and why it is good for the soil. I am also quite aware of its ideological and spiritual dimensions. However, by just looking around me all these years I know the truth, of this "smokeless decay," as Robert Frost puts it, that cooks around us all the time. Walk in the woods in the late fall, see the forest floor blanketed with freshly fallen leaves, or watch ants and other minute creatures of the earth devour fallen limbs or tree stumps and you can see the virtuous necessity of decay. For me, however, it boils down to an aesthetic rooted in a complex yet simple ideology. Keats put is best when he wrote that "Beauty is truth, truth beauty, —that is all/ Ye know on earth, and all ye need to know."

I wanted Sandy to see those compost piles because to me they are profoundly symbolic. I look at them and see much more than piles of weeds and kitchen waste. I see life, beauty, even truth. I feel one with the earth, its soil, its endemic values, values clearly there for anyone to see whose eyes are open. Now, if I could just keep Gabby from rooting about when I am not looking. It boils down to this: I see beauty, she sees grub.

CHAPTER TWENTY FOUR

# Knocking Out Juxtipositions

*Meaningful coincidences*

I AM SITTING IN A MUCH too comfortable folding chair on the deck that wraps around two sides of the small house I built several years ago. Gabby, as usual, has stationed herself approximately ten feet to my left. Interestingly, and it must be some sort of deeply embedded genetic trait, she always positions herself at a crisp forty-five degree angle to wherever I might be, always facing outward. It doesn't matter where I am, in the garden weeding or just sitting here. I usually sit in the same place, so she has an established, well-worn spot as well.

I always begin my stints on the hill with a good sit. It is a ritual that has become an essential prelude to my days here. Actually, sitting quietly before doing anything is a very useful strategy. A writer I did some work with several years ago at Bard College starts all of her sessions with several minutes of 'personal' writing in order to establish a 'presence.' It is a way of warming up for the writing to be done. It is also a way of getting in the right frame of mind. My sitting at the start of every day on the hill is a similar ritual. By sitting quietly and allowing my thoughts free rein the shape of the day makes itself known. Then that moment comes when, as if directed by an invisible force, I hoist myself up out of the chair and just get to work. Hoisting my hefty frame is the hard part!

So, I sit here the morning after cool winds have chased away that horribly oppressive heat, thankful that there is a slight breeze and a threat of rain. While driving up here this morning I couldn't knock the word juxtapositions out of my head. I am not sure why. So I am sitting here trying to figure it out.

I have been staring at the lower left corner of the vegetable garden. A flock of crimson hollyhocks, all started from seed I collected two years ago, crowds that end of the garden. The stalks, heavily laden with blood-red blossoms, sway softly to the rhythms of an invisible breeze whose supple hands orchestrate their movements. On one of my inspection tours of the place several afternoons ago I stopped at that corner of the garden to look more closely at these gorgeous blossoms, something I had never done. I took my glasses off, since I am near-sighted and can get a better view of things close up with them off. There I stood, nose to petal, squinting in order to take it all in. I always marvel at the clarity of vision a squint allows. I remember thinking about Georgia O'Keefe, whose paintings I love, and how her telephoto vision of things, especially flowers, reveals the intricate beauty of their interior spaces. I thought also of the nature of art, whose primary purpose, it seems to me, is to heighten our perception of things. While all this is buzzing through my mind, a bumblebee, dusted with golden flecks of pollen, pushed its way deep into the blossom right next to me. Slathered with pollen from top to bottom, it sucked out all the nectar to be had, then moved swiftly from blossom to blossom as if it were a wine tasting with little time to waste. Interestingly, as the bee flew off into the thick tangle of stems and I lost sight of him, I started thinking about my mother. Which is why, I guess, I have been musing these last few days a bit more ardently than usual about juxtapositions of this very sort.

What was it about a bumblebee awash in pollen working its way in and out of hollyhock blossoms that caused me to start reliving, over the space of several days, and in quite some detail, some of my fondest memories of my mother? I really don't know. I do believe that more is at stake here than the random gestures of neural pathways. Perhaps because the bee seemed to dance and moved with such easy and natural grace that it somehow reminded me that my mother had been a 'modern' dancer, a Twenties bohemian. One of my favorite images of her is a pen and ink drawing by a friend of hers, a painter of some note in those days, Moses Sawyer. Three dancers, obviously exhausted, sit crumpled up in a corner clearly in a state of near collapse. The twinkle in her eye gives mother away. She also loved walking and since we could not afford any of the formal entertainments of the day, the city's streets, gardens, and parks were our living, always very affordable theater. Perhaps that is why I am drawn more than ever to walking today. I can't be sure.

When we lose someone important to us we eventually discover, after the pain has subsided, that she is still with us. Even though she died seventeen years ago, my mother is still very much a part of me. As I sit here looking out at the gardens that Sandy and I have created out of an overgrown pasture, I can see her, stylishly clad in modish garb a bit out of tune with her wizened face and stone gray hair, ambling about the gardens. She nods now and then. A smile brightens her face. She turns to me and says, "lovely Richard, just lovely, it is so charming." Perhaps too she will stroke Gabby's silky coat, look at me and add, "you finally have the dog you always wanted." I do not try to stem the tears; they feel too good. And I will stop trying to figure this connection between mother and the bumblebee out; it just doesn't matter.

CHAPTER TWENTY FIVE

# It's all About Rivets!

*Keeping busy helps keeping it together*

THE EVENTS OF THE PAST SEVERAL WEEKS (9/11) have seen each of us turn inward and outward. At times it has felt like being caught up in the swirl of a horrific hurricane of conflicting emotions. At other times each of us has walked about, blindly, dumbly, feeling as if in the midst of the sunless eye of the very same hurricane. The sunshine that normally suffuses each of our souls with a heavenly warmth instead insulates us from the very heat we so desperately need. We walk about cold, mute, benumbed. I have always felt that life is interesting because of its mysteries and unpredictabilities. I am not as comfortable with that notion right now. As is the case with most of us, there is an awful and frightful tear in our spirits because we cannot fathom the horrors of two weeks ago. It is to our credit that we never will understand how anyone could commit such unspeakable, such obscenely despicable aggression against humanity—and themselves. I find myself wandering about in a daze, yes going about the job of work that is my life, but so many, many times each day reaching for some sort of explanation, some sort of answer. I am not alone, I know for sure. We are all wandering around in a wilderness of a darkness and vastness few of us have ever experienced. I know too, as William Faulkner reminded us in his Nobel address many years ago, that we will more than survive; we will prevail. It is so because we are a strong and resilient people. It is also so because we have no choice. Our profound obligation to the departed is to keep at it, to get back to the task of the living. It does not mean forgetting. No, never, never, never. But it does mean getting on with it. We have no choice. Otherwise it is an admission of defeat. And that is not America's way. It is not a self-righteous confidence at all. Rather, it is what we are all about—about unity, about enterprise, about neighborliness, about an individualism admirably and inextricably wedded to community, to this wonderful village we call America. We are strong because we care about each other and about this country—its land, its people and—most importantly—its ideals. No one of us will ever give in to those who would seek, by whatever means, to destroy America the beautiful—beautiful in so many ways. Our grain is still amber, it ripples in the late summer sun, our skies are as spacious as ever and anyone who might have questioned or doubted the spaciousness of America's collective heart has learned a thing or two.

I have learned some things about myself since these past few days, days that have slogged along far too heavily, far too slowly. I have experienced grief before. Each of us has. Each of us will experience grief again. This is a kind and degree of grief it is impossible to imagine. We hug each other, we fall into sullen silences, we walk about dazed, we look for solace anywhere we can find it. I have found some solace in friendship and in family. I have found it in poetry and music. Marianne Moore reminds us in one poem that poetry's real value is its usefulness. I have rediscovered that usefulness this week. I have found it also in a book that I love and that I have taught to students many times over the last twenty-seven years. It is Joseph Conrad's *Heart of Darkness.*

As I forced myself to keep busy up on the hill in the immediate aftermath of the bombings, so many feelings pulsed through my mind and body. But I knew one thing for sure; I had to keep at it. I love it up here and being busy is what I love most. I love the physical activity as well as the mental activity that accompanies it. It continues to be very, very hard. There are moments when the old joy and lightness pop up, but not for long. But one thing has kept me going. And I think it is the key. It occurred to me several days into last week. In *Heart of Darkness,* Marlowe, the narrator, is stuck in the Congo waiting for rivets to arrive so that he can repair his boat and steam upriver to the 'inner station.' He fights boredom and insanity every day. There is nothing to do. He says, "What did I want? What I really wanted was rivets, by Heaven! Rivets. To get on with the work—to stop the hole. Rivets I wanted." Earlier in his conversation he also says this: "What saves us is efficiency — the devotion to efficiency."

These words have saved me. They are helping me to start filling up the hole, not stop it. Some friends visited from the city this weekend. They just had to get away. I felt honored and grateful that they chose our home. Sandy is away in Florida attending the funeral of an aunt she has loved and been very close to all these years. Uncanny isn't it, the juxtaposition of the natural and the unnatural. Yet the business of the living is living and live we must. Our kids are grown and plying their lives elsewhere. Our neighbors and close friends have sought refuge elsewhere. So it is just Gabby and me for a few more days. Having friends from that devastated city with me, if only for a day, has helped a great deal. We walked the gardens up on the hill and the joy in their son's face erased at least a few moments of despair. I told them that for me it is all about rivets, about keeping busy, about getting on with the work, about keeping in touch with family and friends, about doing all those things I have to do. I know it is the same for all of us.

The sharp edges of grief will pass. Time will blunt them. There will be moments when each of us feels the cold, steely sting of an edge. That is as it should be. It will remind us of what we should never forget. It also will remind us that we must move on, that our tribute to the dead is our commitment to our lives and theirs as well. It will remind us that in life and in death we are all together, and that America the beautiful remains beautiful, spacious, and graced with waves of amber grain that no beast or evil can ever trample. It is about rivets, about work, about efficiency.

Gabby has given me odd looks during the week. She knows that something is different. She goes about her appointed rounds as usual. Her life is unchanged. There have been moments this week, quiet moments up on the hill, when I have looked at Gabby and wished we could trade places, just for a few days.

CHAPTER TWENTY SIX

# Out Walking

*A walk through Nature's gallery*

GROWING UP IN New York City without much money taught me to fend for myself. I spent countless hours walking the streets and by the time I reached college age I had pretty much walked every inch of Manhattan Island. My two-year stint as a cab driver while studying photography is another story—and quite another way of getting around the city. However, when I do drive to the city it takes but a few seconds for the old cabby instincts to take over. I won't go into the details here. Suffice it to say I figure any open gap or lane is just as much mine as anyone else's. To this day, even though my trips to the city are infrequent, I can still feel my way around pretty well. Which is a nice feeling, since I don't experience the alienation or frustration that someone might justifiably feel when confronting the place for the first time. Granted, I am not terribly patient with traffic jams and tie-ups anymore.

On occasion Sandy is forced to muzzle me up a bit, since my mutterings are even too colorful for her ears. My lame excuse is that it is the Navy's fault. Anyone who spends two years aboard a carrier consorting with an unimaginably creative band of linguistically talented old salts can't help but pick up a few useful terms here and there. At any rate, while walking the back roads yesterday with Gabby these thoughts and others preoccupied me. As I have written on several occasions, there is no pastime more physically and mentally rejuvenating than walking. Yesterday's walk lived up to its advance billing.

I think my love of art comes from two primary influences: my mother and the art galleries I wandered in and out of during those peripatetic forays about the city. I was away at boarding school for much of the year, so when I came home for vacations I had no friends nearby and little cash on hand to pay for traditional entertainments. Consequently, when not prostrate on my favorite couch reading or listening to the radio, still my preferred medium, I walked—for hours and hours at a time. I did quite a bit of window-shopping and people watching. Mostly, I walked in and out of art galleries. Some required an admission fee, but most did not. By the time I went off to college my artistic sensibilities had been shaped. I didn't read much about the paintings that I saw. I still do not, for that matter. I would rather just look, enjoy or not enjoy, file away a freely formed mental picture, and then move on. To this day I cannot abide the stuffy, pretentiously stylized commentaries that pass for art criticism.

While out walking yesterday I felt much the same joy and freedom of reaction and expression that I felt years ago when discovering the work of Dufy, Bonnard, Corot, Cezzane, Van Gogh, and others. I think most of us do best when left alone with ourselves to confront our experiences. It is the purest, therefore the most honest, form of artistic interaction.

I saw a lot of great art yesterday. Nature is a wonderful art gallery. It is always open, always free, and no exhibition is ever the same. Turn a corner, look back, and the slant of light will have shifted its angle every so slightly. But the effect will be extraordinary. Lean against the warm trunk of a winter-bare maple as I did yesterday and watch the play of light on golden apples hanging like Christmas bulbs from leafless, wizened branches of a crab apple tree. I passed several apple trees yesterday, some hung with golden pendants, some with red. Others, just as beautiful, came in variations of brown, red, gold, and green. Each, however, has a Calderesque quality. As I walked I thought that as a young man growing up in Pennsylvania, Alexander Calder just might have seen these natural mobiles and perhaps they had helped to shape his extraordinary vision. It doesn't matter if I am right or wrong. It felt good just to think that, to chew on the possibility, then and now. Ultimately, only one's feelings and what one does with them matter. Watch as two small flocks of evening grosbeaks blend with startlingly effortless precision into one lovely unity of movement and motion, an airborne ballet of exquisite grace. Be mesmerized by a headless, side-lighted torso of a tree stump whose lines, textures, and presence mimic, perhaps even surpass, the masterworks of artists past and present.

There is even a wonderfully raw artistry in the design of a beaver hutch. I usually start my walks by heading south so as to pass the swamp just down the road. I was surprised to see that a new hutch has gone up against the far bank. I am sure that it has been there for a while. I just did not see it until yesterday. It is plastered with mud and sticks and looks wonderfully tight and cozy. The beavers are gearing up for a long winter. They have been very busy gnawing away at some pretty sizable maples nearby. I guess the softer stuff is scarce. I suspect that they will have some tasty meals stored up for those long, dark, cold winter nights. I wish them well.

Gabby and I are gearing up for winter too. This year's firewood is cut, cured, split and stacked in the basement. The hill place is bedded down. Snowshoes and skis are at the ready. My winter walking gear is waterproofed and polished. We will walk the roads as often as we can. We will seek the quiet solitude of moonlit nights and the cold warmth of weekend days. I will walk as I did so many years ago, always alert and grateful for the perpetual and protean artistry of nature—pure, honest, and free.

CHAPTER TWENTY SEVEN

# Uncertainty's Allure

*Beware of hidebound ideologues*

I AM MORE CONVINCED THAN EVER that life is a mystery. And I couldn't be any happier. This is not a conviction that has descended upon me as if out of the blue. Rather, it is a conviction felt intuitively for some time now (who knows when these things start?) that seems to be settling in for the long term. It is just that as I have walked many miles along back country roads the past several weeks notions about myself and the world I live in have quietly, as if on cat's feet, insinuated themselves into a more concrete form of being. Perhaps the poet Wordsworth is right. Right in the sense that there comes a time in each of our lives when, impelled by a force no less powerful for its invisibility, each of us starts fitting the puzzling pieces of our disparate lives together. It actually feels quite good. It is not that there isn't some sadness or regret or wistfulness thrown into the equation. That is inevitable. But it sure feels good to sit comfortably astride one's own life. It is not that one miraculously has answers to all the questions that he has asked throughout his life. Ironically, I am at that point in my life when I am quite content with mystery, with a myriad of unanswered and perhaps unanswerable questions. It is that contentment that I am concerned with here.

I do not understand a lot of things. I certainly do not understand what life is or what it is all about. But I do know that I am quite thankful for its being around, however one might like to characterize it. I agree with one writer who has reminded me this week that no one can be certain of anything and anyone who professes such a certainty, no matter the shape and vehemence it takes, must needs be taken with the proverbial grain of salt. This admonition is not limited to life's grander questions and puzzles. During a late evening dinner one night last week I remarked to Sandy that each of us is so steeped in and so blinded by the assumptions that rule our lives that all too often doing what Plato calls 'playing the believing game' is impossible. This notion comes home to roost most vividly with respect to political ideologies. Put a conservative and a liberal in the same room and watch the fireworks. And yet, what each of these individuals has in common far outweighs that which they do not. I have pitched my tent in one of these camps most of my life. I admit to having fanned many an ideological fire over the years. I also know that they are usually inconclusive and can more often than not end in acrimony of a kind that can be ugly. There are many explanations for this behavior. Science offers quite a few, each of which is quite intriguing in its own right.

The so-called softer disciplines offer quite a few alluring explanations themselves. I choose one or the other depending on the state of my mind on any given day. I know enough of history to know that one of the mysteries that we will never solve is our collective inability to be well enough served by its lessons to change our ways. Take a gander about the world these days. I do not see that we have learned too much. In fact, it appears that in many ways we have regressed. The mystery is, frankly, that there is no mystery at all. It is the way things are, period.

There is a white metal chair at the juncture of two paths in our backwoods. I put it there several years ago. It belonged to my father-in-law, who gave it to me when we moved north from the city twenty-eight years ago. We were desperate for furniture of any type, shape, or age. For a time that chair sat in one corner of our Cherry Valley garden. When we moved to the village of Cooperstown it resumed its sentry duty by watching over our small back yard kitchen garden. Several years ago while walking the woods behind our hill place I envisioned the chair at that crossroads and it has been there ever since. It affords me a great deal of comfort.

In a novel I am reading an elderly man who, like me, never knew his father, looks in the mirror and sees his father standing behind him. Of course, when he swings around, his father is not there. But the image his burned into his memory and from that day forward he too sports the red mustache his father wore that day. He claims he still sees his father from time to time and that provides him with a great deal of comfort. When I look at that chair it too provides me with a feeling of solace as well — even joy. I never sit on the chair. My father-in-law was not the kind of man to take kindly to another man sitting on his lap!

I do not understand life. I do not understand death. I do know they are inextricably wedded to one another and that is all there is to it. I also know that when I see the chair I feel a palpable presence. And when I think of my father or look at his picture or take up and rub my fingers along the grain of his pipe, space and time collapse and we are together again for the first time. These are mysteries best left unsolved.

I have said that I do not understand death. It is just one item on a very long and growing list. One of the more pleasurable realities of aging is one's increasing awareness of life's befuddling strangeness, even its contradictory nature. Knowing full well that the news might be unpleasant, I still appreciate not knowing what is around the next corner. We did not know when Sandy's close friend, Don, came to visit us this past summer that within several months he would be married and then fall prey to cancer. Now he is gone. Why? Why, when his career is finally taking off, is a gifted musician taken from family, friends, and a world that might have been just a bit better off for his artistry. As much a mystery is the joy I feel when I look out the on our back yard, even in the chilly throes of winter, and see Don and his son, Evan, playing catch after visiting the Hall of Fame. It is a lovely image, it is forever. Don is gone and not gone and that is a lovely mystery. It is as beautiful a poem as I have ever read.

When we take our walks, Gabby sniffs out her mysteries. I think through mine, always ending up where I started. Gabby seems content with sniffing her way through life. I guess I will do that too, but keep my nose above ground.

CHAPTER TWENTY EIGHT

# Rites and Rituals

*On the necessity of ritual*

RITUALS ARE ESSENTIAL TO OUR LIVES. The older one gets the more one comes to realize and appreciate their value. I have been a long time coming to that. Probably too long. I realize now that what have often seemed empty gestures to me in fact contain a fullness of meaning, significance, and necessity that my self-imposed blinders have prevented me from seeing. Of course, such gestures of rejection are self-defense maneuvers. I am no less culpable on that count. Ironically, I have led a pretty ritualized life all these years, as do most of us. There are habits that characterize the conduct of our daily lives—where we sit at the family dining table, who drives the car, how personal stuff is arranged on dresser tops, who takes out the garbage, where things go in the refrigerator—and on and on it goes. If each of us were to observe ourselves in the course of a day we'd discover a repetitiveness that is as predictable as it is comforting and necessary. Several days ago while puttering around the barn, another ritualized performance, I found myself doing things that I always seem to do about this time of the year. And I do not seem to learn from my mistakes. Oddly enough, there is some comfort in that as well. For instance, no matter how many times I have experienced uncharacteristically balmy mid-March days, I am always fooled. Give me a few warm days and I am out there doing spring things. Inevitably, the eye of the storm passes and there I am wishing I hadn't been such a fool. Such as putting the rain gutter back up on the uphill side of the barn, putting a set of chairs out of the shed deck (after all, one afternoon several weeks ago I basked in the warm glow of sixty degree sunlight!). Suffice it to say, I have done a fair share of outside and inside chores, all of which have proven premature and I suspect that as has been the case in the past, the future holds little hope for me. I am willfully unregenerate. Not all pleasures are to be shunned, perverse or otherwise (so long as each keeps well within clearly defined moral boundaries!). On that account, I feel not at all squeamish about admitting to internal bursts of sweet joy when one of my infamous repeat performances brings these words to the mouths of friends and loved ones: there he goes again! Now, that is a form of notoriety I can live with. So, long live meaningful rituals, as long as there is also room in the existential inn for those wrongly maligned as meaningless. Angle of view is everything!

There are, however, rituals of a more solemn mien. It is to these that I wish to direct some attention. And, in the process, to admit to being more inattentive to them over the years than I should have been. My feelings are an admixture of regret and relief. Regret that I have not on several occasions paid due homage to departed friends and loves ones. And relief that I now realize, not too late I hope, that rituals are forms of closure necessary to all, the living and the dead. There are many wonderful poems that deal with this very reality. Many of these I have read, reread, and even taught. It has taken me this long to actualize the truths they tell in the conduct of my own life.

Several years ago my cousin died. Only forty, she had battled a variety of debilitating diseases. She lost the war in the end; too many odds stacked against her. Invisible assailants, as we all know too well these days, are the toughest to combat. Our mothers, the youngest children in a family of twelve, carried on such a fitful relationship over the years that Sheila and I kidded one another about the fact that our long and close friendship seemed as if it were some sort of covert CIA intrigue. We never parted without reminding one another not to breathe a word to mother. The reasons for their prolonged animosity are far too bizarre to go into here. I suspect that most families wrestle with these internecine conflicts. Our family sure had its fair share. When I returned home from Asia many years ago and lived in New York City for a time we'd meet often for dinner or picnics in Central Park. I have a wonderful picture of one of these picnic lunches. It sits against some books on the shelf above my writing table. My eyes wander to it from time to time. I feel the park, hear the laughter of children playing in the playground nearby and for all practical purpose time escapes itself. I am there again.

I chose not to drive to the city for Sheila's memorial service. Many years have passed and I deeply regret not going. I had my chance and blew it. But I can admit to being wrong, very wrong. And very selfish. Selfish because the service was an essential ritual for both and all of us. I did not want to go because it hurt too badly. I thought going would intensify those feelings. Selfishly, I wanted to protect myself from the pain and hurt I knew I would feel. I should have gone because rituals are transcendent events. They make closure possible. They are necessary. It is why each time a body is pulled out from the rubble of the twin towers all work stops, the workers line up, each saluting in his own way, as the flag draped stretcher is carried solemnly between them to a waiting ambulance.

In the future I may decide against attending a ritual. I hope not. But if I do I will know why. I will know what I am missing. One of my rituals at the end of a workday on the hill is to walk around the outer perimeter. Gabby always tags along. Yesterday I stopped where our two cats, Barney and Beulah, are buried. I brushed the snow away from their gravestones, stood still, thought about them and how much Sandy loved them, and then moved on. Gabby sniffed about the stones a bit, actually seeming to nuzzle each softly. She teaches me things every day that we are together.

CHAPTER TWENTY NINE

# Of Swallows and Bluebirds

*The small stuff matters most*

IT IS TRUE AFTER ALL THAT THE SMALL THINGS IN LIFE DO MATTER a great deal. I relearn that every year up on the hill. Of course, each of us knows that. This is no great or profound insight that I am offering here. Rather, it is an opportunity to reinforce traditional wisdom, something that all too often is relegated to bench warming status in our fast paced, me-centered world. I am a creature of habit and routine and there is no chance at all that I will change much at all. I eat the same cereal for breakfast every morning, a mixture of six grains of various textures and sizes, each theoretically for what does or does not ail me. Now, I could mix it all up in a scrumptious batch, thus saving myself time in the morning. I have thought about it and just as quickly tossed it out as a time saving idea that would rob me of one of my morning's most precious moments. There is something about the daily a.m. mixing routine that gives me a great deal of quiet pleasure. I will not go so far as to describe it as joy, but it does come pretty close. Besides, Gabby is an active and integral player in this morning drama. While I am mixing, she is nosing about the backyard doing her morning business, possibly scaring off unwelcome critters. By the time she gets back I have got her half an apricot and morning biscuit ready for her. You would have to see the look in her eye to appreciate her delight in this daily ritual. But, face it, anybody with a dog acts out a script mutually agreed upon. It is part and parcel of the partnership. The key to having a good day is getting off to a good start. Predictability, pattern, and repetition are essential to the conduct of our daily lives. They provide a framework within which we can then confront the surprises that contribute equally to the fertility of our days.

There are daily patterns that we relish. And then there are seasonal ones. They are particularly tasty because if absence does not necessarily make the heart grow fonder it does do a number on the memory. Most of us have enough trouble getting that feisty mechanism to do an honest day's work. Throw a season into the mix, especially winter, and things get even trickier. Fortunately, help is on the way, even on the wing. We have been putting in some long hours on the hill this week. These abnormally warm days have rolled us out of our winter cocoons. Couple eighty degree-plus days with having a week off and life just does not get any better (Aside: think of all those who paid big bucks to fly to southern climes in search of the very weather we have had this week!). Much of our time has been taken up with drawing thickly matted hay mulch from our daylilies and other perennials. It is an integral part of the spring awakening ritual. Ostensibly, we do this to reassure ourselves that there is indeed life out there—and to open all that latent life to air and sunlight. It is a way of giving the rebirthing process a bit of a leg up.. At first glance all looks well. We thought we might have lost one new acquisition planted well beyond the recommended fall deadline. But as of yesterday morning her head had popped up through the soggy, manurelaced soil and we danced a little celebration jig. Our credo: mulch, mulch, and more mulch.

Several days ago I was working one of the flower beds about ten feet from a bluebird box normally inhabited by Don and Dora, a pair of tree swallows that has summered at our place for several years now. They have always shared the neighborhood with several pairs of bluebirds and a perpetually busy and very chatty pair of house wrens that seemed to show up within minutes of my nailing up their custom-built house several years ago. I sometimes get the feeling that I am being watched. Which serves me right, since I return the favor. At any rate, I looked up just in the nick of time. One of the swallows, unseen or much thought about since last fall, dropped as if by magic out of the sky, flattened its trajectory, and flew a warning sortie within inches of poor Gabby's head. It then shot straight up into the air, tossed in a few playful arabesques, and disappeared into the ether. I am sure that Gabby felt less pleasure about this than I did. She just happened to be lying down a bit too near their turf. Over time this ritual will be repeated, as has been the case every summer.

After a while, all creatures on the place acclimate themselves to one another. Sorties of this sort, each informed by the territorial imperative innate within us all, will occur frequently. But by that time they will have become formal affairs. However, they will have lost their earlier earnestness. As Robert Frost reminds us, good fences do make good neighbors.

The swallows have returned, as have the bluebirds. There are few pleasures in life equal to the first spring bluebird sighting. I caught their chatter for the first time about ten days ago while stacking wood. I leaned back against the woodpile and waited. Within seconds they took off into the late evening sunlight, their luminous backs splashes of sparkling blue gold against a shadowy stand of evergreens. The small things do matter. Bluebirds and swallows are the stuff of dreams. The pattern that is spring is warming its way into its customary rhythms. It will get into full swing soon enough. I can see it in Gabby's eyes. One swallow swoop is all it takes.

CHAPTER THIRTY

## Staying Home

*Charity does begin at home*

THE CONVENTIONAL WISDOM is that people care most about what affects them directly. More specifically, it appears that most Americans are far more concerned about domestic matters close at hand than they are about the shenanigans of a brutal dictator and his lackeys thousands of miles away. It is not an attitude rooted in ignorance or indifference. Rather, it is a collective conviction based on the perfectly understandable belief that while there are always dangers out there, and we should be wary of them, there are more acute dangers not a far remove from our doorsteps. In short, it is always best to mind one's own house first. The recent spate of mindless killings in Maryland and Virginia, not to mention last year's tragedy, are cases in point. From where I sit it appears that we have quite a lot of spring-cleaning to do. And we had best get about it.

As I have puttered about our hill place this past week I too have wrestled with my own territorial imperatives, even given preemption a thought or two. The deer always launch their preemptive strike on our late vegetable crops. They have always been welcome. As Hal Borland points out in his *Book of Days*, come late Fall a man has had enough of hoeing and weeding so let the critters have at it. Spring's another year away. This year, however, the deer managed to munch quite a few of our daylilies plumb down to their soil level crowns, a depredation of a sort we have not ever had to worry about. Sandy is a bit more concerned than I am. We always cut them back anyway, so in one sense they are doing our job for us. Come spring we will have to be vigilant. I suggested to Sandy this morning that since I have yet to convert the barn into a summer cottage perhaps I'll snoop around for a good used popup trailer this winter and move on up there come spring. See, I have my own preemption issues to contend with. I want my daylilies left alone. Whatever tactic I employ, it will not require setting up camp on any neighbor's turf. I will do all I can to work this out amicably. I see myself as a steward, not lord of the manor. However, if I am forced to launch a retaliatory strike of some sort I will not hesitate. No sunshine patriots or summer soldiers on this man's home ground. Without getting into a full blown polemic, a solid case can be made in defense of the proposition that it is precisely because America seems to feel it can willfully people and settle the earth that we find ourselves in the fix we are in. Walt Whitman writes that only humans are industrious over the whole earth.

Perhaps the time has come to pull back on global industriousness and focus on family, home, and community. Perhaps we ought to find ways of staying put and mending the home fences. I have never liked going out much anyway.

There are times when I relish the thought of not having to worry about what is going on beyond self, family, and farm. Rousseau writes poignantly about the constant tension that exists between the individual and society. He wrestled with it throughout his life and writes eloquently about it in *Reveries of a Solitary Walker*. Of course, given the nature of the world we live in becoming an ostrich is not the answer. Ducking the head in some cool, moist sand doesn't sound all that unattractive, actually. There are times, usually after a particularly trying teaching day, when I suggest to Sandy that perhaps the time has come to sell out and head to Nova Scotia. I get the look and that is that. We stay put. The wave of despair that fueled the urge to light out for the far northern territories usually dissipates. The thoughts, however, remain. It is best to wrestle with our ideological demons when tranquility has displaced passion. An agitated state of mind births flimsy, unreflective thought. Ironically, dispassionate thinking is not characterized by the absence of ardor. Rather, it fuels dispassionate thought by burning brightly in memory. Which is why I have not hied myself northward yet. My inclination to cut myself off from the world is ignited by a fleeting urge to disassociate myself from all that is wrong in the world, thus absolving myself of any moral responsibility for any of it. My friend Bartleby in Melville's *Bartleby the Scrivener* prefers not to do anything at all anymore and ends up dead, curled up in the fetal position. Since an untimely demise is not particularly appealing to me, and because I have been raised to believe engagement, not disengagement, is the moral high and proper ground to stake, I resist the urge to find that cool, comfy hillside home overlooking the Bay of Fundy. It is not easy. So I write, and give a great deal of thought to how I can more personally and tangibly contribute to those few causes that I feel deeply about when I retire a year from this June. Unlike the philosopher Peter Singer, I feel that the value of one's contribution to the world is greater by virtue of its palpability. It is easy to send money; we do our fair share of that. Better to dig in the dirt, help build a house, dish out food to hungry people.

I learn a great deal from my dog and the animals that people our place. They define their territories in ways that we can learn from. Stags will defend their territories by butting antlers once in a while. This preemptive locking of horns firms up territorial boundaries and take neither lives nor prisoners. Not bad! Gabby guards the perimeter of her territory—a bark or two usually suffice. By watching the world I learn that it is good to have a home; it is even more important to stay there.

CHAPTER THIRTY ONE

# Beech Leaves

*Why is not always the question to ask*

IT IS NOT POSSIBLE, despite an ample supply of words, to adequately explain why one thing catches one's eye or attention and another does not. In the long run it is not important. Better to just pay attention to what calls attention to itself. For some time now my eyes and ears have been drawn, as if impelled by some primal attraction, to the lovely curved brown leaves that cling to beech trees throughout the winter. Not all of any beech tree's leaves remain, just a select few. And they seem most abundant when they have access to direct sunlight. It is a curious phenomenon whose botanical explanation I have not run into yet. My research methods are rather lax, so there is probably some source out there that could easily clear up a mystery that I seem disinclined to solve. I would never have been a researcher worth a darn since I do not have the temperament for that sort of thing. Numbers both bore and befuddle me. I admire those who find nourishment, a kind of spiritual nutrition, in numbers and statistical data. It has just never been the kind of food that agreed with me. Years ago, before deciding to devote my energies to literary studies, I took a statistics course thinking I might just head in a different direction, one that required that sort of knowledge and its requisite mindset. I barely made it through the first week. You know when you are barking up the wrong tree, so I hightailed it out of there fast. A wise move, since even to this day I find myself mesmerized by the lovely ambiguities of language. For me the aesthetical dimension of any thing or process is far more alluring and meaningful than any description that numbers can ascribe to it. Good thing there is plenty of room, and need, in the world for all of us, those who see value in numbers, and those who value them but prefer to see things through a very different lens. I am happy knowing that there will be beech trees out there every winter whose leaves cling tenaciously to their branches despite the eccentricity of their behavior. It is that eccentricity, that singularity of being that intrigues and captivates me.

Most deciduous trees shed their leafy warm weather dress, but beech trees, for whatever reason, choose to retain some of their summer garb. It is that clinging on, that unwillingness to cave in to the reality of their own passing that so captures my imagination. Certainly there are reasons behind any plant's peculiarities. Plants, not unlike humans, look and act differently because they are different. True difference occurs because it is innate, part and parcel of a thing's essential makeup. We like to clothe natural processes in lengthy and quite fanciful language, but the truth is that each of us, plant, animal, or human acts the way we do because we really have no choice. I am convinced that the conduct of my daily life is determined by a juggernaut of forces well beyond my control. I am not suggesting that one is incapable of making, for instance, moral distinctions. But I am suggesting that just as I cannot help being who and what I am, a beech tree elects not to shed all of its leaves because it too acts according to a set of imperatives that determines its essential nature.

Most likely an explanation for why beech tree leaves hang on the way that they do probably has a great deal to do with chemical processes, about which I know very little. But I am reminded of what that sage of a naturalist Hal Borland reminds us of every so often in his beautifully written books. We are adept at describing and explaining natural phenomena, but we are incapable of determining the nature of the force behind what he so eloquently characterizes as the 'enduring pattern.' It is a pattern indeed. It endures and, for the most part, remains mysterious. Therein lies its beauty.

The recent spate of snowfalls has curtailed my walks, but I was able to put in a few miles here and there last week. Every once in a while I'd be yanked out of a daydream by strange scratching sounds, as if someone were scraping crinkled wads of paper rhythmically across a washboard. I'd look up to see a cluster of copper brown beech leaves, each curled tightly within itself, flapping crisply and in unison on the wings of a soft winter breeze. I have often wondered what an aeolian harp might sound like. I think I have my answer. There is no sound as sweet as the twitter of beech leaves brushed by the wind on a cold winter day. Perhaps Aeolus, the keeper of the winds, is the culprit here. Perhaps one day very long ago as he roamed about looking for places to let his air out a bit, he saw some burnished beech leaves dangling invitingly in the late afternoon sunlight. Captivated by their supple beauty, he played a few tunes on them. He liked what he heard and decided right then and there to keep a few around each winter to practice up on now and then. It is as good an explanation as any, isn't it?

Gabby is usually with me when I walk. She is never quite sure what it is that stops me in my tracks. But on several occasions she has followed suit, perked her little ears up and forward, stood stock still, and not relaxed her attention until the final notes have sounded. We usually look at one another and walk on. One never knows what Aeolus is up to around the next bend.

CHAPTER THIRTY TWO

# Images

*Enduring imprints of experience*

IMAGES HAVE a resiliency that accounts for their strength and vitality. Some pretty bright people have written very interesting books on imagery, language, mind, and the ways in which these things work to produce a range of fascinating effects that comprise essential aspects of our being. As interesting as it all is, I know best what I feel, intuitively, to be true. And that is that images are central to my parallel waking and dreaming lives and that without them existence would be eerily barren indeed. Images come in all sizes and shapes, of course, and are not limited to visual mind pictures. But it seems to me visual images are the strongest because they endure the longest, if not forever. The older I get the more convinced I am that personal experience is the only valid validating tool there is. While driving by a small pond on the way to work several mornings ago something I saw has worked a transforming effect on me. Not only because it was something beautiful in and of itself, but also because it, latched to other transcendently affecting images, has altered my perception of myself and the world in general. What is all the fuss, someone might ask, about a mallard drake paddling across a silvery sheen of early morning water followed by the ever-expanding V of his wake? Where, for instance, does that ever-widening V of a wake disappear to after brushing against the soft grass of the shoreline? Does it stop right there, dead in its watery tracks? Or, does it take on some form of alternate existence ? Does it possess, at its very core, a resonant, ineluctable vitality whose inherent will to live continues on—somehow, somewhere? I remember reading in a wonderful book years ago by Alexander Skutch, a noted naturalist who specialized in hummingbirds, that humankind's primary task in life is to "appreciate the earth." It is as close to a perfect job description for the whole lot of us that I have ever run across. Be nice is more of us did just that. I do not know if that mallard on that crisp, foggy early spring morning took any notice of me at all. But it does not matter a whit. He probably was sailing along giving not much thought at all to thought or the future. Why should he! Frankly, he looked the picture of contentment as he slid noiselessly across the pond towards the far shore. I am sure that he was taking in the world in his way, just as I was taking in the world in my way and that is all that matters. I appreciated him and he appreciated whatever it might have been that preoccupied him at the moment and that is that. I have relived that moment, and countless others, since that morning. I know now what I did not know years ago. That each of these images, not selected randomly, lodges itself in mind because each has something to contribute to one's ongoing perception of self. I am convinced that such images and events as these have a transcendent value that defies traditional logic. Rather, there is a different process at work, one that is intuitive rather than merely logical. It is a higher logic. However I might rant philosophically about this seemingly insignificant sighting, there is no denying its spiritual import—at least to me. I do not feel squeamish about admitting to such thoughts as these because I am convinced that we all experience them. If not, I have never let self-delusion derail my perception of reality before, so why start now?

Yesterday while cleaning the barn for perhaps the third or fourth time this spring (I need another barn!) a male hummingbird bulleted right by my left ear while I bent down to sweep some spilled potting mix into a dustpan (I think I also need one of those shop vacs as well!). These little guys, despite their high-speed flight, can stop and turn on a dime. Good thing, since if it had kept on going it would have been curtains for him. He stopped in his tracks, fluttered in mid air for several seconds, looked me in the eye, thoughtfully it seemed to me, and hightailed it out of there as speedily as he had entered the place. Who knows what guided him through the barn door in the first place. The dustpan is bright orange. Did he think it might be a large, nectar laden geranium blossom? Who knows? But I do know this. That split second communion, that lock of the eyes, that coming together of two minds, however large or small, will remain with me forever. I will never know how much he appreciated me at that moment. I suspect that hummingbirds do not have memories commensurate with ours. That's probably not a bad thing—fewer undecipherable nightmares. No need for an over-priced, jargon-oppressed shrink. In that split second each of us took deep stock of the other. The feeling, and the image, will last forever. It is now added to the mix.

Gabby lay there drowsily while all this went on. She lifted her head slightly when he flew in. When he darted out seconds later she paid him no heed at all. She seemed intent on watching the trees that house the squirrels she so desperately would like to snap into her jaws one of these days. Each of us gets our image jollies in different ways. That is as it should be.

CHAPTER THIRTY THREE

# MoveThem Gooseberries

*Nothing in a garden is forever*

GET RID OF THOSE gooseberries, she said. This just may be the day that I do exactly that. Actually, they have occupied several different niches over the years, finally settling (until today) in at the corner of one of our daylily display beds. I bought them, along with two red currant bushes, quite some time ago when in one of my periodic collecting phases and, if I remember accurately, I had it in my head to pick all those succulent, pale green berries and convert them into a delicious jam. I envisioned myself sending city visitors off with little bottles of the sweet stuff replete with homemade labels. It never happened. Two summers ago I picked every last berry, enough to fill two water buckets, trucked them home, set them outside the back door, and there they stood, fueling their own gradual but sure decay, until I tossed them into the compost heap. As is often the case with me, an idea seems oh so tasty until I have to actually do something about it. The same thing happened with the red currant bushes, although I do have a more plausible explanation for their demise. One died a very natural death. The other I transplanted to our village garden to fill the vacancy left by a rose bush that just couldn't hack our harsh winter climate. An ideal spot for a bush that produces tasty little red berries that someone like me can pick and do fantastically creative things with in the kitchen. It handled winter very well, but come spring for some reason that escapes me, and that is not an uncommon occurrence, I decided to pull it up and chuck it onto the compost heap. Thus ended our first bout with currants. I think I just ran out of interest in the culinary possibilities of currants. With that out of my system there was no reason to keep it around. I am drawn to ornamental shrubs, but the currants that spent a few years with us never lived up to even my low threshold expectations.

Thinking about removing those two gooseberry plants when I get up to the hill gets me to thinking about the way I garden which, it seems to me, is a pretty accurate reflection of the way I lead my life. It is said that nothing is forever. Fact is, some things are and some things are not. We have a little stretch of garden called 'Forever Wild.' Several years ago I ordered some wildflower seed from a place out in Texas, planted it all in this little bed, and watched all that seed come to life - well, not all. The first year most everything came up. Last year a few of the original plantings survived the winter, but this last winter shook the life out of everything so we're back to where we started in the first place—an ever thickening jungle of hardy upstate weeds. Much as I like weeds, and I do, these will very shortly go the way of the gooseberry and currant bushes. When the rain stops, if ever, and the soil dries out a bit, I'll till the patch and plant more daylilies in their stead. At the rate that we seem to be accumulating daylilies we need all the room that we can get. I will miss that unruly potpourri at the bottom of the hill, but the upside is that by planting it with daylilies it will balance out that section of the garden nicely, thus contributing to the overall symmetry of the place.

Symmetry has always interested me, but it has never been a controlling factor in our garden aesthetic. It has always been more of an afterthought. Honoring the haphazard way we go about things by ascribing an aesthetic dimension to it does it an injustice. Some people, and they produce exquisite gardens, plan everything out on paper. We have never been able to do that. Our aesthetic amounts to little more than putting things where there happens to be space, letting them settle in and show their stuff, and then deciding a year or two down the line if this or that should stay put or be packed off to another location. Oddly enough, forced resettlements are rare. However, there are times when we get bees in our bonnets and decide to reconfigure things for no reason other than the sheer joy of shifting things around a bit. Sort of like rearranging the furniture in the living room from time to time.

We put in two fifteen-by-fifty-foot beds in the back part of the meadow last year, thinking it would be nice to have some larger places to plant multiple numbers of daylily varieties. We ordered lots of new plants, put them in the ground, and this spring they all popped up looking as healthy as could be. I had some space left over so I decided to plant some potatoes and squash in one of the beds, thus freeing up space in the vegetable garden for less invasive stuff. Earlier this week I pulled out the daylilies and moved them to existing beds. The squash and potatoes will stay put, but after the fall harvest it will all revert to meadow. Why? Well, I just missed having some meadow back there. It means more mowing, but the meadow was there when we bought the place. Truth is, I just plain miss it. I miss the wildflowers, walking through it, and even mowing it. There are times when it is best just to leave things well enough alone. The older I get the more I realize there is virtue is some hands-off policies. We are back to our original plan of ringing the meadow with display beds. We should have stuck to our original vision. People compliment us on the place when they visit. One lady last summer referred to it as paradise. It is not because of the way it looks, it seems to me, but because of the way it feels. I think of it as a farm, which is why it is called that and not a garden. The latter implies a level of formality at odds with my way of seeing the world. Many of the formalities that characterize our social relations with one another give me the jitters. Maybe that is why Gabby and I get on so well. Our relationship is informal and jitter free.

CHAPTER THIRTY FOUR

# Contemplation

*Thought precedes action*

IT IS MY CUSTOM DURING THE SUMMER months to begin my day up on the hill sitting quietly for half an hour or so just to take stock. It is not a conscious effort to achieve a working harmony between inner and outer realities, but that is a welcome by-product. I look forward to these 'sittings' because they are a way of doing peaceful battle with an innate will to procrastination. I am far too adept at putting things off, so I must constantly find ways of vanquishing the demons that pester me. This is a very pleasant way of doing battle, since it takes little physical energy. Most mornings thirty minutes or so will do and I am off and running, usually non-stop, until a self-imposed late afternoon quitting time. A young colleague twenty-nine years my junior helped me fell quite a few trees last week. Towards the end of the day he commended me for my 'amazing stamina.' The look on his face and the tone of his voice suggested a respectful incredulity. I could hear him thinking, 'not bad for an old guy.' From his perspective I guess I am old - certainly much older than he. Sandy likes to characterize us as 'pre-elderly.' Now there's a nice way of characterizing the transitional stage between middle age and beyond! I pointed out to my young friend that the only diminishment of my physical capabilities that I am aware of, despite the transformation of my outward appearance, seems to be an inability to slog it out from dawn to dusk. These days dusk comes a few hours earlier. I can still run at full throttle most of the day, but come late afternoon I seem more willing to allow fatigue to set in — and more willing to give in to its allure. Besides, it gets me to my customary glass of wine earlier and that is indeed a very good thing.

As I think back on past practices, it is clear that I have grown more contemplative, slowed down a bit. I used to get up, throw on some old clothes, and get right to work. I do not do that anymore. And I do not care to. I still get up early, most mornings before the birds get revved up. But those pre-work hours are filled with quiet work of an actively sedentary nature—reading, writing, thinking, etc. Wordsworth celebrates the contemplative dimension of the aging process. I find myself wishing more and more these days that I had thought things through a bit more in youth and middle age. It is not that I harbor any notion at all that my life might have turned out differently. I am quite happy and content with the way things have worked out. Perhaps there is an inner compass in each of us that points us in the right direction. I do not know. I do know that there is no such thing as potential and that what happens happens because nothing else could have happened. In retrospect, it would have been comforting to know why, for instance, I chose one path over another. Robert Frost is right; it does make a difference. Thing is, the nature of the difference does not make itself known for quite some time. To lean on Wordsworth one more time, I am now at that stage in my life when the 'renovating virtue' of the 'spots of time' that characterize my life are beginning to make some sense.

As I sat watching some routine avian activity several mornings ago, four birds of acutely different color and character darted in and out of my field of view. A scarlet tanager swooped down from the top of a red pine, disappeared into the tall grass, then took off into the underbrush. A few seconds later, a bluebird, its arrival unnoticed, perched on the edge of the nest box hole. It peeked into the box a few times, then flew off to sit on the tip of a poplar branch that leans over my favorite climbing rose on the other side of the garden. A minute or so later a male goldfinch alit atop my pole bean teepee, did a bit of early morning preening, then darted off into a small grove of white ash at the corner of the upper meadow. As if to cap off this early morning parade with a bit of whimsy, a male ruby-throated hummingbird shot out of the pines, flew right across the garden, then screeched to a hovering halt no more than a foot from my face. We locked eyes for several seconds, spoke to one another in that universal language that transcends speech, and he then sped off into the maple grove nearby. I suspect he too needed some time to digest our conversation. I do not know about him, but I am still at it. I have had three memorable encounters with hummingbirds and each one has left me in a sort of existential daze.

In the aftermath of this avian drama, as if each were a cameo appearance in an ongoing play, it slowly dawned on me that I was beginning to understand, finally, what it is that draws me so magnetically to birds —and all of nature's creatures for that matter. I alluded in the last paragraph to being dazed to the core of my being by these hummingbird encounters. I think, and one can never be sure of anything, that each time I see a hummingbird, a scarlet tanager, a bluebird, or a yellow-feathered goldfinch that the pleasure is inevitably conceptual. By that I mean it is not the individual bird that excites me, although it functions as the necessary catalyst. Rather, each bird of a species is emblematic of an idea, a formal notion that takes on a material reality. It is the only way that we can apprehend such ideas. Each sighting, then, of a particular species, becomes just another way of experiencing a whole that is always illusive.

I guess I now understand why squirrels stir Gabby up the way that they do. She does not see a different squirrel; to her they are all the same squirrel. She is a philosopher at heart. Fancy that!

CHAPTER THIRTY FIVE

# Solstice Thoughts

*Feeling rather than fact*

I HAVE WASTED A LOT OF TIME, not uncharacteristically, worrying over how little I know about the solstice. I tend to do that when my ignorance is threatened. I am comforted, perhaps unjustly, by the assumption that others experience similar debilitations. Over the past several weeks I have read a great deal about the solstice, looked at charts and maps, even held a globe in my hand, its north pole in line with the North Star, while rotating it about myself as if I were the sun. I am not sure what is more fun, holding the earth in my hand as if I were Atlas, or pretending to be the sun. I now have an enhanced appreciation of the astronomical phenomena that characterize the solstice. Ironically though, the more I have learned about the sun's habitual dip southward, the less I seem, at a deeper level of consciousness, to know about it. In other words, the facts, as alluring and instructive as they are, in a strange way take me farther away from the solstice than I would like to be. I feel a deep metaphysical kinship with the narrator in Walt Whitman's great poem *When I Heard the Learn'd Astronomer* who, after tiring of the astronomer's charts and diagrams says, "How unaccountable I became tired and sick, / Till rising and gliding out I wander'd off by myself, / In the mystical moist night-air, and from time to time, / Look'd up in perfect silence at the stars." And it was in the silence of a cold, crisp late winter afternoon just a few short days ago, as Gabby and I wandered about the sere winter landscape of our hill place, that thoughts and images of deeper consequence came to mind.

I had gone up to walk, feed the birds, and cut down a tree for the front porch of our village home. After filling the feeders Gabby and I took a walk, the usual loop we make, somewhat abbreviated in winter since she has a hard time getting about when the snow starts piling up. She usually stays right behind me, in my wake, making infrequent forays here and there but always keeping me steadily in her gaze. We are comforted by each other's presence. That is the way it has been ever since my son Tim and I plucked her out of the bottom of a cardboard box, a sleeping furry fuzz ball, when she was just six weeks old. On this day we had a few chores to do, culminating in our cutting down the Norway spruce that would be our front porch tree this Christmas. I cut the tree down and dragged it over to the barn. I had a few other things to bring home, which I nestled into an old blue plastic sled that we keep up there for such contingencies. Once ready, I closed the barn door, grabbed the sled's pull cord with one hand and the tree with the other and started off down the hill towards the truck. I had gotten no more than a few feet when I suddenly felt light as a feather (a stretch for me!). I lost time for what seemed an eternity. In fact, it only took me a minute or two to get from the barn to the truck. But it did seem as if I had journeyed from nowhere to forever and in that space of time it was as if time had stopped, as if there were no time at all, and I was a boy again and it was Christmas Eve and my mother and I were scouring the city streets for a cheap tree to adorn our tiny city apartment. Inveterate bargain hunter that she was, mother always pulled off a good deal. We'd truss the tree up, drag it home, decorate it in a very short time, put our two or three presents underneath, and call it a day. Ours was a spare but festive ritual.

Walking down the hill, tree, dog, and memories in tow, I was aware of moving forward and backward in time. I felt very much part and parcel of time's accordion like expansion and contraction. This sensation of timeless being is part of what Hal Borland so sagely describes as the enduring pattern. The sun comes up, the sun goes down. The earth rotates about its axis bringing day here and night there. We endure dark cold nights even as we edge closer to spring's warm renewal. Everything is a turning and a returning. It is patterned repetition.

The snow shuffled against my boots, the cold air bit deeply into my flesh, my soul seemed to dance freely upon the wind. I floated through time on memory's wings. I was a boy and a man at the same time. The tree I pulled became the tree I carried home for my mother fifty years ago. Time had passed and not passed. I had aged and not aged at all. Gabby's bark waked me out of my walking dream. I remember thinking that perhaps I might be a boy again. One never knows !

This winter's solstice will pass, giving way to the lovely persuasiveness of the universe's immense and unfathomable design. I am glad to be a part of it. And I am glad that in being a part of it I do not understand why it is the way it is. Its rhythms are my rhythms, its music is my music, and its patterns are my patterns. I too have my bright days and my dark days, my short days and my long days. Each life is long and short at the same time. Emerson is right after all. In accepting Nature each of us accepts his own nature. One is a reflection of the other.

CHAPTER THIRTY SIX

## Of Orioles, Swallows, and Time

*Pattern and predictability are comforting*

SPRING SWINGS INTO its full throttle rhythms with a deft hand. As the poet e.e. cummings puts it, "spring is like a perhaps hand." I often think of that wonderful sentence at about this time of the year when spring seems to seep into being almost imperceptibly.

Spring's deft hands are at play everywhere. Each day brings new joys and surprises. Every day up on the hill reaffirms the notion that all is a striving before the wind, that indeed there is nothing new under the sun. There is newness and oldness at the same time. The buds on our fattening lilac bushes are swelling to the bursting point. In a very short time plump yellow and lavender cones of fragrant blossoms will light up the place. I suspect that my nose will take on a somewhat uncharacteristic hue, since I know, same as every year about this time, I will hardly be able to keep my nose to myself. Better to be nosing about one's lilac blossoms than others' business.

Pattern and predictability are comforting. There are those who would disparage such notions, but that is their concern, not mine. It is precisely because there is pattern to things that predictability is possible. And I welcome an ample helping of predictability in my life. There are times when I wish it were possible to predict more, but I take what I can get. On balance, I like the mix that Nature offers. It occurs to me that just as the old and the new share a common heritage, sameness and difference do too. For instance, the birdsong that I hear about the hill as I work are both new and old. Old in the sense that I know that I know those arias I can not yet identify. That within me there is that knowing place that hears and knows at a level deeper than consciousness and that over time that release mechanism that is beyond consciousness will enable me to remember what memory can never forget. It is like having the name of a close friend on the tip of one's tongue and not being able, despite the most strenuous of mental efforts, to spit it out. It comes in time, especially if one is able to put it out of mind so that memory can do its work of remembering unthinkingly.

Several afternoons ago while heading down to the barn to get some tools I had forgotten to toss into the wheelbarrow, something I seem to do with impeccable regularity, a particularly alluring, high pitched avian aria stopped me in my tracks. I stood there, mesmerized, knowing and not knowing at the same time, recognizing and not recognizing. A winter can desensitize any ear's memory, especially a musically challenged ear like mine. It was like that old friend whose name sat there on memory's teasing, elusive edge. I stood still several minutes, listening ever more intently as the song looped lightly across the meadow. Then it came to me. Northern Oriole. Old friends had returned, on schedule, from their winter respite. A melody I know so well yet forget so easily until winter's crust molts and dormant spring memories shake themselves loose, remembering anew who they are and that their time has come. Oriole song fills the air afternoons when I work about the place. I know again what I did not remember I knew and I am buoyed by a joy and 'lightness of being' happily quite impossible to dress down into language.

There are other arrivals. Don and Dora, our resident pair of tree swallows are back. They have been describing circles and figure eights above their nest box for days now, their aerial displays now a fixture above the lower meadow. Best ballet in town; no need to head for Saratoga. Max and Myrna, a pair of Canada geese, are back, nesting and honking away on the pond down the road. Furry goslings will soon be waddling across the road to the pond come early dewy mornings when I stop on my way to work. Time seems so timeless at this time of year. There is, as E.B. White so aptly puts it, time and then there is no time at all. All is well up on the hill. Things are the same and not the same. Old friends are back and yet they may not be the same old friends after all. Gabby knows. She has fallen into her spring routines without the slightest misstep. In fact, so have we all.

CHAPTER THIRTY SEVEN

# Of Absence and Presence

*She's with me even when she's not*

I DO NOT BELIEVE IN GHOSTS. However, I do not rule out the possibility entirely since there is virtue in leaving a bit of wiggle room just in case the assumptions that inform my thinking life, wobbly at best, are not as firmly grounded as I would like to think they are. There is always the chance that something exists, or is possible, yet is forever beyond our grasp. Since I value mystery, that is all right with me. Our species is so intent on finding out things that it often loses itself in the quest. I am not so sure that we know what to do with all the knowledge we claim to have anyway. If there are ghosts out there they have seen fit to stay out of my way and if one deigns to cross my path one of these days I trust we will have a pleasant but brief visit.

There is something ghostly, however, about feeling the presence of someone who happens to be absent from one's life for a time. This thought came to me while taking a shower the other day after a particularly grueling day on the hill. Actually, I am not sure what I look forward to more, the opportunity to play in our gardens all day or that liberating, body-soothing hot shower at the end of a day. It seems to me that I win at both ends. At any rate, absence has been on my mind these past two weeks because Sandy has been in France and I have been keeping myself busy because there is so much work to do on the farm and because work is an antidote to the deep pain of her absence. Some years ago when I kept up with post-modern thought I spent a lot of time wrestling with the issues of absence and presence, as well as that other poster-idea of post-modernism, otherness. They were intellectually exciting times, but it did not take too long for the buzz to dissipate. I am still fascinated by absence and presence. Time and otherness also follow me around, both conceptually and in actuality. I deal with these things differently now. Not as lovely philosophical problems to solve, but as very real, very immediate feelings and sensations. They are as elusive as they have ever been, but they have a palpable presence now that is easier to deal with.

One of our joys up on the hill is working together. We spend a lot of time working at opposite ends of the place, but knowing that we are within earshot of one another is comforting. In short, we are absent and present for one another at the same time. The past several weeks have been very different because of Sandy's physical absence. Yet, she has been there with me every inch and moment of the way. Each of us has our niches and among her many is an uncanny ability to know what plants need to be moved and to where. She is much better at it than I am. She left me pages of notes. I completed most of those chores in a matter of days and then, as new shipments of plants arrived, and as inevitable mysteries and puzzlements occurred, I found myself groping for some sort of assurance that whatever decisions I might make would be all right. Not in the sense of approval or disapproval, since that is not an issue. We have developed an intuitive feel for the place, call it a spiritual kinship. We share an evolved aesthetic that functions outside language, but not beyond presence. That is the key missing ingredient right now. Since she is not here to bounce things off, I forge ahead anyway, as will be the case today. I always keep detailed notes of everything I do, but these past several weeks my note taking has risen to a new anal level! Field note transcriptions into the garden journal at the end of the day, followed up with nifty narratives in my day book. I end every work day with a quiet sit on the bench that Sandy gave me several years ago. It is as close to a meditative state as I ever get. I usually just write for a few minutes to gather in whatever stray thoughts I might have been lucky enough to remember, but since Sandy's temporary absence I have taken to starting out by using my field notes as the raw material for brief explanations of my day to day decisions. The nice thing about gardening, though, is that if you put a plant somewhere and it does not work out you can yank it out and plunk it in somewhere else. In fact, gardening is all about movement and change. A garden is a place that invites temporary permanence.

Absence, it is claimed, makes the heart grow fonder. Perhaps that is the case for some. This man's heart couldn't grow any fonder. It burst at the seams over thirty years ago and still can't seem to contain itself. Fact is, there ain't no substitute for presence, tangible presence, no matter how sweet and lovely memory can make things. As I work my way from flower bed to flower bed today, and until Sandy's return in a few days, I will be buoyed by her incomparably lovely presence all the while all too painfully aware of her absence. I can not wait until Gabby runs those inimitable circles of joy around her when she gets out of the car a few days from now. She runs for both of us.

CHAPTER THIRTY EIGHT

# Birth Tree

*Planting granddaughter Isadora's birth tree*

SEVERAL WEEKS AGO we planted a tree to commemorate the birth of our granddaughter Isadora. It is a beautiful weeping Louisa crab, whose name has taken on added, somewhat spooky significance since learning that Louisa had been one of the names her parents had seriously considered before settling on Isadora. We spend a lot of time planting things up on the hill, but thinking about, locating, then planting 'Izzy's' tree has given us pleasure of a rare kind. Right now things are pre-winter spare up on the hill. Izzy's tree is bare, its branches arching downward as is their wont, seemingly folding in for the winter sleep ahead. Come spring it will burst into life with gorgeous sprays of thick pink flowers. It is planted just behind my bench, the one Sandy had made for me on the occasion of my finally completing work on my doctorate after what now seems like a lifetime of self-imposed hard labor. I sit on that bench at the end of every day and I have already envisioned Izzy and I sitting there in the shade of her tree while we chat about whatever seems important to us at the time. I often end the day by writing in a journal and then reading a poem or two or sifting through a favorite Emerson essay for the umpteenth time. No need right then to explain a lifelong love affair. We get a bit sillier as we get older and I have already imagined some of our conversations, have read her Frost's *Mending Wall* or *After-Apple Picking* when she's asked why I have wood stacked here and there about the place or two ladders, each leaning against the crotch of a tree, their ends "pointing towards heaven still."

Just down from this bench where Izzy and her Grampa will have lifetimes of chats sits her mother's first garden. Of late it has been given over to daylilies (when will we stop!), but bordering the upper run of the raised bed are the old fashioned hollyhocks that her mother planted and loves so deeply to this day. I can tell her all about her mother, how she loved to garden even as a tyke, and how she too can have a garden and plant hollyhocks, since Grampa has made sure to collect plenty of seeds. She might ask about seeds, about what they are, about how one collects them and then plants them. And then we can hoist ourselves up, walk down to the barn (she'll be holding my hand of course!), grab a few handfuls of seed and she can learn by doing which is, after all, still the best way to learn how to do just about anything.

Come vegetable garden planting time we can have a wonderful time. She'll want her own garden, of course, and while her mother's original plot is otherwise occupied, perhaps we'll saunter about the place and she can dowse for the perfect garden location, and then we can get the tiller out (she'll be too small so she'll have to ride my shoulders piggy back and I'll have to bend my knees low so she can hold onto the handles) so as to loosen things up a bit so we can get her very own good earth readied for whatever tickles her fancy. I'll tell her that her mother loves fresh herbs and greens, especially arugula, so we'd best take that into account when deciding on what to plant. I expect that she'll be particular about what goes into her garden, so I'll have to play the role of thoughtful consultant. If she's anything like her mother, and I hope she is (her unique version, of course!) she'll have pretty firm ideas about what's acceptable and what is not. But I like firmness of spirit and mind.

At some point we'll have to take a walk into the woods so I can show her where the stones that form the terraced beds at the top of the driveway came from. I'll tell her that she's actually tracing her father's footsteps, since without his earnest labor and strong back old gramps never would have hauled out enough stone to build those walls. I'll show her the spot where her dad hefted a huge flat stone so easily it made my heart melt with a curious mixture of awe and nostalgia for the days when my back could muster the gumption to do some heavy lifting. Perhaps Izzy will grab a few commemorative stones herself; perhaps birth stones set at the base of her tree. On the way back we'll stop by the barn and I'll tell her how it came about and that with her father's help we set the roof rafters up, made sure they were plumb and square, then nailed them in so we could put the roof on when supplies arrived the next afternoon. We'll sit a bit and I'll explain how the present is all there is but it sure is impossible without the past and her mother and father are as much a part of this place as any of us and whether she knows it or not its got a firm grip on her soul too and from what I know about souls, they hang on pretty tightly to those they take a hankering to. In short, I'll tell her, we're all in this together. It is what this hill is all about.

About this time Gabby will saunter over, curl up at Izzy's feet, look into her eyes and then mine and together we'll know in a world so ripped apart by strife that there is justice after all.

CHAPTER THIRTY NINE

# Hope is on the Wing

*Birdfeeder etiquette as a source of hope*

THOREAU WRITES THAT "joy is the chief condition of life." He is right. It is an elusive bugger, but when joy strikes nothing in the world feels better. Few things in life ardently looked for are ever found. Granted, if I lose a book or tool or favorite pen and I look hard enough for it, chances are I will bump into it. Although, given my penchant for staring things in the face without seeing them there is a pretty good chance that anytime I lose something I will need some help. Joy, however, is a different matter entirely. Ironically, the feeling itself is about as fleeting as anything can be. But genuine, deeply felt joy lasts as memory for a lifetime. One needn't look too far for it either. There are those who jump all over the globe looking for, well, whatever it is they are looking for. Perhaps they find it, perhaps they do not. I can only speak for myself. My round the world travels years ago were interesting, certainly instructive, but I can not recall ever feeling joy's warm fingers wrap around my soul. I did feel it the other day though while filling the bird feeders.

I am certain that Gabby looks forward to these forays just as eagerly as I do. Of course, her interest is not filling feeders. Nor is it the tactile sensation I so enjoy while dipping crinkled coffee cans deep into the sunflower seed stored in metal garbage cans (mouse proofing!). No, she inspects her favorite spots while I go about my bird business. Filling coffee cans does not provide me with the purest of joys, but it is a lot of fun, and certainly a welcome antidote to a day with teenagers for whom the written word in any form is not a cause for celebration. Actually, I prolong the pleasure by playing waterfall, a game I devised several years ago. After filling the can I set it aside. I then reach my hand in, plunge it into the seed, pull up a handful, and then joyfully watch it slide back down through my slightly separated fingers into the heap. It feels great, almost as good as the sand I sifted through my fingers years ago on Jones Beach. I recommend waterfall as effective therapy against the most trying of days. Anything of like consistency will do.

After playing for a while I hoist myself up and head for the feeding station. I hung up a few extra large feeders this year, which is why it is not necessary to check their levels every day. No matter the weather conditions, the show goes on. It rarely changes, which is what appeals to me. The fun comes after the feeders are operating at full capacity. Assuming it is not as frigidly cold as it has been lately, I lean against a white pine a few feet away and watch the action develop.

The chickadees are the first to arrive. I can hear them chatting to one another in the red and white pines across the way. They set the table, so to speak, and if our little hillside colony complement is full, the juncos, hairy and down woodpeckers, white and red breasted nuthatches, and finches pour in from all directions. There are days when small flocks of crows and mourning doves ground feed, but usually before I have arrived. They are less gregarious than these other fellows. They tend to skedaddle when I arrive, or when I get too close for comfort.

The other day I was able to watch the crows feed for several minutes before one of them raised the alarm and they took off for the pine grove across the road, their redoubt of choice. I stood still. A small flock of mourning doves settled in to claim the empty space under the feeders. They pecked away, in their dainty fashion, among the thousands of stray morsels that litter the ground, until a slight movement of mine spooked them. In a matter of seconds the regulars were at it again, trading places, all the while respecting one another's territorial rights and imperatives. It is a remarkable spectacle. Each individual's survival needs are guaranteed in a self-effacing manner characterized by elegance and grace. How neat is that!

Standing against that pine I felt a tingling sensation that can only be described as joy. Not the kind that sends one skipping down the pike to share one's good fortune with friends. No, this is a joy of the quieter sort. Muted, deep, lighter than light itself.

Gabby had returned and was sitting about ten feet from the feeder. The birds paid her no mind. I watched these variously garbed winged creatures share this remarkably tight space without the least hint of hostility or animosity. And each species is so different from all the others. They do diversity a heck of a lot better than we do, I thought. We write about it, preach about, and argue about it. They do it. The momentary joy I felt was rooted, I think, in the hope this particular moment educed. Thousands of people die every year simply because of their differences—religious, ethnic, racial, ideological, etc. The visitors to our feeder are as different from one another as any living creatures can be. Theirs is not a perfect world. They do have their snippy moments. But for the most part they have a found a harmony that has escaped us. I did not want to lose the moment. I nodded to Gabby, she headed down the path to the car, and we drove home.

CHAPTER FORTY

# More Than Just a Walk

*No walk is ever the same*

A WALK IS MORE THAN JUST A WALK. Each walk has the potential to be a significant episode in one's life. Rare is the walk that does not have, at least at some level of consciousness, what Wordsworth so aptly describes as a "renovating virtue." Now that the weather offers brief breaks of warmth and sunshine now and then, I hit the back roads a bit more frequently. We cross-country ski and snowshoe a bit, but there really is nothing better than a good walk to air out the spirit and give the legs a natural workout. A walk Gabby and I took last weekend has stuck with me, given me plenty to mull over since then.

I found myself caught in an aged sugar maple's gaze a few days ago. It stands tall against the road, its bark rivers of craggy runnels shrouding its immense girth. The morning sunlight, filtered through its outstretched limbs, cast eerie shadows across the glistening dirt road, as if snakes were writhing hurriedly out of danger. There is something about an old tree standing tall against time. Such a tree represents something more than strength, something just the other side of stolidity. It is more than a matter of mere survival. It is a matter of standing one's ground. Standing under this old fellow's gnarled arms I felt something more than its commanding presence, I felt something of its wisdom, its integrity perhaps. Integrity has to do with soundness, values, absolute honesty. It may seem silly to suggest that one might feel such things, but in retrospect I do not think so. To walk in the shade of such an imposing presence is to feel a mixture of humility and awe. We do not stand in awe of nature and its forms often enough. As a culture we value motion, not stillness. Too few of us stand firm on home ground anymore. Ironically, we leave home thinking we have left it behind. We have not.

While walking back to the hill that morning I thought of Loren Eisley, who writes about traveling back to Nebraska to see the cottonwood sapling he and his father planted together with his toy spade and bucket when he was a very young boy. His father had promised him that they would not move anymore, that this place was home. They would stand their ground there. It did not work out.

Years later Eisley returned to see once again the tree that they had planted together. As he puts it, "it had been growing in my mind all those years." It was not there. But in the strange way that such events shape our lives, it lived in his mind and when he returned to that spot he felt the tree's presence. It became as venerable a tree as any oak or sugar maple could be. He reminds us that without time and place we are lost, without them "man is lost, not only man but life."

In his Confessions, Rousseau writes about a walnut tree planted on the terrace by his ward when a young lad of sixteen. He and his cousin wanted a tree of their own so they cut a willow slip and planted it a few feet away from the walnut tree. The walnut tree was watered daily. The boys contrived a way to detour the water away from the walnut to their willow by building an underground channel. When they were found out, their ward was so impressed by their ingenuity that punishment was out of the question. The willow did not make it. Interestingly enough, Rousseau writes that "if only I should return to those blessed spots and find my dear walnut tree still alive, I should water it with my tears."

Eisley has his cottonwood, Rousseau his walnut, and I have a rose bush and a willow tree. I also now have my granddaughter's birth tree and the several lilacs that we have planted to commemorate the lives of those whose lives gave us meaning and continue to do so. When we lived in Cherry Valley there were two slope-shouldered willows in the back yard. Many a time I'd just sit against one or the other and take time and thought, even sleep, as they came. I still hear their music, the soft shushing sound as the wind pushed their feathery boughs back and forth. And then there is the rose bush within sight of the kitchen window of my aunt's farmhouse. It has never left my sight, never been far from view. It occupies a special place in my 'inward eye.'

I filled out my tree order a few days ago. Twenty willow saplings will arrive come early spring. I will put a few in sight of the house we are going to build soon. I'll put a rose bush within view too. Come spring I'll drive to the farm, take a few cuttings, root them, and hope that at least one takes. If at least one rose shoot takes hold that means it is comfortable with its new home ground. I will think often of Rousseau and Eisley. They have reminded me of what matters most in life. Gabby reminds me of that every day. When we rested under the shade of that sugar maple she chased its shadows. I will chase its shadows for the rest of my life.

CHAPTER FORTY ONE

# The Teaching Life

*Teachers do make a difference*

THIRTY YEARS AGO when I somewhat reluctantly took a teaching job at a local school it never occurred to me that it might be anything more than a stopgap measure, a way of marking time until I figured out what I really wanted to do in life. Among the options I had considered were international reporting for a newspaper or perhaps the Foreign Service. Both a far cry from teaching school in rural communities in upstate New York. My wife, whose prescience in such matters still astounds me, opined that since I enjoyed teaching, and over the years had taught English to adults in Vietnam, photography in New York, and horseback riding for several summers when we first moved to Cherry Valley, teaching just might be my calling. Not having much else on my plate I decided to give it a go. That was thirty years ago. In a few short days my teaching life, or at least that part of it, will come to an end as I make my long planned walk home from Fort Plain on what I hope is a sunny but not too humid day in late June. Outfitted with fancy new hiking shoes and the walking stick my son used on a Boy Scout trip to the Grand Canyon what seems like an eternity ago, I will amble my way home afoot. Thoreau writes that walking is the swiftest form of travel. He is right if one's destination is not a place but a state of mind. My hope is that I cover the twenty-five plus miles in a highly animated imaginative state unimpeded by blisters, fatigue, or darkness. At any rate, it will be a fitting coda to a thirty-year stint characterized by far more joys than displeasures.

Yesterday while clearing the area up on the hill that will be our future new and forever home, I revisited some of my old teachers, the ones that still to this day continue to affect the way I think, see the world and, as I have discovered through reflection, the way I also teach. At times, while aiming the chain saw at the core of a tree, hoping for a perfect forty-five degree angle, I could feel a smile break out across my face in response to a memory of a particular teacher. I hope no one was looking! Picture a bearded guy with a whirring chain saw in hand grinning from ear to ear for no apparent reason at all. Scary thought ! It is obviously a good idea to focus on the job at hand in such instances. Fortunately, things worked out and I was able to accomplish both tasks. The one rather abstract, the other starkly concrete. When reflecting on all this later I admitted to myself that despite my devotion to the curative powers of reflection, there are times better suited to such thoughts.

After clearing away some brush I sat for a bit to think a bit more about some of my former teachers. My eleventh grade English teacher, Bill Carhart, dazzled us with his erudition without overpowering us. Demanding but never condescending, he taught us how to think. He showed us that a mind indeed is a terrible thing to waste. He did it with humor, an infectious zaniness, and a willingness to let genuine thought thread its way along whatever paths it chose. Our discussions were always rooted in the particular texts that we were reading. As long as our discussions were earnest and genuine, he allowed us free rein. I have described this willingness to veer off track as 'the art of purposeful digression,' and I have always allowed my own students the very same freedoms. Without that, reading, which ought to be a very personal and inventive activity, becomes a dull and dead experience indeed. One of the things I have enjoyed most about teaching is the unpredictability. One just never knows what responses students will have, what questions they might ask, or what practices or values they might question. Students these days are much bolder than they used to be. Such moments make for great teaching fun. Most of the time !

Our first headmaster, Burke Boyce, required that after Sunday dinner, a very formal occasion in those days, we gather at his feet (literally) in the large common room adjacent to the dinning hall to be read to (all one-hundred and twenty-five of us). It is not hard to imagine what most of us thought about such an idea. But over time the soft modulations of his voice hauled us in and before long even the most recalcitrant among us began to look forward to these half-hour readings. Robert Browning was one of his favorite poets, so we got a healthy dose of him. He read short stories, poems, excerpts from novels, even (I think) snippets of philosophy from time to time. I read to my students often. In fact, they fight me tooth and nail when I have the temerity to suggest they read. As is the case with most human interactions, we compromise. They know I love occupying center stage, so my protestations are often less convincing than they should be. They know that I know what they are up to. Ah, the games we play.

There are other teachers. We all have them. We take what they give us, spin it about in our own internal, very subjective souls, add to it, and then hope that our students will return the favor to others, whether they become teachers or plumbers. It does not matter. What does matter is that students come away from their brief interludes with us better able to stand on their own two intellectual feet. If I have learned one thing over the years it is that teachers do not transfer knowledge. If that were its sole purpose, teaching would be an awfully insipid business. Students ultimately teach themselves. A teacher's primary job is, as Mortimer Adler wrote several years ago, to prepare students for a lifetime of learning. I have tried to do that. As I edge closer to my retirement day I can sneak off into the sunset knowing I have given it all that I have. It is a good feeling.

While sawing away Gabby sat not far away. That is not her normal behavior. Usually when she sees me carrying the saw she saunters off to be as far away from that ear shattering noise as she can be. Perhaps she knew what I was thinking. The look in her eye suggested that she did. She continues to be one of the best teachers that I have ever had. What I like best about her method is she never assigns papers. Now, that is a teaching chore I will not miss.

CHAPTER FORTY TWO

# Idealism

*Idealism should trump ideology*

THINGS ARE PROGRESSING about on schedule up here on the hill. The vegetable garden, altered a bit as the result of our picking up a few tricks in Italy, is well on its way to providing us with another summer of fresh, organic produce. The daylily beds, especially after all that rain, have filled out exponentially and while I have been setting in foundation plantings around the new house, Sandy has been doing battle with legions of weeds. The end of one bed looks more like a hayfield than a flower bed. I will attack that bed as soon as some house chores are reckoned with. As any land dweller knows, there is never a shortage of tasks to attend to. Some things need to be looked after right away. Others lend themselves well to being put off into a near future that often turns into much more than that. I often find myself approaching jobs around here in the same way that I tackle tree pruning. I carry pruning shears around with me every day. There are ideal times for pruning, at least from a horticultural standpoint. Rare is the season that I adhere strictly to ideals. Having always been partial to ideals, as well as abstractions of all sorts, an inclination embedded since reading quite a bit of Plato over the years, I know the value of striving to reach them. It is said that a journey's end is less pleasing than the journey itself. The euphoria one feels after having accomplished an especially arduous but aesthetically invigorating task is short lived, but the journey, step by step, has, at least for me, a longer shelf life. When I putter about the place my head is crammed with all sorts of ideal notions of what ought to be done. I figure as long as I stay the course, all the while inching closer to the ultimately unattainable, things will work out. One garden writer whose work I like for its earthy common sense, writes that the best time to tackle any gardening job is when you happen to be there, wherever that is, and it just seems like the right time to get at it.

Watching others at work, normally when I should be otherwise occupied, is one of my least attractive qualities. By others I am referring, primarily, to the various non-human inhabitants of this place. For instance, while taking frequent breaks up here at the house the last several days (I have to use a pick axe to loosen the rock-laden clay soil) I have watched with no small degree of intensity the comings and goings of a pair of nesting bluebirds and their neighbors, an equally frenetic pair of tree swallows that occupied one of the hill's prime bluebird houses before their blue-mantled buddies arrived. Their respective methods differ, but only in kind, certainly not degree. I am an enthusiastic dabbler in evolutionary theory, an explanation whose basic premises seem quite valid to me without negating other less materialistic ways of thinking about the multi-dimensional nature of being. Our culture lauds its work ethic, usually referred to as Protestant. I suspect that our collective approach to labor does echo some protestant principles, but it seems to me that a good case can be made for our having placed a high value on honest labor by virtue of its obvious merits. I also suspect that genetics plays no small part in the game. Neither bluebirds nor tree swallows have enjoyed the benefit of theologically rooted moral training, yet they seem to get by rather nicely. They have their little spats from time to time, but blood is not shed. In light of the present state of the world that seems a minor miracle. Perhaps they, and their avian cohorts, by whatever process, know what we humanoids seem incapable of realizing at this point in our evolution: blood spilled in the name of ideology begets more blood, nothing more, nothing less. Given our alleged intelligence, the barbarity of our methods leaves one wondering about the nature of intelligence itself. In nature there is predation. Clearly, all is not pretty out there. With some exceptions, if blood is shed it is in search of food and, at times, a territorial imperative. Generally, however, bluebirds can share their space with tree swallows and vice versa with relative ease. A squawk or two when a territorial dispute arises is normally all that it takes. It is also worth pointing out that tree swallows do not try to convert bluebirds to Swalloism, and bluebirds do not try to convert tree swallows to

Bluebirdism. Seems to me there is a lesson there. Each species plays out its ideological bents unfettered by the other.

One of conservatism's basic tenets used to be an unalloyed protection of individual freedom. While watching mom and dad bluebird forage for insects at the base of their house yesterday, my arms still ringing after hitting a boulder sized rock with the pick axe, it occurred to me, and not for the first time, that conservatism seems to have lost its way. Ironically, there are some aspects of traditional conservatism that this so-called liberal can buy. The right of individuals to live their lives as they please, and with whomever they please, is one of them. As if empty legislative proclamations ever hold sway over reality! The extent to which conservatism of late has sought to arrogate to itself the right to impose its religious and social views on the rest of us is both scary and downright inconsistent. I am reminded of what Walt Whitman said when someone pointed out a few contradictions in his poetry. He said, "If I contradict myself, therefore I contradict myself." Fine. For poetry. Not so good for the construction of sound social and political theory.

Atop the tall ash tree just to the right of my window two tree swallows sit looking out on the world. A chipping sparrow, a level down from them, sits quietly, alone with his thoughts. Below him, about ten feet off the ground and not far from their nest box, my bluebird friends are doing a bit of preening. Sort of a tree of life. Now, that is the kind of world Gabby and I want to live in. We hope the idea spreads.

CHAPTER FORTY THREE

# Of Time and a Grandson's Birth

*Planting Grant's birth tree*

THIRTY-THREE YEARS AGO, and in a pretty excited state, I called my mother from the delivery room at Bassett to tell her of the birth minutes before of her grandson. A week ago our son called us with the news of his own son's birth. Since that moment, when I have not been doting on the many pictures we have, or dreamed of the walks we might take together or those moments when I can do my part to help him make way in this sometimes difficult and complicated world, I have thought of time and how, as E.B. White once put it, there is time and then again there is no time at all. I can remember the moment of my son's birth as if it were just moments ago. And here it is, thirty-three years later, and the miracle has repeated itself for both he and his wife. It makes one think a bit about the nature of life and the meaning of existence itself. Unlike some people, my own life, while rooted in a few certainties, has always been characterized by a healthy array of uncertainties. Those so certain of their beliefs and place in the order of things have always seemed a bit disingenuous to me. But I suppose it is comforting to at least feel as if one has all the answers. To the contrary, I am comforted by knowing that there are mysteries that I will never solve. I also know, as my mother used to say, that what is good for one goose may not be the answer for another. People and geese have a lot in common.

I do know that in the years ahead, as long as we stay healthy, we will experience the joy of being grandparents. We already know something about that since our granddaughter, who will turn five in September, has been an infinite and growing source of joy for us. She looks forward to showing her cousin the ropes, perhaps giving him a helping hand now and then in ways that parents and grandparents can not. Isadora and I were meandering through the gardens yesterday just chatting about this and that. We stopped by her birth tree and then sauntered over to her cousin's, which Sandy and I planted a few days ago. She stood alongside it, rubbed her fingers along one of its leaves, smiled, and said, "This is Grant's tree, isn't it?" I said, "Yup, it is." There was no need for further discussion so we moved on. In my mind's eye I saw a nine-year-old girl and a four-yearold boy walking down the hill together followed by a six-year-old retriever having a grand old time enjoying a purity of being reserved for the young. I have always felt that adulthood is best experienced when spiced with a bit of youthful innocence. C.S. Lewis writes about being surprised by joy later in life. When he stopped fighting it and gave into it, completely and unabashedly, life took on new and extraordinary meanings. Lewis found solace in the church; others find it elsewhere. It does not matter. But in many ways it is a process of looking backward, of reclaiming what has been lost. I think I enjoy grandparenthood so much because it gives me a chance to recover lost joys. It may seem silly to say this, but in many ways we adults take adulthood too seriously. Actually, we take so much so seriously that we complicate our lives unnecessarily. Spending an afternoon with a four-year-old planting flowers and vegetables and explaining the need to turn over compost piles reminds one of what life can be like. It is no wonder I find myself paying less and less attention to the news these days. Thoreau was right. Names and places and circumstances change, but day after day the news varies but a little.

While I can not determine the course of my grandson's life, I hope that I can influence the way he sees and thinks about the world. He will grow up in a world where technology rules the roost, where rather than sit down and really talk to one another, people twitter and tweet. I am reminded of a Native American woman in a Jim Harrison novel who sits quietly for many minutes before answering a question put to her. When her friend wonders aloud why she sits speechless for so long she says, "Talking is not thinking."

We live in a world where thought counts less than talk. Communication these days seems characterized by thoughtless chirping and tweeting. One bit of advice I would give to my grandchildren is to leave the tweeting to the birds. I hope they think things through honestly and deeply. I want them to think for themselves. I hope they will value civility and cling to it even when differing sharply with others. I trust they will become active in the life of whatever community they choose to settle in. But they must do so realizing that no one ever gets his way all the time and that our collective survival depends on working things out. We find ourselves in some of these horrible pickles because we take sides and assume a winner-take-all posture. The Middle East is a vivid example of self-destructive ideological intransigence. I look forward to a few days next week when I will hold my grandson in my arms. I will sing and hum the same tunes to him that I did to his father thirty-three years ago. It is true. There is time and there is no time at all.

CHAPTER FORTY FOUR

# Katie

*Katie's birth is a reason not to give up on hope*

One of our rituals up here on the hill is the planting of a birth tree to celebrate the arrival of a grandchild. It is an occasion of great joy. Thus far we have planted three, the most recent on the occasion of the birth of my stepson Eric's daughter Katherine Louise. Eric and family visited several weekends ago and not only were we able to show off the tree, but Katie got to latch on to its sole, not yet red cherry. One cherry does not make a market basket, but since we did not expect any fruit for several years the appearance of just one fruit is perhaps an omen—one suggesting that Katie's life will be, well, fruitful. One never knows what shape a life will take. One of my basic beliefs is that life's many mysteries are what make it so fascinating, so filled with hopeful anticipation. One of the many joys of grandparenthood is watching these new lives journey their way through a world fraught with as much reason for hopefulness as anxiety over the oft ill-conceived behaviors of individuals and societies. Each new life brings with it the possibility that perhaps succeeding generations will fulfill the extraordinary potential for good that humanity is capable of. Were it not the case, the future would look awfully bleak. I am always on the lookout for reasons to hope for the best. Pessimism all too often forces itself upon me.

Several years ago Scott Russell Sanders, one of my favorite writers, was hiking in Colorado with his son. As they walked Sanders unwittingly offered up some pretty gloomy thoughts about our fate, much of his negativism rooted in our culture's destructive indifference to the very environment that sustains it. At one point his son, in exasperation, turns to his father and asks him to at least try to give him some reason to believe that the future just might hold some rejuvenating bright spots for his and future generations. The outcome of that hike was *Hunting For Hope,* Saunders's thoughtful examination of his own basic assumptions with a view to offering up some reasons for his son to believe that the future might not be as bleak as he anticipates. Perhaps the most promising reality is that we do have the capacity to fix things. We can undo the damage we have so willfully done to the environment. We can shift our national cultural paradigm to one that values the planet, that sees the immense value in leading environmentally sustainable lives. The challenge, as has always been the case, is to commit to doing so. In short, we need to devote ourselves to our own salvation. It is a challenge we have only fitfully committed ourselves to thus far.

Katie's birth gives me reason for hope. She has wonderful parents who share the hopes for the future that I have mentioned here. If there is any place to look for a reason to believe that the future does hold promise for humankind one need look no farther than Katie. She was born into a world that has the intelligence, the imagination, the inventiveness, and the capacity to do great things. That is the challenge she and her contemporaries face. I am banking on them.

# REGULATING UTILITIES IN AN ERA OF DEREGULATION

*Also by Michael A. Crew*

THE ECONOMICS OF PUBLIC UTILITY REGULATION (*with Paul R. Kleindorfer*)
PUBLIC UTILITY ECONOMICS (*with Paul R. Kleindorfer*)
THEORY OF THE FIRM
PAYING BY DEGREES (*with Alistair Young*)
PROBLEMS IN PUBLIC UTILITY ECONOMICS AND REGULATION (*editor*)
ISSUES IN PUBLIC UTILITY PRICING AND REGULATION (*editor*)
REGULATORY REFORM AND PUBLIC UTILITIES (*editor*)
ANALYZING THE IMPACT OF REGULATORY CHANGE (*editor*)

# Regulating Utilities in an Era of Deregulation

Edited by
Michael A. Crew
*Professor of Economics*
*Graduate School of Management, Rutgers University*

St. Martin's Press New York

Scholarly & Reference Division,
St. Martin's Press, Inc., 175 Fifth Avenue, New York, NY 10010

First published in the United States of America in 1987

Printed in Great Britain

ISBN 0–312–00527–X

Library of Congress Cataloging-in-Publication Data
Regulating utilities in an era of deregulation.
Bibliography: p.
Includes index.
1. Public utilities—Government policy.
I. Crew, Michael A.
HD2763.R43 1987 363.6'0973 86–29639
ISBN 0–312–00527–X

# Contents


*List of Figures and Tables* vii

*Preface and Acknowledgements* ix

*Authors and Discussants* xi

1 Introduction to Regulating Utilities in an Era of Deregulation 1
*Michael A. Crew*

2 Productivity Incentives and Rate-of-Return Regulation 7
*Michael A. Crew and Paul R. Kleindorfer*

3 Regulatory Policy under Uncertainty: How Should the Earned Rate of Return for a Public Utility Be Controlled? 25
*Howard E. Thompson*

4 Governance Costs of Regulation for Water Supply 43
*Michael A. Crew, Paul R. Kleindorfer and Donald L. Schlenger*

5 Public Utility Equity Financing Practices: A Test of Market Efficiency 63
*Cleveland S. Patterson and Nancy D. Ursel*

6 Ramsey Pricing in Telecommunications Markets with Free Entry 77
*Donald J. Brown and Geoffrey M. Heal*

7 An Analysis of Ramsey Pricing in Electric Utilities 85
*Jon P. Nelson, Mark J. Roberts and Emsley P. Tromp*

8 An Analysis of Pricing and Production Efficiency of Electric Utilities by Mode of Ownership 111
*Paul M. Hayashi, Melanie Sevier and John M. Trapani*

9 Residential Electricity Demand Modelling with Secret Data 137
*Christopher Garbacz*

10 A Life-Cycle Study of Commercial Cogeneration/Cooling: A State-of-the-Art Gas Technology 155
*Richard L. Itteilag and Christina A. Swanson*

11 Estimation and Linking of Economic and Financial Costs in Telecommunications 171
*James H. Alleman and Veena Gupta*

*Index* 197

# List of Figures and Tables

**Figures**


| | | |
|---|---|---|
| 2.1 | The incentive function $\gamma B\,(M, H)$ | 17 |
| 3.1 | Sample path of rate of return and rate case initiations | 29 |
| 3.2 | Solution to valuation equation with different regulatory controls, $x_1$ | 31 |
| 3.3 | Solution to valuation equation with different regulatory controls, $x_u$ | 32 |
| 4.1 | Welfare and transactions costs | 49 |
| 11.1 | Econometric cost models without financial models | 179 |
| 11.2 | Economic cost models integrated with financial models | 134 |
| 11.3 | Structure for TFM integration | 192 |


**Tables**


| | | |
|---|---|---|
| 2.1 | Illustrative values for the productivity incentive scheme | 18 |
| 3.1 | The cost of capital as a function of $x_l$ and $x_u$ | 33 |
| 3.2 | The expected time to the next rate case | 34 |
| 3.3 | Relative revenue requirements associated with control | 35 |
| 3.4 | Maximum and minimum stock prices associated with control | 36 |
| 3.5 | Probability of earning $x$ before initiating a rate case from $x_1$ | 37 |
| 3.6 | The effects of earned rate of return variability | 38 |
| 4.1 | Welfare effects of transactions costs | 50 |
| 4.2 | Prisoner's Dilemma model | 51 |
| 4.3 | Requested versus allowed return on equity | 54 |
| 4.4 | Costs per customer for most current rate case | 55 |
| 4.5 | Average time between filing and award | 56 |
| 4.6 | Outside consulting expenses by category | 56 |
| 4.7 | Involvement of state appointed intervenor | 56 |
| 4.8 | Definition of variables | 57 |
| 4.9 | Results of regression runs | 59 |
| 5.1 | Public utilities' common stock issues | 64 |
| 7.1 | Multi-product cost function parameter estimates | 95 |
| 7.2 | Estimated marginal cost by customer class | 96 |
| 7.3 | Cost interdependency at the expansion point | 97 |

7.4 Parameter estimates for Ramsey numbers 98
7.5 Pricing hypothesis tests 98
8.1 Estimates of selected parameters of translog cost function in private firms 120
8.2 Estimates of selected parameters of translog cost function in public firms 121
8.3 Marginal cost estimates in private firms 122
8.4 Marginal cost estimates in public firms 123
8.5 Data for evaluating pricing efficiency in private firms 125
8.6 Data for evaluating pricing efficiency in public firms 126
8.7 Relative social welfare weights 127
8.8 Mean value of selected cost variables 129
8.9 Cost comparisons for evaluating production efficiency 130
9.1 Variable definitions 139
9.2 Direct elasticities - demand equation 143
9.3 Direct elasticities - demand equation: new results 144
9.4 Elasticity estimates - new models (adjusted data) 146
9.5 Elasticity estimates - new models (unadjusted data) 147
9.6 Direct elasticities - demand: pooled cross-section results 149
9.7 The model without restrictions 151
9.8 Test of the appropriate price variable 152
10.1 Performance and cost parameters for gas-fired chillers/heaters and electric chillers 162
10.2 Ratio of the annualised energy costs of gas cooling to electric cooling 166
10.3 Ratio of the annualised life-cycle costs of gas cooling to electric cooling 166
10.4 Ratio of the annualised energy costs of gas cogeneration/cooling to electric cooling: 500-ton units 168
11.1 Contribution format of the income statement 174
11.2 Balance sheet 175
11.3 Funds statement 177

# Preface and Acknowledgements

This book is a result of two seminars held at Rutgers - The State University of New Jersey on 1 November 1985 and 2 May 1986 entitled 'Regulating Utilities in an Era of Deregulation'. Eight previous seminars in the same series resulted in *Problems in Public Utility Economics and Regulation* (1979), *Issues in Public Utility Pricing and Regulation* (1980), *Regulatory Reform and Public Utilities* (1982), and *Analyzing the Impact of Regulatory Change in Public Utilities* (1985).

Like the previous seminars, these seminars received financial support from leading utilities companies. The views expressed, of course, are those of the authors and do not necessarily reflect the views of the sponsoring companies. I thank Atlantic Electric Company, Commonwealth Water Company, Elizabethtown Gas Company, Elizabethtown Water Company, Garden State Water Company, GTE Service Company, Hackensack Water Company, Jersey Central Power & Light Company, Middlesex Water Company, Monmouth Consolidated Water Company, New Jersey Bell Telephone Company, New Jersey Natural Gas Company, New Jersey Water Company, New York Telephone Company, Northeast Utilities Company, NYNEX Service Company, Public Service Electric and Gas Company, Rockland Electric Company, Shorelands Water Company, South Jersey Gas Company and United Telephone Company of New Jersey. The support went far beyond financial assistance. Company managers freely gave their time and advice and on several occasions provided information about their industries. Their wise counsel was especially useful to me in striving to achieve clarity of exposition and relevance to industry and regulatory problems both at the seminars and in the chapters of this book. I especially thank James Alleman, George Baulig, Bert Blewitt, Frank Cassidy, Bill Cobb, Lawrence Codey, Larry Cole, Frank Delany, A. Noel Doherty, Russ Fleming, Edward Jones, Pat Keefe, James Lees, Clifford Mastrangelo, Edwin Overcast, Henry Patterson III, Glenn Phillips, Don Schlenger, Joseph Schuh, Paul Schumann, Neal Stolleman, Richard Tompkins, Michael Walsh and George Wickard.

Many thanks are owed to the distinguished speakers and discussants, listed on pages xi and xii, for their cooperation in making the seminars and this book possible. They all worked very hard in achieving deadlines, without which the speedy publication of this book would have been impossible.

I would like to thank Linda Brennan and Nanette Freitas for their secretarial and research assistance.

The usual disclaimers are applicable. None of the people named here is responsible for any errors. The views expressed are the views of the authors and not of the sponsoring companies.

MICHAEL A. CREW

# Authors and Discussants

**James H. Alleman**, Telecommunications Economist, International Telecommunications Union, Geneva, Switzerland.

**Miles O. Bidwell**, Chief, Economic Research, New York State Public Service Commission.

**Jeremy A. Bloom**, Senior Staff Analyst, GPU Service Company

**Joseph Bowring**, Research Economics, New Jersey Board of Public Utilities.

**Edward Boyer**, Staff Manager, Mathematical Modeling, Bell Atlantic.

**Donald J. Brown**, Chairman, Economics Department, Yale University.

**Robert J. Camfield**, Economic Analyst, Georgia Power Company.

**Lawrence Cataldo**, District Manager, Bell Communications Research.

**Mark Crain**, Associate Professor of Economics, George Mason University.

**Michael A. Crew**, Professor of Economics, Graduate School of Management, Rutgers University.

**Barbara Curran**, President, State of New Jersey Board of Public Utilities.

**Dillard L. Edgemon**, Vice President, Rates and Revenue, American Water Works Service Company.

**Christopher Garbacz**, Professor of Economics, University of Missouri-Rolla.

**Robert N. Guido**, Commissioner, New Jersey Board of Public Utilities.

**Veena Gupta**, Manager, Economics, GTE Service Corporation.

**Paul M. Hayashi**, Professor of Economics, University of Texas at Arlington.

**Geoffrey M. Heal**, Professor of Economics, Graduate School of Business, Columbia University.

**Melvin Heuer**, President, Energy Initiatives.

**Richard L. Itteilag**, Director, Gas Demand Analysis, American Gas Association.

**Paul R. Kleindorfer**, Professor of Decision Sciences and Vice Dean, The Wharton School, University of Pennsylvania.

**Charlotte Kuh**, District Manager, Economic Analysis, AT&T.

**Clifford Mastrangelo**, Assistant Vice President, Revenue Requirements, New Jersey Bell.

**Eileen A. Moran**, Manager, Finance and Investments, Public Service Electric and Gas Company.

**James G. Mulligan**, Assistant Professor of Economics, University of Delaware.

**Jon P. Nelson**, Professor of Economics, Pennsylvania State University.

**Richard Norgaard**, Professor of Finance and Director of the Bureau of Public Utility Research, University of Connecticut.

**Cleveland S. Patterson**, Associate Professor and Chairman, Department of Finance, Concordia University.

**Tony Pusateri**, Manager, Cost Methods, New Jersey Bell.

**Mark J. Roberts**, Associate Professor of Economics, Pennsylvania State University.

**James D. Rodgers**, Head, Department of Economics, Pennsylvania State University.

**Donald L. Schlenger**, Vice President, United Water Resources.

**Melanie Sevier**, Strategic Planning Analyst, Middle South Services.

**Patricia B. Smith**, Assistant Professor of Finance, Rutgers University.

**Christina A. Swanson**, Manager, Special Demand Studies, American Gas Association.

**Howard E. Thompson**, Professor of Business, Graduate School of Business, University of Wisconsin-Madison.

**John M. Trapani**, Professor and Chairman, Department of Economics, University of Texas at Arlington.

**Emsley P. Tromp**, Staff Economist, Bank of the Netherlands Antilles.

**Nancy D. Ursel**, Doctoral Candidate, Department of Finance, Concordia University.

# 1 Introduction to Regulating Utilities in an Era of Deregulation

Michael A. Crew

The papers in this volume reflect the rapid and dramatic changes that are currently taking place in the regulation of public utilities. Although changes are occurring in all utilities there is little doubt that telecommunications is currently undergoing more upheaval than the other public utilities - gas, electricity and water. The underlying approach to regulation of natural monopoly has changed. Presumably, the overwhelming economies of scale and scope, that were assumed to arise from a single supplier, now take second place in the minds of policy-makers who extol the benefits of entry and competition. Thus, because of changes in policy at the federal level, state regulators are no longer able to guarantee and protect a utility's franchise from entry. In the case of telecommunications and electricity, entry and competition has been fostered by federal government policy. The divestiture by the American Telephone and Telegraph Company of the Bell operating companies on 1 January 1984 is a landmark in this process. Similarly, the Public Utility Regulatory Policies Act 1978 (PURPA) encouraged competition from cogenerators for electric utilities. With the deregulation of gas at the well-head in 1984 several new competitive contracting arrangements have become possible in the gas industry.

In part, this collection of essays attempts to throw light on why such fundamental changes are taking place. The fundamental change in attitudes and approach stems partly from a (perhaps) unjustified dissatisfaction with regulatory institutions and policies. In addition, it stems from the effects of technological change which may be undermining the foundations upon which the scale and scope economies are based. To apply past regulatory practices in the current situation causes considerable problems. For example, regulatory commissions still regulate prices. Under current practice companies have to obtain the permission of the regulators before they can change their prices. Thus, in the current competitive environment, utilities may be hampered by the need for regulatory approval in the speed and extent to which they respond to competitive threats. The changed situation demands new regulatory policies and institutions. Accordingly, some of the following chapters address the new instruments available in the changed circumstances.

Chapter 2 by Crew and Kleindorfer, Chapter 3 by Thompson, and Chapter 4 by Crew, Kleindorfer and Schlenger, are concerned with the operation of existing regulatory institutions and provide clues as to where the current dissatisfaction may have arisen. Chapter 5 by Patterson and Ursel, and Chapter 9 by Garbacz investigate the nature of actual behaviour in regulated industries. Chapter 6 by Brown and Heal, Chapter 7 by Nelson, Roberts and Tromp, and Chapter 8 by Hayashi, Sevier and Trapani examine the important proposed reform in public utility pricing known as Ramsey pricing. Chapter 10 by Itteilag and Swanson, and Chapter 11 by Alleman and Gupta are by practitioners working in the gas and telecommunications industries respectively. They throw light on the effects of the changed environment upon their industries.

Thompson examines the fundamental problem of rate of return regulation, namely the determination of the cost of capital of the firm. He expands on his earlier work, (Thompson, 1985), in examining how regulators can affect the capital market's valuation of the firm and therefore its cost of capital, by setting the allowed rate of return companies may earn. Thompson's results suggest an asymmetric regulatory policy that is responsive in providing prompt rate relief when the firm's rate of return is under pressure and slow to respond in cutting prices when earnings are good and in excess of the allowed rate of return. Such a policy has the benefit of minimising the cost of capital and revenue requirements.

A further advantage of Thompson's asymmetric regulatory policy may be the beneficial effect it has on the transactions costs of governance. Regulatory schemes have costs associated with their operation. These costs are not insignificant, at least in the case of water companies, as shown by Crew, Kleindorfer and Schlenger in their examination of the costs incurred by water companies in presenting their rate cases, based upon a nationwide survey. Thompson's policy would tend to reduce the frequency of rate cases, which from the Crew-Kleindorfer-Schlenger analysis, would result in lower transactions costs.

Advocates of regulation, while arguing that it was intended to preserve the scale and scope economies available from single firm operation, have recognised the potential for inefficient operation along the lines of Averch, Harvey and Johnson (1962) and Leibenstein (1966). One of the advantages of competition is that it would eliminate, or at least considerably mitigate, such inefficiencies. Crew and Kleindorfer take a different view. While recognising the potential for such inefficiencies as well as governance costs inefficiencies, they are desirous of retaining the scale and scope economies of monopoly. Their paper, therefore, examines the role of incentive schemes, for example, total-factor-productivity incentives and automatic adjustment policies. Such policies are currently being employed in the new British Telecom. While such schemes promise reductions in governance costs and improvements in productivity, problems of assuring product quality and the like lead the authors to be less than sanguine about their potential benefits.

Patterson and Ursel examine how electric utilities have raised the vast amounts of capital over the last few years. They find that the rights issue has effectively disappeared as a financing device. They show that there appears to be little support for this phenomenon in terms of the efficient market hypothesis. Additionally, this phenomenon appears to have been overlooked by regulators who have become increasingly concerned with other aspects of utility finance over the years. Patterson and Ursel's work suggests another possibly fruitful area where regulators and companies may have to devote attention if the regulation of utilities is to become more efficient.

The papers on Ramsey pricing provide insights into how the pricing of utilities may be made more efficient. None of the papers deal with the important issue of sustainability – if regulators allow entry, will competitors be able to undercut selectively the economically-efficient Ramsey prices? Despite this, all the papers have important implications for the current regulation of utilities. Brown and Heal's paper is particularly relevant to the issue of the regulated telecommunications industry. Like Crew and Kleindorfer (1986) they show that because of the complementary nature of the demands for access and usage that access may indeed be priced under its marginal cost. At first sight this may be a discouraging result for an industry which claims that its prices for local telephone service are far below cost. On reconsideration, however, it may support the industry position. Local service has two components, access and usage. Currently the general practice is to bundle access and local usage together in terms of a flat rate. Under Ramsey pricing these would become unbundled, and subscribers may end up paying no more for access than the current flat rates but paying for usage at a rate significantly above marginal costs.

Hayashi, Sevier and Trapani examine pricing efficiency and costs in both privately owned and publicly owned utilities. Although some of their findings are relatively favourable to the publicly owned utilities, their results are by no means sufficiently strong so as to counter previous work that indicated that publicly owned utilities were less efficient than privately owned utilites. In contrast, Nelson, Roberts and Tromp are concerned only with privately owned electric utilities. Both papers are in agreement that Ramsey pricing of electricity has not yet arrived. Whether increased entry by cogenerators will hasten the adoption of Ramsey pricing is beyond the scope of their papers.

Itteilag and Swanson are concerned with cogeneration, not from the usual electric utility point of view, which often sees it as a threat to its franchise with the potential for disrupting the operation of its system, but from the point of view of the gas industry. New absorption chillers and small gas-powered engines make cogeneration an attractive technology in smaller scale commercial operations. This development is clearly seen as an opportunity for the gas industry to sell gas in new markets. From the electric utility point of view it is important. To the extent that the prices charged commercial customers of electricity are significantly more than Ramsey prices, the new technologies examined by Itteilag and Swanson may promote changes in current tariffs in the direction of the Ramsey prices.

Alleman and Gupta provide an introductory description of how their company, GTE, is attempting to integrate economic data and accounting data. In view of the limited knowledge of most economists about financial accounting data, this is clearly an important topic. From the company's and the industry's point of view, such exercises are of increased potential significance given the competitive environment. Economists have the tools to assist management in their response to competition, but accountants have the data on a day-to-day basis. The importance of linking the economists with the data of the financial accountants is clear.

This book has only covered a few, perhaps idiosyncratic aspects, of the problem of regulating utilities in an era of deregulation. On obvious omission is how utilities might diversify into unregulated business and the implications of this for the regulators. This and other fertile topics will have to be left for another occasion. One thing is clear: the problem is not likely to go away soon.

**References**

AVERCH, Harvey and JOHNSON, L. L. (1962) 'Behavior of the Firm under Regulatory Constraint', *American Economic Review*, vol. 52, December, pp. 1052–69.

CREW, Michael A. and KLEINDORFER, Paul R. (1986) *The Economics of Public Utility Regulation* (London: Macmillan).

LEIBENSTEIN, H. (1966). 'Allocative versus X-Efficiency', *American Economic Review*, vol. 56, June, pp. 392–415.

THOMPSON, Howard E. (1985) 'Estimating Return Deficiencies of Electric Utilities 1963–1981', in M. A. Crew (ed.), *Analysing the Impact of Regulatory Change* (Lexington, Mass.: Lexington Books).

# 2 Productivity Incentives and Rate-of-Return Regulation

Michael A. Crew
and Paul R. Kleindorfer

Rate-of-return (RoR) regulation has been the subject of much criticism on the grounds of economic inefficiency. According to Averch and Johnson (1962), it can result in input distortions in the form of a capital bias. Another criticism has been that regulation induces rent seeking which results in a further dissipation of resources (Crew and Rowley, 1986). Williamson (1976, 1984), however, argues that these kinds of criticisms of regulation are incomplete to the extent that they ignore transactional due process and equity issues. He argues that before economists condemn regulation out of hand they should perform a comparative institutional assessment to determine how regulation shapes up against other governance structures. In Crew and Kleindorfer (1986) we performed such a comparative institutional assessment. The result of this assessment was relatively favourable for traditional RoR regulation but did indicate the need for additional incentives for economic efficiency.

The purpose of this paper is to examine in more detail some proposals for adding efficiency incentives to traditional RoR regulation. We shall not consider in this paper the role which deregulation could play as an incentive for efficiency, although this has been much discussed in recent literature. We will rather confine ourselves to a discussion of efficiency incentives within the administered contract context of traditional RoR regulation.

Our reasons for doing this are that complete deregulation of the utility sector seems unlikely, so that some significant part of the utility sector will doubtless remain regulated in the long run. Within this context, therefore, an investigation of efficiency incentives under administered regulation seems an important continuing problem.

This chapter will proceed as follows. Section 2.1 will review the potential for improving existing RoR regulation, including a number of incentive-based schemes proposed in recent literature. Since the fundamental problem with RoR regulation is its arguable lack of incentives for efficiency, we consider in Section 2.2 a generic proposal for productivity incentives within the RoR framework. Section 2.3 evaluates the implementability of these schemes and concludes that a simple Consumer Price Index (CPI)-based automatic adjustment rule is the most promising of recent proposals. However, several problems remain to be solved in theory and practice before any of these proposals can be validated as workable and efficient.

## 2.1 OPPORTUNITIES FOR IMPROVING RoR REGULATION

In this section we review the nature of RoR regulation and its strengths and weaknesses in terms of the attributes of efficiency and equity. In addition, we briefly describe and provide a critique of some incentive schemes either tried or proposed for public utility regulation. First, however, we will sketch the concepts of efficiency which we employ. We consider four categories of economic efficiency: allocative efficiency, X-efficiency, dynamic efficiency, and governance cost efficiency.

*Allocative efficiency* is the traditional measure of static efficiency used by economists. Prices are set so that total benefits less total costs (net benefits) are maximised. This can be expressed in the form of a simple expression:

$$\text{maximise } W = TR + S - TC \tag{2.1}$$

where $W$ = net benefit
$TR$ = total revenue
$S$ = consumer's surplus
$TC$ = total costs.

The maximization of $W$ (allocative efficiency) leads to price equal to marginal cost. Returns to scale and the need to cover costs mean that second-best (or Ramsey) pricing may have to replace simple marginal cost pricing. Regulation may be viewed as an institution to implement such optimal second-best prices.[1] However, regulation may have undesirable side effects in the form of X-inefficiency.

*X-efficiency* is a concept introduced by Leibenstein (1966) and refers to the losses in benefits that occur when firms fail to combine inputs efficiently, thus resulting in higher costs. At first sight, allocative efficiency appears to preclude X-inefficiency. However, in the context of a regulated firm this may not be the case. The regulator may attempt to enforce the optimal pricing rules which are necessary for allocative efficiency but may have to take the cost estimates from the firms it is regulating. These cost estimates may be high because of the presence of X-inefficiency.

By *dynamic efficiency* we mean the ability to accommodate growth and change. More specifically it may be asked, does the system encourage the adoption of innovation and invention? Is it accommodating to changes in tastes and preferences? It is important that regulation be judged not just in static efficiency terms but in dynamic terms as well.

*Governance cost efficiency* is the fourth category. Of concern in evaluating alternative governance structures for monopoly regulation is the efficiency of the governance structure itself. If a given governance structure requires considerable input (for example, of lawyers, accountants and the utilities themselves) in order to function properly, then these transactions costs of the government structure need to be accounted for in the net benefit associated with the regulatory institution in question. An examination of regulatory governance costs for RoR regulation is presented in Crew and Kleindorfer (1985) and Crew, Kleindorfer and Schlenger (1986).

RoR regulation is the predominant form of commission regulation in the United States today. Before a utility can change its prices it has to make an application to its State Commission. It then has to file testimony, present evidence and go through a process of administrative hearings. This is an adversarial process with the case against the rate increase usually presented by some publicly-appointed intervenor or rate counsel. The proceedings typically centre on the issue of a 'fair' price. Fairness has also been the historical and legal basis for the 'cost-plus' nature of regulation. The idea is that the regulated company should not be able to make excessive profits from its monopoly but should recover its costs plus a fair return. Thus, in rate proceedings, one issue is the amount of the costs, the 'cost of service', that the utility will incur in the course of its operations. Such cost-plus mechanisms have a long history of promoting inefficiency as documented in the defence contracting area by Cross (1968) and Williamson (1967), for example. RoR regulation, relying as it does on cost plus, is thus unlikely to be strong on efficiency. However, issues of economic efficiency are not completely absent from the proceedings. Expert witnesses may be called to testify to the need for the company to be allowed a particular rate of return so that it can attract capital to maintain its continued operations. Less commonly, economists are called to testify on the efficiency properties of the rate structure proposed. However, it is not clear that commission decisions are significantly affected by such efficiency arguments. Despite the improved eloquence of economists' testimony on efficiency, equity is likely to remain the driving force underlying commission decisions for a number of reasons. Thus RoR testimony, while ostensibly based on the principles of financial economics, is unlikely to be decided on the merits of the arguments, but much more likely on the basis of some decision rule intended to be 'fair' like splitting the difference between the witnesses provided by both sides. As the process is dominated by lawyers - many commissioners are lawyers as well as local politicians - the decisions are going to be much more sensitive to judicial and political considerations than to 'esoteric' economic arguments. Thus, the strengths of the regulatory process are not economic efficiency but rather due process, making monopoly acceptable and the like.

Given this perspective, the comparative institutional assessment of Crew and Kleindorfer (1986) found unsurprisingly that the weaknesses of RoR regulation lay in areas of X-efficiency, dynamic efficiency and governance costs, while its strengths are in the due process, equity and fairness dimensions. Indeed, as it currently operates, regulation provides few if any effective incentives for efficiency.[2] The prime purpose of incentive-based regulatory schemes is to promote efficiency without exploding governance costs or undermining fairness. For incentive-based regulation to be effective it needs to pass a number of tests apart from improving allocative and X-efficiency. It needs primarily to be understood by the participants of the regulatory game and accepted by the public at large. This is not easy. It is possible to devise schemes with strong incentives for efficiency but which would not come close to passing these tests, (for example, Loeb and Magat (1979)). Our aim here is to examine schemes that may stand a chance of passing these understandability and acceptability tests.

A number of incentive schemes have been proposed and used in a limited way over recent years. We will now briefly review and critique some of these.

### 1. Automatic Fuel Adjustment Clause (AFC)

Most electric and gas utilities tariffs contain an AFC. From an efficiency point of view the benefits of AFC are largely in terms of transactions cost economy. When fuel costs are rising or falling rapidly, being required to go through a full rate case would be exceedingly costly for companies and commissions alike. In addition, the issues would almost always be the same. Thus the AFC is a means whereby fuel cost changes are taken outside the formal proceedings and compensated for by a simple mechanical formula. Clearly, in terms of reduced regulatory activity, the AFC has considerable benefits in economising on regulatory transactions costs. However, it would at best appear to provide no incentives for allocative efficiency, X-efficiency, or dynamic efficiency. Indeed several authors have argued that the cost-plus nature of the AFC may induce inefficient fuel usage.[3]

Another problem with AFCs has been the perception that AFC provides price increases that lack the due process stamp of the commission. As they are automatic, they change every month, sometimes fluctuating wildly from month to month. This leads to bad consumer reaction and claims that the increases are unfair. In response, some regulators have modified automatic increases so that they are averaged over several months or a year to avoid monthly fluctuations in fuel costs on the customer's bill.

In any case, AFCs represent only a piecemeal approach to efficiency incentives. Indeed, the automatic fuel adjustment clause approach arguably promotes only governance cost efficiency, perhaps at the expense of allocative and X-efficiency.

### 2. Production Oriented Incentives

A number of incentives to improve individual power plant performance have been considered. For example, the allowed rate of return for the company may be made a function of average plant factor (or the percentage of the time the plant operates). Similarly, attempts may be made to economise on construction costs by adjusting the amount in the rate base as actual construction costs diverge from an agreed target. Such schemes have the advantage of being simple and apparently easily understood. However, they may be too simple to be effective. For example, the construction cost incentive requires that the target be set correctly, but the regulator and the company may have insufficient information to set it. In addition, construction costs may get out of the control of the company because of regulatory requirements imposed by several agencies. The Nuclear Regulatory Commission is an obvious case in point.

## 3. Industry Benchmarks

The apparent success of diagnostic-related groups (DRG) in reducing the costs of medical care has led to proposals for industry benchmarks as incentives, for example Shleifer (1985). The Achilles' heel of industry benchmarks is clearly the idiosyncratic nature of each utility. Shleifer (1985) points out for a static model that certain kinds of heterogeneity can be dealt with through industry benchmarks, namely those that can be related to underlying, observable causal factors. However, it is very dubious that the differing performance, demand and cost characteristics of public utilities in any sector could be explained by externally observed factors such as the number of subscribers, average temperature in their franchise area, the CPI index in the region involved, and so on.[4] Public utilities appear to be considerably more complicated than this.

## 4 Total Factor Productivity Incentives

Total factor productivity indices have formed the basis for a number of actual and proposed incentive schemes. Perhaps the most simple of these was the scheme employed in Michigan for the period 1980–82. A similar scheme is being used at British Telecom. These schemes allow the company automatic price increases, that is price increases without a formal rate proceeding, equal to some general standard of inflation (for example the CPI) minus an offset for total factor productivity improvements.[5] The total factor productivity offset is agreed to before the fact for an extended period into the future. If the company meets the agreed upon productivity objectives, it will be allowed price increases exactly sufficient to meet the impact of inflation. If it more than meets these productivity objectives, it will gain a corresponding advantage in its allowed price increases. In any case, the company, the commissioner and the consumers are saved the additional governance costs of frequent rate hearings. In the next section we discuss an extension to this type of scheme which aims at providing additional incentives to the firm for accurately assessing its expected total factor productivity improvements.

## 2.2 PRODUCTIVITY INCENTIVES

This discussion extends Crew, Kleindorfer and Sudit (1979). We imagine a multi-product RoR firm producing outputs $y_1, \ldots, y_n$ with respective output prices $p_1, \ldots, p_n$. The firm uses inputs $x_1, \ldots, x_m$ which it purchases at prices $w_1, \ldots, w_m$. Assuming that revenues are fully distributed to factor owners, the following identity results:

$$\sum_j p_j y_j = \sum_i w_i x_i. \tag{2.2}$$

The variables in Equation (2.2) vary with time. Denoting by a ' . ' over a variable the change or derivative of that variable with respect to time (for example $\dot{p} = dp/dt$), we have the following identity:

$$\sum_j \dot{p}_j y_j + \sum_j p_j \dot{y}_j = \sum_i \dot{w}_i x_i + \sum_i w_i \dot{x}_i. \tag{2.3}$$

Or multiplying and dividing each $\dot{p}_j, \dot{y}_j, \dot{w}_i, \dot{x}_i$ by, respectively $p_j, y_j, w_i, x_i$, and dividing by the left- and right-hand side of Equation (2.2),

$$\sum_j \beta_j \left(\frac{\dot{p}_j}{p_j}\right) = \sum_i \alpha_i \left(\frac{\dot{w}_i}{w_i}\right) - H \tag{2.4}$$

where $\alpha_i$ and $\beta_j$ are the respective costs and revenue shares for input $i$ and product $j$, that is,

$$\alpha_i = \frac{w_i x_i}{\sum_k w_k x_k} \qquad \beta_j = \frac{p_j y_j}{\sum_k p_k y_k} \tag{2.5}$$

and where total factor productivity change H is given by

$$H = \sum_j \beta_j \left(\frac{\dot{y}_j}{y_j}\right) - \sum_i \alpha_i \left(\frac{\dot{w}_i}{w_i}\right). \tag{2.6}$$

The general scheme we have in mind involves an automatic adjustment formula involving three main elements: allowed changes in the prices of inputs and outputs, a minimum expected rate of improvement in productivity $M$, and the actual rate of productivity improvement achieved $H$. The general form of the relationship we have in mind for these quantities is that rate of growth of output prices should be a function of the rate of growth in input prices ($\dot{w}/w$), of expected improvement in productivity ($M$), and of the actual rate of growth in productivity ($H$), that is

$$\frac{\dot{p}}{p} = F\left(\frac{\dot{w}}{w}, M, H\right). \tag{2.7}$$

For example, Equation (2.7) might be specified so that the firm's prices would be allowed to change according to the rule

$$\Sigma\, \beta_j \frac{\dot{p}_j}{p_j} = \Sigma\, \alpha_i \frac{\dot{w}_i}{w_i} - T \tag{2.8}$$

where

$$T = M + \phi(H - M)^{+} \tag{2.9}$$

with $\phi < 1$ and $x^{+} = \text{Max}\,[x, 0]$. The parameter $\phi$ specifies the sharing rule between the firm and its customers for productivity improvements in excess of the predicted value $M$. This formula would require the firm to achieve productivity growth of at least $M$ (or face corresponding losses via (2.8)). The firm would receive additional benefits if $H > M$ is achieved. When $H > M$, the consumer continues to benefit since the firm is only allowed a price increase corresponding to $(1 - \phi)M + \phi H$, which is less than the true productivity increase $H$ when $M < H$. Thus, the consumer shares in the firm's productivity growth, both when $H < M$ and when $H > M$.

In order to implement a productivity incentive scheme like (2.8)-(2.9), four problems must be addressed: how to measure input price inflation, how to structure output price increases, how to measure total factor productivity growth, and how to set the minimum productivity growth standard ($M$). We briefly consider each of these in turn.

### 1. Measuring Input Price Inflation

The choices here are essentially twofold, either use a general index like the CPI or use a more industry-specific index. We suggest the former, quite simply for reasons of consumer and regulatory consensus and acceptability.

## 2. Structuring Output Price Increases

Here the question is how to translate total allowed price increases across all products (as defined by the right-hand side of (2.8)) into allowed increases for each individual product ($\dot{p}_j/p_j$ on the left-hand side of (2.8)). Again for reasons of simplicity and acceptability, we suggest equal price increments (that is if (2.8) indicates that the total allowed weighted increase for the next period for all products is 5 per cent, then each product's price would be increased 5 per cent - $\dot{p}_j/p_j = \dot{p}_k/p_k$ for all $j, k$).

## 3. Measuring Total Factor Productivity Growth

There are still significant problems with standardising a methodology for measuring total productivity growth (see, for example, Diewert (1985)). Some of these can be alleviated through industry standards, especially in the more homogeneous industries such as electricity, gas and water, where reasonable measurement methodologies already exist. However, this issue is likely to remain a central problem for productivity incentives, as we discuss further in the final section of this paper.

## 4. Setting $M$, the Minimum Expected Productivity Improvement

There are several methods available for setting $M$, including using the CPI (or other general index), comparisons with other firms, and through productivity improvement standards particular to the firm in question. Although there has been some recent theoretical work (see Shleifer (1985)) on comparative productivity benchmarks, the general verdict of practitioners and others has been that these are most difficult to apply (see Olley and Le (1984)). The reasons why comparative benchmarks for setting minimum productivity standards have been problematic are not hard to find. Basically, idiosyncratic conditions in the firm's market place, cost conditions, and technology make comparisons very difficult. Added to this is the adversarial nature of the regulatory process which requires, in the language of Vogelsang (1986) and Sappington and Sibley (1985), that the regulatory mechanism in question be (easily) verifiable by third parties. This is unfortunately very difficult in the comparative productivity domain. For these reasons we will pursue the alternative course of dealing with benchmarks for minimum productivity improvement based on the particular firm in question.

Within the specific firm benchmark, there are also several possibilities. These include historical extrapolations of total factor productivity improvements (see Diewert (1985) and Denny and Fuss (1983)) as well as self-revealed minimum productivity standards. We will assume here that it is difficult for the regulators to understand the cost and technology conditions of the firm without the firm's help so we are essentially in the self-revealed game in any case. *Ex post facto*, of course, actual total factor productivity can be monitored (subject to a set of difficulties we note below) but we are dealing here with the setting of productivity standards *ex ante.*

Thus, consider the general procedure (2.7) where $M$ is self-revealed by the firm. It is clear that one concern one must have with such self-revealed standards is strategic misrepresentation by the firm. However, one can use results from the decentralised planning literature (for example Weitzman (1976) and Tam (1985) in ameliorating these problems. Specifically suppose that rule (2.7) is implemented as follows:

$$\sum_j \beta_j \left(\frac{\dot{p}_j}{p_j}\right) = \sum_i \alpha_i \left(\frac{\dot{w}_i}{w_i}\right) - \gamma B(M,H) \tag{2.10}$$

where $\gamma < 1$ is a sharing parameter (analogous to $\phi$ in (2.9)) and

$$B(M,H) = H + a(M-H)^+ + b(H-M)^+ \tag{2.11}$$

where $x^+ = \text{Max}[x,0]$ and $a, b$ are parameters between 0 and 1.

The properties of the function $B(M,H)$ are shown in Figure 2.1 below. From this and the form of $B$ it can be shown that the minimum of $B(M,H)$ over $M$, for any fixed $H$, is $M = H$. This implies truthful revelation of the minimum expected productivity improvement $M$ for any actual expected productivity improvement $H$. We can also represent the benefits associated with any revelation of expected productivity $M$, given an expected total factor productivity increase of $H$. Using the regulatory rule (2.10)-(2.11), the firm's benefits would clearly be the amount of the total factor productivity increase which the firm is allowed to keep. This is then equal to $H - \gamma B(M,H)$. As can be seen from Equation (2.11),

$$\frac{\partial \gamma B(M,H)}{\partial H} = \begin{cases} \gamma(1-a) < 1 & \text{if } M > H \\ \gamma(1+b) & \text{if } M < H \end{cases} \tag{2.12}$$

which means that the benefits associated with increased productivity are always positive with the firm, so long as $\gamma(1 + b)$ is less than 1. Thus, the proposed regulatory adjustment mechanisms for pricing induces the truthful revelation of expected minimum productivity improvements $M$ for any projected actual rate of productivity $H$. Moreover, once $M$ is set, the firm has continuing incentives to strive for increased productivity in the sense that its benefits will continue to increase, whatever $M$ it has declared, for any increases in actual total factor productivity $H$ achieved.

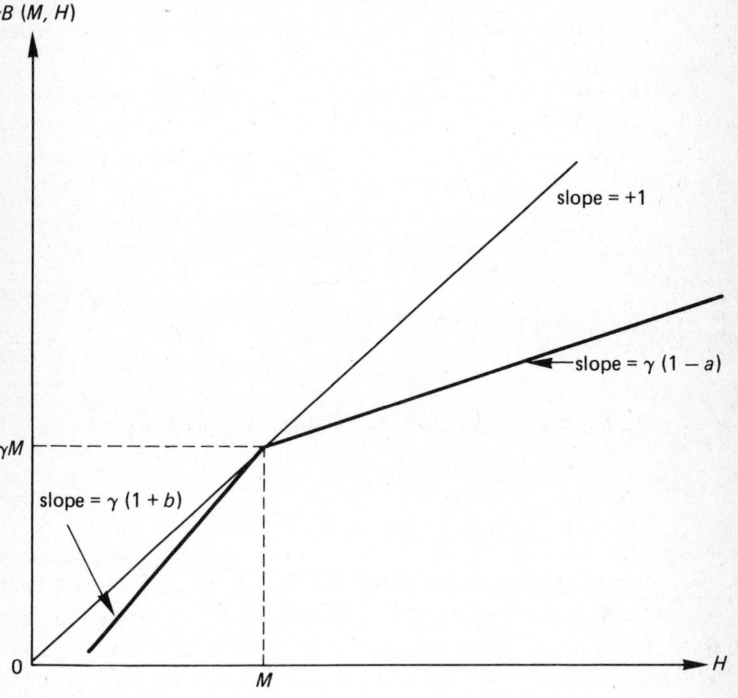


*Figure* 2.1 The incentive function $\gamma B\ (M, H)$

Table 2.1 below shows the effect of the proposed regulatory scheme (2.8)-(2.10). In the example shown we assume that weighted input price increases are 5 per cent and that the firm expects and therefore declares a minimum productivity improvement over the next year of 3 per cent. The table shows the percentage price increase allowed to the firm as a function of the actual productivity results achieved of either 2 per cent or 4 per cent. The table also shows as a percentage the net benefits $\Delta B$ which remain to the firm as a result of its productivity increases. As is well known from the productivity literature (see Denny and Fuss (1983)), these net percentage productivity benefits translate into before-tax dollars by multiplying them by the base period cost. The net benefits to the consumer are simply the total factor productivity increase (times base-period costs) minus the net benefits to the firm. Clearly both the firm and the consumer benefit in this scheme.

*Table* 2.1 Illustrative values for the productivity incentive scheme (2.10)–(2.11)

$$\sum \frac{\dot{w}_i}{w_i} \alpha_i = 0.05 \qquad M = 0.03$$

$$\Delta P = 100 \left( \sum \frac{\dot{p}_j}{p_j} \alpha_j \right) \qquad \Delta B = 100\,(\mathrm{H} - \gamma \mathrm{B})$$

| *Parameters* $(\gamma, a, b)$ | $H = 0.02$ $\Delta P$ | $\Delta B$ | $H = 0.04$ $\Delta P$ | $\Delta B$ |
|---|---|---|---|---|
| 0.5 0.5 0.2 | 3.75 | 0.75 | 2.90 | 1.90 |
| 0.6 0.5 0.2 | 3.50 | 0.50 | 2.48 | 1.48 |
| 0.5 0.5 0.2 | 3.75 | 0.75 | 2.90 | 1.90 |
| 0.5 0.6 0.2 | 3.80 | 0.80 | 2.90 | 1.90 |
| 0.5 0.5 0.2 | 3.75 | 0.75 | 2.90 | 1.90 |
| 0.5 0.5 0.3 | 3.75 | 0.75 | 2.85 | 1.85 |

Example: for the parameter values (0.5, 0.5, 0.3)

$$\Delta P = \frac{w_i}{w_i} \alpha_i - \gamma\,[H + a(M - H)]$$

$$= 5.00 - 0.5\,[2.00 + 0.5(3.00 - 2.00)] = 3.75$$

Summarising, the most promising productivity scheme may be use of CPI to measure input price inflation, equal percentage increases in output prices and self-revealed minimum standards $M$ coupled with (2.10)–(2.11). Under this proposal, the firm would be allowed price increases equal to the CPI, minus a fixed productivity offset agreed to at the beginning of the planning period. If the firm did not achieve its minimum expected productivity growth ($M$ in the above formulation), it would simply absorb the difference. The argument then would be over the agreed upon productivity standard *ex ante* (that is at the beginning of, say, a three-year planning period) as well as on measurement of productivity improvement ($H$) *ex post.*

There are clearly several possible extensions of this type of scheme, all having the same general structure (2.10)-(2.11). That is, some benchmark for input factor price inflation is required (firm-specific or economy-wide) and some measure of expected and some measure of actual improvement in productivity growth is required. The fundamental problem is to obtain these figures with reasonable transactions costs while maintaining sufficient accuracy so as to provide real incentives for productivity growth for the firm. This problem is very difficult, as we now discuss.

## 2.3 APPLICATION OF THE PRODUCTIVITY INCENTIVE SCHEME

The above theoretical description can easily be translated into a more practical scenario. This would follow similar such schemes as implemented, for example, in Michigan. First, a general rate case would be instituted to determine the appropriate rate of return following traditional utility economics methods. In the same case a company productivity study would be introduced to establish the expected productivity improvement $M$ in the above formula. The commission would set the sharing parameters $a$, $b$ and $\gamma$ to effect the appropriate risk sharing and benefit sharing between the firm and the consumer. The above table points out some of the trade-offs involved in this process.

Annual rate adjustments would be based on the prior years productivity improvements and the agreed upon minimum productivity standards for the period in question. Such rate increases would be determined by the regulatory adjustment scheme (2.10)-(2.11). The plan would run for a specified period, for example three years with no stated upper or lower limits on the rate of return during this period. Only significant exogenous events, for example new accounting rules or tax rules, would interrupt this automatic adjustment procedure.

It is to be emphasised that the firm should be entirely free to use the gains from its productivity efforts to provide extra compensation for employees and managers. This would be particularly important in the case of senior managers. They could be rewarded by substantial bonuses which would make top management positions at least as attractive as similar positions in the private sector. This is similar in spirit to the several recent schemes that have been proposed for managerial incentives (see Vogelsang (1986) and Tam (1985)).

Recall from Section 2.1 and Crew and Kleindorfer (1986) that the purpose of the productivity incentives discussed is to promote X-efficiency, dynamic efficiency and transactions cost efficiency. By providing incentives to the firm to improve its productivity clearly all the traditional efficiency measures should improve. Moreover, transactions cost of governance should decrease because of the less complicated rate proceedings. However, it is clear that some of this is achieved at the cost of fairness and price control aspects of regulation in that consumers may feel that a more hands-off attitude with respect to the regulated firm may provide less control than is desirable and may leave questions as to whether the profits which are earned are in fact due to the productivity improvement efforts of the firm or to some exogenous chance events, the benefits of which the consumers should have shared more greatly.

As it turns out, these fairness issues are not the only problems with respect to the productivity incentive schemes proposed. Indeed, general lack of implementation of such productivity incentives in regulated industries should make us somewhat suspicious. Several problems can be mentioned as key in this regard.

### 1. Measurement Problems Related to Total Factor Productivity

The presence of scale effects, the unique difficulties of measuring capital, the problems of defining the product set, and problems of properly segregating and measuring inputs are but a few of the traditional problems that have been mentioned in respect to the measurement of the total factor productivity. On the other hand, if we cannot measure total productivity accurately (that is verifiably in an adverserial environment) clearly the above scheme will not work at all.

### 2. Productivity Incentives

One of the *desiderata* for any automated regulatory mechanism is that it provide proper incentives for a firm to innovate and choose the proper technology and product set. With respect to the technology and the plant mix, the above scheme probably is in the right spirit. However, it is not clear that the automated adjustment scheme proposed will provide the proper incentives for the firm to select the right product set, including the introduction of new products. In particular, until now we have completely suppressed the problem of measuring product quality, certainly a fundamental attribute of each product. It is clear, however, that regulators would have to establish minimum quality standards for each output in order to have an identifiable standard output against which to measure total factor productivity (improvements). This raises many questions on the appropriate measurement of product quality in an adversarial environment. In many instances in electricity and telecommunications, there may be verifiable quality measures for many of the products offered. In other instances, especially with respect to new product offerings, product quality may be very difficult to measure. Without valid and verifiable measurement, however, the product set cannot be said to be well defined and this is essential if the above scheme is to work.

## 3. Regulatory Problems

We have already mentioned fairness and the issue of a legitimated process which traditional RoR regulation provides. In particular, consumers have an opportunity to have their complaints and concerns reviewed under present procedures. The automated productivity scheme proposed, while compatible with traditional RoR regulation tools and processes, would clearly present fewer opportunities for review by consumer groups.

The basic issue addressed here is the introduction of productivity incentives into the regulated rate of return regulated firm. This is essential in combating the fundamental weakness of RoR regulation on traditional efficiency dimensions and transactions costs. At the same time, the above caveats and reservations with respect to productivity measurement and control suggest that productivity measures will be extremely difficult to introduce as an external regulatory tool. Of the above proposals, it would seem that simple productivity benchmarks, such as the CPI method discussed at the end of Section 2.2, are the least problematical in terms of inducing productivity gains while not exploding transactions cost of governance or undermining consumer trusts.

In view of the problems discussed here, perhaps the strongest defensible recommendation for regulatory policy at this time would be to require the filing of productivity growth plans on a periodic basis with regulatory commissions. This would encourage the internal management use of productivity analysis techniques and perhaps promote inter-firm rivalry across franchises through the informal (but public) comparison of productivity growth among utilities. One might view this as a sort of 'gossamer invisible hand' inducing utilities to strive for better comparative performance. Such a requirement for filing productivity plans might also contribute to standardisation of productivity measurement and thus to the eventual implementability of some of the schemes discussed here. The major short-run benefit, however, would clearly be to promote better internal productivity measurement and management by utilities.

## Acknowledgements

Comments on an earlier version by our discussants D. L. Edgeman of the American Waterworks Service Company and C. M. Mastrangelo of New Jersey Bell are gratefully acknowledge.

## Notes

1. See Crew and Kleindorfer (1986) for a detailed examination of theoretically optimal departures from marginal cost pricing.
2. To the extent that the allowed rate of return is less than the cost of capital or the firm is not earning its allowed rate, there will be strong incentives for productivity improvement in the short run. This is clearly not a viable approach to productivity incentives in the long run; at best it will cause excessive resources being devoted to 'working' the regulatory process and may threaten the very viability of the firm.
3. For an examination of such issues, see Scott (1980) and Baron and Taggart (1980), for example.
4. As one group of practitioners (Olley and Le, 1984, p. 118) noted in the context of productivity measurement for regulated industries: 'Given the state of the art, inter-firm (productivity) level comparisons are not meaningful in any known sense.'
5. Our understanding of the Michigan experiment owes much to a presentation by Howard Face at Rutgers Advanced Workshop on Public Utility Economics and Regulation, 19 April 1985.

## References

AVERCH, H. and JOHNSON, L. L. (1962) 'Behavior of the Firm under Regulatory Constraint', *American Economic Review*, vol. 52, pp. 1052–69.

BARON, D. P. and Taggart, R. A. (1980) 'Regulatory Pricing Procedures and Economic Incentives', in M. A. Crew (ed.) *Issues in Public-Utility Pricing and Regulation* (Lexington: Lexington Books).

CREW, M. A. and KLEINDORFER, P. R. (1985a) 'Governance Costs of Rate-of-Return Regulation', *Journal of Institutional and Theoretical Economics*, vol. 141, no. 1, March, pp. 104–23.

CREW, M. A. and KLEINDORFER, P. R. (1986) *The Economics of Public Utility Regulation* (London: Macmillan).

CREW, M. A., KLEINDORFER, P. R. and SCHLENGER, D. L. (1986) 'Governance Costs of Regulation for Water Supply', in M. A. Crew (ed.) *Regulating Utilities in an Era of Deregulation* (London: Macmillan).

CREW, M. A., KLEINDORFER, P. R. and SUDIT, E. F. (1979). 'Incentives for Efficiency in the Nationalised Industries: Beyond the 1978 White Paper', *The Journal of Industrial Affairs*, vol. 7, pp. 11–15.

CREW, M. A., and ROWLEY, C. K. (1986) 'Deregulation as an Instrument of Industrial Policy', *Journal of Institutional and Theoretical Economics*, vol. 142, no. 1, March. pp. 52–70.

CROSS, J. G. (1968) 'A Reappraisal of Cost Incentives in Defense Contracts', *Western Economic Journal*, vol. 6, June, pp. 205–25.

DENNY, M. and FUSS, M. (1983) 'A General Approach to Intertemporal and Interspatial Productivity Comparisons', *Journal of Econometrics*, vol. 23, no. 3, pp. 315–30.

DIEWERT, W. E. (1985) 'Efficiency Improving Incentive Schemes for Regulated Industries', *Discussion Paper 85–34*, Department of Economics, University of British Columbia, November.

LEIBENSTEIN, H. (1966), 'Allocative Efficiency Versus X-Efficiency', *American Economic Review*, vol. 56, June, pp. 392–415.

LOEB, M. and MAGAT, W. A. (1979) 'A Decentralized Method for Utility Regulation', *Journal of Law and Economics*, vol. 22, October, pp. 58–73.

OLLEY, R. E. and LE, C. D. (1984) 'Total Factor Productivity of Canadian Telecommunications Carriers', Project Report to the Department of Communications and to the Members of the Canadian Telecommunications Carriers Association, February.

SAPPINGTON, D. and SIBLEY, D. (1985) 'Regulatory Incentive Schemes using Historic Cost Data', Working Paper at Bell Communications Research, August.

SCOTT, F. A. (1980) 'Fuel Adjustment Clauses and Profit Risk', in M. A. Crew (ed.) *Issues in Public-Utility Pricing and Regulation* (Lexington: Lexington Books).

SHLEIFER, A. (1985) 'A Theory of Yardstick Competition', *The Rand Journal of Economics*, vol. 16, pp. 319–27.

TAM, M. S. (1985) 'Reward Structures in a Planned Economy: Some Further Thoughts', *Quarterly Journal of Economics*, vol. 100, no. 1, pp. 279–89.

VOGELSANG, I. (1986) 'A Little Paradox in the Design of Regulatory Mechanisms', Boston University Department of Economics Working Paper, January.

WEITZMAN, M. (1976) 'The New Society Incentive Model', *Bell Journal of Economics*, vol. 7, no. 1, pp. 251–7.

WILLIAMSON, O. E. (1967) 'The Economics of Defense Contracting Incentives and Performance', in Roland N. McKean (ed.) *Issues in Defense Economics* (New York: National Bureau of Economic Research).

WILLIAMSON, O. E. (1976) 'Franchise Bidding for Natural Monopolies in General and with Reference to CATV', *Bell Journal of Economics*, vol. 7, no. 1, pp. 73–104.

WILLIAMSON, O. E. (1984) 'The Economics of Governance: Framework and Implications', *Journal of Institutional and Theoretical Economics*, vol. 140, March, pp. 195–223.

# 3 Regulatory Policy Under Uncertainty: How Should the Earned Rate of Return for a Public Utility be Controlled?

Howard E. Thompson

## 3.1 INTRODUCTION

Much of the analysis of the effects of rate-of-return regulation on public utilities has centered on the 'Averch–Johnson (A–J) problem' first introduced in 1962. Simply stated, the A–J problem saw the firm choosing its inputs - labour and capital - so as to maximise profits subject to rate of return regulation in a static and deterministic environment. Within this framework they demonstrated that if the allowed rate of return exceeds the cost of capital the firm will choose to employ a higher capital-to-labour ratio than it would under cost minimisation. In other words, the regulatory process will cause social welfare inefficiencies.

The A–J model not only suggested these social inefficiencies but lead to the uncomfortable conclusion that as the allowed rate of return approached the cost of capital from above the optimal capital stock for the firm tended to infinity. However, at equality there were many firm optimal decisions; the solution was indeterminate. These results from the A–J model appeared to suggest that the traditional practical regulatory rule that the allowed rate of return should be equal to the cost of capital was ineffective.

But subsequent analysis has shown that the conclusions suggested by the A-J framework were weak and subject to substantial modification as the framework was brought 'closer to reality'. Klevorick (1971) focused on the conditions, within the A-J framework, which may be present to rescue the traditional practical regulatory rule. He found that there were cases where the social welfare would be enhanced if the allowed rate of return was set equal to the cost of capital as well as cases where setting the allowed rate of return to exceed the cost of capital was socially optimal.

Extensions outside of the A-J framework further weakened the conclusions and strengthened the traditional approach to regulation. Perrakis (1976) argued that in the presence of probabilistic demand the A-J capital-labour inefficiency conclusion did not hold. Bawa and Sibley (1980) introduced uncertain regulatory reviews, with probability of occurrence dependent on the difference between the allowed and actual rates of return, and test-year calculation of prices. They concluded that if the regulator sets the allowed rate of return equal to the cost of capital, the firm will be efficient in producing its output. The optimal regulatory policy is apparent.

The literature thus far reviewed suggests that the appropriate regulatory policy under uncertainty is to set the allowed rate of return equal to the cost of capital. This literature, however, does not discuss the way in which regulatory behaviour will affect the risk of the firm and hence how it will affect the cost of capital of the firms. The role of regulation on risk and the cost of capital was suggested by Leland (1974) and Marshall, Yawitz and Greenberg (1981) who argue that setting prices so that the value of the firm equals the rate base leads to both efficient input combinations and a fair rate of return to investors.

The point of view expressed in this chapter is that the appropriate regulatory rule to follow in the presence of uncertainty is to set the allowed rate of return in such a way that the value of the firm is virtually equal to the rate base at the time of the review. Furthermore, since the literature suggests that efficiency issues are unimportant in this framework, the effect of regulation on the cost of capital emerges as the main social welfare aspect of rate regulation. Since the procedure for specifying the allowed rate of return is the traditional one, the regulatory decisions for initiating a rate case constitute the only instruments by which the cost of capital and hence social welfare can be controlled.

In this chapter we analyse how regulatory controls on the earned rate of return (for initiating a rate case) affect the cost of capital, the revenue requirements and the variability of stock price for the utility. Section 3.2 describes the valuation equation used as well as the nature of the regulatory policy that is followed. The model developed in this section is numerically evaluated in Section 3.3. Section 3.4 suggests a regulatory policy that has a number of socially optimal characteristics.

The conclusions of this chapter suggest a regulatory policy that is quick to help out a company whose rate of return falters but is tolerant of 'good' earnings and hence is not quick to reduce rates when the company is more profitable. On the surface, this conclusion seems manifestly 'unfair' in its treatment of stockholders and rate payers but it will be argued that this is not the case.

## 3.2 THE FRAMEWORK FOR ANALYSIS

### 1. The Valuation Equation

The framework for analysis of the problem of effective regulation is the continuous time valuation model of Brennan and Schwartz (1982) as extended by Thompson (1985b). These papers both look at the firm as a going concern and concentrate on the dynamic effects of regulation on value and risk. In these papers it is vividly seen that it is not possible to determine risk, and hence the cost of capital, for a regulated firm without a model of regulation. The traditional approach of determining the risk of the firm and from it establishing the cost of capital without reference to regulatory policy is seen as being inadequate to the task.

Regulation affects the value of the firm through both the rate setting policy and the policy for initiating rate reviews. In this chapter the rate setting policy will be largely confined to the simple rule that the allowed rate of return is set in such a way that the market value of the firm will be slightly in excess of the book value of the rate base at the time of the rate case. The 'excess' will be such that the net proceeds from any shares issued at the time of the rate case will be equal to the book value to prevent dilution of the earning power of the existing investors. The policy for initiating rate reviews will be what Brennan and Schwartz call 'deterministic' regulation where rate reviews are initiated when the earned rate of return on book value hits either an upper or lower control limit. The study of how the placing of these upper and lower limits affects the cost of capital and social welfare is the purpose of this chapter.

The basic sources of uncertainty which are present in the subsequent model are in the earned rate of return and the growth of rate base. Given the upper and lower control limits, the uncertainty in the earned rate of return determines the probability that a rate case will be initiated. The particular factors which affect the earned rate of return – for example demand and costs - are not specified. Rather, the earned rate of return, $x$, is assumed to be exogenously determined by the process

$$dx = \mu dt + \sigma_1 dz_1 \tag{3.1}$$

where $\mu$ is the expected change in the earned rate of return, $\sigma_1$ a measure of variability and $dz_1$ a Wiener process with mean zero and variance $dt$.

In addition to uncertainty in the earned rate of return the process governing the growth of rate base, $B$, is also exogenous and given by

$$dB = gBdt + \sigma_2 Bdz_2 \tag{3.2}$$

where $gB$ is the expected growth in rate base and $\sigma_2 B$ is the variance of growth; $dz_2$ is a second Wiener process with mean zero and variance $dt$. Again, the cause of the uncertainty in $B$ is not specified be it because of population growth, usage habits, or other factors.

The market price of a share, $S(x, B, n)$, where $n$ is the number of shares is to be determined. Before developing a value for $S$ it should be noted that since both $x$ and $B$ evolve as stochastic processes it follows that $n$ will also follow a stochastic process. From the sources and uses of funds equation we have

$$dB = (x - \bar{p}x)\,Bdt + fSdn \tag{3.3}$$

where $\bar{p}$ is the dividend payout ratio and $f$ is the net proceeds-to-market price ratio on new stock issues. Substituting (3.2) into (3.3) and solving for $dn$ yields

$$dn = \frac{g - (1 - \bar{p})x}{fS}\,Bdt + \frac{\sigma_2 B}{fS}\,dz_2 \tag{3.4}$$

as the stochastic process governing the growth of shares.

Adapting the valuation approach of Cox, Ingersoll and Ross (1978) as applied by Brennan and Schwartz, the homogeneity property $S(x, B, n) = y(x)B/n$, and deterministic regulation, Thompson (1985b) obtains the fundamental differential equation for the market price to book value ratio

$$\frac{1}{2}\sigma_1^2 y'' + (\mu - \sigma_1\lambda)y' + (g - r)y - \frac{[g - (1 - (1 - f)\bar{p})x]}{f}$$
$$- \frac{\sigma_2^2}{f} + \frac{\sigma_2^2}{f_y^2} = 0 \tag{3.5}$$

where $r$ is the risk free rate and $\lambda\sigma_1$ is the covariance of $x$ with market return. The boundary conditions to this problem follow from the upper and lower regulatory control limits and are

$$y(x_l) = \frac{1}{f} \text{ and } y(x_u) = \frac{1}{f} \tag{3.6}$$

In Equation (3.6) $x_l$ is the lower control limit on the rate of return and $x_u$ is the upper control limit. If $x_l < x < x_u$ no rate case will be started. When $x = x_l$ or $x = x_u$ a rate case is initiated and the allowed rate of return set to $x^*$ so that the market-to-book ratio is $1/f$. Figure 3.1 illustrates one possible sample path of the rate of return - from Equation (3.1) and the initiation of rate cases.

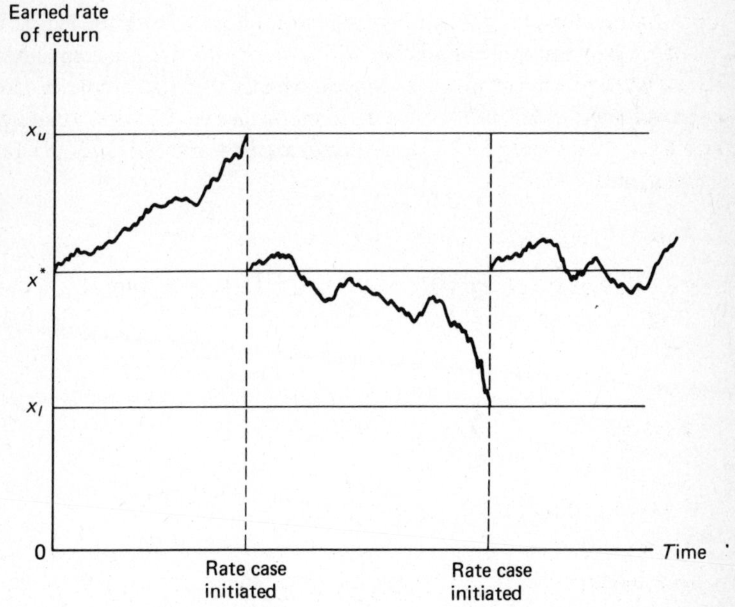


*Figure* 3.1 Sample path of rate of return and rate case initiations

Part of the analysis of regulatory policy is done by selecting a set of values for $x_l$ and $x_u$ and then solving (3.5) subject to (3.6). This produces the function $y(x)$. The cost of capital is defined as that value $x = c$ where $y(c) = 1/f$. The solution to (3.5) is done by numerical methods.[1]

## 2. The Welfare Function

To select a reasonable regulatory policy the regulator must consider the revenue requirements in addition to the cost of capital and the behaviour of the market price of the stock of the firm. Minimum revenue requirements have a significant appeal as a social welfare function. Symbolically the revenue requirement is

$$R(x_l, x_u) = E\left[R_1 + R_2(x_l, x_u) + \frac{Bc(x_l, x_u)]}{1-\tau}\right] \tag{3.7}$$

where $R_1$ is that part of the revenue requirement that is unaffected by the choice of $x_l$ and $x_u$ - operating expenses, depreciation, and cost of debt; $R_2$ is the cost of preparing the rate cases during the year including both company and commission costs which are allocated to the company; and $c$ is the cost of equity (with $1 - \tau$ transforming it to a before tax basis).

Since the earned rate of return, $x$, is modelled by Brownian motion the expected time between rate cases is given (see Karlin and Taylor (1975), p. 360) by

$$E[T \mid x_1, x_u] = \frac{1}{\sigma_1^2}[x_u - c(x_l, x_u)]\,[c(x_l, x_u) - x_l]. \tag{3.8}$$

If the cost to conduct a rate case is $K$ then the rate case cost per unit time (year) is

$$E[R_2(x_l, x_u)] = \frac{K}{E[T \mid x_l, x_u]}. \tag{3.9}$$

Given (3.7) and (3.9) the relative (to rate base) revenue requirements associated with control (RRAC) are

$$RRAC = \frac{R - R_1}{B} = \frac{K}{BE[T \mid x_l, x_u]} + \frac{c(x_l, x_u)}{1-\tau}. \tag{3.10}$$

In Section 3.3 the effects of $x_l$ and $x_u$ on RRAC will be analysed along with their effects on $c$ and $y(x)$.

## 3.3 THE EFFECT OF REGULATORY CONTROLS ON $c, y(x)$, AND RRAC

The analysis of regulatory policy which follows focuses on the effect of controls $x_l$ and $x_u$ on the revenue requirements at the time of a rate case. The inclusion of $c$ in RRAC in equation (3.10) imposes a constraint that the firm should be allowed to earn the cost of capital at the time of the rate case. In addition to studying RRAC we will also examine the effects of $x_l$ and $x_u$ on $c$ and the variability of the stock price.

The solution to Equations (3.5) and (3.6) is time consuming, taking on the order of 6–8 minutes on an IBM PC for each $x_l$ and $x_u$ combination. Therefore, a single set of parameters - that is $\mu$, $\sigma_1$, $\sigma_2$, $\lambda$, $\bar{p}$, $f$, $r$ - has been chosen to make the calculations which are presented in subsection 1. The way in which changes in these parameters affect the outcomes will be discussed in subsection 2 below.

The control parameters $x_l$ and $x_u$ have noticeable effects on the cost of capital, the revenue requirements and the variability of stock price. The effects of $x_l$ and $x_u$ on the cost of capital and stock prices are illustrated in Figures 3.2 and 3.3.

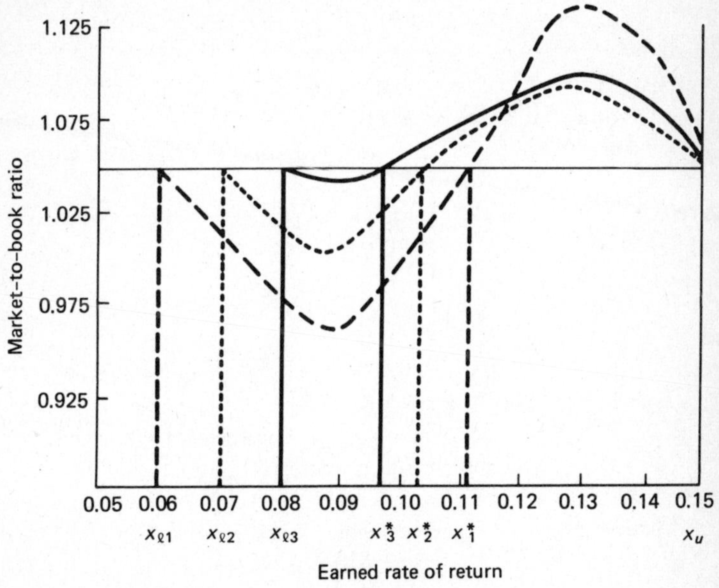


*Figure* 3.2 Solution to valuation equation with different regulatory controls, $x_l$

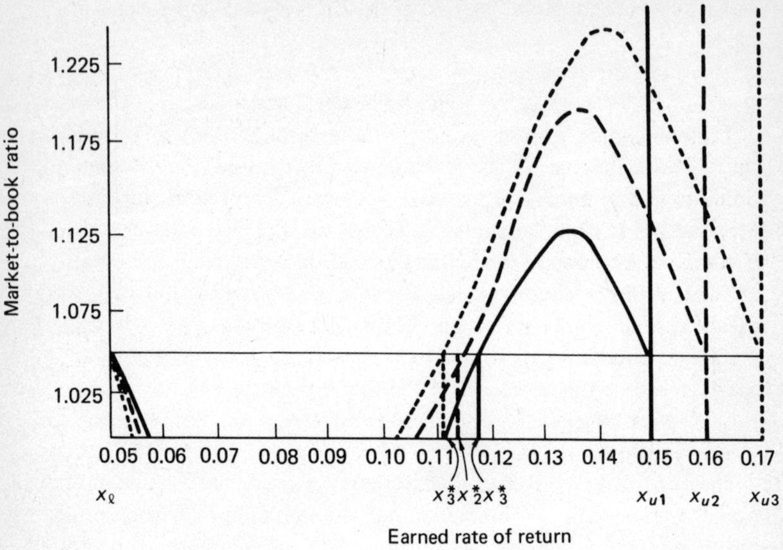


*Figure* 3.3 Solution to valuation equation with different regulatory controls, $x_u$

Figure 3.2 shows the market-to-book ratio solutions to the valuation equations and cost of capital for three values of $x_l$ (0.06, 0.07, 0.08) for a given value of $x_u = 0.15$. Note that the cost of capital, $x^*$, is lower when $x_l$ is higher and the variability of market-to-book ratio is greater when $x_l$ is lower.

There are some general conclusions that can be drawn from investigation of the roles of $x_l$ and $x_u$. The most important ones are:

1. The cost of capital itself is affected by the regulators' choice of $x_l$ and $x_u$.
2. As either $x_l$ or $x_u$ approach the cost of capital the revenue requirements become large due to the increased frequency of rate cases.
3. The lowest cost of capital and revenue requirements will occur when $x_l$ is slightly below the cost of capital and $x_u$ is quite far above it.
4. The lowest stock price that will be attained is largely determined by $x_l$ and little affected by $x_u$. The highest stock price that will be attained is largely determined by $x_u$ and little affected by $x_l$.

These effects and others will be illustrated in the next section using a numerical example.

## 1. A Numerical Example Illustrating the Effects of $x_l$ and $x_u$

In this section Equations (3.5) and (3.6) were solved with $\sigma_1 = 0.01$, $\sigma_2 = 0.005$, $\lambda = 0.14$, $\bar{p} = 0.7$, $f = 0.95$, $r = 0.1$, $\tau = 0.5$, and K/B = 0.007.

Table 3.1 is designed to illustrate the effect of $x_l$ and $x_u$ on the cost of capital. Note that as one moves across a row from left to right the cost of capital declines. This illustrates the fact that for a given upper control an increased lower control will reduce the cost of capital since the probability of the firm 'wandering' at lower earned rates of return, before the next rate case, is diminished as $x_l$ increases. Likewise, reading down any column reveals a declining cost of capital. This follows from the fact that it is *possible* to 'wander' in a 'higher' rate of return region before the next rate case.

*Table* 3.1 The cost of capital as a function of $x_l$ and $x_u$

| | $x_l$ | | | | | | |
|---|---|---|---|---|---|---|---|
| $x_u$ | *0.03* | *0.04* | *0.05* | *0.06* | *0.07* | *0.08* | *0.09* |
| 0.13 | $x$ | $x$ | $x$ | 0.12310 | 0.11434 | 0.10522 | 0.09562 |
| 0.14 | 0.13620 | 0.12997 | 0.12328 | 0.11606 | 0.10820 | 0.09958 | 0.09006 |
| 0.15 | 0.12910 | 0.12371 | 0.11780 | 0.11120 | 0.10377 | 0.09534 | $x$ |
| 0.16 | 0.12434 | 0.11951 | 0.11420 | 0.10775 | 0.10054 | 0.09216 | $x$ |
| 0.17 | 0.12116 | 0.11661 | 0.11136 | 0.10528 | 0.09878 | 0.08979 | $x$ |
| 0.18 | 0.11895 | 0.11457 | 0.10947 | 0.10350 | 0.09645 | 0.08803 | $x$ |
| 0.19 | 0.11740 | 0.11312 | 0.10812 | 0.10222 | 0.09520 | 0.08674 | $x$ |
| 0.20 | 0.11630 | 0.11210 | 0.10716 | 0.10130 | 0.09430 | 0.08580 | $x$ |
| 0.21 | 0.11553 | 0.11137 | 0.10647 | 0.10065 | 0.09365 | 0.08572 | $x$ |
| 0.22 | 0.11498 | 0.11086 | 0.10599 | 0.10018 | 0.09319 | 0.08463 | |

Assumptions: $\mu = 0$, $\sigma_1 = 0.01$, $\sigma_2 = 0.005$, $\lambda = 0.14$, $\bar{p} = 0.7$, $f = 0.95$, $r = 0.1$, $\tau = 0.5$

The boxes marked by $x$'s denote illogical control sets. For example, the box $x_l = 0.03$, $x_u = 0.13$ would have a cost of capital greater than 0.13. Thus the control limits would suggest that the earned rate of return was controlled between two limits, both of which were less than the cost of capital. Thus the market value of the stock would never reach $1/f$. The $x$'s in the column labelled 0.09 illustrate cases where both control limits are above the cost of capital, thus causing market values to be always above $1/f$. More will be said later about the boxes marked with $x$'s.

If the object of regulation was merely to reduce the cost of capital, Table 3.1 suggests some interesting observations. Since the cost of capital declines along rows – until hitting $x$'s – and since it also declines along columns, it seems as if optimal regulation would occur when $x_l$ is quite large - just less than the cost of capital - and $x_u$ is quite large (one might be tempted to guess infinity for $x_u$). But notice that the rate of change of the cost of capital, as $x_u$ is increased, declines as $x_u$ gets larger thus suggesting some asymptotic behaviour. Since the absence of an upper control seems intuitively implausible, we will not extend the table but rather focus on other issues in exploring reasonable regulatory policy.

Table 3.2 shows the expected time to a rate case given that the allowed rate of return is set at the cost of capital in the present rate case. The table (or rather what is not in the table) must be interpreted carefully. As the cost of capital nears one of the control limits the expected time to a rate case gets smaller. Reference to Table 3.1 for $x_l = 0.09$ and $x_u = 0.13$ shows $x_l$ being within 0.00562 of the cost of capital and producing an expected time to a rate case of 1.93 years. On the other hand, for $x_l = 0.03$ and $x_u = 0.19$ the expected time to a rate case is 63.45 years - virtually no regulation. Since Table 3.2 is given only for integer values of the controls and since the $x$'s denote illogical cases, we can conclude that, say, between $x_l = 0.08$, $x_u = 0.15$ and $x_l = 0.09$, $x_u = 0.15$, there is a value for $x_l$ for which the expected time to the next rate case is zero. Indeed had many more calculations been made, each row would have read a zero before the cell containing an $x$. This fact has a bearing on the interpretation of Table 3.3.

*Table* 3.2 The expected time to the next rate case

| | $x_l$ | | | | | | |
|---|---|---|---|---|---|---|---|
| $x_u$ | *0.03* | *0.04* | *0.05* | *0.06* | *0.07* | *0.08* | *0.09* |
| 0.13 | $x$ | $x$ | $x$ | 4.35 | 6.94 | 6.25 | 1.93 |
| 0.14 | 4.03 | 9.02 | 12.25 | 13.42 | 12.15 | 7.91 | 0.03 |
| 0.15 | 20.77 | 22.01 | 21.83 | 19.87 | 15.64 | 8.38 | $x$ |
| 0.16 | 33.64 | 32.19 | 29.44 | 24.95 | 18.16 | 8.25 | $x$ |
| 0.17 | 44.52 | 40.90 | 35.98 | 29.31 | 20.24 | 7.85 | $x$ |
| 0.18 | 54.30 | 48.79 | 41.94 | 33.28 | 22.10 | 7.39 | $x$ |
| 0.19 | 63.45 | 56.21 | 47.59 | 37.06 | 23.89 | 6.96 | $x$ |
| 0.20 | 72.23 | 63.38 | 53.07 | 40.76 | 25.69 | 6.62 | $x$ |
| 0.21 | 80.80 | 70.39 | 58.46 | 44.45 | 27.52 | 6.39 | $x$ |
| 0.22 | 89.25 | 77.34 | 63.83 | 48.14 | 29.41 | 6.27 | $x$ |

Assumptions: $\mu = 0$, $\sigma_1 = 0.01$, $\sigma_2 = 0.005$, $\lambda = 0.14$, $\bar{p} = 0.7$, $f = 0.95$, $r = 0.1$, $\tau = 0.5$

*Table* 3.3 Relative revenue requirements associated with control

| | $x_l$ | | | | | | |
|---|---|---|---|---|---|---|---|
| $x_u$ | *0.03* | *0.04* | *0.05* | *0.06* | *0.07* | *0.08* | *0.09* |
| 0.13 | x | x | x | 0.24781 | 0.22971 | 0.21156 | 0.19486 |
| 0.14 | 0.27416 | 0.26072 | 0.24713 | 0.23264 | 0.21698 | 0.20004 | 0.41373 |
| 0.15 | 0.25838 | 0.24774 | 0.23592 | 0.22275 | 0.20839 | 0.19151 | x |
| 0.16 | 0.29889 | 0.23924 | 0.22828 | 0.21518 | 0.20147 | 0.18517 | x |
| 0.17 | 0.24248 | 0.23339 | 0.22291 | 0.21080 | 0.19671 | 0.18047 | x |
| 0.18 | 0.23803 | 0.22928 | 0.21911 | 0.20721 | 0.19322 | 0.17701 | x |
| 0.19 | 0.23491 | 0.22636 | 0.21639 | 0.20463 | 0.19069 | 0.17449 | x |
| 0.20 | 0.23270 | 0.22431 | 0.21445 | 0.20277 | 0.18887 | 0.17266 | x |
| 0.21 | 0.23115 | 0.22284 | 0.21306 | 0.20146 | 0.17133 | 0.17133 | x |
| 0.22 | 0.23004 | 0.22181 | 0.21209 | 0.20051 | 0.18662 | 0.17038 | x |

Assumptions: $\mu = 0$, $\sigma_1 = 0.01$, $\sigma_2 = 0.005$, $\lambda = 0.14$, $\bar{p} = 0.7$, $f = 0.95$, $r = 0.1$, $\tau = 0.5$, $K/B = 0.007$

Table 3.3 shows the relative revenue requirements associated with control. They tend to decline across rows. However, as the box with an $x$ is reached the relative revenue requirements will eventually rise dramatically. This occurs when the expected number of rate cases per year increases dramatically (or when the time between rate cases declines toward zero). Thus for every row there is a value of $x_l$ that minimises the relative revenue requirements. No minimum exists in the columns.

Table 3.4 shows the maximum and minimum values of the stock price given the control limits. The top number in each cell is the maximum value of the market-to-book ratio while the bottom number is the minimum value. Note that the maximum value market-to-book ratio varies little across rows while the minimum value varies considerably. Looking down the columns the roles are reversed. Stated simply, we see the $x_l$ value controlling the minimum value of stock price and the $x_u$ value controlling the maximum value. Obviously, the range of variability of the stock rise is controlled by the range between $x_l$ and $x_u$. The smaller the range the less the variability in the stock price.

The revenue requirements and the stock price function are likely to be two factors that influence regulators. The range of the stock price for $x_l = 0.08$ and $x_u = 0.22$ is greater than the range for $x_l = 0.08$ and $x_u = 0.14$. However, the revenue requirements are lower for the case of $x_u = 0.22$. The gremlin on the left shoulder of the regulator would be arguing for $x_u = 0.14$ while the gremlin on the right shoulder would whisper '$x_u$ = 0.22'. What should the regulator do? One fact that may help is the proba-

*Table* 3.4 Maximum and minimum stock prices associated with control

| | $x_l$ | | | | | | |
|---|---|---|---|---|---|---|---|
| $x_u$ | *0.03* | *0.04* | *0.05* | *0.06* | *0.07* | *0.08* | *0.09* |
| 0.13 | *x* | *x* | *x* | 1.055 | 1.064 | 1.073 | 1.079 |
| | | | | 0.940 | 0.997 | 1.035 | 1.052 |
| 0.14 | 1.053 | 1.061 | 1.072 | 1.086 | 1.101 | 1.112 | 1.117 |
| | 0.659 | 0.769 | 0.864 | 0.943 | 1.002 | 1.039 | 1.053 |
| 0.15 | 1.091 | 1.107 | 1.125 | 1.143 | 1.159 | 1.170 | *x* |
| | 0.660 | 0.771 | 0.868 | 0.947 | 1.007 | 1.043 | |
| 0.16 | 1.163 | 1.183 | 1.203 | 1.221 | 1.237 | 1.247 | *x* |
| | 0.662 | 0.774 | 0.872 | 0.952 | 1.011 | 1.046 | |
| 0.17 | 1.260 | 1.280 | 1.290 | 1.318 | 1.332 | 1.340 | *x* |
| | 0.664 | 0.777 | 0.825 | 0.956 | 1.015 | 1.048 | |
| 0.18 | 1.376 | 1.395 | 1.413 | 1.430 | 1.443 | 1.451 | *x* |
| | 0.666 | 0.780 | 0.878 | 0.959 | 1.018 | 1.049 | |
| 0.19 | 1.507 | 1.524 | 1.541 | 1.556 | 1.568 | 1.575 | *x* |
| | 0.668 | 0.782 | 0.880 | 0.961 | 1.020 | 1.050 | |
| 0.20 | 1.651 | 1.667 | 1.682 | 1.696 | 1.706 | 1.712 | *x* |
| | 0.669 | 0.783 | 0.882 | 0.963 | 1.022 | 1.051 | |
| 0.21 | 1.806 | 1.820 | 1.834 | 1.846 | 1.855 | 1.860 | *x* |
| | 0.620 | 0.784 | 0.833 | 0.965 | 1.023 | 1.051 | |
| 0.22 | 1.971 | 1.984 | 1.996 | 2.006 | 2.015 | 2.019 | *x* |
| | 0.671 | 0.785 | 0.884 | 0.965 | 1.023 | 1.051 | |

Assumptions: $\mu = 0$, $\sigma_1 = 0.01$, $\sigma_2 = 0.005$, $\lambda = 0.14$, $\bar{p} = 0.7$, $f = 0.95$, $r = 0.1$, $\tau = 0.5$

bility of initiating a rate case from $x_l = 0.08$ before reaching given levels of $x$ on the high side. These probabilities can be easily calculated.

Again, using the properties of Brownian motion as developed by Karlin and Taylor (1975, p. 360), we find this probability to be

$$\Pr[\text{reaching } x_l \text{ before } x] = \frac{C(x_l, x_u) - x_l}{x - x_l}$$

Table 3.5 tabulates these probabilities for the two cases along with the stock price values corresponding to each earned rate of return. From Table 3.5 it can be seen that the probabilities of achieving some of the higher earnings levels before initiating a rate case from $x_l$ are very low for the wide range controls. This, of course, reflects the fact that it is much more probable to initiate a rate case from the lower limit when the cost of capital is close to that lower limit. Note that for the wider range controls the probability of reaching the maximum stock price before a rate case is approximately 0.04. Note also that the probability of reaching 1.11 times book value is more than twice as great with $x_u = 0.14$ than it is with $x_u = 0.22$.

*Table* 3.5 Probability of earning $x$ before initiating a rate case from $x_l$

| Earning Level | $x_l = 0.08$, $x_u = 0.14$, $C = 0.09958$ | | $x_l = 0.08$, $x_u = 0.22$, $C = 0.08463$ | |
|---|---|---|---|---|
| $x$ | *Stock price* | *Probability* | *Stock price* | *Probability* |
| 0.10 | 1.0539 | 0.979 | 1.1143 | 0.232 |
| 0.11 | 1.0817 | 0.650 | 1.1925 | 0.154 |
| 0.12 | 1.1075 | 0.488 | 1.2938 | 0.116 |
| 0.13 | 1.1077 | 0.390 | 1.4125 | 0.093 |
| 0.14 | 1.0526 | 0.325 | 1.5519 | 0.077 |
| 0.15 | | | 1.6868 | 0.066 |
| 0.16 | | | 1.8146 | 0.058 |
| 0.17 | | | 1.9323 | 0.051 |
| 0.18 | | | 2.0042 | 0.046 |
| 0.19 | | | 2.0116 | 0.042 |
| 0.20 | | | 1.9128 | 0.038 |
| 0.21 | | | 1.6157 | 0.036 |
| 0.22 | | | 1.0526 | 0.033 |

Assumptions: $\mu = 0$, $\sigma_1 = 0.01$, $\sigma_2 = 0.005$, $\lambda = 0.14$, $\bar{p} = 0.7$, $f = 0.95$, $r = 0.1$, $\tau = 0.5$

The development in Table 3.5 suggests that a policy that yields quick regulatory reactions when earned rate of return slips and slow reaction when earnings soar may not be an unreasonable policy. This idea will be discussed in more depth later. But first the next section examines the effects of various parameters on both the calculations and conclusions of this section.

## 2. Regulatory Response to Various Firms

The numerical analysis of the previous section serves as a base for analysis of the way the firm characteristics affect the nature of reasonable regulation. In this section the effects of $\mu$, $\sigma_1$, and $K/B$ on the cost of capital, revenue requirements and stock prices will be examined. The base analysis was done with $\mu = 0$, $\sigma_1 = 0.01$, and $K/B = 0.007$. This type of firm might be characterised as one with no trends in the earned rate of return, moderate variability in the rate of return, and relatively small rate case costs. A change in each of these characteristics will be discussed here.

*Trends in the Earned Rate of Return*

Firms with positive values of $\mu$ tend to have lower costs of capital. The intuition for this case is straightforward. With $\mu < 0$ we would expect that between the present and the next rate cases the average earnings level would be greater than when $\mu = 0$ (if in both cases the same starting $x$ was used). This will tend to raise the market-to-book ratio at the time of the present case. Then in order to move the market-to-book ratio back to $1/f$, the cost of capital must fall. Furthermore, we find that the maximum stock price is affected little but the minimum stock price is affected. When $\mu < 0$ effects symmetric to these take place.

These effects suggest that a regulatory policy that has a lower lower control limit is appropriate when variability increases.

*Variability in the Rate of Return*

Some interesting effects take place as variability changes. Thompson (1985b) has shown that the cost of capital may decrease as the variability increases. Table 3.6 shows the cost of capital, expected time to a rate case, and the maximum and minimum stock prices as a function of the variability. The reason for the ultimate decline in cost of capital can be explained by noting that as $\sigma_1$ increases the time to the next rate case falls. This means that there is a shorter period of time that the company has a possibility of earning deficient returns. Thus they are 'put back on course' at shorter intervals of time. Also note that as $\sigma_1$ increases the stock price variability narrows. This is also a function of shorter time interval between rate cases.

*Table* 3.6 The effects of earned rate of return variability

| $\sigma_1$ | *C(0.05, 0.15)* | *E[T* \|*0.05, 0.15]* | *Max y(x)* | *Min y(x)* |
|---|---|---|---|---|
| 0.005 | 0.1153 | 90.64 | 1.298 | 0.630 |
| 0.010 | 0.1178 | 21.83 | 1.125 | 0.868 |
| 0.020 | 0.1172 | 5.51 | 1.073 | 0.995 |
| 0.030 | 0.1159 | 2.50 | 1.062 | 1.026 |

Assumptions: $\mu = 0$, $\sigma_2 = 0.005$, $\lambda = 0.14$, $f = 0.95$, $\bar{p} = 0.7$, $g = 0.06$, $r = 0.1$, $x_l = 0.05$, $x_u = 0.15$

Finally, it should be noted in Table 3.6 that although $C(x_l, x_u)$ declines as $\sigma_1$ increases the decline is negligible. The main effect is in $E[T \mid x_l, x_u]$ which is reduced. Thus the rate case costs will rise with the net effect of a slight decrease in the lower control limit in a reasonable regulatory policy.

*Cost of a Rate Case*

The relative cost of a rate case, *K/B,* has no effect on the cost of capital but it does affect the revenue requirements. Clearly, if each case is more costly the relative revenue requirements associated with a given control plan will increase. Thus we will find the control limits affected. Basically, this will be a reduction in the lower control limit.

## 3.4 SUMMARY AND CONCLUSION

This chapter has been concerned with regulatory policy under uncertainty. The subtitle of the paper poses the essential question: How should the earned rate of return for a public utility be regulated? The literature growing out of the Averch–Johnson problem, after more than two decades of refinement, seemed to settle in on the conclusion that it was socially optimal to set the allowed rate of return equal to the cost of capital. The literature suggested that if this were done the capital:labour ratio for the utility would be set at the social optimum.

But an optimal capital to labour ratio does not signal the end of issues associated with rate of return regulation. The literature stemming from Averch–Johnson almost without exception takes the cost of capital as given. But more than twenty years ago Leventhal (1965) noted that regulation affected the cost of capital, thus pointing out an embarrassing gap in the literature that still exists today. The methodology for studying the relationship between regulation and value was developed by Brennan and Schwartz who adapted the stochastic equilibrium models of Cox, Ingersoll and Ross to regulated firms. Thompson (1985b) extended these models to the study of the cost of capital and its determinants. In that study, one important determinant was regulatory policy.

This chapter was originally conceived as an effort to determine optimal regulatory policy. Simply stated, it was concerned with calculating upper and lower control limits (on the earned rate of return) which minimised revenue requirements. This social welfare function seemed entirely reasonable – and perhaps still is reasonable – but turned out to be unobtainable.

In exploring the revenue requirements as a social welfare function, it was evident that for any given upper limit, $x_u$, on the earned rate of return there was a value of the lower limit, $x_l$, which minimised revenue requirements. The striking characteristic of this value was that it was close to, but slightly below, the cost of capital, reflecting the fact that as the lower control approached the cost of capital the rate case costs tended to rise rapidly, thus increasing the revenue requirements. But while there was a minimising value of $x_l$ given $x_u$ there was no minimising value of $x_u$ given $x_l$. Thus an optimal selection of $x_l$ and $x_u$ was unavailable.

Even though no revenue requirements minimising value of $x_u$ was evident some interesting aspects of the welfare function were observed. First, for a given value of $x_l$ the cost of capital and revenue requirements tended to approach asymptotes as $x_u$ was increased. Thus loose regulation at the upper level was desirable but the 'marginal benefit of looseness' was a declining function.

The general conclusion that emerged from the analysis was that the lower control should be 'tight' and the upper control 'loose'. This kind of regulation would tend to minimise both the cost of capital and the revenue requirements. In one sense, this is a startling conclusion (and indeed one which I am forced to question myself)! But it has some support. First, let me suggest that it is the type of policy that the companies have advocated. Secondly, Thompson (1985a), in analysing return deficiencies over the 1963–81 period, has shown that companies which tended to have smaller return deficiencies or favourable regulation, had lower costs of capital.

**Acknowledgements**

I thank John L. Thompson and Dr Chang Mo Ahn for assistance with the calculations.

**Notes**

1. See Thompson (1985b) for a discussion of the solution procedure.

**References**

AVERCH, H. and JOHNSON, L. L. (1962) 'Behavior of the Firm Under Regulatory Constraint', *American Economic Review*, vol. 52, no. 5, pp. 1062–9.

BAWA, V. S. and SIBLEY, D. S. (1980) 'Dynamic Behavior of a Firm Subject to Stochastic Regulatory Review', *International Economic Review*, vol. 21, no. 3, pp. 627–42.

BRENNAN, M. J. and SCHWARTZ, E. S. (1982) 'Consistent Regulatory Policy Under Uncertainty', *The Bell Journal of Economics*, vol. 13, no. 2, pp. 506–21.

COX, J. C., INGERSOLL, J. E. and ROSS, S. A. (1978) 'A Theory of the Term Structure of Interest Rates', Stanford University Research Paper No. 4680, August.

KARLIN, S. and TAYLOR, H. M. (1975) *A First Course in Stochastic Processes.* 2nd edn (New York: Academic Press).

KLEVORICK, A. K. (1971) 'The "Optimal" Fair Rate of Return', *Bell Journal of Economics and Management Science*, vol. 2, no. 1, pp. 122–53.

KLEVORICK, A. K. (1973) 'The Behavior of a Firm Subject to Stochastic Regulatory Review', *Bell Journal of Economics and Management Science*, vol. 4, no. 1, pp. 57–88.

LELAND, H. E. (1974) 'Regulation of Natural Monopolies and the Fast Rate of Return', *Bell Journal of Economics and Management Science*, vol. 5, no. 1, pp. 3–15.

LEVENTHAL, H. (1965) 'Vitality of the Comparable Earnings Standard for Regulation of Utilities in a Growth Economy', *The Yale Law Journal*, vol. 74, May, pp. 989–1018.

MARSHALL, W. J., YAWITZ, J. B. and GREENBERG, E. (1981) 'Optimal Regulation Under Uncertainty', *Journal of Finance*, vol. 36, no. 4, pp. 909–22.

PERRAKIS, S. (1976) 'On the Regulated Price-Setting Monopoly Firm with Random Demand Curve', *American Economic Review*, vol. 66, no. 3, pp. 410–16.

THOMPSON, H. E. (1985a) 'Estimating Return Deficiences of Electric Utilities: 1963–1981', in M. A. Crew (ed.) *Analyzing the Impact of Regulatory Change in Public Utilities* (Lexington: DC Heath & Company).

THOMPSON, H. E. (1985b) 'Uncertainty, "Deterministic Regulation" and the Cost of Capital to Public Utilities', Wisconsin Working Paper 2–85–6, Graduate School of Business, University of Wisconsin-Madison, February.

# 4 Governance Costs of Regulation for Water Supply

Michael A. Crew, Paul R. Kleindorfer
and Donald L. Schlenger

## 4.1 INTRODUCTION

Theory and practice of regulation of natural monopoly have extended traditional concerns with allocative efficiency to include the transactions costs associated with setting up and operating regulatory institutions. Originally, with single-product natural monopoly, the objective of regulation was just a matter of allocative efficiency, the idea being to promote the maximisation of net benefit as expressed by the excess of total consumer and producer surplus over production costs. However, the nature of efficiency concerns has become broader, and now involves such considerations as X-efficiency (see Leibenstein (1966)) and transaction costs.

X-efficiency, as an all-embracing term, is useful when broad notions of welfare losses from monopoly and regulation are being discussed. However, institutional design requires that we be more specific about the nature and source of these inefficiencies. Here transactions costs enter the picture through the new institutional economics pioneered by Williamson (1975). Production costs are seen as one aspect of the total costs of performing a set of transactions. The broader study of transactions involves comparison of all of the costs associated with the transaction, including contracting, administration and regulatory costs. The thrust of the new institutional economics is the comparison of alternative governance structures (the contractual and technological arrangements for performing the relevant set of transactions) as to their relative efficiency, including all relevant transactions costs. Governance mode A may have high production costs and low transactions costs. Mode B may have high transactions costs and low production costs. The total is what is relevant. Thus, X-inefficiency, when precisely measured, would refer to the excess of production and transactions costs of a particular governance structure over and above the optimal governance mode.

These considerations suggest a more sophisticated version of the traditional net benefits measure. This is achieved by incorporating transactions costs in the net benefits maximisation across alternative regulatory institutions and policies, that is, measuring net benefits as

Net Benefits = Total Consumer and Producer Surplus Less Production Costs Less Transactions Costs

A major concern raised by this broadened perspective is the nature and measurement of transactions costs. This chapter examines this issue with a particular focus on rate-of-return regulation for investor owned water companies in the United States. Our purpose will be to understand the specific nature and magnitude of those (transactions) costs resulting from the ongoing interaction between regulators and regulated firms. Our analysis is both theoretical and empirical, the empirical work being based on a national survey of investor owned water utilities. This survey, conducted with the cooperation of the National Association of Water Companies (NAWC) and Hackensack Water Companies, aimed at throwing light on the costs and consequences of regulation. Of the companies surveyed, 86 responded to our detailed questionnaire. The companies varied considerably in size, with 50 companies that we classified as small with an average of 10 000 customers, 24 classified as medium with an average of 43 000 customers, and 12 large companies averaging about 153 000 customers.

The results of the survey revealed very high costs of governance for small companies at \$7.10 per customer per annum based upon the latest rate case, compared to \$1.03 for large companies. Thus, for small companies a significant part of an average customer's bill goes on rate cases. As we will show, this is rather high and probably exceeds any benefits provided by regulation. One important implication of these results is that regulation of water utilities, and especially of smaller companies, should be radically reformed to reduce regulatory transactions costs.

The chapter proceeds as follows. Section 4.2 is concerned with an analysis of the governance cost of regulation, extending our earlier (1985) work by employing the work on rent seeking of Tullock (1967) and Crew and Rowley (1986). This suggests extending of the theory of rent seeking to include the effects of barriers to entry in the rent-seeking sector. Section 4.3 is concerned with an analysis of our survey results, including the testing of various hypotheses that were generated in Section 4.2 as to who benefits and why the structure continues to exist. Section 4.4 is by way of concluding discussion, stressing especially the possible implications of this approach for regulatory policy and alternative governance structures.

## 4.2 THEORY OF GOVERNANCE COSTS AND REGULATION

According to Williamson (1976) and Goldberg (1976), regulation is intended to ensure that society achieve the scale and/or scope economies available from natural monopoly and at the same time protect the consumer from monopoly exploitation. Regulation involves a contract between the regulated firm, the regulator and the public, which gives the firm an incentive to make the necessary investment in a highly transaction-specific fixed plant and makes the monopoly acceptable to the public by establishing control over prices. In view of the considerable size of the transaction-specific investment, without the safeguards provided by regulation, the firm could be 'held up' for the transaction-specific investment along the lines envisaged by Klein, Crawford and Alchian (1978). To provide this assurance to both consumers and the producer so that neither will be exploited is not costless. A governance mechanism has to be devised and operated. X-inefficiencies and allocative inefficiencies may arise as a result of the operation of a governance mechanism, like regulation. Transactions costs of governance will also be incurred in operating the governance structure for natural monopoly.

Regulation, as the pioneering work of Tullock (1967) has shown, provides opportunities for rent seeking. Artificial scarcities are created by government attempts to regulate economic activity. The associated rents created by regulation will not go unnoticed. They will be sought by rent seekers who will expend resources to get them and may induce others to spend resources to hold on to them. The focus of this chapter is how such rent seeking and associated transactions costs occur under rate-of-return (RoR) regulation. We will not be concerned here with how RoR regulation behaves compared to other governance structures, as such issues have been examined in, for example, Williamson (1976) and Crew and Kleindorfer (1986a). Rather we will take RoR regulation as a given and examine the transaction costs of this particular governance structure in detail.

RoR regulation's ostensible aims are to protect the consumer and at the same time provide the firm with a 'fair' rate of return. These aims of regulation are overseen and interpreted by the legal system. The likelihood that the legal system makes conspiracy and enrichment by the principals difficult does not, however, prevent rent seeking from occurring under RoR regulation. Before a public utility is allowed to change its prices, it has to seek approval of its state regulatory commission. It must file its case and then be prepared to be examined on it. While the procedure varies in different states, the example of New Jersy will suffice for our purposes. Following the filing by the company, intervenors have the opportunity to object to the company's case. Intervenors, principally the state-appointed Rate Counsel, then file their own testimony criticising the company's case. The options then are for the two sides either to discuss their differences and agree to a 'stipulation' which has to be approved by the regulators, or to litigate the case before an administrative law judge. The litigation, if such occurs, involves almost all the features of normal court proceedings, such as cross examination, rebuttal and the like. The judge then prepares his report, which goes to the commission (in New Jersey, the Board of Public Utilities) for a final decision. The board specifies its decision on the amount of money it is going to allow the company through a target revenue R as in Equation (4.1).

$$R = O + s(V - D) \tag{4.1}$$

where

$R$ = revenue requirements
$O$ = operating expenses, including current depreciation
$s$ = allowed rate of return
$V$ = gross value of utility's property (that is rate base)
$D$ = accumulated depreciation.

It when passes the case to the board staff who work out rates they consider will be just sufficient to raise the desired sum of money.

When all the figures in (4.1) are agreed by the board and corresponding rates derived, an order is issued which allows the company to charge these rates. If the company believes that the order treats it grossly unfairly in the sense that it believes it can show failure of due process, it may appeal to the appellate court, the state supreme court, and even to the United States Supreme Court if federal law is involved. More likely, however, it will begin working on preparing for another rate case to enable it to expedite filing. In any event, the company will continue working on a day-to-day basis with the regulators. This continuing contact is important in establishing what regulators are likely to accept and also for behind the scenes lobbying for positions the company wishes to institute in the future.

The process described above can be costly, involving considerable expenditure of resources by the company, the regulators and intervenors. Moreover, given the quasi-judicial nature of the process, the company has little control over the outcome. The process described also appears to provide little incentive toward economising scarce resources, because of the cost-plus nature of the process, and it generates a considerable potential for rent-seeking activities:

1. rent seeking by managers to indulge their preferences for certain expenses - the notion of expense preference developed by Williamson (1967);
2. rent seeking by hourly paid workers through the activities of their unions;
3. rent seeking by intervenors;
4. rent seeking by commissioners;
5. rent seeking by expert witnesses;
6. rent seeking by certain customers and suppliers of the utility;
7. rent seeking by stockholders.

We might summarise current theories on rent seeking and regulation of natural monopolies as saying that the prospect of appropriating rents generates considerable interest in setting up and controlling a monopoly franchise. Given that the legal system is ultimately responsible for adjudicating the allocation of such rents, notions of due process (see Mashaw (1985)), and fairness slowly permeate the regulatory institutions set up to protect/control/oversee the monopoly franchise. These institutions may be viewed in steady state as an institutional embodiment of the equilibrium of the various contenders for available rents. Given the nature and importance of public utilities, these institutions must also be able to legitimate the outcomes of the ongoing administered contract between regulators, firms and consumers. This legitimation process gives rise to transactions costs which may be large enough to make the net benefits of regulation negative.

Let us now consider the transactions costs of regulation in more detail, using first a simple two-agent model along the lines of our (1985) paper. In that paper we examined both the above issues and we found that in terms of the net-benefit approach, at least in the case of water companies in New Jersey, little seemed to be gained from the regulatory process because the visible transactions costs, to say nothing of the invisible transactions costs, exceeded the benefits of price control provided by regulation. We also found that there was some evidence to suggest that both the companies and the Rate Counsel did, however, cooperate on occasion in an attempt to mitigate each side's, and therefore rate payers', losses. This might imply that the limits are adaptively set to the rents that are remaining. We now present our (1985) model and summarise our empirical results.

We first expand the definition of the traditional social welfare function to include transaction costs:

$$W = TR + S - C - (G_1 + G_2) \tag{4.2}$$

where

$W$ = net benefit
$TR$ = total revenue
$S$ = consumer's surplus
$C$ = total cost, excluding the transactions costs of governance
$G_1$ = the firm's regulatory transactions costs
$G_2$ = the consumers' representative's regulatory transactions costs.

The aim of the actors in rate proceedings is for the firm to get as high a price as it can (subject to an assured maximum of the monopoly price), and for the consumers' representative to keep the price increase as low as possible.

In Figure 4.1, $P^0$ is the price before the company begins rate proceedings. $P^1$ is the price awarded as a result of the rate case. The firm's gain is given by the shaded area $P^1AFP^0 + DEFB$. The consumers' loss is given by $P^1AEP^0$. Thus, if we ignore transactions costs, $ABC < CDE$ implies that the firm's gain exceeds the consumers' loss and the price increase will result in a net benefit. The first thing to note is that the net gains, $ABC$ and $CDE$, are rather small in relation to the loss by consumers.

This may be illustrated by means of a simple example. We assume a linear cost function $C(Q) = cQ$, and constant elasticity demand function $Q = AP^{-\eta}$. Let total regulatory transactions costs be denoted $G = G_1 + G_2$. Then, if $G$ is expended to arrive at a price $P$, total welfare at the pair $(P, G)$ is

$$\begin{aligned} W(P, G) &= \int^{Q(P)} (x/A)^{-1/\eta}\, dx - cQ(P) - G \\ &= [\eta P/(\eta - 1) - c]\, Q(P) - G \end{aligned} \tag{4.3}$$

We now use (4.3) to illustrate the impact of regulatory transactions costs.

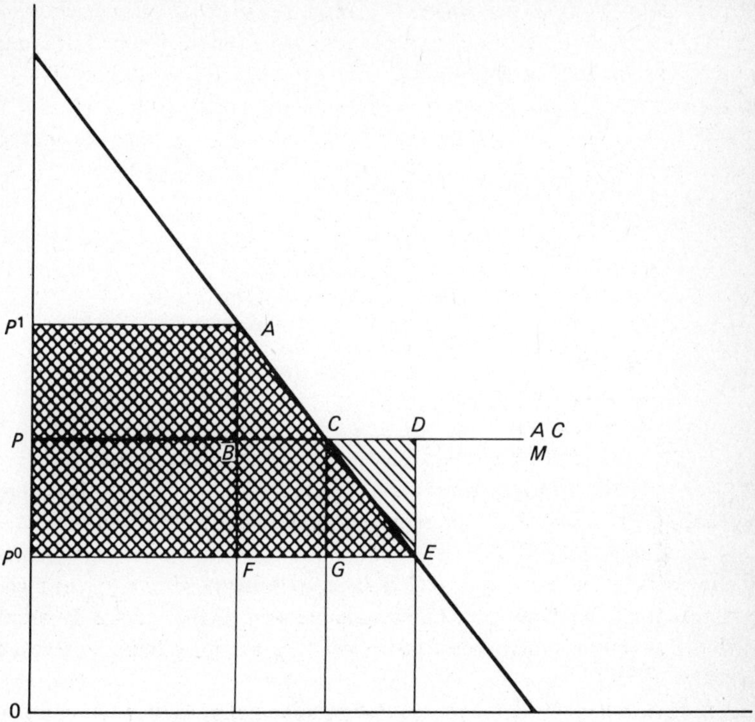


*Figure* 4.1 Welfare and transactions costs

First, let us compare the $(P, G)$ pairs $[kc, 0]$ and $[(1+t)c, G]$, where $0 \leqslant k < 1$ and $t = [G/(cQ(1+t)c)]$. The pair $[P, G] = [kc, 0]$ corresponds to a firm operating at a loss, recovering only the fraction $k$ of its costs. The firm can either continue at this price level (with lump-sum subsidies) or it can achieve a price increase through a rate proceeding. Suppose the total transactions cost of this proceeding are $G$ and the resulting price $P$ is just sufficient to recover total cost $cQ(P)$ plus $G$, that is, $P = c + G/Q(P) = c(1 + G/cQ(P)) = c(1 + t(c, G, P))$. Comparing the welfare resulting from these two cases, one computes for the present example that $W((w+t)c, G) = W(kc, 0)$ when

$$t = k[(1-(1-k)\eta/k]^{1/(1-\eta)} - 1. \tag{4.4}$$

Table 4.1 shows illustrative values of $\eta$, $k$, and $t$ for which (4.4) holds. If $t$ (that is, $G$) is larger than that achieving equality in (4.4), then welfare losses will be incurred by instituting the rate proceeding.

*Table* 4.1 Welfare effects of transactions costs

| | $\eta \cong 1$* % | $\eta = 0.5$ % |
|---|---|---|
| $k = 0.9$ | 0.56 | 0.28 |
| $k = 0.95$ | 0.14 | 0.07 |

*Note*: *(4.3) is not defined for $\eta = 1$, but it has the limit indicated as $\eta$ approaches 1.

Transactions costs $t = G/cQ$ as a percentage of total costs ($cQ$) sufficient to make the welfare effects of a break-even price change equal to zero at selected values of $k$ and $\eta$.

The results in Table 4.1 suggest that only small expenditures of regulatory transactions costs are justified, because any increase in transactions costs above these levels will make net benefits ($W$) in (4.2) negative. Thus, such regulatory expenses, at least with this simple measure of efficiency, quickly eat up the benefits associated here with them.

In view of the way even small transactions costs offset the benefits arising from the regulatory process, we will now briefly examine how transactions costs arise in the process. The adversary process results in the utility's attorneys facing usually a publicly appointed intervenor, which we will call the public advocate. The situation they face at first sight is akin to that of the Prisoner's Dilemma. Each party would be better off if they were able to cooperate to the extent that each side's transactions costs would be reduced and the point $C$ in Figure 4.1 that maximised net gain, $W$, would be achieved. However, to the extent that the process may be characterised as a Prisoner's Dilemma, the two parties may have incentives not to cooperate. We will now illustrate how this may happen with the aid of Table 4.2. The firm's strategies are shown in the far left column and intervenor's strategies in the top row. We denote the firm's profits by $U(P) - G_1 = TR - C_1 - G_1$ and consumer surplus by $S(P) - G_2$, where $P$ is price resulting from the regulatory process and $G_1$, $G_2$ are the transactions costs paid by the firm and intervenor in negotiating $P$. We assume that the firm and public intervenor attempt to maximise $U(P) - G_1$, and $S(P) - G_2$, respectively. If both parties cooperate, total welfare is maximised with $W = U(P) - g_1 + S(P) - g_2$. This is greater than the situation where each agent independently maximises with $W = U(P \pm \delta) - G_1 + S(P \pm \delta) - G_2$. This is because where both cooperate each incurs lower transactions costs of $g_1$ for the firm and $g_2$ for the intervenor, and the price would likely be set close to the optimal $P$ in Figure 4.1. Where each independently maximises his respective objective function, the resulting $P$ might lie anywhere between $P + \delta$ and $P - \delta$, where $\delta$ is small in absolute value, and where $G_1$ and $G_2$ are assumed large relative to $g_1$ and $g_2$. If, however, one party cooperates and the other does not, gains arise for the non-cooperating party. In the case of the firm, it results in the higher price $U(P + \Delta)$ less the transactions cost $G_1$, while the intervenor loses with $S(P + \Delta) - g_2$, saving only on transactions costs. Similarly, when the intervenor maximises and the firm cooperates, the firm loses with $U(P - \Delta) - g_1$ and the intervenor gains with $S_2(P - \delta) - G_2$. If each follows the minimax solution - as expected - both are worse off, as shown in the bottom right cell. Each therefore has, in this application of the classic Prisoner's Dilemma, an incentive not to cooperate, although both would lose if both do not cooperate (that is, if the rate case is litigated).

*Table* 4.2 Prisoner's Dilemma model

| *Firm's strategy* | *Intervenor's strategy* | |
|---|---|---|
| | *Cooperate* | *Maximise independently* |
| Cooperate | $U(P) - g_1, S(P) - g_2$ | $U(P - \Delta) - g_1, S(P - \Delta) - G_2$ |
| Max. independently | $U(P + \Delta) - G_1, S(P + \Delta) - g_2$ | $U(P + \delta) - G_1, S(P + \delta) - G_2$ |

*Note*: where $\Delta$, $G_1$, $G_2$ are large and where $\Delta \gg |\delta|$, $G_1 \gg g_1$, and $G_2 \gg g_2$.

It is conceivable that the Prisoner's Dilemma may not apply in the simple form outlined above. In view of the fact that, in practice, frequent interaction may and does occur between companies and the advocate, it is arguable that some modified form of the Prisoner's Dilemma, such as the 'repeated prisoner's Dilemma' as examined by Axelrod and Hamilton (1981) and Axelrod (1984), applies. Here other strategies rather than simple cooperation or cheating may arise, and may even dominate. One such strategy is tit-for-tat, which in Axelrod and Hamilton's experiments was a very robust strategy. Tit-for-tat involves 'cooperating on the first move and then doing whatever the other player did on the preceding move' (Axelrod and Hamilton, 1981, p. 1393). Whether tit-for-tat is efficient and stable depends upon the probability of further interaction between the parties, the higher the probability the more likely tit-for-tat is to be efficient and stable. In the case of utilities and a permanent public advocate, the chance of meeting again would presumably be large, implying that tit-for-tat is a (Pareto efficient) Nash equilibrium in the repeated

Prisoner's Dilemma game. With other intervenors the probability would be lower and the non-cooperative strategy may be the only Nash strategy in the repeated game.

The above two-party game can be generalised to include the other rent seekers in the regulatory process. Let the set of all such rent seekers be denoted by $N$, and denote the preferences of $i \in N$ by $V_i(x_i, r_i)$, where $x_i$ is some privately held resource (that is expertise) which has an opportunity cost if applied to rent seeking; $r_i$ denotes total rents appropriated by agent $i \in N$.

Let $\rho(x)$ be the total rents produced when agents $i \in N$ allocate the vector of resources $x = \{x_i \mid i \in N\}$ to rent seeking activities. Total rents $\rho(x)$ may be as great as total consumer surplus less total costs if perfect discrimination can be implemented. In the usual (Tullock, 1967) case of uniform pricing, $\rho(x)$ can be represented as

$$\rho(x) = P(x)Q(P(x)) - C(Q(P(x)), x),$$

where we have indicated a dependence of both revenues and costs on actions of rent seekers. For example, managers of the firm may choose to allocate their managerial expertise to reducing costs or to achieving greater revenue by obtaining the consent to price changes. Similarly, we can model the effects of increased legal expenditures as in the two-party model above.

The rent seeking game (RSG) emerging from the above is the game characterised by the following givens:

$$\{V_i(x_i, r_i) \mid i \in N\}, \{X_i \mid i \in N\}, \rho: X \rightarrow R,$$

where $X_i$ is the feasible action space of agent $i \in N$, $X = \prod_N X_i$, and where every solution $\{(X_i, r_i) \mid i \in N\}$ to *RSG* must satisfy

$$x_i \in X_i, i \in N, \sum_{i \in N} r_i = \rho(x).$$

The fact that the $r_i$ are not constrained (for example to be non-negative) assumes that there is some residual stakeholder, here the investor, who absorbs all residual (positive or negative) rents. The important thing to note about *RSG* is that rent seekers influence both the size of the pie ($\rho(x)$) as well as its distribution.

On repeated plays of *RSG*, the same Prisoner's Dilemma incentives analysed above arise in this more general setting. Although the analytics of this remain to be studied, it should be clear, as in Axelrod (1984), that there are incentives for cooperation in assuring the continuing creation of rents $\rho(x)$ and in devising distribution mechanisms (to divide $\rho(x)$ among $i \in N$) which attenuate the dissipation of these rents.

An important issue raised by the above is the extent to which the rent seeking game bars new entrants. When entry barriers are low relative to expected rents, one may expect stronger competition to dissipate more of the rents than when entry costs are high relative to expected rents. In water supply, entry barriers are arguably high relative to expected rents for new rent seekers. This rests on the cost of information to play the game, the average (small) size of the typical water company, and the likelihood that potential rents are already completely distributed to existing participants in the rent seeking game.

The above theory gives rise to several hypotheses for rent seeking and regulation in water supply. These can be roughly structured in two categories:

1. Who benefits from the current structure?
2. Why does the current structure continue to exist?

As we show in the next section, lawyers are the principal beneficiaries of the present process. We hypothesise that the process continues to exist because it provides a means of sharing the rents that arise, which satisfies the aspirations of those who have the power to change the process, namely the lawyers. Unlike the traditional rent seeking assumptions of Tullock (1967), we argue that there is not perfect competition among rent seekers. Indeed, we will argue that in view of the repeated Prisoner's Dilemma nature of the game, cooperation is the rule rather than the exception. To the extent that this results in a less than complete dissipation of the rents, the weaker the competition the smaller the welfare loss in rent seeking situations in contrast to the effects of competition in traditional markets.

## 4.3 ANALYSIS OF SURVEY RESULTS

To test the hypotheses developed in Section 4.2, we employ two approaches:

1. an analysis of descriptive statistics, and
2. regression analysis.

As a result, we are able to throw new light on some of the institutional details of the process and the effects on the various actors.

## 1. Analysis of Descriptive Statistics

Table 4.3 and 4.4 throw some light on how and which companies gain from the regulatory process. Table 4.3 shows that small companies requested somewhat more than large companies (the difference being significant at a 10 per cent level), but that they got no more. This may be indicative that small companies are less well schooled in the nature of the game. It may also imply that because they offer very little rents to the other players that they get few rents themselves out of the process. Almost certainly, smaller companies are more risky than larger companies, implying that their request for a higher allowed rate of return is not unjustified. However, the fact that they are awarded on average only the same as large companies implies that their case goes unrecognised by commissions. This may be because commissions believe that few potential rents are to be gained from allowing small companies higher returns. Table 4.4, on the other hand, shows that small companies spent considerably more on a per customer basis than did large or medium-sized customers. The very high expenditure by small companies offers some support for the notion that few rents remain to be dissipated in the case of small companies. If this is the case, regulators would feel constrained in allowing small companies a higher rate of return. Further indication of the relatively unfavourable treatment for smaller companies may be seen in Table 4.5, which shows that rate cases for smaller companies took somewhat longer than rate cases for large and medium companies. This may arise from the lack of expertise of small companies as well as their failure to provide sufficient rents to

*Table* 4.3 Requested versus allowed return on equity.

| *Size of company* | *Number of companies* | *Return on equity requested %* | *t-test values* |
|---|---|---|---|
| | Requested % return on equity by company size | | |
| Small | 48 | 17.15 | 0.47 |
| Medium | 24 | 16.49 | 1.39 |
| Large | 12 | 15.70 | |
| All companies | 84 | 16.50 | |
| | Allowed % return on equity by company size | | |
| Small | 46 | 14.70 | 0.01 |
| Medium | 24 | 14.56 | 0.40 |
| Large | 12 | 14.69 | |
| All companies | 82 | 14.45 | |

*Table* 4.4 Costs per customer for most current rate case

| *Size of company* | *Number of companies using consultants* | *Average for companies using consultants* $ | *t-test values* |
|---|---|---|---|
| | *Costs per customer for outside consultants* | | |
| Small | 49 | 7.13 | 3.47 |
| Medium | 24 | 1.33 | 0.64 |
| Large | 12 | 1.11 | |
| Weighted average all companies | 85 | 1.99 | |
| | *In-house costs per customer* | | |
| Small | 46 | 3.45 | 2.95 |
| Medium | 18 | 1.36 | 1.34 |
| Large | 8 | 0.79 | |
| Weighted average all companies | 72 | 1.36 | |
| | *Total rate cases expenses per customer* | | |
| Small | 45 | 10.74 | 3.65 |
| Medium | 18 | 2.39 | 1.44 |
| Large | 8 | 1.68 | |
| Weighted average all companies | 72 | 3.15 | |

regulators, attorneys and others which would provide the inducement to move the process along, thereby leaving some rents for the residual rent seekers, the stockholders.

Table 4.6 shows the categories of expense incurred in rate cases. Lawyers were used in 72 cases, nearly one and a half times as frequently as the next most frequently used expertise, rate-of-return consultants. In addition, the amount spent on lawyers, $2 094 912, far exceeds the amount spent on any other kind of consultants. The expenditure on rate-of-return consultants was $572 369, a little more than a quarter of what was spent on lawyers. Lawyers clearly were the biggest beneficiaries among the outside contractors. Large companies were subject to much more attention by public advocates and publicly appointed intervenors, as shown in Table 4.7. This may seem to imply socially efficient behaviour on the part of public advocates. It is not necessarily the case, since it does not necessarily follow that small-company cases have less significant public-interest qualities than large-company cases. However, it is clear that there are many fewer rents to soak up in small company cases than in large-company cases.

*Table* 4.5 Average time between filing and award

| *Size of company* | *Number of companies* | *Average time for case (in months)* | *t-test values* |
|---|---|---|---|
| | Duration of most recent rate case | | |
| Small | 49 | 9.6 | |
| Medium | 24 | 7.8 | 1.59 |
| Large | 11 | 8.5 | 0.96 |
| All companies | 84 | 9.0 | |
| | Duration of second most recent rate case | | |
| Small | 35 | 11.3 | |
| Medium | 17 | 8.5 | 2.04 |
| Large | 6 | 10.5 | 0.57 |
| All companies | 58 | 10.3 | |
| | Average time between most recent and second most recent rate case | | |
| Small | 35 | 18.2 | |
| Medium | 17 | 19.5 | 0.45 |
| Large | 6 | 19.5 | 0.00 |
| All companies | 58 | 18.7 | |

*Table* 4.6 Outside consulting expenses by category

| *Type of consultants* | *Number of companies engaging consultants by type* | *Average amount spent by companies engaging consultants* $ |
|---|---|---|
| Forecasting | 4 | 16 404 |
| Costing | 4 | 16 059 |
| System planning | 2 | 3 360 |
| Financial | 15 | 29 560 |
| Rate design | 33 | 15 003 |
| Rate of return | 49 | 11 681 |
| Legal | 72 | 29 096 |
| Other | 18 | 17 906 |

*Table* 4.7 Involvement of state appointed intervenor

| *Size of company* | *Number of companies* | *Percent of all companies* % | *t-test values* |
|---|---|---|---|
| Small | 18 | 36 | |
| Medium | 11 | 46 | 0.79 |
| Large | 11 | 92 | 3.44 |
| All companies | 40 | 47 | |

## 2. Regression Analysis

An econometric analysis of survey returns was also undertaken using ordinary least squares. Definitions of variables are given in Table 4.8.

*Table* 4.8 Definition of variables

| | | |
|---|---|---|
| TIME | = | Time elapsed in months since last rate case. |
| NUMINT | = | Number of intervenors (including the Public Advocate) involved in the rate case. |
| AMTREQ | = | Amount requested (annual revenue increase) in the rate case. |
| AMTALL | = | Amount allowed (annual revenue increase) as a result of the rate case. |
| CUST | = | Number of customers in most recent year preceding rate case. |
| FIRMTC | = | Transactions costs for the given rate case for the firm. This consisted of a subjective estimate of the value of internal management time spent on the rate case. |
| PADVTC | = | Transactions costs for the given rate case by a publicly appointed intervenor. |
| INTVTC | = | Transactions costs for the given rate case of all non-public intervenors. |
| EXTTC | = | PADVTC + INTVTC = Transactions costs for all external intervenors. |
| TOTALTC | = | FIRMTC + PADVTC + INTVTC = Total transactions costs of rate case. |
| LITIG | = | A dummy variable which was 1 if the case was litigated and 0 if the case was stipulated. |

The three basic equations to be estimated were:

$$\text{AMTALL} = a_0 + a_1\,\text{TIME} + a_2\,\text{NUMINT} + a_3\,\text{AMTREQ} + a_4\,\text{CUST} + a_5\,\text{FIRMTC} + a_6\,\text{EXTTC} + a_7\,\text{LITIG} \tag{4.5}$$

and

$$\text{TOTALTC} = b_0 + b_1\,\text{TIME} + b_2\,\text{NUMINT} + b_3\,\text{AMTREQ} + b_4\,\text{CUST} + b_5\,\text{LITIG} \tag{4.6}$$

and

$$\text{FIRMTC} = c_0 + c_1\,\text{TIME} + c_2\,\text{NUMIT} + c_3\,\text{AMTREQ} + \tag{4.7}$$

$$c_4 \text{ SALES} + c_5 \text{ EXTTC} + c_6 \text{ LITIG}$$

The above three equations were estimated using two data sets:

$S$ = small firms with sales not exceeding 25 000(000) gals/year (50 rate cases);

$K$ = medium and large firms with sales exceeding 25 000(000) gals/year (36 rate cases).

The results are shown in Table 4.9.

These results are consistent with the earlier analysis of Crew and Kleindorfer (1985) whereby most of the variation in amount allowed is explained by the amount requested. This is consistent, for the larger firms at least, with the scenario described in Crew and Kleindorfer (1985) whereby regulators and companies behave as if they were participants in a game in which the commission grants them some fixed fraction of what they request minus a flat-rate deduction (the intercept). For the small firms the intercept term was not significant, but the amount requested (AMTREQ) was highly significant, with approximately three-quarters of the request being allowed. Nothing else was significant in the case of the small firms. In contrast, for the large firms, the LITIG, EXTC, CUST and TIME variables were also significant. The LITIG variables's positive sign implies a good understanding of the process by the larger firms. They got more when they litigated. Although they were not affected by the number of intervenors, they were affected negatively by the amount spent by the intervenors (EXTC). This is consistent with our theory, supporting the notion that the large companies and the publicly appointed intervenors are in a well-understood game, the results of which depend in part on the amount expended. The lack of significance of this term in the case of the small companies is also consistent with our hypothesis that they have less of a grasp of the rules of the game. Similarly, the significantly positive TIME term for the large companies showed their understanding of the process. This is consistent with their being able to make reasoned business judgements as to how long to wait between cases. The longer they wait between cases the more they ultimately get, but of course the more they forego awaiting rate approval.

The equations for total transactions costs (TOTALTC) and firm transactions cost (FIRMTC) provided weaker results. For the small companies TIME and ANTREQ are both significantly positive, possibly implying that they move together. The longer a company waits, the more it needs and

*Table* 4.9 Results of regression runs

| *Dependent variable* | *CONSTANT* | *TIME* | *NUMINT* | *AMTREQ* | *CUST* | *FIRMTC* | *EXTTC* | *LITIG* | *F-STAT* | $R^2$ | $R^2$ *ADJ* |
|---|---|---|---|---|---|---|---|---|---|---|---|
| AMTALL(*S*) | −52238.2<br>(−0.42) | 31060.2<br>(1.03) | 15503.3<br>(0.62) | 0.7747<br>(11.01)** | −5.6345<br>(−1.11) | −0.8238<br>(−0.77) | 0.1158<br>(1.39) | −24096.0<br>(−0.44) | 33.73** | 84.89 | 82.38 |
| AMTALL(*L*) | −1639400.0<br>(−2.70)** | 845625.3<br>(3.53)** | 6807.0<br>(0.11) | 0.2754<br>(3.78)** | 9.0893<br>(3.26)** | −0.6915<br>(−0.43) | −0.6892<br>(−2.12)* | 439280.7<br>(2.52)** | 22.24** | 84.75 | 80.94 |
| TOTALTC(*S*) | 439946.6<br>(3.37)** | 96772.8<br>(2.36)** | −20296.4<br>(−0.64) | 0.2129<br>(2.36)** | 2.5454<br>(0.37) | | | −205470.0<br>(−3.05)** | 4.78** | 35.20 | 27.84 |
| TOTALTC(*L*) | 565160.3<br>(2.55)** | −258680.0<br>(−1.79)* | 26481.4<br>(1.23) | −0.0006<br>(−0.02) | −0.0374<br>(−0.03) | | | 41026.5<br>(0.69) | 1.33 | 18.21 | 4.58 |
| FIRMTC(*S*) | 7011.8<br>(0.39) | 1229.5<br>(0.28) | 6837.9<br>(2.02)* | 0.0236<br>(2.52)** | 0.4208<br>(0.58) | | 0.0389<br>(3.79)** | 5545.1<br>(0.72) | 6.34** | 46.97 | 39.57 |
| FIRMTC(*L*) | 62237.8<br>(0.89) | 12182.2<br>(0.43) | 1104.6<br>(0.15) | 0.0217<br>(2.91)** | −0.1933<br>(−0.59) | | 0.0146<br>(0.38) | −6145.0<br>(−0.30) | 2.62* | 35.22 | 21.81 |

*Notes*: 1. The number of observations was $S$ = small = 50; $L$ = large = 36.
2. $t$-values are in parentheses; * and ** respectively indicates 0.05 and 0.01 level of significance (for testing hypothesis $H0$: $\beta^i = 0$, $H1$: $\beta^i \neq 0$).

the more it needs to spend on presenting its case. In contrast, for the large companies the TIME variable has a negative sign. Again this is consistent with a better understanding of the game. Large companies have a much smaller variance in the time between rate cases. Where they delay, they are able to present their case more convincingly and at less expense. The fact that this variable is insignificant for the FIRMTC variable is indicative of the intervenor's showing some recognition of the added strength given to the firm's case by extending the time between cases. For small companies FIRMTC was increased if external intervenors spent more. Again this may reflect small companies' lack of understanding of the game that large firms have. Small firms may get into relatively more conflict with publicly appointed intervenors than large firms.

## 4.4 CONCLUDING DISCUSSION AND IMPLICATIONS FOR REGULATION

The implications of this study for regulation are fairly clear. Prescriptions as to what to do about them are much less clear. For regulated water companies transactions costs of governance are quite high. This is particularly so in the case of small companies. In the case of large companies these costs are apparently much lower. We cannot be certain, however, that even for large companies governance costs are not excessive, because our survey grossly understates the in-house costs of companies. In the case of large companies these may be much higher than in the case of small companies. Departments and employees that have no direct connection with the rate case may be required to 'drop everything' to provide input for the rate case at some critical stage. It is highly unlikely that such expenses would be reported in our survey. It is possible that companies carry extra capacity in such departments to deal with these kinds of eventualities. Our survey has certainly revealed how limited our knowledge is on the effects of the process of regulation on the internal operation of companies. Further study is required to give us even a rudimentary knowledge of such effects.

Even given the problem of our inadequate knowledge of in-house costs, it would appear that the costs of regulating smaller companies are too high and need to be reduced. We can also, from our discussion of rent seeking, be aware of the reason why costs are too high, and suggest that governance structures be modified to attenuate rent seeking in the case of small companies. Deregulation would clearly get rid of many of the transactions costs of the current governance mode. However, in the case of water there is little alternative, and the problems of monopoly exploitation and transaction specificity would still remain. Deregulation may be like throwing the baby out with the bath water. Devising alternative, more efficient, governance structures is difficult, requiring considerably more research. There may also be significant intangible benefits from regulation (for example those arising from the assurance of due process), as argued by Mashaw (1985) and Crew and Kleindorfer (1985, 1986b). Consider, for example, the following proposal to regulate all small utilities based upon the rate of return and adjustments to the various items in the cost of service as determined in the rate cases for the larger companies. Small companies would not be required to have a formal rate case if they were prepared to utilise the percentage adjustments derived from the large-company cases. Any competent intervenor with standing would, of course, still be allowed to instigate a full hearing. This proposal could be expected to significantly reduce the number of rate cases and associated transactions costs. None the less, there are several difficulties. One of these is the problem of the base period. If the base period were one in which cost of service was overstated, the effect of automatic adjustments based upon what larger companies got could eventually result in prices converging to the monopoly price. This would still have the advantage that many fewer rents would be dissipated than currently. However, it would completely fail to protect the consumer from monopoly pricing.

The net result is that although the analysis and empirical results of this paper have pointed toward areas where reform might take place, they have also underlined the problem of making *ad hoc* adjustments to the regulatory process. While this chapter has thrown light on the complex interactions of rent seekers, it is beyond its scope to prescribe precise reforms. Clearly, regulation of small companies takes place at a very high cost and alternative governance structures or modifications to the existing governance structures are needed. However, because of the complexities of the process we cannot do more than propose further study of the problem at this point. A first modest objective of such study would be to determine regulatory institutions and procedures which are compatible with legal precedents and which do not dissipate more net benefits than they yield.

**Acknowledgements**

The authors gratefully acknowledge helpful comments on an earlier draft by W. Mark Crain and James Rodgers, as well as the assistance of Frank Gradilone of the Hackensack Water Company in collecting and analysing questionnaire data, and of Jae Sik Lee for statistical assistance.

**References**


AXELROD, R. (1984) *The Evolution of Cooperation* (New York: Basic Books).

AXELROD, R. and HAMILTON, W. D. (1981) 'The Evolution of Co-operation', *Science*, vol. 211, no. 4489, pp. 1390–6.

CREW, M. A. and KLEINDORFER, P. R. (1985) 'Governance Costs of Rate-of-Return Regulation', *Journal of Theoretical and Institutional Economics*, vol. 141, March, pp. 104–23.

CREW, M. A. and KLEINDORFER, P. R. (1986a) 'Governance Structures for Natural Monopoly: A Comparative Institutional Assessment', Forthcoming in *Journal of Behavioral Economics.*

CREW, M. A. and KLEINDORFER, P. R. (1986b) *The Economics of Public Utility Regulation* (London: Macmillan).

CREW, M. A. and ROWLEY, C. K. (1986) 'Regulation as an Instrument for Industrial Policy', *Journal of Institutional and Theoretical Economics*, vol. 142, no. 1, March, pp. 52–78.

GOLDBERG, V. P. (1976) 'Regulation as an Administered Contract', *Bell Journal of Economics*, vol. 7, no. 2, pp. 426–48.

KLEIN, B., CRAWFORD, R. G. and ALCHIAN, A. A. (1978) 'Vertical Integration, Appropriable Rents, and the Competitive Contracting Process', *Journal of Law and Economics*, vol. 21, October, pp. 297–326.

LEIBENSTEIN, H. (1966) 'Allocative Efficiency Versus X-Efficiency', *American Economic Review*, vol. 56, June, 392–415.

MASHAW, J. (1985) *Appropriate, Competent and Dignified: Due Process Ideals for an Administrative State* (New Haven, Conn.: Yale University Press).

TULLOCK, G. (1967) 'The Welfare Costs of Tariffs, Monopolies, and Theft', *Western Economic Journal*, vol. 5, June, pp. 224–32.

WILLIAMSON, O. E. (1967) *The Economics of Discretionary Behavior: Managerial Incentives in the Theory of the Firm* (Chicago: Markham).

WILLIAMSON, O. E. (1975) *Markets and Hierarchies: Analysis and Antitrust Implications* (New York: Free Press).

WILLIAMSON, O. E. (1976) 'Franchise Bidding for Natural Monopolies – In General and With Respect to CATV', *Bell Journal of Economics*, vol. 7, no. 1, pp. 73–104.

# 5 Public Utility Equity Financing Practices: A Test of Market Efficiency

Cleveland S. Patterson and Nancy D. Ursel

## 5.1 INTRODUCTION

One of the persistent challenges facing financial researchers is to find a set of satisfactory answers to the related questions:

1. Why do firms acquire new equity capital via public underwritten issues rather than employing the apparently less costly non-underwritten rights offering alternatives?
2. Why do those firms which do employ rights offerings not set the subscription price sufficiently low so that the risk of failure is effectively reduced to a negligible level?

Both Brealey and Myers (1984) and Jensen and Smith (1984) list this 'equity issue paradox' as being among the most important unsolved problems in finance.

The paradox has been particularly evident in the public utility industry in the United States which has undergone a massive shift from rights issues to underwritten issues during the past two decades, as can be seen in Table 5.1.

If the use of underwriting is relatively inefficient, as suggested by financial theory, then this shift may be very costly given that 'an allowance for flotation costs of anywhere up to one percentage point is often factored into allowed rates of return on equity.

*Table* 5.1 Public utilities' common stock issues 1963–83

| *Period* | *Average number of issues per year* | *% Rights issues* | *% public underwritten issues* |
|---|---|---|---|
| 1963–69 | 25 | 55 | 45 |
| 1970–76 | 77 | 15 | 85 |
| 1977–83 | 92 | 4 | 96 |

*Source*: Moody's Public Utility Manuals.

Section 5.2 reviews the theoretical reasons why rights issues may be superior to underwritten public issues while Section 5.3 reviews the attempts to explain the predominant use of underwriting which have been advanced in the literature to date.

Section 5.4 summarises the results of a survey sent to the chief financial officers of large United States electric utilities. The purpose of the survey was to investigate their degree of agreement with the theoretical assumptions underlying the normative rights preference model and also to solicit their reasons for the financing choices they had made in recent years.

Based on the survey, it is apparent that at least one important reason why financial managers may shy away from rights issues is that many do not believe that financial markets are efficient as assumed by the rights preference model. When stock is issued through rights at a discount from market, book values per share and, for a given rate of return, earnings per share are lower than they would be if the same amount of capital were to be issued at or close to market through a public underwritten issue. This per share dilution, often referred to as a quasi-split effect, is in theory exactly compensated for by the market value of the rights received by the firm's investors so that the total value of their holdings is unaffected. In an efficient market, investors will look through the reduction in reported earnings per share caused by the rights issues in the same manner as they normally look through the effects of a stock split which does not affect the value of their holdings. However, if markets are not efficient with respect to the information contained in historical growth rates in per share data then the quasi-split effect of a rights issue may result in a reduction in the total value of the shares relative to the value that they would have if the same amount of new capital were raised through a public issue. Section 5.5 tests this hypothesis empirically and concludes that markets, at least with respect to utilities during the period studied, may in fact be inefficient as postulated.

Section 5.6 summarises the conclusions of the chapter and its implications.

## 5.2 THEORETICAL RELATIONSHIPS IN RIGHTS ISSUES

When shares are issued through a rights issue, investors are given one right for each share they own. $N_S$ rights, either received from the issuing firm or purchased in the market, entitle the holder to purchase one new share at a subscription price $S$. For a given amount of new equity raised, $N_S$ is a function of $S$. If the rights-on market price is $M$, then it is easily shown that the market value of a right, $R$, is given by:

$$R = \frac{M - S}{N_S + 1} \tag{5.1}$$

and the market value per share of the stock after the issue, $P_S$, on the assumption that the new capital is invested in projects with *NPV* equal to zero, is

$$P_S = \frac{MN_S + S}{N_S + 1}\,. \tag{5.2}$$

$P_S$ is less than $M$ if $S$ is less than $M$ so that the value of each share originally held by an investor will be less after the issue when stock is raised through rights than it is when raised at or close to $M$ in a public issue. However, despite this decline in *per share* value, the total value of the investors' holdings is unaffected by the choice of financing method since they receive a right for each share held so that their wealth remains equal to $M$ in either case.

$$\text{Total wealth per share} = \frac{MN_S + S}{N_S + 1} + \frac{M - S}{N_S + 1} = M \tag{5.3}$$

While total wealth is unaffected, earnings, dividends and book value per share are all lowered by the sale of shares at $S$ rather than at $M$ and the greater the discount from $M$, the greater will be the reduction in reported per share data. Hawk and Thatcher (1971) show that this quasi-split effect is equivalent to a stock split of $y$ to 1 where

$$y = 1 + \frac{1}{S/R + N_S} \tag{5.4}$$

or, alternatively, to a stock dividend of $y - 1$.

When a firm implements one or more stock splits or declares a series of material stock dividends during some historical period, its reported growth rates in per share earnings, dividends, and book value per share for the period are reduced. However, investors are generally aware that no real change in value has occurred and it is common practice to adjust reported earnings to account for the splits or stock dividends in a consistent manner. Thus, while a two-for-one split may result in reported earnings per share of \$2.00 in year $t$ and \$1.10 in year $t + 1$, investors will generally see through the data and value the shares as if reported earnings were \$2.00 and \$2.20 respectively. In theory, investors should treat the quasi-split effect of a rights issue in an identical manner since in this case, as in the case of splits and stock dividends, the total value of their holdings is unaffected by the event.

The purpose of selling new shares to an underwriter in a public issue is to ensure that 100 per cent of the issue will be taken up at the agreed price as well as to employ the selling ability of the banking group. In a rights issue, the same end can be achieved by setting $S$ at a very large discount from $M$. Most shares will be sold in a rights issue as long as $M$ remains sufficiently above $S$ throughout the subscription period to ensure that $R$ is greater than the transaction costs of exercising or selling the rights. A few investors, through apathy or absence, may neither exercise nor sell their rights but the opportunity cost penalty of such inaction can be increased by setting $S$ low enough to make $R$ a large number approaching $M$ in magnitude. Thus the decision to use public underwritten issues rather than rights issues becomes a question of the relative cost of the two financing methods, where costs are defined in a broad sense to refer to all potential penalties inherent in each method.

## 5.3 REVIEW OF PREVIOUS LITERATURE

The principal arguments that have been made at various times in favour of underwritten public issues can be summarised as follows:[1]

1. Rights offerings are allegedly more costly than underwritten offerings.
2. Underwritten offerings can be more easily timed to take advantage of favourable market conditions and proceeds are available sooner than in a rights offering.
3. Underwriters help to stabilise market prices around the offer date or affect prices positively through implied certification of the bona fides of the issue.

4. Underwritten offerings reduce the uncertainty about the proceeds.
5. Underwritten offerings to the general public widen the distribution of shareholdings relative to an issue made through rights to existing shareholders.
6. Underwritten issues provide management with certain perquisites not available in non-underwritten issues.
7. Rights offerings lower the share price of the issuing firm relative to the price that would prevail in an equal size underwritten issue.

Assertion 1, that rights offers are more costly, has been exhaustively researched by Smith (1977), Hansen and Pinkerton (1982) and Bhagat (1983) as well as by a number of studies by the Securities and Exchange Commission and others. Smith found that rights offerings appeared to be significantly less costly than underwritten offerings even when unreported opportunity costs of the firm's employees' time and taxes and transaction costs imposed on shareholders as well as direct out-of-pocket expenses were taken into account. Smith also analysed and dismissed most of the other arguments listed above. Hansen and Pinkerton (1984) criticised Smith's cost comparisons on the grounds that there is a systematic difference in the sample of firms using each type of financing method. Specifically, they argued that rights offerings are advantageous for closely-held firms but that the majority of firms, which are not closely held, benefit from lower costs in an underwritten issue.[2]

A counter-assertion, that rights issues are less costly because there is no apparent concession to the pre-issue market price in a rights issue while underwritten issues are often made at a slight discount, has been shown to be unfounded by Parsons and Raviv (1985).[3]

Bhagat (1983) tested the relative cost question indirectly by studying the effects on shareholder wealth of removing pre-emptive rights requirements from corporate charters. His evidence is that such amendments, when announced, decrease wealth and concludes that, while underwritten offers may be in the best interests of managers, they are not beneficial to shareholders.

Heinkel and Schwartz (1984) attempted to provide a resolution to the paradox by assuming the existence of asymmetric information between investors and firms. In this model, higher quality firms signal their true value by setting relatively high subscription prices in rights offers while lower quality firms remain indistinguishable to investors by making fully underwritten issues.

Empiricial studies of price changes around the announcement date of rights and underwritten issues have been made by Smith (1977), Heinkel and Schwartz (1984) and Dann and Mikkelson (1984). All of these event studies indicate that abnormal returns around rights issues are marginally higher than those around underwritten issues. This evidence can be interpreted as either being consistent with the signalling hypothesis (that is the rights issue announcement conveys positive new information about quality) or with the cost hypothesis (that is the announcement tells investors that the lower cost method of acquiring capital has been chosen). However, both interpretations proceed from the assumption that the financing decision is a relatively infrequent random event that reflects a choice by management that cannot be anticipated. Moreover, the comparisons between the two groups assumes that there are no systematic differences between their characteristics other than the differences hypothesised.

A related but different question concerning the effects on value of rights issues is the following. If we take a relatively homogeneous group of companies each of which typically issues new equity frequently in the ordinary course of business and which tends to follow either a rights policy or an underwritten policy in a predictable manner over a period of time, is it possible to distinguish between them in terms of the way they are valued? Specifically, in the context of the discussion in Section 5.2, are the earnings or dividend streams of companies which primarily issue through rights valued differently from those which primarily issue through underwritten issues and, if so, does the valuation vary with the subscription price? This question, unlike the event studies referred to, requires cross-section analysis rather than time series studies.

## 5.4 RESULTS OF UTILITY SURVEY

In order to investigate the attitudes and understanding of financial managers involved in frequent equity financing decisions, a questionnaire was sent to the Chief Financial Officer's (CFO's) of the seventy largest electric utilities. This group was selected because all of the companies have been very active in the market in the past decade and also because the response rate in a previous mailing to the same group (Patterson, 1984) had been a gratifying 70 per cent. The purpose of the questionnaire was to:

1. Investigate whether the understanding of rights issues and their effect on the firm was congruent with the assumptions of finance theory.
2. Investigate why the firms had chosen the vehicle, either rights or public, that they had utilised.

In designing and sending out the questionnaire it was recognised that the useful response rate was likely to be low because of the nature of the investigation and because, as indicated in Table 5.1, few of the firms at this point in time are likely to be making conscious choices in the sense of giving serious consideration to rights issues. Virtually all firms now choose underwritten issues as a matter of course.

Nevertheless, the results were disappointing and any conclusions are necessarily tenuous at best since only forty utilities replied and, on average, more than half of those indicated 'no opinion' or 'don't know' in response to the majority of questions. The reasons for this are strikingly apparent in the answers to the question which asked: 'Did you give any consideration to a rights issue instead of an underwritten public issue?' Only six firms affirmed that they had considered this alternative but explicitly rejected it, and only four firms actually issued shares through rights in the past decade. All of the other responding firms either did not consider the rights alternative at all or did not know if they had ever looked at this method explictly. One respondent noted that 'many companies and most investors are totally uneducated about rights issues'.

Those firms which did answer the questions, however, tended to be fairly uniform in their responses and for that reason the results of the questionnaire are of some value. The questions and and responses are therefore shown below:

1. Do you agree that: 'When a firm issues shares through a rights issue the value of rights received will always exactly compensate existing investors for the reduction in value per share caused by the fact that the subscription price is below the rights-on price. This is true no matter what level the subscription is set at.'

   Agree 18; disagree 2.

However, twelve of the agreeing firms indicated that while true in theory the statement might not be true in practice because of market imperfections, transactions costs, or shareholder apathy.

2. Do you agree that: 'The lower the subscription price is set in a rights issue, the lower the risk that the issue may not be fully subscribed. If the price is set low enough, the risk can be effectively eliminated.'

   Agree 14; disagree 5.

3. Do you agree that: 'It is generally true that the total after-tax expenses of a rights issue are less than the total of the after-tax expenses and underwriting costs of an underwritten public issue.'

   Agree 9; disagree 6.

However, several of those agreeing noted that costs of a rights issue could mount rapidly if a large number of rights were not exercised for any reason.

4. Do you agree that: 'Because the subscription price is below the rights-on price, rights issues cause a quasi-split effect by reducing earnings per share below what they would have been if the stock had been sold at market. The lower the subscription price, the greater the quasi-split effect.'

   Agree 16; disagree 2.

5. Do you agree that: 'Stock dividend payments and stock splits are usually adjusted for in published historical reports on a company's performance but the quasi-split effect of a rights issue is not.'

   Agree 14; disagree 1.

6. Do you agree that: 'Even when the quasi-split effect is not adjusted for in published reports, informed investors generally make such adjustments themselves when calculating historical growth trends or when valuing a security.'

   Agree 5; disagree 11

However, two of those agreeing noted that the statement might not be true in practice for the majority of individual, as opposed to institutional, investors.

7. Do you agree that: 'All things being equal (that is ignoring differences in out-of-pocket expenses and underwriting costs), the value of a firm should be the same whether it issues a given amount of equity through rights with a low subscription price, issues through rights with a high subscription price, or issues at market through a public underwritten issue.'

   Agree 18; disagree 2.

In a separate series of questions, responding firms who had explicitly rejected the use of rights offerings were asked to identify possible reasons for their choice. The principal reasons indicated were:

1. 'Desire to widen shareholder distribution.' (10)
2. 'Concern that value of existing shareholders' equity would be diluted by the lower subscription price in a rights issue.' (7)
3. 'Greater out-of-pocket costs in a rights issue than expenses and underwriting costs in a public issue.' (8)

   Regulatory or legal constants were also mentioned by four respondents.

The conclusion to be drawn from this very limited sample of opinions is:

1. Not only do frequent issuers of equity not choose to use rights, contrary to normative theory, they appear not even to *consider* this option as being a viable alternative to be explored and have little apparent knowledge of its ramifications.
2. Those expressing an opinion appear generally to be in accord with the usual assumptions of financial theory (questions 1, 2, 4, 5, 7) but are split on the questions of relative cost (question 3) and generally disagree that markets 'look through' unadjusted quasi-split effects (question 6). Two of the three reasons given for preferring underwritten issues are consistent with the latter two concerns. The third reason frequently given is a desire to widen distribution.

## 5.5 EMPIRICAL TEST OF MARKET EFFICIENCY

In an efficient market, prices will be set by investors who 'see through' the quasi-split effect on the value of the firm's equity. However, it is apparent from the results of the survey as well as anecdotal evidence (see Smith (1977) and Bhagat (1983)) that there is considerable concern on the part of managers that the quasi-split effect may in fact have a negative effect, contrary to the efficient market hypothesis. To investigate whether or not this concern is legitimate, we tested the effects of the quasi-split effect on the value of a group of electric utilities many of which had issued shares through rights during the period 1963–81. The investigation is both a test of the hypothesis that the quasi-split effect is a contributing factor to the 'equity issue paradox' and a test of the efficiency of the market in reacting to public information about utility shares.

The public utility sector was chosen for the study because it provides a large and relatively homogenous cross-section of firms and because, as indicated in Table 5.1, companies in this industry typically enter the equity markets regularly and frequently. Study of the industry is also of interest in its own right because inefficiency in the choise of financing method impacts directly on the cost of service under regulation.

The sample for the study consisted of approximately one hundred United States electric utilities which had data available during the study period. Because of the relative stability of earnings growth for companies in this industry it is possible to use the simple Gordon growth model to segregate the effects of historical growth patterns on price, that is

$$\frac{D}{P} = k - g^e \tag{5.5}$$

where $P$ is the current price per share, $D$ is the current indicated dividend rate, $k$ is the investors' discount rate and $g^e$ is the expected rate of growth in dividends per share.

If historical growth, $g$, is used by investors as a proxy for expected growth, then the quasi-split effect can be investigated by breaking $g$ into two parts:

1. $g_u$: the reported rate calculated without adjustment for the quasi-split effect of any rights issues made during the historical growth period, and;
2. $g_r$: the difference between total growth, $g_t$, calculated using data which is adjusted for the quasi-split effect, and $g_u$.

The regression model to be estimated is then:

$$\frac{D}{P} = a_0 + a_1\, g_u + a_2\, g_r + e \tag{5.6}$$

where $a_0$, $a_1$, and $a_2$ are regression coefficients and $e$ is an error term.

Under the hypothesis of market efficiency, investors make no distinction between $g_r$ and $g_u$ and therefore $a_1 = a_2$. If this is true, financial managers should have no concern about the quasi-split effect on value. However, if markets are inefficient so that investors estimate future growth based only on reported figures without any explicit adjustment, then $a_2$ will equal zero.

The hypotheses to be tested are therefore

$$H_0: a_1 \geqslant a_2$$
$$H_a: a_1 < a_2$$

that is, the null is that $g_r$ is given at least as much weight in investors' evaluations as $g_u$, while the alternative hypothesis is that investors totally or at least partially ignore $g_r$ so that its weight in their evaluation is less than that of $g_u$.

To calculate $g_u$, historical five-year growth rates for book value per share were calculated for each company ending in the cross-section years 1968, 1974, and 1980.[4] Data was taken from Compustat as well as from Moodey's Utility Manual which reports adjustments for stock splits and stock dividends but not for the quasi-split effect of rights issues. To calculate $g_r$ for those firms which had employed rights offerings during the calculated growth period, it was necessary to adjust the reported book value per share figures upwards using Equation (5.4), where $R$ was calculated from Equation (5.1) based on the average price of the shares on the day rights warrants were distributed, as reported in Moody's Dividend Record. The growth rate $g_r$ was then arrived at by subtracting $g_u$ from the total growth rate calculated from the adjusted data.[5]

The three non-overlapping cross-sectional sets of data were pooled to increase the efficiency of the regression and two dummy variables, $D_1$ and $D_2$, were added to reflect differences in economic conditions which might have affected dividend yields in the different years. The regression coefficients $a_0 \ldots a_4$ for the pooled regression over 281 observations were ($t$-statistics in parentheses):

| $a_0$ | $a_1 g_u$ | $a_2 g_r$ | $a_3 D_1$ | $a_4 D_2$ | $R^2$ |
|---|---|---|---|---|---|
| 0.058 | −0.314 | 4.089 | 0.058 | 0.067 | 0.69 |
| (14.06) | (−4.77) | (2.37) | (16.90) | (16.85) | |

The estimated coefficient of $g_u$, $a_1$, was negative and significantly different from zero, as predicted by the Gordon model.[6] However, the estimated coefficient of $g_r$, $a_2$, was significantly positive at the 5 per cent level. More importantly for our purposes, the $t$-statistic for the difference between the estimated values of $a_1$ and $a_2$ was 6.52 implying that the null hypothesis that $a_1 \geqslant a_2$ could be rejected with high confidence.

A pooled regression over the non-overlapping years 1969, 1975 and 1981 produced similar results, with a $t$-statistic of 2.62.

| $a_0$ | $a_1 g_u$ | $a_2 g_r$ | $a_3 D_1$ | $a_4 D_2$ | $R^2$ |
|---|---|---|---|---|---|
| 0.070 | −0.349 | 1.692 | 0.017 | 0.051 | 0.73 |
| (24.59) | (−7.47) | (1.34) | (6.64) | (17.69) | |

Thus in both cases, the results of the regression are consistent with the hypothesis that investors distinguish between reported growth $g_u$ and the rights adjustment $g_r$ and that the latter is valued less highly. In fact, as indicated by the significantly positive value of $a_2$ in one case, it may even be negatively valued.

In order to provide some assurance that the results obtained were in fact due to investors' reaction to quasi-splits and were not simply due to some statistical aberration, we also selected a sample of firms which did not have rights issues during the growth period and then created artificial rights adjustments for them. In contrast to our expectations with the original sample of rights issues that $a_1 < a_2$, the expectation for this sample is that $a_2 = a_1$ since the distinction between $g_r$ and $g_u$ is truly an artifact and we would expect both growth terms to be equally valued by investors.

The artificial rights growth adjustment was done as follows: Let $N$ equal the number of firms in the original sample and $n$ equal the number which had rights issues and therefore had positive $g_r$ terms. Of the $N - n$ firms which did not have rights issues, $n/N$ per cent were randomly selected to receive artificial rights adjustments and $(n/N)(N - n)$ actual $g_r$ terms from the original sample were randomly selected to be applied to those firms. $g_u$ for each firm was then calculated by subtracting its artificial $g_r$ term from its total growth rate $g_t$. The result of the pooled regressions for this control sample were:

| $a_0$ | $a_1 g_u$ | $a_2 g_r$ | $a_3 D_1$ | $a_4 D_2$ | $R^2$ |
|---|---|---|---|---|---|
| 1968, 74, 80 (239 observations) | | | | | |
| 0.057 | −0.316 | 0.733 | 0.055 | 0.068 | 0.71 |
| (13.16) | (−4.49) | (0.35) | (15.29) | (16.57) | |
| 1969, 75, 81 (240 observations) | | | | | |
| 0.070 | −0.359 | 0.528 | 0.018 | 0.070 | 0.75 |
| (21.87) | (−7.03) | (0.42) | (6.57) | (16.34) | |

The $t$-statistics for the null hypothesis that $a_1 \geqslant a_2$ were 0.25 and 0.51 respectively so that the null hypothesis could not be rejected, as anticipated.

## 5.6 CONCLUSION

A possible reason for the 'equity issue paradox' with respect to the strong disinclination of firms to use rights issues despite their apparent cost advantage is that rights issues cause a quasi-split effect on per share data and thus reduce reported growth rates. In an efficient market, investors will see through this effect so that it should have no influence on the value of the firm. However, if markets are not efficient, and if investors' expectations are influenced by historical trends, then a rights issue may negatively affect value relative to an underwritten issue. Moreover, the degree of loss will be a direct function of the subscription price discount from market price.

The conclusions of the chapter are consistent with the concerns of managers that markets, at least for utilities, are in fact inefficient in this sense and that there is a 'cost' in a rights issue that varies with the discount and is not present in an underwritten issue. This result both provides an explanation of the paradox and is also indicative of another anomaly in the efficient markets literature.

The results also have implications for regulatory decisions regarding management's choice of financing methods. If only out-of-pocket costs are considered, it can probably be demonstrated in most instances that utilities' increasing use of underwritten public issues, as illustrated in Table 5.1, imposes an unnecessary burden on revenue requirements when firms are allowed to recover costs through rate of return adjustments. However, if markets are inefficient, as suggested by the study, then the use of rights may have an offsetting upward effect on the firm's cost of equity which, in fact, justifies the choices being made in the industry.

**Notes**

1. For detailed discussion of the argument, see Smith (1977) and Bhagat (1983).
2. For a criticism of the empirical methodology of this study, and a reply, see Smith and Dhatt (1984) and Hansen and Pinkerton (1984).
3. Studies by Marsh (1979) and White and Lusztig (1980) show that price pressure in rights issues is negligible.
4. Growth rates in dividends per share and earnings per share were also used but they generally had less explanatory power than growth in book value per share. In addition, the model was tested with several other variables, including leverage, beta, percentage of sales from electricity, and Argus regulatory rating. None of these additional variables was found to be consistently significant.
5. This procedure may slightly underestimate $g_r$ since Equation (5.4) only provides a floor to the value of a right. If investors regard the right as a call on the stock with an exercise price of $S$, the value of the right may exceed $R$ by a small premium.

6. The model, as depicted by Equation (5.5), predicts that $a_1 = a_2 = -1$. A value closer to $-0.3$ is, however, typical in empirical studies and has been explained by Gordon (1974) as being due to a relationship between $k$ and $g$.

## References


BHAGAT, S. (1983) 'The Effect of Pre-emptive Rights Amendements on Shareholder Wealth', *Journal of Financial Economics*, vol. 12, November, pp. 287–310.

BREALEY, R. and MYERS, S. (1984) *Principles of Corporate Finance*, 2nd edn. (New York: McGraw Hill).

DANN, L. Y. and MIKKELSON, W. K. (1984) 'Convertible Debt Issuance, Capital Structure Change and Financing-related Information', *Journal of Financial Economics*, vol. 13, June, pp. 157–86.

GORDON, M. J. (1974) *The Cost of Capital to a Public Utility* (East Lansing, Michigan: MSU Public Utility Studies).

HANSEN, Robert and PINKERTON, J. M. (1982) 'Direct Equity Financing: A Resolution of a Paradox', *Journal of Finance* 37, June, pp. 651–65.

HANSEN, Robert and PINKERTON, J. M. (1984) 'Direct Equity Financing: A Resolution of a Paradox: A Reply', *Journal of Finance*, vol. 39, December, pp. 1619–24.

HAWK, S. L. and THATCHER, L. W. (1971) 'The Treatment of Rights Offerings in Common Stock Valuation', *Public Utilities Fortnightly*, 11 November, pp. 23–31.

HEINKEL, R. and SCHWARTZ, E. S. (1984) 'Rights versus Underwritten Offerings: an Asymmetric Information Approach', UBC Working Paper No. 1033, November.

JENSEN, M. C. and SMITH, C. W. (eds) (1984) *The Modern Theory of Corporate Finance* (New York: McGraw-Hill, 1984).

MARSH, P. (1979) 'Equity Rights Issues and the Efficiency of the U.K. Stock Market', *Journal of Finance*, vol. 34, no. 4, September, pp. 839–62.

PARSONS, J. and RAVIV, A. (1985) 'Underpricing of Seasoned Issues', *Journal of Financial Economics*, vol. 14, September, pp. 377–98.

PATTERSON, C. S. (1984) 'The Financing Objectives of Large U.S. Electric Utilities', *Financial Management*, vol. 13, no. 2, pp. 15–23.

SMITH, C. W. (1977) 'Alternative Methods for Raising Capital: Rights Versus Underwritten Offerings', *Journal of Financial Economics*, vol. 5, December, pp. 273–307.

SMITH, R. L. and Dhatt, M. (1984) 'Direct Equity Financing: A resolution of a Paradox: Comment', *Journal of Finance*, vol. 39, December, pp. 1615–18.

WHITE, R. and LUSZTIG, P. (1980) 'The Price Effects of Rights Offerings', *Journal of Financial and Quantitative Analysis*, vol. 15, March, pp. 25–39.

# 6 Ramsey Pricing in Telecommunications Markets with Free Entry

Donald J. Brown and Geoffrey M. Heal

A standard normative model of optimal regulated pricing is Ramsey pricing. Ramsey prices are those prices which maximise the indirect social welfare function subject to the regulated firm breaking even at those prices. Faulhaber (1975), first observed that requiring a regulated multiproduct monopoly to use Ramsey pricing may be incompatible with allowing free entry into some of the regulated firm's markets. He argues that, in general, Ramsey prices produce cross-subsidisation in that if the cost function describing the monopolist's technology is additively separable - hence the average cost of production for each product is well defined - then in some markets the Ramsey prices exceed the average cost of production and in other markets (the subsidised markets) the Ramsey prices are less than the average cost of production. Consequently, firms will enter those markets which are being taxed relative to the average cost of production and produce those commodities at a price less than the Ramsey price. This will leave the regulated firm with insufficient revenue to subsidise consumption in those markets where it is pricing below average cost. The resulting mix of regulated prices and market prices will not be socially optimal.

An obvious way to prevent cream-skimming, that is entry into a regulated market and pricing above average costs but below the regulated price, is simply to forbid entry. This policy fails to discriminate between entrants possessing a more efficient technology and those firms having the same technology as the regulated firm but making a profit on the regulatory wedge between the regulated price and the average cost of production. In a similar vein, an entry fee or licence to produce in regulated markets will deprive society of those technologies whose profitability falls short of the amount of the entry fee.

In his seminal paper, Faulhaber also gave a definition of prices·for multi-product firms without additively separable cost functions which are free of cross-subsidies. A special case of subsidy-free prices, as they were called by Faulhaber, is the notion of supporting prices introduced by Sharkey and Telser (1978). Given a menu of outputs, supporting prices are those prices such that (1) the firm breaks even at those prices and (2) any production plan with less of the given outputs makes a non-positive profit at these prices.

A cost function is said to be supportable if supporting prices exist for every menu of outputs.[1] Supportable cost functions generalise additively separable cost functions, where each good is produced with decreasing average costs. In this special case, the average costs of production constitute a family of supporting prices. Another important example of a supportable cost function is an additively separable cost function, where each good is produced with constant marginal cost and there is a common fixed cost of production.[2]

In a recent paper, Brown and Heal (1985) prescribed a policy designed to encourage cost reducing innovation, to promote efficient production and to eliminate cream-skimming in markets served by a regulated multi-product firm, where the firm's technology is given by a supportable cost function. They propose that (1) markets served by the regulated firm be open to free entry and (2) an excise tax be imposed on commodites produced in these markets. This tax is the difference between the socially optimal Ramsey prices and the prices which support the socially optimal demand, generated at the Ramsey prices.

Consumers face Ramsey prices but the regulated firm and potential entrants face supporting prices in the Brown–Heal model. Consequently, no firm with the same technology as the regulated firm will find it profitable to enter and produce at prices less than the supporting prices. Firms with more efficient technologies will enter and make positive profits.

This mode of regulation differs fundamentally from the traditional model of regulatory Ramsey pricing. In the standard model, the regulated firm is required to be a price-taker, that is required by the regulator to sell the firm's outputs at the Ramsey prices and both firms and consumers face the same prices.

In the Brown–Heal model, the regulated firm first estimates and announces the Ramsey prices. Then the firm computes the supporting prices for the socially optimal demand or equivalently the excise taxes such that the Ramsey prices net of the excise taxes equal the supporting prices. Any firm may enter the markets served by the regulated firm and sell its output at prices less than those announced by the regulated firm. The regulated firm is required to meet any residual demand in the event of entry, at its announced prices.

The Ramsey prices facing households can be interpreted as the sum of the supporting prices plus an excise tax. This excise tax prevents cream-skimming in that only firms which can produce more cheaply than the regulated firm will enter. Since the socially optimal demand breaks even at both the Ramsey and the supporting prices, we see that the excise taxes simply constitute a family of transfers.

In this chapter, we specialise the Brown–Heal model to telecommunications markets, where we focus on the issue of access pricing. In particular, we address the following questions:

1. Prior to divestiture, was the practice of pricing long distance service above average cost and subsidising local service socially optimal?
2. Post divestiture, is it socially optimal for local telephone companies to price access to long distance service above average cost for the purpose of subsidising local service?

Our model is a simple general equilibrium model: there is a single factor, labour/leisure, which is the *numéraire* good and is untaxed; several products; a single representative consumer;[3] a single regulated firm with a supportable cost function; finally, there are potential entrants, having access to the technology of the regulated firm. The regulator maximises the indirect utility function of the representative consumer over those prices which break even. Ramsey prices are defined as the solution to this maximisation problem.

Our major assumption is that, prior to divestiture, the consumer demands for the products of the regulated firm are independent, that is zero cross-price elasticities. This assumption seems reasonable if we define the products to be the various telephone services such as interstate, intrastate, local, and so on and we ignore access which is complementary to each of the telephone services. For simplicity, we assume only two products: local service, denoted $G$, and long-distance service, denoted $E$. The first order condition for Ramsey prices are given by:

$$\eta_{EE} = \left[\frac{q_i - MC_i}{q_i}\right] = \left[\frac{q_G - MC_G}{q_G}\right] \eta_{GG}$$

where the $q$'s are the Ramsey prices, $MC$ is the marginal cost and $\eta$ is the demand price elasticity.

Sharkey and Telser (1978), show for a supportable cost function, $C(E, G)$, that $C(E, G) \geqslant MC_E\,E + MC_G\,G$. Since Ramsey prices must break even, we see that $q_E \geqslant MC_E$ and $q_G \geqslant MC_G$. In this general case, we cannot say more about $q_E$ and $q_G$ relative to $P_E$ and $P_G$, the supporting prices for the optimal social demand $(\bar{E}, \bar{G})$. So suppose $C(E, G) = K + \alpha E + \beta G$, then $MC_E = \alpha$ and $MC_G + \beta$. In this case, $q_E > \alpha$ and $q_G > \beta$ follows from the first order condition. Moreover, it is easy to show for this cost function that $q_E$ and $q_G$ are, in fact, supporting prices for $(\bar{E}, \bar{G})$. Hence there is no need to impose an excise tax to prevent cream-skimming. Entry into these markets at the Ramsey prices to produce outputs $(E, G) \leqslant (\bar{E}, \bar{G})$, at prices less than the Ramsey prices, can only mean that the entrant possesses a more efficient technology than the regulated firm.

An excise tax is necessary, if we assume that the cost function is additively separable. Suppose $C(E, G) = C_1(E) + C_2(G)$ where $C_1(E) = \alpha E$ and $C_2(G) = K + \beta G$. Then $q_E > \alpha = MC_E = AC_E$, the average cost of $E$. Hence by the break even condition, $q_G < AC_G$, the average cost of $G$; and at the social optimum, local service is subsidised. This example has two important features:

1. The commodity produced with increasing returns is subsidised or equivalently the commodity produced with constant returns is taxed, independent of the demand elasticities.
2. Supporting prices for this example are $P_E = \alpha$ and $P_G = \frac{K}{\bar{E}} + \beta$. In general, $P_E \neq q_E$ and $P_G \neq q_G$. Hence an excise tax is necessary to prevent cream-skimming in this case.

In the post-divestiture world, where one of the commodities produced is access, denoted $F$, we drop the assumption of independent demands and allow some of the cross price elasticities to be non-zero. But the separability of the cost function seems a more realistic assumption than previously. With three products, two of which are complementary to the third, qualitative properties of the Ramsey prices can only be determined numerically. The first-order conditions are given below:[4]

$$\theta_E \eta_{EE} + \theta_F \frac{Fq_F}{Eq_E} \eta_{FE} + \theta_G \frac{Gq_G}{Eq_E} \eta_{GE} = \tag{6.1}$$

$$\theta_F \eta_{FF} + \theta_E \frac{Eq_E}{Fq_F} \eta_{EF} + \theta_G \frac{Gq_G}{Fq_F} \eta_{GF} = \tag{6.2}$$

$$\theta_G \eta_{GG} + \theta_F \frac{Fq_F}{Gq_G} \eta_{FG} + \theta_E \frac{Eq_E}{Gq_G} \eta_{EG}. \tag{6.3}$$

In addition we require that:

$$q_E E + q_G G + q_F F = C(E, F, G) \tag{6.4}$$

where $E, F, G$ are the market demands as functions of $q_E, q_F$, and $q_G$ for local service, access, and long-distance service, respectively; and

$$\theta_i = \frac{q_i - MC_i}{q_i} \text{ for } i = E, F, \text{ or } G.$$

Erickson (1985), has computed Ramsey prices and supporting prices in this model where he assumes that access is produced with constant returns to scale, as is long-distance service, but local service is produced with a fixed cost and constant marginal cost. He uses two different demand structures: one where the demand for long-distance service depends on the price of access and one where it does not; in both cases, the demand for local service depends to some extent on the price of access.

Erickson also considers two different Ramsey models: a simplified case where cross-price elasticities are ignored, as well as the complete Ramsey model presented above. His results indicate that when the demand for a telecommunications service depends on the price of access, the complete Ramsey model will produce a higher price for that service and a lower price for access relative to the prices produced by the simplified model. Furthermore, in the case where the demand for long distance service depends on the price of access, the direction of subsidisation is actually altered: whereas in the simplified model access and long-distance service subsidise local service, the complete model produces a situation where local usage and long distance subsidise access. In sum, Ramsey pricing is compatible with free entry in telecommunications markets served by a regulated firm, if the firm's technology is given by a supportable cost function.

Intuitively, supportable cost functions allow the regulated firm to allocate costs in a fashion which is free of cross subsidies and hence remove the potential for cream-skimming, if there is free entry. A number of such cost allocation schemes have recently been proposed. In particular, Aumann–Shapley prices are supporting prices for cost functions exhibiting cost complementarity, Mirman, Tauman and Zang (1983). It is worth noting for additively separable cost functions with a common fixed cost that the Aumann-Shapley prices reduce to the imputations derived from the attributable cost method (ACM) of fully distributed cost (FDC) pricing, as discussed in Brown and Sibley (1985).

Since supporting prices will in general not meet the first-order conditions necessary for Pareto optimality, consumers' welfare can be improved by commodity taxation, thereby altering the prices which face consumers. In fact, our model shows that these excise taxes can be chosen optimally, that is such that the consumer prices, the sum of the excise taxes and the supporting (producer) prices, are the Ramsey prices.

**Acknowledgements**

The authors would like to thank the participants of the seminar on 'Regulating Utilities in an Era of Deregulation' for their many helpful comments and suggestions. In particular, we wish to thank Larry Cataldo, Larry Cole, Michael Crew, Ken Curry, and Charlotte Kuh.

**Notes**

1. A sufficient condition for a cost function be supportable is cost complementarity, that is the second mixed partials of the cost function with respect to outputs are non-positive.
2. See Faulhaber for an interesting example of a cost function which is not supportable.
3. These assumptions are made only for ease of exposition. A more realistic model with many consumer types and several factors of production can be analysed by numerical methods. In this more general model, the indirect social welfare function assigns weights to the various consumer types. These weights, which are the outcome of some political process, determine the optimal distribution of products in the regulated markets.
4. K. Spier, in a personal communication, provided a derivation of conditions (6.1) through (6.3).

**References**

BROWN, D. and HEAL, G. (1985) 'The Optimality of Regulated Pricing: A General Equilibrium Analysis', in *Advances of Equilibrium Theory*, vol. 244 (Berlin, Springer Verlag).

BROWN, S. and SIBLEY, D. (1985) *The Theory of Public Utility Pricing* (New York: Cambridge University Press).

ERICKSON, C. (1985) 'Ramsey Pricing in Regulated Markets with Free Entry', Senior Essay (New Haven, Conn.: Yale University).

FAULHABER, G. (1975) 'Cross-Subsidization: Pricing in Public Enterprise', *American Economic Review*, vol. 65, December, pp. 966–77.

MIRMAN, L. TAUMAN, Y. and ZANG, I. (1983) 'Supportability, Sustainability, and Subsidy Free Prices', Northwestern Discussion Paper 563, June.

SHARKEY, W. and TELSER, L. (1978) 'Supportable Cost Functions of a Multiproduct Firm', *Journal of Economic Theory*, vol. 18, no. 1, pp. 23–37.

# 7 An Analysis of Ramsey Pricing in Electric Utilities

Jon P. Nelson, Mark J. Roberts
and Emsley P. Tromp

## 7.1 INTRODUCTION

One of the main purposes of electric utility regulation is to determine the price of electricity to be charged to a utility's residential, commercial, and industrial customers. While the price of electricity for each of these customer groups is not determined by market forces, information on the customer's demand structure and the firm's costs of production is generally used in the rate-setting process. Since these output prices are crucial in determining the level and pattern of electricity usage as well as the level of firm costs and profits, it is important to analyse whether these regulated prices satisfy desirable economic criteria. The goal of this paper is to examine whether prices for the three major electricity customer groups satisfy the economic efficiency requirements embodied in the Ramsey pricing rule.

As developed and refined by Baumol and Bradford (1970), the Ramsey pricing rule is a criteria for determining the economically efficient set of prices that achieve some desired minimum level of profit for the producing firm. Maximising the sum of consumer and producer surplus subject to the minimum profit constraint yields the basic result that the deviation between price and marginal cost for each of the firm's outputs should be inversely proportional to the product's elasticity of demand. If this pricing criterion is not satisfied, it is possible to increase total consumer surplus without altering firm profits, by raising the price of some outputs while lowering the price of other outputs.

In this chapter we develop an econometric model of electric utility pricing and use it to test whether observed patterns of output prices satisfy the Ramsey criteria. The model is applied to a sample of 66 utilities in 1970 and 1978 and is also used to test the hypotheses of monopolistic and marginal cost pricing. We then use results from the econometric model to calculate the set of Ramsey output prices for each utility and estimate the welfare gain or loss which would accrue to each customer class if Ramsey pricing was adopted. The use of data from 1970 and 1978 allows us to compare our results with the studies of Ramsey pricing in electric utilities by Meyer and Leland (1980), Nelson (1982), Eckel (1983) and Hayashi, Sevier and Trapani (1985). These studies use data from the mid-1960s and the early 1970s. It also allows us to draw some conclusions about changes in pricing patterns which may have resulted from industry and regulatory changes occurring in the 1970s.[1]

The empirical results indicate that, on average in 1970, actual prices to residential customers were less than Ramsey prices while commercial and industrial customers faced prices which were higher than Ramsey prices. Adoption of Ramsey pricing in 1970 would have required an average increase in residential prices of 25.6 per cent and an average decrease of 20.0 and 14.8 per cent for commercial and industrial customers. In 1978, average residential prices were still found to be below Ramsey prices but prices to commercial customers did not diverge substantially from the efficient levels. Actual industrial prices were significantly above Ramsey levels. If the Ramsey pricing rule was adopted in 1978, average prices for the three outputs would change by a positive 13.5 and 4.1 per cent for residential and commercial customers and by a negative 20.6 per cent for industrial customers. Despite substantial reallocations of consumer surplus among customer groups, the net gain in surplus from moving to the Ramsey optimum is relatively small, equalling 3.7 per cent of utility revenue in 1970 and 4.0 per cent in 1978.

In Section 7.2 we develop the econometric model of Ramsey pricing and identify the pricing hypotheses to be tested. Section 7.3 discusses the necessary data and estimation techniques and Section 7.4 reports the empirical results. The welfare gains from Ramsey pricing of electricity are reported in Section 7.5, and summary and conclusions are offered in the final section.

## 7.2 AN ECONOMETRIC MODEL OF ELECTRICITY PRICING

The Ramsey rule, as derived by Baumol and Bradford (1970), describes the set of uniform output prices that maximise the sum of equally-weighted producer and consumer surplus subject to a minimum profit constraint. It requires that the difference between the price and marginal cost of each output be inversely proportional to the elasticity of demand for the product.[2] More specifically, the prices must satisfy the condition that, for all outputs $j$,

$$t_j \equiv \left[\frac{P_j - MC_j}{P_j}\right] \eta_j = t(\pi) \tag{7.1}$$

where $P_j$, $MC_j$, and $\eta_j$, are the price, marginal cost, and demand elasticity for output $j$, respectively. The elasticity-weighted mark-up, $t_j$, is often referred to as the Ramsey number for output $j$. The set of prices which satisfy Equation (7.1) are the quasi-optimal or Ramsey prices and result in equal Ramsey numbers across all outputs. At the quasi-optimal set of prices, the Ramsey numbers for each output equal $t(\pi)$ which is an increasing function of the minimum required level of profit, $\pi$, for the firm.

Given a set of observed prices for a regulated, multi-product producer it is useful to ask whether or not the Ramsey rule is satisfied in practice. If not, then it is possible to increase the total surplus by altering the set of output prices. Empirical examination of the Ramsey rule involves estimation of the marginal cost and demand elasticity for each output, construction of the Ramsey number for each output using (7.1), and a statistical test of the equality of the Ramsey numbers across outputs. While this framework provides the basis for most studies of Ramsey pricing, the specific methods used to estimate marginal costs, demand elasticities and Ramsey numbers, and to test hypotheses differ substantially. In this section of the paper we develop an econometric model to simultaneously estimate the firm's cost structure and Ramsey numbers. By relying on estimating equations which characterise the firm's output markets it is possible to estimate more accurately the marginal costs of each firm's outputs. In addition, parametric tests which allow us to examine whether or not the Ramsey pricing conditions are satisfied by all firms in the sample are developed. This method of testing the hypothesis of Ramsey pricing contrasts with the testing methods used in other studies.

The empirical model of electricity pricing begins with a specification of the firm's technology. Electric utilities are modelled as producing output for residential, commercial, and industrial customers.[3] In general, the marginal cost of supplying additional power to each customer group can vary due to differences in the time pattern of demand by the group, transmission losses, and the mix of transmission and distribution equipment necessary to serve each group.[4] Each utility is assumed to purchase inputs of capital, labour, and fuel in competitive markets to minimise the cost of producing a given mix of the three outputs. The firm's technology can be represented by the multi-product cost function $TC(w_K, w_L, w_F, Q_R, Q_C, Q_I)$, where $w_K$, $w_L$, and $w_F$ are the prices of capital, labour, and fuel, $Q_R$, $Q_C$, and $Q_I$ are the output of kilowatt hours (KWH) sold to residential, commercial, and industrial customers, and $TC$ is total cost.[5]

Empirical estimation of the technology requires that a particular functional form be chosen for the multi-product cost function. It is especially important that the empirical cost function not place severe restrictions on the estimates of marginal costs. The translog multi-product cost function satisfies this criteria. The translog form can be viewed as a second-order Taylor series approximation to an arbitrary twice differentiable cost function and places no *a priori* restrictions on the first or second derivatives of the cost function.[6] The translog multi-product cost function is written as

$$lnTC = \beta_0 + \sum_i \beta_i \, lnw_i + \sum_j \beta_j \, lnQ_j + \tfrac{1}{2}\sum_i\sum_k \gamma_{ik} \, lnw_i \, lnw_k +$$

$$\tfrac{1}{2}\sum_j\sum_l \gamma_{jl} \, lnQ_j \, lnQ_l + \sum_i\sum_j \gamma_{ij} \, lnw_i \, lnQ_j \qquad i,k = K,L,F \qquad j,l = R,C,I \qquad (7.2)$$

The marginal cost of each output can be constructed from (7.2) as

$$\frac{\partial TC}{\partial Q_j} = \frac{TC}{Q_j} \cdot \frac{\partial lnTC}{\partial lnQ_j} = \frac{TC}{Q_j} \cdot \left(\beta_j + \sum_l \gamma_{jl} \, lnQ_l + \sum_i \gamma_{ij} \, lnw_i\right) \qquad (7.3)$$

$$i = K,L,F \qquad j,l = R,C,I$$

The estimated marginal cost of serving each customer class is a function of the firm's actual output mix and factor prices and will therefore differ for each firm in the sample. A change in the output level of one customer class is permitted to affect the marginal cost of all other outputs.

While the cost function (7.2) contains all necessary information on the firm's technology, more precise parameter estimates can be obtained by including additional equations summarising the firm's input choice. A set of estimable factor demand equations, written in cost share form, can be constructed from (7.2) by applying Shephard's lemma:

$$\frac{\partial lnTC}{\partial lnw_i} = S_i = \beta_i + \sum_k \gamma_{ik} \, lnw_k + \sum_j \gamma_{ij} \, lnQ_j \qquad i,k = K,L,F \qquad j = R,C,I \qquad (7.4)$$

where $S_i$ is input $i$'s share of the total expenditure on all three inputs. Equations (7.2) and (7.4) have been used frequently to estimate the technology of electric power production and provide a particularly useful framework for estimating the marginal costs of each firm's outputs.

One practical difficulty with using Equations (7.2) and (7.4) to estimate marginal costs for residential, commercial, and industrial outputs is that several important parameters ($\beta_j$, $\gamma_{jl}$ where $j, l = R, C, I$) appear only in Equation (7.2) and statistical estimates of these parameters are often imprecise. In order to estimate more accurately the marginal cost of each output it is useful to augment equation system (7.2) and (7.4) with additional estimating equations describing pricing behaviour in the firm's output markets.

The price schedule of electricity for each customer class is determined by state regulatory commissions after consideration of demand conditions, utility costs, and required levels of profit for the utility. The use of the Ramsey rule requires that, after determination of the minimum required level of profit, prices be set so that the divergence between price and marginal cost for each output be inversely related to the output's demand elasticity. Even if Ramsey prices are set by the regulatory commission for each firm, the divergence between price and marginal cost and therefore the firm-specific Ramsey number $t(\pi)$ will differ across utilities with differences in the minimum required level of profit. It is possible to develop empirical equations which summarise output market conditions while allowing Ramsey numbers to vary across firms and customer classes.

Equation (7.1) for a single firm can be rewritten as

$$P_j = \frac{\partial TC}{\partial Q_j} (1 - t_j(\pi) \frac{1}{n_j} )^{-1} \qquad j = R, C, I. \tag{7.5}$$

where $t_j(\pi)$ indicates that the divergence between price and marginal cost for customer class $j$ will vary with the firm's required level of profit. Substituting the parametric expression for marginal cost (7.3) into (7.5) and rewriting yields the set of Ramsey revenue share equations for a single firm

$$\frac{P_j Q_j}{TC} = (\beta_j + \sum_l \gamma_{jl} \, lnQ_l + \sum_i \gamma_{ij} \, lnw_i) (1 - t_j(\pi) \frac{1}{\eta_j} )^{-1}$$

$$i = K, L, F$$

$$j, l = R, C, I \tag{7.6}$$

Equations (7.6) express the ratio of revenue from customer class $j$ to total cost as the product of the output-cost elasticity and a mark-up factor which depends on the demand elasticity and Ramsey number for output $j$.

The output market equations given by (7.6) will allow the Ramsey number for each customer class to be estimated parametrically together with the parameters of the cost function and will provide the basis for the tests of Ramsey, monopolistic, and marginal cost pricing. In addition, they provide cross-equation restrictions on the parameters $\beta_j$ and $\gamma_{jl}$ ($j, l = R, C, I$) which are useful in providing more accurate estimates of the marginal cost of each output.[7] Before Equation (7.6) is estimated, a parametric form for $t_j(\pi)$ must be adopted. We assume the Ramsey number for each customer class is a quadratic function of the firm's profit level so that

$$t_j(\pi) = \alpha_j + \delta_{1j} \cdot \pi + \delta_{2j} \cdot \pi^2 \qquad j = R, C, I \tag{7.7}$$

The parameters $\alpha_j$, $\delta_{1j}$ and $\delta_{2j}$ are allowed to vary across customer classes but are assumed to be the same across all firms in the sample. Thus, Equation (7.7) allows the estimated Ramsey numbers for each customer class to vary across firms with differences in each utility's level of profit.

The complete estimating system consists of the multi-product cost function (7.2), input share Equation (7.4) for capital, labour and fuel, and Ramsey revenue share Equation (7.6) for residential, commercial, and industrial outputs where $t_j(\pi)$ is given by (7.8).[8] This empirical model allows a large set of hypotheses concerning the nature of electricity production and pricing to be examined. In particular, the parametric specification of the Ramsey number for each output in (7.7) allows us to test the pricing hypotheses jointly for all firms in the sample.[9] The necessary parameter restrictions for each hypothesis to be tested are developed below.

### Ramsey Pricing

Quasi-optimal or Ramsey pricing requires that the Ramsey numbers $t_j$ given by (7.7) be equal across customer classes. A necessary and sufficient condition for Ramsey pricing to hold for all sample firms is that $\alpha_R = \alpha_C = \alpha_I$, $\delta_{1R} = \delta_{1C} = \delta_{1I}$, and $\delta_{2R} = \delta_{2C} = \delta_{2I}$. These six restrictions guarantee that the Ramsey numbers are equal across customer classes for each utility. The Ramsey numbers are still allowed to vary across utilities with differences in the level of firm profit.

### Constant Ramsey Numbers

The hypothesis that the Ramsey number for customer class $j$ is constant across all sample utilities is tested with the parameter restrictions $\delta_{1j} = \delta_{2j} = 0$. If the Ramsey number for each customer class is constant across all firms then $\delta_{1R} = \delta_{1C} = \delta_{1I} = \delta_{2R} = \delta_{2C} = \delta_{2I} = 0$. In this case the Ramsey numbers do not vary across utilities with differences in firm profits. This implies that the elasticity-weighted mark-ups for each output, given by $\alpha_R$, $\alpha_C$ and $\alpha_I$, are constant across firms.

**Monopoly Pricing**

The hypothesis that the price of output $j$ is set at the monopoly level can be tested by restricting $t_j = 1$ for all sample firms. This requires the three parameter restrictions $\alpha_j = 1$, $\delta_{1j} = \delta_{2j} = 0$. To test that all output prices are set at monopoly levels the necessary parameter restrictions are $\alpha_R = \alpha_C = \alpha_I = 1$, $\delta_{1R} = \delta_{1C} = \delta_{1I} = \delta_{2R} = \delta_{2C} = \delta_{2I} = 0$.

**Marginal Cost Pricing**

If the output price for a customer class is set equal to marginal cost then the Ramsey number for that customer class equals zero. Marginal cost pricing of output $j$ requires that $\alpha_j = \delta_{1j} = \delta_{2j} = 0$. Marginal cost pricing of all outputs requires that $\alpha_R = \alpha_C = \alpha_I = \delta_{1R} = \delta_{1C} = \delta_{1I} = \delta_{2R} = \delta_{2C} = \delta_{2I} = 0$.

Given the empirical model developed in this section, a detailed set of hypotheses concerning electric utility pricing can be tested. Results from the estimated cost model and hypothesis tests are reported in Section 7.4.

## 7.3 DATA AND ESTIMATION METHODS

The empirical model developed in Section 7.2 requires data on the quantities and prices of capital, labour and fuel inputs, the quantities and prices of output to residential, commercial and industrial customers, and the demand elasticity for each customer class. The data, particularly the capital input, must apply to all operations of the firm including transmission and distribution activities as well as generation. The inclusion of transmission and distribution activities is important because this part of the production process substantially affects the relative marginal costs of the three outputs.[10]

The necessary data are constructed for a sample of 66 privately owned electric utilities for the years 1970 and 1978. The two cross-sections are estimated separately. Two time periods are examined because of the substantial changes in both the cost of production and the firm's regulatory environment during the 1970s. The earlier year also allows for easier comparison of the results with other studies. To insure a homogeneous sample of firms, the sample is restricted to vertically integrated firms participating in generation, transmission, and distribution activities. Publicly owned firms, members of holding companies, firms which make significant wholesale power purchases, and combination gas and electric companies are excluded.

**Fuel**

The quantity of fuel input is constructed as the sum of BTUs purchases by each plant owned by the firm as reported in *Steam-Electric Plant Construction Cost and Annual Production Expenses.* The average price per BTU is constructed as the total expenditure on fuel inputs divided by the total quantity of BTU's.

**Labour**

The quantity of labour input is defined as the sum of full-time plus one-half the number of part-time employees reported in the *Statistics of Privately Owned Electric Utilities in the United States* (hereafter, *Statistics*). The price of labour is constructed by dividing annual labour expenditure, the sum of wages, salaries and employee pensions and benefits, by the quantity of labour input.

**Capital**

The service price of capital input is constructed according to methods originally described by Christensen and Jorgenson (1969). The service price is a Tornqvist price index over the service prices of seven different capital assets. Each asset service price is a function of capital gains, the service life of the asset, its depreciation rate, tax policy, and the firm's opportunity cost of capital. The quantity of capital input is constructed using the perpetual inventory method and gross investment data from the *Statistics.* Capital stocks are constructed for each of the seven asset classes and the capital input is constructed as the residual Tornqvist quantity index.

**Output**

The quantity of each of the three types of output is measured as total KWH's sold to final consumers from the *Statistics.* The price of output for each customer class is measured as the average price of a KWH in each customer class. In studies of consumer demand for electricity, researchers have argued that, because of the declining block nature of electric utility rates, the marginal price rather than the average price is relevant for the individual consumer.[11] This concern has led to the use of several proxies for the marginal price including the price in the block which contains the largest number of consumers and the price in the last block. From the point of view of the firm, the price of the marginal unit of output cannot be measured because it will depend on the customer who purchases it. As a result, we have chosen to use the average price for each customer class. The hypothesis tests performed in the next section therefore examine whether or not the observed prices for each customer class, on average, correspond to the uniform prices which would be required for efficiency.

**Demand Elasticities**

The demand elasticity for each customer class is taken from the estimates derived by Mount, Chapman and Tyrell (1973). They estimate long-run demand elasticities by customer class which vary across states. On average, in the sample, the demand elasticities for residential, commercial, and industrial customers are 1.25, 1.45, and 1.73, respectively. The sample range is 0.96 to 1.34 for residential users, 1.34 to 1.50 for commercial users and 1.38 to 2.02 for industrial users. Ramsey pricing would therefore indicate that the smallest proportional deviations between price and marginal cost, on average, should apply to industrial customers, while residential customers would face the largest proportional deviations between price and marginal cost.[12]

**Estimation and Testing Methods**

Each of the seven estimating equations is assumed to be subject to random errors that are normally distributed with a zero mean and constant variance. The errors are assumed to be contemporaneously correlated across equations. Zellner's seemingly unrelated regression technique is used to estimate the system of equations. Because the input share equations sum to one at each observation the variance-covariance matrix of disturbances across equations is singular. The labour share equation is deleted prior to estimation and the Zellner estimator is iterated until convergence to guarantee that the parameter estimates are invariant to the equation that is deleted. The likelihood ratio test statistic is used to test the pricing hypotheses.

## 7.4 EMPIRICAL RESULTS

The complete empirical model developed in Section 7.2 is estimated separately for 1970 and 1978. The multi-product cost function parameters are reported in Table 7.1. Twenty-one of the parameters are estimated directly and the remaining seven are constructed from the linear homogeneity restrictions. The parameters that measure the interactions between outputs and input prices are generally insignificant. The first-order parameters and the parameters that measure the interactions among input prices and among the output levels are virutally all significant. This last set of parameters is particularly important because it indicates that the marginal cost of serving any customer class is significantly affected by changes in the output of the other customer classes.

The monotonicity and concavity conditions are checked at each data point after estimation. Monotonicity is satisfied at every data point in both years. Concavity is satisfied at 65 of the 66 data points in 1970 and every data point in 1978.

### Structure of Production and Marginal Cost Estimates

Information about several important aspects of the multi-product technology can be derived from the parameter estimates in Table 7.1. The degree of multi-product scale economies is defined as[13]

$$S \equiv \left( \sum_i \frac{\partial lnTC}{\partial lnQ_i} \right)^{-1} \qquad i = R, C, I.$$

A value of $S$ greater than one indicates scale economies are present or that an equal proportional increase in all three outputs results in a decline in ray average cost.[14] In 1970 the estimates of $S$ vary from a low of 1.07 to a high of 1.12. While all sample firms are estimated to be producing in an increasing returns to scale region, the hypothesis that all firms produce under constant returns to scale cannot be rejected.[15] In 1978, $S$ varies from 0.96 to 1.18 with eight firms producing in a decreasing returns to scale region.[16] In this case the hypothesis of constant returns to scale is rejected.

Estimates of the marginal cost for each customer class, as functions of the firm's input prices and output mix, can be constructed from the estimated cost functions. The mean and range of the marginal cost estimates

*Table* 7.1 Multi-product cost function parameter estimates (standard errors in parentheses)

| *Parameter* | *1970* | | *1978* | |
|---|---|---|---|---|
| $\beta_0$ | 11.993 | (0.021)* | 12.974 | (0.023)* |
| $\beta_K$ | 0.651 | (0.006)* | 0.450 | (0.007)* |
| $\beta_F$ | 0.191 | (0.006)* | 0.423 | (0.009)* |
| $\beta_L$ | 0.158 | (0.004)* | 0.127 | (0.004)* |
| $\beta_R$ | 0.436 | (0.033)* | 0.382 | (0.030)* |
| $\beta_C$ | 0.250 | (0.026)* | 0.285 | (0.027)* |
| $\beta_I$ | 0.232 | (0.017)* | 0.254 | (0.022)* |
| $\gamma_{KK}$ | 0.185 | (0.025)* | 0.157 | (0.025)* |
| $\gamma_{KF}$ | −0.088 | (0.016)* | −0.121 | (0.018)* |
| $\gamma_{KL}$ | −0.097 | (0.019)* | −0.036 | (0.017)* |
| $\gamma_{KR}$ | 0.014 | (0.011) | 0.012 | (0.012) |
| $\gamma_{KC}$ | 0.001 | (0.008) | 0.004 | (0.008) |
| $\gamma_{KI}$ | −0.017 | (0.008)* | −0.016 | (0.010) |
| $\gamma_{FF}$ | 0.078 | (0.017)* | 0.162 | (0.021)* |
| $\gamma_{FL}$ | 0.010 | (0.010) | −0.041 | (0.008)* |
| $\gamma_{FR}$ | −0.008 | (0.009) | −0.019 | (0.011) |
| $\gamma_{FC}$ | −0.011 | (0.006) | −0.002 | (0.008) |
| $\gamma_{FI}$ | 0.024 | (0.007)* | 0.019 | (0.012) |
| $\gamma_{LL}$ | 0.087 | (0.020)* | 0.076 | (0.015)* |
| $\gamma_{LR}$ | −0.005 | (0.009) | 0.007 | (0.008) |
| $\gamma_{LC}$ | 0.009 | (0.007) | −0.002 | (0.006) |
| $\gamma_{LI}$ | −0.007 | (0.006) | −0.003 | (0.006) |
| $\gamma_{RR}$ | 0.168 | (0.011)* | 0.179 | (0.013)* |
| $\gamma_{RC}$ | −0.080 | (0.008)* | −0.088 | (0.008)* |
| $\gamma_{RI}$ | −0.084 | (0.008)* | −0.111 | (0.011)* |
| $\gamma_{CC}$ | 0.130 | (0.011)* | 0.142 | (0.011)* |
| $\gamma_{CI}$ | −0.051 | (0.007)* | −0.068 | (0.009)* |
| $\gamma_{II}$ | −0.140 | (0.009)* | 0.160 | (0.014)* |

*Note:* *Significantly different from zero at the 0.05 level with a two-tailed test.

are reported in Table 7.2. On average for both years, the marginal cost of serving residential customers is the highest among the three groups followed by commercial and industrial customers. Between 1970 and 1978 the average estimate of marginal cost in the sample increased 60.0 per cent for residential output, 94.7 per cent for commercial output, and 110.0 per cent for industrial output. In addition, the range of marginal cost estimates across firms increased substantially between 1970 and 1978 indicating less homogeneity across firms in the latter year.

The interdependency of output production can be examined by measuring the impact of a change in the level of one output on the marginal cost of the other outputs. In the case of the translog cost function this is measured as

$$\frac{\partial^2 TC}{\partial Q_i \partial Q_j} = \frac{TC}{Q_i Q_j}\left[\frac{\partial lnTC}{\partial lnQ_i}\cdot\frac{\partial lnTC}{\partial lnQ_j} + \gamma_{ij}\right] \quad i,j = R, C, I \quad i \neq j \qquad (7.8)$$

At the point of expansion, where the output levels and factor prices equal one, (7.8) equals

$$\frac{\partial^2 TC}{\partial Q_i \partial Q_j} = \frac{TC}{Q_i Q_j}[\beta_i \beta_j + \gamma_{ij}] \qquad i,j = R, C, I \quad i \neq j. \qquad (7.9)$$

The second derivative in (7.9) will have the same sign as the expression in brackets. The estimated value of $\beta_i \cdot \beta_j + \gamma_{ij}$, together with its standard error, is reported for each output pair in Table 7.3. For 1970 all of the estimates are positive indicating that an increase in any output raises the marginal cost of the other two outputs. The residential-commercial and residential-industrial estimates are significantly different from zero. The 1978 estimates for the residential-industrial and commercial-industrial pairs are small and statistically insignificant. The residential-commercial interdependency is positive and significant. This positive pattern of cost interdependency is contrary to what we would expect if there were economies of scope in the production process.[17]

*Table* 7.2 Estimated marginal cost by customer class (dollars/KWH)

| *Customer class* | *Mean (standard deviation)** | *Sample range* |
|---|---|---|
| | 1970 | |
| Residential | 0.025 (0.002) | 0.021–0.032 |
| Commercial | 0.019 (0.002) | 0.014–0.024 |
| Industrial | 0.010 (0.002) | 0.007–0.013 |
| | 1978 | |
| Residential | 0.040 (0.006) | 0.029–0.056 |
| Commercial | 0.037 (0.008) | 0.011–0.054 |
| Industrial | 0.021 (0.009) | 0.014–0.035 |

*Note*: *This is the standard deviation of the estimated marginal cost values across the sample firms.

*Table* 7.3 Cost interdependency at the expansion point (standard error in parentheses)

| | *1970* | | *1978* | |
|---|---|---|---|---|
| Residential-commercial | 0.030* | (0.007) | 0.021* | (0.007) |
| Residential-industrial | 0.018* | (0.007) | −0.015 | (0.008) |
| Commercial-industrial | 0.007 | (0.004) | 0.005 | (0.006) |

*Note*: *Statistically different from zero at the 0.05 level.

**Customer Pricing Patterns and Ramsey Number Estimates**

In addition to estimates of marginal cost which vary by firm and customer class, the empirical model of production provides parametric estimates of the Ramsey numbers which vary by firm and output. The estimates of the parameters $\alpha_j$, $\delta_{1j}$ and $\delta_{2j}$ are reported in Table 7.4. Two patterns are present in the parameter estimates. First, $\delta_{1j}$ and $\delta_{2j}$ measure the effect of an increase in the utility's profit on the markups for each output. The positive, statistically significant values of $\delta_{1j}$ and the negative, significant values of $\delta_{2j}$ indicate that increased profit raises the mark-up for each output but at a declining rate. As expected, the customer class markups vary with the firm's level of profit. The second pattern in the coefficients in Table 7.2 is the fact that $\alpha_R$, $\alpha_C$ and $\alpha_I$ are positive in all but one case. This indicates a positive mark-up across customer classes for most firms. The large, significant positive estimates for $\alpha_I$ indicate a fairly substantial base mark-up for industrial customers.

Using the coefficients in Table 7.4 it is possible to test if the observed mark-up patterns correspond to Ramsey, monopolistic, or marginal cost pricing levels. The test statistics for the pricing hypotheses are reported in Table 7.5. The broad results of the tests are straightforward. All restrictions corresponding to Ramsey pricing as well as monopolistic or marginal cost pricing for individual outputs or all outputs simultaneously are rejected at the 0.05 significance level. The hypothesis that the mark-up for each customer class can be treated as a constant across all firms is also rejected in favour of the alternative that it varies with the firm's profit level. The rejection of the hypothesis of Ramsey pricing for all firms is relatively weak in 1970 while the rejection of monopolistic pricing, particularly for residential consumers, is very strong.

On average across the sample, the Ramsey numbers in 1970 for residential commercial, and industrial customers are −0.089, 0.251, and 0.252, respectively. This indicates that on average residential customers

*Table* 7.4 Parameter estimates for Ramsey numbers (standard errors in parentheses)

| *Parameter* | *1970* | | *1978* | |
|---|---|---|---|---|
| Residential | | | | |
| $\alpha_R$ | −0.057 | (0.095) | 0.105 | (0.091) |
| $\delta_{1R}$ | 0.010 | (0.002)* | 0.087 | (0.020)* |
| $\delta_{2R}$ | −0.0001 | (0.00003)* | −0.009 | (0.003)* |
| Commercial | | | | |
| $\alpha_C$ | 0.271 | (0.125)* | 0.168 | (0.120) |
| $\delta_{1C}$ | 0.005 | (0.002)* | 0.090 | (0.019)* |
| $\delta_{2C}$ | −0.0001 | (0.0001) | −0.005 | (0.002)* |
| Industrial | | | | |
| $\alpha_I$ | 0.301 | (0.105)* | 0.381 | (0.113)* |
| $\delta_{1I}$ | 0.013 | (0.003)* | 0.192 | (0.050)* |
| $\delta_{2I}$ | −0.0002 | (0.0001)* | −0.020 | (0.008)* |

*Note*: *Significantly different from zero at the 0.05 level with a two-tailed test.

*Table* 7.5 Pricing hypothesis tests

| *Hypothesis* | *Number of restrictions* | *Test statistics 1970* | *1978* | $\chi^2$ *critical value** |
|---|---|---|---|---|
| Ramsey pricing ($\alpha_j = \alpha_k, \delta_{1j} = \delta_{1k}, \delta_{2j} = \delta_{2k}$ for $j, k = R, C, I$) | 6 | 13.40 | 24.68 | 12.59 |
| Constant Ramsey numbers ($\delta_{1j} = \delta_{2j} = 0, j = R, C, I$) | | | | |
| Residential | 2 | 31.03 | 16.52 | 5.99 |
| Commercial | 2 | 22.23 | 33.65 | 5.99 |
| Industiral | 2 | 15.92 | 13.82 | 5.99 |
| All customer classes | 6 | 55.11 | 55.85 | 12.59 |
| Monopoly pricing ($\alpha_j = 1, \delta_{1j} = \delta_{2j} = 0, j = R, C, I$) | | | | |
| Residential | 3 | 172.20 | 143.44 | 7.82 |
| Commercial | 3 | 47.90 | 65.92 | 7.82 |
| Industrial | 3 | 80.87 | 45.89 | 7.82 |
| All customer classes | 9 | 430.66 | 347.746 | 16.92 |
| Marginal cost pricing ($\alpha_j = \delta_{1j} = \delta_{2j} = 0, j = R, C, I$) | | | | |
| Residential | 3 | 31.13 | 22.75 | 7.82 |
| Commercial | 3 | 24.35 | 35.50 | 7.82 |
| Industrial | 3 | 22.55 | 30.42 | 7.82 |
| All customer classes | 9 | 68.35 | 102.156 | 16.92 |

*Note*: *0.05 significance level.

faced prices below marginal cost while commercial and industrial customers faced similar positive elasticity-weighted mark-ups. On average, the Ramsey numbers are substantially closer to zero than to one which indicates that the prices are closer to competitive rather than monopolistic levels. In 1978, the pattern of average Ramsey numbers differs, with the values for residential, commercial, and industrial customers being 0.155, 0.239, and 0.496, respectively. All mark-ups have increased, which reflects a higher average level of nominal economic profit for these sample firms in 1978. The increases have fallen primarily on residential and industrial customers. In particular, average industrial prices are half-way between competitive and monopolistic levels. The other customer groups have prices closer to marginal cost with residential customers again having the lowest elasticity-weighted mark-ups.

Given that the hypothesis of quasi-optimal or Ramsey pricing is rejected in both years it is therefore possible to alter output prices to increase total consumer surplus while holding the firm's profit level constant. In the next section we examine how the actual output prices compare with the set of Ramsey prices for each firm and estimate the potential welfare gains or losses by customer group which would result from adopting Ramsey prices.

## 7.5 ESTIMATING THE WELFARE GAINS FROM RAMSEY PRICING

The hypothesis that all firm's prices satisfy the Ramsey criteria was rejected in Section 7.4 implying that prices can be adjusted to increase the sum of producer and consumer surplus. In this section the set of Ramsey optimal prices is calculated for each sample firm and compared with the utility's actual prices. The potential welfare gain by customer class is then estimated.

In order to calculate the Ramsey price and corresponding consumption level for each customer class a system of six equations is solved for each of the sample firms. The equations require that the three Ramsey numbers be equal, that the price and quantity changes represent movements along the firm's demand curves, and that the firm's level of economic profit be unchanged.

The first two equations in the system are:

$$\left|\frac{P_R - \dfrac{\partial TC}{\partial Q_R}}{P_R}\right| \eta_R = \left|\frac{P_C - \dfrac{\partial TC}{\partial Q_C}}{P_C}\right| \eta_C$$

$$\left|\frac{P_R - \dfrac{\partial TC}{\partial Q_R}}{P_R}\right| \eta_R = \left|\frac{P_I - \dfrac{\partial TC}{\partial Q_I}}{P_I}\right| \eta_I \tag{7.10}$$

These two equations guarantee that the three Ramsey numbers will be equal at the computed optimum. It is important to emphasise that the marginal cost for each customer class in (7.10) is expressed as a function of the firm's output mix using Equation (7.3) and the estimated translog cost function parameters. As the firm's output levels are changed, the marginal cost of serving each customer class will also change. The marginal cost for any customer class is not assumed to be constant when computing the Ramsey optimum.

The next three equations in the system guarantee that movements in the price and quantity for each customer class correspond to movements along their demand curve. It is assumed that the demand curve for each customer class takes the constant elasticity form

$$Q_i = \beta_i P_i^{-\eta_i} \qquad i = R, C, I \tag{7.11}$$

where $\eta_i$ is the observed firm demand elasticity and $\beta_i$ is a firm specific intercept which captures all non-price effects. Since all other variables that affect demand are assumed to be fixed when calculating the Ramsey optimum, firm $j$'s demand curve constraints can be rewritten as

$$\Delta lnQ_i = \eta_i(\Delta lnP_i) \qquad i = R, C, I. \tag{7.12}$$

The $\Delta$ operator represents the difference between the original level of $P_i$ or $Q_i$ and the Ramsey optimum.

The final equation in the system is the firm's profit constraint. Each level of the profit constraint corresponds to a different set of Ramsey prices. In this case the firm is constrained to earn the level of economic profit that it actually earned in the year being examined. The profit constraint is written as

$$\sum_i P_i Q_i - TC(Q_R, Q_C, Q_I) = \pi_0 \qquad i = R, C, I. \tag{7.13}$$

where $\pi_0$ is the firm's observed level of economic profit. Total cost is measured as the exponential of the estimated translog cost function and therefore changes in the level and mix of the firm's three outputs affect the firm's total cost as well as its revenues. For each of the 66 sample firms in both 1970 and 1978, the six equations given in (7.10), (7.12), and (7.13) are solved simultaneously for the three prices and three output levels which satisfy the Ramsey criteria.[18]

In 1970 movement to the Ramsey optimum generally requires an increase in residential prices and a decrease in commercial and industrial prices. This is consistent with the earlier finding that, on average, residential prices were approximately 7 per cent below marginal cost in 1970 while commercial and industrial prices were approximately 17 and 14 per cent above marginal cost. Of the 66 sample utilities, movement to the Ramsey optimum requires higher residential prices for 64, higher commercial prices for 7, and higher industrial prices for 19. On average, prices to residential customers would have to increase 25.6 per cent to 3.11 cents/KWH. Commercial prices would fall by 20.0 per cent to 1.9 cents/KWH and industiral prices would fall by 14.8 per cent to 1.0 cents/KWH, on average. At the optimum the average Ramsey number for all customer classes is 0.087 which implies that prices for residential, commercial, and industrial prices, respectively, are 6.9, 6.0, and 4.9 per cent above marginal cost.

In 1978 the movement from actual to Ramsey prices requires a slightly different pattern of adjustments. It is still the case that residential prices would rise for virtually all utilities but commercial prices would now be increased for a substantial number of utilities. In the sample, residential prices would increase for 62 or the 66 utilities and commercial prices would rise for 46 utilities. Only three sample utilities would increase industrial prices when moving to the Ramsey optimum. The largest difference between 1970 and 1978 is that, in the latter year, substantially more utilities have a price for commercial customers which is less than the Ramsey price. This pattern is also revealed by examining the average price changes for each customer class which are required to move from the actual 1978 prices to the Ramsey optimal prices. Residential and commercial customers would face prices that, on average, were 13.5 per cent and 4.1 per cent higher than actual, while industrial prices would be lowered an average of 20.6 per cent. At the Ramsey optimum the average prices for residential, commercial, and industrial customers would be 5.3, 4.7 and 2.5 cents/KWH. The average Ramsey number across all sample firms is 0.247 which indicates the prices exceed marginal cost by 19.6, 17.1 and 14.0 per cent for residential, commercial and industrial customers.

In both sample years, adoption of Ramsey prices requires a substantial readjustment of prices across consumer groups. This will result in a reallocation of consumer surplus among the groups as well as an increase in the total level. In order to calculate the welfare gains from adopting the set of Ramsey prices we calculate the change in the sum of producer and consumer surplus. Because the equations used to calculate the Ramsey prices and quantities constrain the firm to earn its observed level of economic profit there is no change in producer surplus. The total gain in welfare will be approximated by the sum of the changes in consumer surplus for the three customer groups. Using the constant elasticity demand curves in (7.11) the change in consumer surplus is measured by the integral of the demand curve between the original and Ramsey optimal prices.[19] The formula for the change in consumer surplus for customer group $i$ is:

$$\Delta CS_i = \left| \frac{P_i^* Q_i^*}{1 - \eta_i} \right| \left| 1 - \left( \frac{P_i}{P_i^*} \right)^{(1-\eta_i)} \right| \qquad i = R, C, I \qquad (7.14)$$

where $P_i$ is the original price and asterisks are used to denote the Ramsey prices and quantities.

Ramsey pricing requires higher prices on average for residential customers and lower prices for commercial and industrial customers in 1970. The loss in consumer surplus for residential users would, on average, equal 25.7 per cent of their actual expenditure on power. In the sample this loss averages \$17.1 million per utility. This loss to residential consumers is more than offset by a gain in consumer surplus for commercial and industrial customers which averages \$14.9 million and \$7.9 million per utility. As a percentage of total revenue from these two customer groups the welfare gains are 30.1 and 19.1 per cent. While there is a substantial reallocation of consumer surplus among customers the average net welfare gain per utility of \$5.7 million represents only 3.7 per cent of total revenue for the average utility in this sample.

This pattern is not significantly altered when we examine the welfare gains in 1978. The average change in consumer surplus is a negative \$27.2 million for residential purchasers and a positive \$1.5 million and \$45.7 million for commercial and industrial customers. These changes represent 14.2, 1.0 and 29.6 per cent of the total revenue from each class for the average utility in the sample. As in 1970, residential customers would face higher prices and less consumer surplus under Ramsey pricing but now industrial rather than commercial customers would be the largest gainers. The total increase in consumer surplus for the customers of the average utility in the sample is again not large. The net gain in consumer surplus from adopting Ramsey prices in 1978 would be approximately \$20 million per utility but this represents only 4 per cent of an average utility's total revenue.

To summarise, the adoption of Ramsey prices in either 1970 or 1978 would have required average price changes for individual customer groups which range between 4 and 25 per cent. While some customer groups, particularly commercial in 1970 and industrial in 1978, would realise substantial increases in welfare the net gain in consumer surplus in the two years represents only 3.7 and 4.0 per cent of an average firm's total revenue in the two years. It is worth repeating that these results represent an average of the changes across all sample utilities and that the level of firm profit is being held fixed. Furthermore, the net welfare estimates ignore any possible change in the resource costs which are incurred in the regulatory process.

## 7.6 SUMMARY AND CONCLUSIONS

Analysis of the pattern of residential, commercial and industrial electricity prices for a sample of 66 utilities in 1970 and 1978 indicates that actual prices across utilities deviate from Ramsey prices in a fairly systematic way. Prices faced by residential customers are consistently found to be lower than Ramsey levels in both 1970 and 1978. Industrial prices are greater than Ramsey prices in both years while commercial prices are higher in 1970 and lower, on average, in 1978.

Turning to other empirical studies, a similar pattern for residential prices has been reported by Hayashi, Sevier and Trapani (1985) and Eckel (1983) using 1965 and 1970 data. Using 1973 data, both of these studies, as well as Nelson (1982), also find commercial rates to be higher than would be indicated by the Ramsey criteria. Meyer and Leland (1980) combine industrial and commercial outputs and report cross-subsidisation in favour of residential customers in 1969, although this pattern diminishes in 1974. The results reported in this chapter are in agreement with these earlier studies, although we find residential customers in 1970 to be even more strongly favoured than has generally been the case.

With respect to industrial customers, results of these studies are in less agreement. Our results indicate that actual prices industrial customers faced in 1970 were slightly higher than at the Ramsey optimum and this divergence increased between 1970 and 1978. Using marginal prices, Eckel (1983) finds that industrial customers had the highest elasticity-weighted mark-ups in 1970 while Hayashi, Sevier and Trapani (1985) find that industrial prices would have to be increased slightly if Ramsey pricing was adopted. Nelson (1982) reports approximately equal elasticity-weighted mark-ups for residential and industrial customers in 1973.

In addition to calculating the set of Ramsey prices for each firm in our sample we also estimate the welfare gains or losses by customer class which would result from the adoption of Ramsey pricing. In total, residential customers would face a loss in consumer surplus equal to 25.7 per cent of their expenditure on electricity in 1970 and 14.2 per cent in 1978. Commercial customers would have welfare gains equal to 30.1 and 1.0 per cent of expenditure in the two years while the corresponding gains for industrial users would be 19.1 and 29.6 per cent. While there is substantial reallocation among customer groups, the net gain in consumer surplus is relatively small, equalling 3.7 and 4.0 per cent of total customer expenditure for the average utility in 1970 and 1978, respectively. Regulation, as suggested by Stigler (1971) and Peltzman (1976), seems to be dominated by redistribution concerns. However, these net estimates ignore the transactions costs of regulation which have been emphasised by Posner (1975), Crew and Kleindorfer (1985) and others. Given the magnitude of the redistribution estimates, these costs can, on theoretical grounds, be expected to be substantially greater than the allocative effects of electricity regulation.

**Acknowledgements**

We are grateful to Michael Crew, Frank Gollop, Randy Nelson, and George Sweeney for helpful comments.

**Notes**

1. See Joskow (1974) and Joskow and MacAvoy (1975) for discussion of changes in the regulatory environment.
2. This version of the Ramsey rule assumes that the demand for each output is independent of the prices of all other outputs produced by the firm. Electric utilities produce outputs for residential, commercial, and industrial customers, and an assumption of zero cross-price effects is very reasonable because purchasers cannot shift from one customer class to another in response to price changes. Theoretical work which relaxes the assumption of zero cross-price effects is reported in Baumol and Bradford (1970), Braeutigam (1979), and Sherman and George (1979). The Ramsey rule has also been modified to allow for equity considerations by Feldstein (1972), Munk (1977) and Willig and Bailey (1981).
3. Nelson (1982) uses the same three customer groups in his analysis. Meyer and Leland (1980) aggregate commercial and industrial customers into a single group. Eckel (1983) and Hayashi, Sevier and Trapani (1985) assume that residential and commercial customers have identical marginal costs and aggregate the two groups when estimating the firm's technology. The model developed here treats the three customer groups separately and allows for both dif-

ferences in production costs and regulatory treatment across the groups.

4. Data on each customer classes' purchases that occur during peak and off-peak periods does not exist for these firms. If the data did exist the firm could be modelled as producing six outputs, peak and off-peak power for each of the three customer classes, with different marginal costs for each. Any discussion of Ramsey pricing in this framework would require modelling cross-price elasticities of demand because each customer class could substitute between peak and off-peak purchases. Given the available data, we are limited to inferences concerning the marginal cost of supplying each customer class given the existing time pattern of demands. The papers contained in Aigner (1984) provide detailed analysis of the welfare gains from time-of-day pricing using results of experimental programmes set up by several utilities. There is some evidence from this work that time-of-day pricing may not be cost effective in many parts of the country.
5. A single-output cost function has been used extensively in recent years to examine the technology of electric power production as well as regulatory effects. Christensen and Greene (1976) use it to measure scale economies, Stevenson (1980) examines technical-change biases, Gollop and Roberts (1980, 1983) measure sources of productivity growth and quantify the cost effects of environmental regulation, and Nelson (1984) examines capital stock vintage and regulatory effects.
6. See Brown, Caves and Christensen (1979) for a detailed discussion of the multi-product translog cost function.
7. Fuss and Waverman (1981) estimate equations similar to (7.6) in a study of the structure of production of Bell Canada. They assume that the firm acts as a monopolist in each output market so that all $t_j$ are set equal to one.
8. Restrictions which guarantee that the estimated cost function is linear homogeneous in factor prices are imposed prior to estimation. The parameter restrictions are: $\sum_i \beta_i = 1$, $\sum_i \gamma_{ik} = 0$, and $\sum_i \gamma_{ij} = 0$, where $i, k = K, L, F$ and $j = R, C, I$. Symmetry restrictions are also imposed prior to estimation. No restrictions on the degree of returns to scale are imposed. Monotonicity and concavity of the estimated cost function are checked after estimation.
9. Previous studies of Ramsey pricing in utilities have only tested for equality of the average Ramsey numbers across all sample firms or for equality when evaluated at the mean prices and output levels. The difficulty with this approach is that the sample means of $t_i$ and $t_j$ could be equal without $t_i$ and $t_j$ being equal for any sample firm. The testing procedure developed here avoids this problem.
10. See Roberts (forthcoming) for an empirical examination of the effect of a firm's output mix and service area characteristics on cost, scale economies, and the demand for transmission and distribution inputs.

11. See Taylor (1975) for a summary of earlier demand studies and discussion of this issue.
12. An alternative to treating the demand elasticities as data is to specify them as parameters and estimate them in Equation (7.6). In order to identify both the Ramsey number and demand elasticity for each customer class in (7.6), it would be necessary to include the demand equations in the estimating system and rely on the cross-equations restrictions. This would significantly increase the number of parameters in the estimating model because, at a minimum, variables for income and the price of substitute energy types would have to be included in each of the output demand equations. These additional parameters are not directly relevant to the pricing hypotheses being tested and, since detailed estimates of demand elasticities are already available, we have chosen to simplify this dimension of the model. Hayashi, Sevier and Trapani (1985) model the cost function, input share equations, and demand equations and estimate the (constant) customer-class demand elasticities together with the cost function parameters.
13. See Panzar and Willig (1977) for derivation.
14. See Bailey and Friedlaender (1982, pp. 1029–30) for a discussion of the relationship between multi-product scale economies and ray average cost.
15. The parameter restrictions are $\sum_i \beta_i = 1$, $\sum_i \gamma_{ij} = 0$ where $i = R, C, I$ and $j = R, C, I, K, L, F$.
16. If $S > (<) 1$ then marginal cost pricing will lead to negative (positive) economic profits (Bailey and Friedlaender, 1982, p. 1030). For those firms producing in the decreasing returns-to-scale region, a uniform price equal to marginal cost would be the first-best pricing solution. While these firms would earn positive economic profits there is no guarantee they would earn the level of accounting profit established by the regulatory commission.
17. Baumol, Panzar and Willig (1982, pp. 74–5) show that weak cost complementaries $\left(\frac{\partial^2 TC}{\partial Q_i \partial Q_j} \leqslant 0\right)$ are a sufficient condition for economies of scope. In electricity production it is most likely that economies of scope would arise from the joint production of peak and off-peak power. This would be difficult to quantify using total output for each customer class unless the classes had very different demand patterns.
18. The six equations are non-linear in the prices and quantities. As starting values, the best direction of change for each of the three prices is calculated using the economic gradient technique developed by Willig and Bailey (1977, 1979). The current prices are changed by 10 per cent in the direction indicated by the gradient method. Overall, the gradient method is quite accurate in indicating the final direction of price change to the Ramsey optimum. In 1970 and 1978, respectively, it correctly indicated the final direction of price change for all three customer classes for 56 and 48 of

the 66 sample firms. For the remaining firms in each year it correctly indicated the direction for two of the three price changes.

19. The area under the Marshallian demand curve is used, as it is in most applied welfare studies, rather than the area under the income-compensated Hicksian demand curve. Willig (1976) argues that in most circumstances this measure of consumer surplus will provide a good approximation to the equivalent and compensating variations, the theoretically correct measures of welfare change.

## References

AIGNER, D. J. (ed) (1984) 'Welfare Econometrics of Peak-Load Pricing for Electricity', *Annals of the Journal of Econometrics*, vol. 26, nos 1–2, pp. 1–15.

BAILEY, E. E. and FRIEDLAENDER, A. F. (1982) 'Market Structure and Multiproduct Industries', *Journal of Economic Literature*, vol. 20, no. 3, pp. 1024–48.

BAUMOL, W. J. and BRADFORD, D. F. (1970) 'Optimal Departures from Marginal Cost Pricing', *American Economic Review*, vol. 60, no. 2, pp. 350–65.

BRAEUTIGAM, R. (1979) 'Optimal Pricing with Intermodal Competition', *American Economic Review*, vol. 69, no. 1, pp. 38–49.

BROWN, R., CAVES, D. and CHRISTENSEN, L. R. (1979) 'Modelling the Structure of Cost and Production for Multiproduct Firms', *Southern Economic Journal*, vol. 46, no. 1, pp. 256–71.

CHRISTENSEN, L. R. and GREENE, W. H. (1976) 'Economies of Scale in United States Electric Power Generation', *Journal of Political Economy*, vol. 84, no. 4, pp. 655–76.

CHRISTENSEN, L. R. and JORGENSON, D. W. (1969) 'The Measurement of U.S. Real Capital Input, 1929–1967', *Review of Income and Wealth*, vol. 5, no. 4, pp. 292–320.

CREW, M. A. and KLEINDORFER, P. R. (1985) 'Governance Costs of Rate of Return Regulation', *Journal of Institutional and Theoretical Economics*, vol. 141, no. 1, pp. 104–23.

ECKEL, C. M. (1983) 'Customer-Class Pricing by Electric Utilities', unpublished PhD dissertation, University of Virginia.

FELDSTEIN, M. (1972) 'Distributional Equity and the Optimal Structure of Public Prices', *American Economic Review*, vol. 62, no. 1, pp. 32–6.

FUSS, M. and WAVERMAN, L. (1981) 'Regulation and Multiproduct Firm: The Case of Telecommunications in Canada', in G. Fromm (ed.), *Studies in Public Regulation* (Cambridge: The MIT Press) pp. 277–313.

GOLLOP, F. M. and ROBERTS, M. J. (1980) 'The Sources of Economic Growth in the U.S. Electric Power Industry', in T. G. Cowing and R. E. Stevenson (eds), *Productivity Measurement in Regulation Industries* (New York: Academic Press) pp. 107–43.

GOLLOP, F. M. and ROBERTS, M. J. (1983) 'Environmental Regulations and Productivity Growth: The Case of Fossil-Fueled Electric Power Generation', *Journal of Political Economy*, vol. 91, no. 4, 654–74.

HAYASHI, P. M., SEVIER, M. and TRAPANI, J. M. (1985) 'Pricing Efficiency Under Rate-of-Return Regulation: Some Empirical Evidence for the Electric Utility Industry', *Southern Economic Journal*, vol. 51, no. 3, pp. 776–92.

JOSKOW, P. (1974) 'Inflation and Environmental Concern: Structural Change in the Process of Public Utility Price Regulation', *Journal of Law and Economics*, vol. 17, no. 2, pp. 291–328.

JOSKOW, P. and MacAVOY, P. W. (1975) 'Regulation and Financial Condition of the Electric Power Companies in the 1970s', *American Economic Review*, vol. 65, no. 2, pp. 295–301.

MEYER, R. A. and LELAND, H. E. (1980) 'The Effectiveness of Price Regulation', *Review of Economics and Statistics*, vol. 62, no. 4, pp. 555–66.

MOUNT, T., CHAPMAN, L. and TYRELL, G. (1973) 'Electricity Demand in the United States: An Econometric Analysis', Oak Ridge National Laboratories, ORNL-NSF-EP-49.

MUNK, K. J. (1977) 'Optimal Public Sector Pricing Taking Distributional Aspects into Consideration', *Quarterly Journal of Economics*, vol. 91, no. 4, pp. 639–50.

NELSON, R. A. (1982) 'An Empirical Test of the Ramsey Theory and Stigler-Peltzman Theory of Public Utility Pricing', *Economic Inquiry*, vol. 20, no. 2, pp. 277–90.

NELSON, R. A. (1984) 'Regulation, Capital Vintage, and Technical Change in the Electric Utility Industry', *Review of Economics and Statistics*, vol. 66, no. 1, pp. 59–69.

PANZAR, J. C. and WILLIG, R. D. (1977) 'Economies of Scale in Multi-Output Production', *Quarterly Journal of Economics*, vol. 91, no. 3, pp. 481–93.

PELTZMAN, S. (1976) 'Toward a More General Theory of Regulation', *Journal of Law and Economics*, vol. 19, pp. 211–40.

POSNER, R. (1975) 'The Social Costs of Monopoly and Regulation', *Journal of Political Economy*, vol. 83, no. 5, pp. 807–27.

SHERMAN, R. and GEORGE, A. (1979) 'Second-Best Pricing for the United States Postal Service', *Journal of Public Economics*, vol. 1, no. 1, pp. 45–72.

STEVENSON, R. E. (1980) 'Measuring Technological Bias', *American Economic Review*, vol. 70, pp. 163–73.

STIGLER, G. J. (1971) 'The Theory of Economic Regulation', *Bell Journal of Economics and Management Science*, vol. 2, no. 1, pp. 3–21.

TAYLOR, L. D. (1975) 'The Demand for Electricity: A Survey', *Bell Journal of Economics and Management Science*, vol. 6, no. 1, pp. 74–110.

WILLIG, R. (1976) 'Consumer's Surplus Without Apology', *American Economic Review*, vol. 66, no. 4, pp. 589–97.

WILLIG, R. and BAILEY, E. (1977) 'Ramsey-Optimal Pricing of Long Distance Telephone Services', in J. T. Wenders (ed.), *Pricing in*

*Regulated Industries: Theory and Application* (Denver: Mountain States Telephone and Telegraph Co.), pp. 68–97.

WILLIG, R. and BAILEY, E. (1979) 'The Economic Gradient Method', *American Economic Review*, vol. 69, no. 1, 96–101.

WILLIG, R. and BAILEY, E. (1981) 'Income-Distribution Concerns in Regulatory Policymaking', in G. Fromm (ed.), *Studies in Public Regulation* (Cambridge, Mass.: The MIT Press) pp. 79–102.

# 8 An Analysis of Pricing and Production Efficiency of Electric Utilities by Mode of Ownership

Paul M. Hayashi, Melanie Sevier
and John M. Trapani

## 8.1 INTRODUCTION

Assessing the welfare consequences of public versus private ownership in the provision of electricity in the United States requires an analysis of two important aspects of static efficiency; the relative production efficiency as measured through cost of production and the efficiency of the pricing of output as measured by Ramsey type pricing rules. These two aspects of efficiency are not, however, independent since the pricing of output will be influenced by the absolute and relative costs of production as well as the motivation of regulators and managers of the utilities.

The purpose of this paper is to evaluate the pricing behaviour of a sample of publicly owned and privately owned utilities operating in the United States and assess the importance of differences in production cost in determining the prevailing tariff structures by customer class. This will involve estimating the demand and cost structures for the two modes of ownership. The analysis will cover the time period 1965–80 so that pricing responses to both absolute cost changes (due to the oil embargo) as well as relative cost differences (due to mode of ownership) may be observed.

A number of recent studies have provided empirical evidence on the relative production efficiency of public and investor owned electric utilities. Using alternative measures of costs and specifications of the cost functions a number of these studies have found that publicly owned firms have lower costs than privately owned electric utilities including Meyer (1975), Neuberg (1977), Pescatrice and Trapani (1980) and Fare, Grosskopf and Logan (1985). Other studies have found public firms to be less efficient or found no significant difference in efficiency associated with mode of ownership including De Alessi (1974) and Atkinson and Halversen (1984). Differences in relative production efficiency may be attributed to X-inefficiency of managers of publicly owned utilities or rate-of-return regulation induced inefficiencies of privately owned utilities or some combination of the two.

With regard to pricing efficiency De Alessi (1974) has examined public and private rate structures and generally found public firms have lower prices and less complex price structures. In examining rate structures of privately owned utilities second-best welfare maximising pricing rules for multiple output firms have been developed for firms facing various forms of a regulatory constraint and pursuing varying objectives (Sherman, 1981; Marino, 1981). Recent empirical research on the pricing of electricity by customer class for privately owned electric utility firms reveals that their price structures are not quasi-optimal when evaluated by these second-best criteria (Meyer and Leland, 1980; Hayashi, Sevier and Trapani, 1985). This reflects the function for maximising consumer surplus, $W(p_i)$, subject to a fixed profit constraint.

$$Z = W(p_i) + \lambda [\Sigma p_i q_i - C(q) - \pi_0] \tag{8.1}$$

where

$p_i = p_i(q_i)$ = price of the $i$th product
$C(q)$ = multi-product cost function
$p_i q_i$ = revenue equation.

The quasi-optimal prices for independent demands developed from this optimisation problem[1] are given by the familiar Ramsey pricing rule

$$\frac{P_i - MC_i}{P_i} = \frac{\lambda - 1}{\lambda} \frac{1}{\epsilon_i} \qquad i = 1, 2, \ldots, n. \tag{8.2}$$

This pricing rule states that the percentage mark-up of price over marginal cost for each output produced should be equal to the reciprocal of the price elasticity weighted by $(\lambda - 1)/\lambda$.

The circumstances under which the managers of publicly owned utilities would choose this optimal price structure have been explored by Funkhouser and MacAvoy (1979). This outcome is assured, for example when the public firm maximises social utility, which is assumed to be a function of the various outputs products, subject to a resource endowment and a fixed profit constraint. However, the property rights model of public production would suggest that this type of objective would be unlikely (De Alessi, 1974). It is argued that under public ownership there is little incentive for owners to police managerial efficiency and therefore managers inability of rate-of-return regulation to bring about welfare maximising solutions. The departure of the prevailing price structures from the quasi-optimal structure may reflect that the objectives of regulators of the privately owned firms involve the maintenance of political support and thus take account of the political power of various groups (De Alessi, 1974; Funkhouser and MacAvoy, 1979). In a recent paper, Ross (1984) develops a procedure whereby the regulator's social welfare weights assigned to various beneficiaries may be estimated from prevailing pricing behaviour.

When a utility is publicly owned or controlled then its objectives may become entangled with those of the manager and its goals may or may not result in efficient production and /or a socially desirable price structure. It has been suggested that managers of public firms might choose a price structure to maximise output, charging lower prices, and would be less concerned with maintaining political support (De Alessi, 1974). The relative performance of publicly owned utilities in achieving welfare maximising price structures has not been evaluated.

## 8.2 WELFARE MAXIMISING PRICE STRUCTURES

In this section we will identify the welfare-maximising criterion for pricing various outputs of a multi-product firm. Given this criterion we will analyse the prevailing price structure of public and private utilities, test for efficient pricing, and then determine the implied social welfare weights assigned to the customer classes by the regulators of private firms and managers of public firms. Consider the objective of public firms will have greater opportunity to pursue policies which increase their own welfare. The pursuit of these policies may be modelled as the manager choosing a set of prices to maximise some weighted sum of consumer surplus subject to a profit constraint (Ross, 1984). If weights, $\alpha_i$, are assigned to customer groups, then the objective function may be written as

$$Z = \Sigma\alpha_i W_i(P_i) + \lambda[\Sigma p_i q_i - c(q_i) - \pi_0] \tag{8.3}$$

and the optimum prices are given by

$$\frac{P_i - MC_i}{P_i} = \frac{\lambda - \alpha_i}{\lambda} \frac{1}{\epsilon_i}. \tag{8.4}$$

It is important to note from (8.4) that the pricing choice, and therefore total consumer surplus, will be influenced by marginal production cost, $MC_i$, the social welfare weights assigned to each customer class, $\alpha_i$, and the price elasticity of demand, $\epsilon_i$. This price structure is different from the Ramsey quasi-optimal prices unless $\alpha_i$ equals unity for all customer classes.

Under private ownership it is also unlikely that the price structure resulting from profit maximisation subject to a rate-of-return constraint would be quasi-optimal. Nor is it probable that the prices set by the regulators of private firms will be optimum if the regulators have to take political support into their objective function. Assuming regulators may also maximise the weighted sum of consumer surplus subject to a rate-of-return constrain then their objective function may be written as

$$Z = \Sigma\alpha_i W_i(P_i) + \lambda[\Sigma p_i q_i - C(q_i) - (s - r)K(q_i)] \tag{8.5}$$

where

$s$ = allowed return on capital
$r$ = market cost of capital
$K$ = capital stock

and the optimum prices are given by

$$\frac{P_i - MC_i}{P_i} = \frac{\lambda - \alpha_i}{\lambda} \frac{1}{\epsilon_i} + \frac{(s - r)}{P_i} \frac{\partial K}{\partial q_i}. \tag{8.6}$$

The important thing to note from (8.6) is that in the presence of rate-of-return regulation total consumer surplus will be additionally influenced by the allowed rate-of-return on capital. The additional term $[(s - r)/P_i] \cdot \partial K_i/\partial q_i$ reflects the effect of varying $P_i$ on the firm's allowable profit under rate-of-return regulation. If $s$ is equal to $r$, then this new term vanishes from (8.6). However, if $s$ is greater than $r$ and $K$ is a normal input then the presence of the regulatory constraint will require a greater difference between price and marginal cost at the optimal solution. We should also note from this formulation that the allowed rate-of-return, $s$, which enters explicitly into the quasi-optimal price expression is assumed to be selected by the regulator before the price structure is determined. Thus, we envision a two-stage process whereby the regulator selects $s$, 'the fair return to capital' and then selects (or influences the selection of) the price by customer class.

Ross (1984) has shown that the relative social welfare weights assigned to customer groups may be extracted from the mark-ups and demand elasticity values. For the fixed profit constraint case the relative weights are given by

$$\frac{\alpha_1}{\alpha_2} = \frac{1 - M_1 \epsilon_1}{1 - M_2 \epsilon_2} \tag{8.7}$$

where

$$M_i = \frac{P_i - MC_i}{P_i} .$$

To measure the social welfare weights for the rate-of-return constraint case, we rewrite the optimal price structure as

$$\frac{P_i - MC_i^r}{P_i} = \frac{\lambda - \alpha_i}{\lambda} \frac{1}{\epsilon_i} \tag{8.8}$$

where

$$MC_i^r = MC_i + (s - r)\, \partial K / \partial q_i .$$

We refer to $MC_i^r$ as regulated marginal cost which may be viewed as the marginal cost to society involving $MC_i$, the product cost incurred under rate-of-return regulation, plus the excess valuation of additional capital employed. Thus, for the regulated firm we express the relative weights as

$$\frac{\alpha_1}{\alpha_2} = \frac{1 - M_1^r \epsilon_1}{1 - M_2^r \epsilon_2} \tag{8.9}$$

where

$$M_i^r = \frac{P - MC_i^r}{P_i}$$

Given that the incentive structures in which both the managers of public firms and the regulators of private firms operate are unlikely to produce the socially desirable price structure,[2] the nature of prevailing prices in relation to optimal prices and the implied distribution of benefits (social welfare weights) is of considerable importance in assessing the welfare consequences of these firms providing electric power. In the following section we develop a procedure to estimate marginal cost and the price elasticity of demand for each output and then evaluate utility pricing structures using a cross-section sample of publicly and privately owned firms operating in the United States. These pricing structures are then analysed in light of the differences in cost of production over time and across modes of ownership.

## 8.3 EMPIRICAL MODEL SPECIFICATION

For the purpose of the empirical analysis conducted here we specify the multi-product firm cost by a translog function, which is a second-order Taylor series approximation to an arbitrary cost function. The translog form of the function is given by

$$\begin{aligned} lnC = \alpha_0 &+ \sum_i \beta_i lnq_i + 1/2 \sum_i\sum_j \beta_{ij} lnq_i lnq_j + \sum_i\sum_j \theta_{ij} lnP_i lnq_j \\ &+ 1/2 \sum_i\sum_j \lambda_{ij} lnP_i lnP_j + \sum_i \phi_i lnP_i t + \phi t \end{aligned} \qquad (8.10)$$

where

$q_1$ = residential kilowatt/hour sales
$q_2$ = commercial kilowatt/hour sales
$q_3$ = industrial kilowatt/hour sales
$P_1$ = firm's market cost of capital ($r$)
$P_2$ = average labour wage rate ($w$)
$P_3$ = fuel price ($f$)
$t$ = an index of technical change.

This form is estimated for both the publicly and privately owned firms without imposing the restrictions that the cost function is linearly homogeneous in factor prices. Cost-minimizing behaviour is not a maintained hypothesis for either form of ownership and a likelihood ratio test is conducted to determine if the constraint is appropriate. For the privately owned firms, total cost is measured as production cost plus allowable profit (regulated cost) and the allowed rate of return is included on the right hand side of (8.10). This form of the cost function is appropriate for analysis of the social welfare weights implied by prevailing price structures.[3]

Marginal cost is derived from the total cost function as follows:

$$lnC/lnq_i = MC_i\,(q_i/C) = \beta_i + \sum_j \beta_{ij} lnq_j + \sum_j \theta_{ij} lnP_i \tag{8.11}$$

so that the marginal cost curve is given by

$$MC_i = [\beta_i + \sum_j \beta_{ij} lnq_j + \sum_j \theta_{ij} lnP_i]\, C/q_i. \tag{8.12}$$

Therefore, an estimate of the translog cost function provides the basis for an estimate of Equation (8.12).

In order to estimate the price elasticity of demand, the demand functions for output by customer type were specified as follows. For residential customers the demand equation is

$$\begin{aligned} lnq_1 &= \beta_{11} + \beta_{12}\, lnPIR + \beta_{13}\, lnNR + \beta_{14}\, lnPGR + \beta_{15}\, lnYP \\ &\quad + \beta_{16}\, CSAT \cdot ln(CDD) + \beta_{17}\, HSAT \cdot ln(HDD) \end{aligned} \tag{8.13}$$

where

| | | |
|---|---|---|
| $q_1$ | = | kilowatt/hour sales, residential |
| $PIR$ | = | price instrument for electricity, residential |
| $NR$ | = | number of residential customers |
| $PGR$ | = | price of gas to residential users |
| $YP$ | = | per capita personal income |
| $CSAT \cdot ln(CDD)$ | = | appliance saturation weighted cooling degree days |
| $HSAT \cdot ln(HDD)$ | = | appliance saturation weighted heating degree days. |

For commercial customers the demand equation estimated is

$$\begin{aligned} lnq_2 &= \beta_{21} + \beta_{22}\, lnPIC + \beta_{23}\, lnNC + \beta_{24}\, lnPGC + \beta_{25}\, lnENMPC \\ &\quad + \beta_{26}\, ln(CDD) + \beta_{27}\, ln(HDD) \end{aligned} \tag{8.14}$$

where

$q_2$ = kilowatt/hour sales, commercial
$PIC$ = price instrument for electricity, commercial
$NC$ = number of commercial customers
$PGC$ = price of gas to commercial users
$ENMPC$ = per capita non-manufacturing employment
$CDD$ = cooling degree days
$HDD$ = heating degree days.

For the industrial demand equation the following specification was employed:

$$ln q_3 = \beta_{31} + \beta_{32}\, lnPII + \beta_{34}\, lnNI + \beta_{35}\, lnPGI + \beta_{36}\, ln VA \qquad (8.15)$$

where

$q_3$ = kilowatt/hour sales, industrial
$PII$ = price instrument for electricity, industrial
$NI$ = number of industrial customers
$PGI$ = price of gas to industrial users
$VA$ = value added by manufacturer.

The use of instrumental variables for the price variable in each demand equation is based upon the fact that decreasing block pricing results in price being endogenous even though the rate schedule may be set by a regulator.[4] The use of number of customers in each equation is to pick up scale effects of varying market size on total customer demand. The inclusion of the price of gas, income, and the weather variable is a fairly standard specification of electricity demand.[5] The inclusion of non-manufacturing employment in the commercial equation and value added by manufacturing in the industrial equation is to pick up variations in the demand for power by commercial/industrial customers which may be associated with the level or type of activity as opposed to the number of customers. The measurement of all variables is treated in the data appendix.

The data employed to estimate all equations are for a cross-sectional sample of 32 privately owned electric utility firms and 22 publicly owned firms. The firms selected employ only conventional fossil fuel methods of production and have an insignificant amount of purchased power. The appropriate data were collected for the eight years, 1965, 1966, 1969, 1970, 1974, 1975, 1979, and 1980. The measurement of variables is discussed in the appendix. The models were estimated for the public and private firm samples separately for the four pooled samples combining the 1965-66 data, the 1969-70 data, the 1974-5 data, and the 1979-80 data.[6]

## 8.4 COST EQUATION RESULTS

The coefficients of Equation (8.10) were estimated for public and private firms using the four cross-section samples. The linear-homogeneity restrictions were imposed on the estimated model and the log of the likelihood function was compared for the restricted and unrestricted models. For both the public and private firms we had to reject the hypothesis that these restrictions were appropriate at the 95 per cent confidence level.[7] Therefore the cost equations were estimated without the linear homogeneity constraints and the reported coefficients in Tables 8.1 and 8.2 are the unrestricted estimates. A number of alternative specifications were estimated varying the functional form of the cost equation. The estimates of selected parameters of the model are given in Table 8.1 and 8.2. Overall the statistical results are satisfactory, however, several points should be noted.

Residential and commercial output we combined into the single output variable, $q_1$. This procedure was mandated by the extent of multi-collinearity in the model when residential and commercial output were treated separately. Thus, we are assuming that cost of production is the same for these two outputs. Second, the statistical model selected and presented here has constrained the factor price-output interactive terms to be zero. The choice of this form of the model is based upon our statistical analysis of various alternatives with the interaction terms included. Their inclusion added little to the significance of the model and presented some additional problems of multi-collinearity. In addition, the estimated values of marginal cost (evaluated at the sample mean) were unaffected by their exclusion.

The marginal cost equations implied by these results are given in Tables 8.3 and 8.4 with the values of marginal cost calculated at the sample means reported below each equation. The estimates of marginal cost are consistent across the four samples for private firms with higher marginal cost for residential and commercial users than for industrial users. For public firms, marginal cost for industrial users tends to be greater (at the sample mean) than that for non-industrial users. This latter result is due to the smaller scale of industrial output for public firms. That is, while the cost elasticities of non-industrial output are always greater than those for industrial output the mean marginal cost estimates are less for industrial users due to the relatively small scale of industrial output provided by publicly owned firms.

We also note that the mean estimate of marginal cost for non-industrial production is greater for privately owned firms while those for industrial power tend to be significantly higher for public firms. Since the public and private firms differ significantly in scale of production and cost of inputs, this difference in estimated marginal cost at the sample mean really says nothing about relative efficiency. However, these absolute differences in marginal cost are essential to the analysis of pricing structures. We examine the issue of relative efficiency in a later section.

*Table* 8.1 Estimates of selected parameters of translog cost function in private firms

| | *1965/66* | *1969/70* | *1974/75* | *1979/80* |
|---|---|---|---|---|
| $lnq_1$ | 0.6786* | 0.6938* | 0.78284* | 0.71368* |
| | (27.101) | (33.970) | (26.744) | (17.311) |
| $lnq_2$ | 0.3301* | 0.2423* | 0.23518* | 0.32874* |
| | (12.829) | (12.296 | (7.5737) | (6.5345) |
| $lnq_1, lnq_2$ | 0.0070 | 0.0292* | 0.03079* | −0.022437 |
| | (0.4579) | (2.723) | (1.9791) | (0.95914) |
| $lnr$ | 0.5268* | 0.2663* | 0.25678* | 0.46412* |
| | (7.659) | (3.199) | (2.5472) | (2.5696) |
| $lnw$ | 0.0672 | −2.9236* | 0.23967 | 0.16582 |
| | (0.0661) | (2.298) | (1.2177) | (0.35293) |
| $lnf$ | −0.1842* | −0.0566 | 0.22724 | 0.12033 |
| | (3.504) | (0.5129) | (0.77181) | (0.22017) |
| $lnr \cdot t$ | 0.0014* | 0.00122 | 0.000855 | −0.0008619 |
| | (2.125) | (1.497) | (0.79145) | (0.65118) |
| $lnw \cdot t$ | 0.0292* | 0.0595* | 0.006398* | −0.003970 |
| | (3.452) | (5.604) | (2.9148) | (1.0779) |
| $lnf \cdot t$ | 0.00179* | 0.0039* | 0.000124 | −0.006001* |
| | (3.346) | (3.882) | (0.03463) | (1.6610) |
| $t$ | −0.0270* | −0.0608* | −0.00699 | 0.03268* |
| | (3.298) | (5.220) | (0.64225) | (2.1809) |

*Note*: Numbers in parentheses are $t$-ratios under the null hypothesis that the coefficient is zero. The coefficients on the squared and cross-product price terms are omitted from the table even though they were estimated. An asterisk indicates the variable is significant at the 95% confidence level.

*Table* 8.2 Estimates of selected parameters of translog cost function in public firms

| | *1965/66* | *1969/70* | *1974/75* | *1979/80* |
|---|---|---|---|---|
| $lnq_1$ | 0.5588* | 0.5005* | 0.5505* | 0.4766* |
| | (17.156) | (20.378) | (13.320) | (6.170) |
| $lnq_2$ | 0.3347* | 0.4271* | 0.4331* | 0.4107* |
| | (7.002) | (12.518) | (8.543) | (4.361) |
| $lnq_1 \cdot lnq_2$ | −0.0067 | −0.0165* | 0.0049 | 0.0495* |
| | (0.6173) | (1.953) | (0.2716) | (1.664) |
| $lnr$ | 0.3798* | 0.8932* | 0.4928* | 0.6348* |
| | (2.037) | (5.780) | (4.159) | (2.468) |
| $lnw$ | −0.1188 | 0.3081* | −0.1427 | −0.4334 |
| | (0.6589) | (1.653) | (0.3392) | (0.6606) |
| $lnf$ | −5.4306* | −6.005* | 0.1093 | −1.203* |
| | (5.442) | (5.944) | (0.0995) | (4.346) |
| $lnr \cdot t$ | −0.00159 | −0.00147 | 0.00018 | 0.00134 |
| | (1.129) | (1.585) | (0.2538) | (1.453) |
| $lnw \cdot t$ | −0.00167* | −0.00037 | 0.0025 | 0.0060* |
| | (1.708) | (0.3651) | (1.1085) | (2.399) |
| $lnf \cdot t$ | 0.0293* | 0.01879* | −0.01855* | 0.0027 |
| | (2.654) | (2.108) | (2.554) | (1.118) |
| $t$ | −0.0373* | −0.0313* | 0.04739* | −0.0232 |
| | (2.579) | (2.482) | (2.478) | (1.148) |

*Notes*: Numbers in parentheses are $t$-ratios under the null hypothesis that the coefficient is zero. The coefficients on the squared and cross-product price terms are omitted from the table even though they were estimated. An asterisk indicates the variable is significant at the 95% confidence level.

Finally, we note the way in which the vintage of plant and equipment (technical change index) impacts cost of production. Newer plant for both types of firm embodied fuel using technology in the earlier years as indicated by the positive and significant coefficients on the variable $lnf \cdot t$. During the 1960s fuel costs were falling so that fuel-using technology would have been cost effective. During the 1970s this pattern appears to have changed in that plant embodied technology was either neutral or discouraged fuel consumption. This finding is consistent with the trend in fuel price during the later sample periods.

*Table* 8.3 Marginal cost estimates in private firms

| | Residential/commercial | Industrial |
|---|---|---|
| 1965/66 | $MC_1 = [0.67865 + 0.00701 lnq_2]\ C/q_1$<br>17.63<br>(0.454) | $MC_2 = [0.33015 + 0.00701 lnq_1]\ C/q_2$<br>10.95<br>(0.419) |
| 1969/70 | $MC_1 = [0.69382 + 0.02922 lnq_2]\ C/q_1$<br>16.95<br>(0.242) | $MC_2 = [0.24231 + 0.02922 lnq_1]\ C/q_2$<br>9.71<br>(0.358) |
| 1974/75 | $MC_1 = [0.78284 + 0.03079 lnq_2]\ C/q_1$<br>33.436<br>(1.1585) | $MC_2 = [0.23518 + 0.03079 lnq_1]\ C/q_2$<br>20.259<br>(2.3233) |
| 1979/80 | $MC_1 = [0.71368 - 0.02244 lnq_2]\ C/q_1$<br>47.549<br>(2.7846) | $MC_2 = [0.32874 - 0.02244 lnq_1]\ C/q_2$<br>34.661<br>(5.9489) |

*Note*: Numbers below each equation are the values of *MC* (measured in mils per KWH) when the equation is evaluated at the sample mean of all variables and the standard errors of *MC* shown in parentheses. The standard errors were computed treating the mean of *C* and *q* as constant.

*Table* 8.4 Marginal cost estimates in public firms

| | Residential/commercial | Industrial |
|---|---|---|
| 1965/66 | $MC_1 = [0.5588 - 0.00673 lnq_2]\ C/q_1$<br>10.672<br>(0.7415) | $MC_2 = [0.3347 - 0.0067 lnq_1]\ C/q_2$<br>13.356<br>(1.3966) |
| 1969/70 | $MC_1 = [0.5005 - 0.0165 lnq_2]\ C/q_1$<br>10.475<br>(0.5061) | $MC_2 = [0.4271 - 0.0165 lnq_1]\ C/q_2$<br>16.252<br>(1.3966) |
| 1974/75 | $MC_1 = [0.5506 + 0.0049 lnq]\ C/q$<br>21.079<br>(2.0089) | $MC_2 = [0.4332 + 0.0049 lnq]\ C/q$<br>32.972<br>(3.9969) |
| 1979/80 | $MC_1 = [0.4766 + 0.0496 lnq]\ C/q$<br>29.30<br>(4.7970) | $MC_2 = [0.4108 + 0.496 lnq]\ C/q$<br>46.162<br>(13.9007) |

*Note*: Numbers below each equation are the values of *MC* (measured in mils per KWH) when the equation is evaluated at the sample mean of all variables and the standard errors of *MC* shown in parentheses. The standard errors were computed treating the mean of *C* and *q* as constant.

## 8.5 DEMAND ELASTICITIES

Separate demand equations were estimated by customer class for both public and private firms. The equations were estimated using an instrumental variable approach to account for the endogeneity of the price of electricity. For residential customers the elasticity estimates ranged from −1.08156 to −1.10891 for private firms and from −0.7743 to −0.8082 for public firms. The estimated demand elasticities for commercial users were between −1.70955 and −2.3702 for private firms and between −1.3738 and −2.1316 for public firms. Finally, the estimates for industrial customers ranged between −2.2562 and −3.3180 for private firms and −3.2496 and −3.3090 for the public firms in our sample.

A recent survey of demand elasticity estimates published by EPRI reported long-run price elasticity estimates for residential demand between −0.44 and −1.89. For commercial demand the range of estimates was −0.56 to −1.60 and for industrial demand, −0.51 to −1.82. All estimates reported in the survey were based upon aggregated data. It is interesting that these estimates do not conform to the widely held view that industrial demand would be most elastic, due to availability of substitutes, and residential demand would be least elastic. Our results lie within the range of estimates for residential demand but are somewhat larger for commercial and industrial demand. The implications of these elasticity estimates for the tests of pricing efficiency are considered in the analysis which follows.

Overall the estimated demand equations were satisfactory on statistical grounds. The explanatory power was best for the residential model and worst for the industrial model. However, even for the industrial model our specification explained 60–75 per cent of the variation in sales.

## 8.6 EVALUATING PRICING EFFICIENCY

Given the estimates of marginal cost reported in Tables 8.3 and 8.4 and the price elasticity of demand estimates by class of customers discussed above, we can test for quasi-optimal pricing by public and private firms using condition (8.4).[8] The data required and test results are summarised in Tables 8.5 and 8.6. Table 8.5 reports the weighted and unweighted price mark-up by customer class for the privately owned firms. The mark-up of price over marginal cost in the 1965–66 and 1969–70 samples are in the range of 18 to 27 per cent for residential and commercial users but significantly less for industrial customers.[9] Quasi-optimal pricing is rejected for both of these samples.[10] A dramatic difference in pricing behaviour is observed in the samples during the 1970s. In these years we find prices are not significantly different from marginal cost for all customer classes. This change in pricing structure is undoubtedly the result of oil price shocks and the effects of extensive inflation on the regulatory pricing process. It reflects the inability of private utilities to keep rates adjusted to rapidly changing fuel and capital costs. Indeed, prices were set so close to marginal costs in those years that we cannot reject optimal pricing for the 1979–80 sample.

*Table* 8.5 Data for evaluating pricing efficiency in private firms

| | *1965/66* | *1969/70* | *1974/75* | *1979/80* |
|---|---|---|---|---|
| Residential | | | | |
| $(P - MC)/P$ | 0.2756 | 0.2331 | −0.0548 | 0.0316 |
| | (0.0187) | (0.0113) | (0.0401) | (0.0623) |
| $[(P - MC)/P]\epsilon$ | 0.2981 | 0.2343 | −0.0607 | 0.0035 |
| | (0.0540) | (0.0570) | (0.0426) | (0.0628) |
| Commercial | | | | |
| $(P - MC)/P$ | 0.2446 | 0.1788 | −0.0881 | 0.0155 |
| | (0.0195) | (0.1170) | (0.0867) | (0.1335) |
| $[(P - MC)/P]\epsilon$ | 0.4181 | 0.4124 | −0.2031 | 0.0359 |
| | (0.0835) | (0.0750) | (0.0937) | (0.1337) |
| Industrial | | | | |
| $(P - MC)/P$ | −0.0223 | 0.0699 | 0.0010 | 0.0153 |
| | (0.0384 | (0.0345) | (0.3803) | (0.5612) |
| $[(P - MC)/P]\epsilon$ | −0.0504 | 0.2320 | 0.0034 | 0.0508 |
| | (0.0859) | (0.1260) | (0.3803) | (0.5613) |
| *F*-test | | | | |
| Ramsey pricing | 393.88* | 40.83* | 12.95* | 0.312 |

*Note*: The numbers in parentheses below the weighted and unweighted mark-ups are standard errors of the estimate. The value of the *F*-statistic reported in the bottom row is computed for the null hypotheses that the weighted mark-ups for each customer class are equal. An asterisk indicates that we reject the null hypotheses at the 95% confidence level.

For the public firms we also find a decline in the price-marginal cost mark-up after 1974 but with a somewhat different effect on the absolute level. Prior to 1974, the mark-ups for non-industrial customers ranged

*Table* 8.6 Data for evaluating pricing efficiency in public firms

| | *1965/66* | *1969/70* | *1974/75* | *1979/80* |
|---|---|---|---|---|
| Residential | | | | |
| $(P - MC)/P$ | 0.461 | 0.425 | 0.217 | 0.312 |
| | (0.0293) | (0.0227) | (0.0603) | (0.0959) |
| $[(P - MC)/P]\epsilon$ | 0.357 | 0.343 | 0.175 | 0.252 |
| | (0.1476 | (0.1226) | (0.0861) | (0.0999) |
| Commercial | | | | |
| $(P - MC)/P$ | 0.477 | 0.490 | 0.243 | 0.318 |
| | (0.0512) | (0.0300) | (0.0804) | (0.7794) |
| $[(P - MC)/P]\epsilon$ | 0.655 | 0.554 | 0.275 | 0.360 |
| | (0.3306) | (0.1065) | (0.1900) | (0.8113) |
| Industrial | | | | |
| $(P - MC)/P$ | −0.197 | −0.474 | −0.727 | −0.446 |
| | (0.6477) | (0.4019) | (0.6470) | (1.348) |
| $[(P - MC)/P]\epsilon$ | −0.640 | −1.465 | −2.247 | −1.378 |
| | (0.6556) | (0.4764) | (0.7567) | (1.369) |
| *F*-test | | | | |
| Ramsey pricing | 98.389* | 554.194* | 421.968* | 42.405* |

*Note*: The numbers in parentheses below the weighted and unweighted mark-ups are standard errors of the estimate. The value of the *F*-statistic reported in the bottom row is computed for the null hypotheses that the weighted mark-ups for each customer class are equal. An asterisk indicates that we reject the null hypotheses at the 95% confidence level.

between 42 and 49 per cent whereas for industrial customers we observe price less than marginal cost suggesting a favoured treatment of the industrial customer class. After 1974 the mark-ups for non-industrial customers drop in the face of rising fuel and capital costs but prices are maintained above marginal costs of production in the range of 20–30 per cent. Public firms appear to be more reluctant to pass on higher costs of production to industrial customers than they are to non-industrial customers. All of this meant lower mark-ups to non-industrial customers and larger subsidies to industrial customers. Quasi-optimal pricing is rejected for public firms in all samples.

The social welfare weights implied by these pricing structures are presented in Table 8.7. For the privately owned firms, the implied social welfare weights indicate that residential and industrial customers were

*Table* 8.7 Relative social welfare weights

| | *Private firms* | *Public firms* |
|---|---|---|
| 1965/66 | | |
| $\alpha R/\alpha C$ | 1.206* | 1.864 |
| | (1.803) | (1.363) |
| $\alpha R/\alpha I$ | 0.6680* | 0.392* |
| | (4.213) | (2.051) |
| $\alpha C/\alpha I$ | 0.5540* | 0.210* |
| | (4.64) | (2.206) |
| 1969/70 | | |
| $\alpha R/\alpha C$ | 1.316* | 1.473* |
| | (2.77) | (2.375) |
| $\alpha R/\alpha I$ | 0.997 | 0.266* |
| | (0.022) | (4.163) |
| $\alpha C/\alpha I$ | 0.757* | 0.181* |
| | (2.000) | (5.975) |
| 1974/75 | | |
| $\alpha R/\alpha C$ | 0.882 | 1.138 |
| | (1.269) | (0.593) |
| $\alpha R/\alpha I$ | 1.064 | 0.254* |
| | (0.1572) | (3.542) |
| $\alpha C/\alpha I$ | 1.207 | 0.223* |
| | (0.4417) | (3.058) |
| 1979/80 | | |
| $\alpha R/\alpha C$ | 1.001 | 1.169 |
| | (0.0068) | (0.177) |
| $\alpha R/\alpha I$ | 1.017 | 0.315 |
| | (0.0296) | (1.547) |
| $\alpha C/\alpha I$ | 1.016 | 0.269 |
| | (0.0273) | (0.820) |

*Note*: The numbers below the relative weights are *t*-ratios computed under the null hypothesis that this ratio is equal to unity. An asterisk indicates that the ratio of the weights is significantly different from unity at the 95% confidence level.

favoured relative to commercial users in the earlier years but that after 1974 the relative weights approach unity. This implies equal treatment of the customer classes by regulators and is consistent with the previous test results for Ramsey pricing.

For the public firms the estimated relative weights indicate favoured treatment of industrial customers over non-industrial customers throughout our sample period. The weights also suggest that residential and commercial customers are treated equally except during the 1974/75 sample period when residential customers received preferred price treatment.[11]

Overall, the pricing efficiency analysis suggests three major findings. For private firms the trend during our sample period has been toward efficient pricing and involving a movement away from favoured treatment of residential and industrial uses. For public firms their pricing pattern has been consistently different from the quasi-optimal one favouring treatment of industrial users. Finally, for both public and private firms, prices have moved closer to marginal costs of production (smaller mark-ups) during the 1970s, however, public firms have always charged lower overall rates. The differences in the pricing patterns by mode of ownership are clearly the result of a combination of factors including the regulatory process facing private firms and the political pressures on their regulators, the incentives of public managers, and differences in absolute and relative costs of production. In the next section we provide some evidence related to differences in cost efficiency of the public and private firms.

## 8.7 EVALUATING PRODUCTION EFFICIENCY

Table 8.8 reports the mean values for average cost of production for both types of firms in our sample and the major components of these costs. Looking simply at average cost, public firms in our sample have had lower cost of production during the 1960s but this differential is reversed in the later years. The cost advantage of public firms prior to 1974 appears to be attributable to capital costs. Following 1974 the difference between capital expenses for public and private firms diminishes as the relative per unit cost of the public firm's rise. Differences in operation expense appear to be due to differences in fuel costs which were higher for public than private firms except for the 1979–80 sample when they were approximately the same. Maintenance expense is also somewhat lower for private firms further supporting the inference that the cost advantage of public firms comes from the capital expense area.

*Table* 8.8 Mean value of selected cost variables

| | *1965/66* | *1969/70* | *1974/75* | *1979/80* |
|---|---|---|---|---|
| Average cost | | | | |
| Public | 9.9263 | 9.7711 | 19.7445 | 37.5631 |
| Private | 11.0440 | 10.5134 | 19.8346 | 32.9015 |
| Operation expense | | | | |
| Public | 6.056 | 5.999 | 13.442 | 22.725 |
| Private | 5.303 | 5.292 | 11.919 | 21.401 |
| Maintenance expense | | | | |
| Public | 1.014 | 0.9768 | 1.4227 | 2.587 |
| Private | 0.8941 | 0.8693 | 1.2369 | 2.3906 |
| Capital expense | | | | |
| Public | 3.299 | 3.504 | 6.008 | 9.665 |
| Private | 5.227 | 4.959 | 7.149 | 10.138 |

*Note*: All mean values are in mils per KWH. Capital expense includes depreciation, interest and dividend payments.

The upward trend in average cost indicated in Table 8.8 is consistent with the trends in marginal cost and the declining mark-ups charged by both public and private firms previously discussed. However, a remaining question is whether the lower tariffs charged by public firms throughout our sample are due to differences in factor costs (primarily capital costs) or if some part is attributable to differences in efficiency of production between mode of ownership. This latter question is difficult to answer within our sample because of differences in scale of production and structure of customer bases across the public and private firms. However, some insights may be gained by comparing costs of production. One way to do this is to project private (public) cost using the public (private) firms' cost structure and then compare these estimates to actual costs.[12] Table 8.9 presents the results of this comparison. The results indicate that during the 1960s public firms were more efficient in that private firms could lower their total cost by adopting the public firm's cost structure. This pattern of efficiency is reversed during the 1974–75 and 1979–80 samples when private firms appear to have an efficiency advantage. These findings are consistent with the trends in per unit cost discussed above in that private firms' relative cost position was improving in the 1970s. They further suggest that the pattern of cost change may be in part due to changes in relative efficiency as well as changes in factor prices. That is, the cost differences implied by the results of Table 8.9 essentially hold factor prices fixed (across mode of ownership) and are, in principle, attributable to differences in efficiency in use of the factors.

*Table* 8.9 Cost comparisons for evaluating production efficiency

| | *1965/66* | *1969/70* | *1974/75* | *1979/80* |
|---|---|---|---|---|
| Public coefficients/ public data | 14.032 | 18.855 | 49.186 | 105.11 |
| Private coefficients/ public data | 17.448 | 23.112 | 37.696 | 88.751 |
| Private coefficients/ private data | 59.536 | 85.354 | 232.645 | 488.72 |
| Public coefficients/ private data | 46.244 | 73.949 | 265.686 | 509.89 |

*Note*: The cost comparisons are conducted by estimating the parameters of the same specification of the translog cost function for both public and private firms.

The fact that private firms have become relatively more efficient may be the result of several factors. It could be that they were more able to adjust to rising fuel costs than the publicly owned firms due to differences in the structure of their customer base with larger industrial users. This change would be captured in the estimated coefficients of the cost function. However, it is also possible that private firms were forced to produce more efficiently during the 1970s due to regulatory lag in allowing rates to adjust to rising fuel and capital costs. As Bailey (1974) has shown, regulatory lag can be effective in forcing firms to become more efficient and adopting a more efficient combination of resources. That is, the relative production inefficiency of private firms in the 1960s could be explained by profit maximisation under rate-of-return regulation and the fact that they could earn allowable profits. In the 1970s with the fall in mark-ups and the decline in profitability, increased production efficiency appears to have become essential.

## 8.8 CONCLUSIONS

The purpose of this chapter has been to evaluate the pricing behaviour of public and private utilities operating in the United States and assess the importance of differences in cost of production in determining the prevailing price structures. Our study covers the period 1965 to 1980. Our results regarding pricing behaviour involve tests for Ramsey pricing and an analysis of weights assigned to various customer classes. Our findings here are the following. For private firms the trend during our sample period has been toward efficient pricing and a movement away from favoured treatment of residential and industrial uses. For public firms the pricing patterns have not been Ramsey efficient but have favoured treatment of industrial users. For both public and private firms, prices have moved closer to marginal costs of production (smaller mark-ups) during the 1970s but public firms have maintained lower overall rates.

The analysis of cost of production revealed several things. Public firms had an absolute cost advantage over private firms during the 1960s due primarily to capital cost differences and they appear to have been relatively more efficient producers during this period. During the 1970s, the absolute cost advantage of public firms eroded with the declining capital cost differential between public and private firms and the private firms became the relatively more efficient producers. The improved efficiency of private firms during this period of rising fuel and capital costs may be the result of regulatory lag. That is, the lag in price adjustments to rising input costs may have induced these firms to choose a more efficient combination of resources.

## Appendix

The following data were employed to estimate the econometric models in this paper.

*Output*, $q_i$, is measured as kilowatt hour sales (in billions) to each customer class. Data for residential, commercial, and industrial kilowatt hour sales is available, by firm, for each year in the Federal Power Commission's *Statistics of Privately (Publicly) Owned Electric Utilities in the United States.*

*Wage rate*, $w$, is measured as the average wage rate of manufacturing employees in the state where the utility firm is located. These data are available in the Bureau of Labor Statistics, *Employment and Earnings.*

*Price of fuel*, $f$, is measured by fuel cost per kilowatt hour of electricity produced. These data are reported by firm, for each year in the Federal Power Commission's *Steam Electric Plant Construction Costs and Annual Production Expenses.*

*Price of capital*, $r$. The user cost of capital is estimated by the weighted average interest payment on debt for the publicly owned firms. For private firms the following cost of capital was estimated.

$$r = \frac{S}{S+P+D} k_e + \frac{P}{S+P+D} k_p + (1-t) \frac{D}{S+P+D} k_d$$

where

$S$ = the market value of equity
$P$ = the market value of the preferred stock
$D$ = the market value of the debt
$k_e$ = the cost of equity funds
$k_p$ = the cost of debt, and
$t$ = the marginal corporate income tax rate.

Data on interest and dividend payments, debt and equity, capital and depreciation are reported by firm for each year in *Statistics of Privately (Publicly) Owned Electric Utilities in the United States* and Moody's *Public Utility Manual.*

*Allowable rate of return*, $s$, is estimated by an average of the actual rates earned by the firm during the current and previous two years. Actual rates of return are available in *Statistics of Privately Owned Electric Utilities in the United States.*

*Technology index*, $t$. The index of technology employed here measures the vintage of the firm's generating equipment. It is computed as the weighted average age of generating equipment used by the firm where the weights are the percentage of total capacity installed at a given date. Installation dates and generating capacity of the various plants are available in *Steam Electric Plant Construction Costs and Annual Production Expenses.*

*Cost of production*, C, is computed as the sum of operation, maintenance, depreciation and interest and dividend expenses. Distribution and transmission expenses are included in operation expenses. Data required are available in *Statistics of Privately (Publicly) Owned Electric Utilities in the United States.*

*Price instrument*, $PI_i$. A price instrument for average price of electricity sold to each customer class was computed. The basic series on average price was computed by dividing dollar sales in each customer class by kilowatt hour sales to that class. The variable was then regressed on all exogenous variables used in the cost and demand equations. The data on sales by class of customer are available in *Statistics of Privately Owned Electric Utilities in the United States.*

*Number of customers*, $N_i$, is reported for each firm and for each year in *Statistics of Privately (Publicly) Owned Electric Utilities in the United States.*

*Price of gas*, $PG_i$. The price of gas incorporated in the demand equations is calculated as the ratio of total gas revenues in each customer class to total gas sales within the same class. The components of the ratio are available by state and are published in the American Gas Association, *Gas Facts.*

*Per capita personal income*, YP, is the relative value of the personal income in a state to its total resident population. Total personal income figures may be obtained from the Bureau of Economic Analysis, *National Income and Product Accounts of the United States.* Population figures are available from the Bureau of the Census, *Current Population Reports, Series P–25.*

*Appliance saturation weights*, CSAT, HSAT. CSAT reflects the proportion of homes with central air-conditioning in a given state. HSAT gauges the proportion of homes in the state with electric heat. These ratios were calculated from data published by Taylor, *et al.* in *Residential Demand for Energy (Electric Power Research Institute EA–1572).*

*Weather degree days*, CDD, HDD. Cooling degree days (CDD) are a measure of the extent to which climatic temperature exceeds 65°F while heating degree days (HDD) captures temperature deviations below 65°F. This information is available from the *National Oceanic and Atmospheric Administration.*

**Acknowledgements**

We would like to thank our discussants Robert Camfield and James Mulligan for their very helpful suggestions and insightful comments on this research project. We also wish to thank Michael Crew and the participants of the 2 May 1986 workshop at Rutgers University entitled 'Regulating Utilities in an Era of Deregulation'.

**Notes**

1. This pricing rule has been developed by Baumol and Bradford (1970).
2. Some recent research has been concerned with designing incentive mechanisms to induce quasi-optimal (Ramsey) pricing by natural monopolies (Tam, 1985).
3. We estimate the regulated cost function for the private firms for the purpose of testing the pricing behaviour. However, for the purpose of comparing production efficiency we contrast the basic translog cost function estimates under the alternative modes of ownership and use of the same form of the cost function.
4. See Taylor (1975) for a discussion of this problem. Price instruments were developed using the average price of electricity regressed on all exogenous variable determining cost of production and customer demand. Halvorsen (1975) demonstrates that log-linear estimation of demand and average price (instrument) equations will result in elasticities of demand which are equal to those that would be obtained with marginal price data.

5. For a survey of electric demand models see Taylor (1975) and Bohi (1982).
6. The pooling of two years of data in each sample required that we deflate all variables measured in dollars. For this purpose we deflated the appropriate variables using the GNP price deflator. Our base year was the first year in each of the four samples.
7. To assess further the presence or absence of cost minimising behaviour, the constant-output factor demand elasticities were evaluated at the sample means of the data. For the private firms all demand elasticities were negative during the 1970s which is consistent with cost minimising behaviour. During the 1960s the constant-output fuel demand elasticity was found to be positive while those for capital and labour were negative. For the public firms input demand for capital was always found to be negative and those for fuel were consistently positive. Labour's demand elasticity was negative except for one sample.
8. The pricing rule applied to the private firms in our sample is that given by condition (8.8).
9. Our estimate of the variance of the weighted mark-up term was

$$VAR[(P - MC)/P]\,\epsilon_i = [(1/P)\epsilon_i]^2\, VAR(MC) + \\ + [(P - MC)/P]^2\, VAR(\epsilon_i) \\ + 2[(1/P)\epsilon_i]\,[(P - MC)/P]\, COV(MC, \epsilon_i)$$

where $P$ and $MC$ are evaluated at their sample mean values and

$$VAR(MC_i) = (C/q_i)^2\, VAR(\beta_{ii}) + (C/q_i \cdot lnq_j)^2\, VAR(\beta_{ij}) \\ + 2(C/q_i)(C/q_i \cdot lnq_j) COV(\beta_{ii}, \beta_{ij}).$$

10. The test statistic employed was $F = MST/MSE$

where $$MST = \sum_i^k n_i(\bar{X}_i - \bar{X})^w/(k - 1)$$

$$MSE = (n_i - 1)\sum_i^k S_i^2/(n - k)$$

and $$\bar{X} = 1/k \sum_i \bar{X}_i,\ S_i^2 = VAR(\bar{X}_i) \text{ and } n = kn_i.$$

11. The inferences regarding pricing efficiency were re-examined using the average price elasticity estimates reported in Mount, Chapman and Tyrell (1973) which are smaller for commercial and industrial users than our estimates. These estimates for residential, commercial and industrial customers are 1.25, 1.45 and 1.73 respectively. Our conclusions about Ramsey pricing and the relative social welfare weights are unaltered by the use of these alternative demand elasticity estimates.

12. A potential difficulty with forecasting the cost of one sample using the estimated cost structure of the other is that the estimated structure is an approximation near the sample mean values of the variables. Given that the public firm's output is smaller than that of private firms, a potentially large error of forecast may hamper these cost comparisons. To mitigate this problem we have made our comparisons using both estimated cost structures and found our forecasts of costs to be consistent. This consistency suggests that our estimated cost functions do properly capture the effects of scale of output on cost of production and permit reasonably accurate projections of cost while varying the scale of output produced.

## References

ATKINSON, S. E. and HALVORSEN, R. (1984) 'A New Hedonic Technique for Estimating Attribute Demand – An Application to the Demand for Automobile Fuel Efficiency', *Review of Economics and Statistics*, vol. 66, no. 3, pp. 417–26.

AVERCH, Harvey and JOHNSON, Leland L. (1962) 'Behaviour of the Firm Under Regulatory Constraint', *American Economic Review*, vol. 52, no. 5, December, pp. 1053–69.

BAILEY, Elizabeth (1974) *Economic Theory of Regulatory Constraint* (Lexington: Lexington Books).

BAUMOL, William J. and BRADFORD, David F. (1970) 'Optimal Departures from Marginal Cost Pricing', *American Economic Review*, vol. 60, no. 3, pp. 265–83.

BOHI, Douglas R. (1982) *Price Elasticities of Demand for Energy-Evaluating Estimates* (Palo Alto: Electric Power Research Institute).

COWING, Thomas G. (1978) 'The Effectiveness of Rate-of-Return Regulation: An Empirical Test Using Profit Functions', in M. Fuss and D. McFadden (eds), *Production Economics: A Dual Approach to Theory and Applications* (Amsterdam: North Holland).

COWING, Thomas G. (1982) 'Duality and Estimation of a Restricted Technology', in *Advances in Applied Micro-Economics*, Vol. 2, V. K. Smith (ed.) (Greenwich, Conn.: JAI Press).

DE ALESSI, T. (1974) 'An Economic Analysis of Government Ownership and Regulation: Theory and the Evidence from the Electric Power Industry', *Public Choice*, vol. 19, no. 1, pp. 1–42.

FARE, R., GROSSKOPF, S. and LOGAN, J. (1985) 'The Relative Performance of Publicly-Owned and Privately-Owned Electric Utilities', *Journal of Public Economics*, vol. 26, no. 1, pp. 89–106.

FUNKHOUSER, R. and MacAVOY, P. W. (1979) 'A Sample of Observations on Comparative Prices in Public and Private Enterprises', *Journal of Public Economics*, vol. 11, no. 3, pp. 353–68.

HAYASHI, P., SEVIER, M. and TRAPANI, J. (1985) 'Pricing Efficiency Under Rate-of-Return Regulation: Some Empirical Evidence of the

Electric Utility Industry', *Southern Economic Journal*, vol. 51, no. 3, January, pp. 776–92.

HALVORSEN, Robert (1975) 'Residential Demand for Electric Energy', *Review of Economics and Statistics*, vol. 57, no. 1, February, pp. 12–18.

MARINO, Anthony M. (1981) 'Optimal Departures from Marginal Cost Pricing: The Case of a Rate of Return Constraint', *Southern Economic Journal*, vol. 48, no. 1, July, pp. 37–49.

MEYER, Robert A. (1975) 'Publicly Owned Versus Privately Owned Utilities: A Policy Review', *Review of Economics and Statistics*, vol. 57, no. 4, pp. 391–9.

MEYER, Robert A. and LELAND, Hayne E. (1980) 'The Effectiveness of Price Regulation', *Review of Economics and Statistics*, vol. 62, no. 4, November, pp. 555–66.

MOUNT, T., CHAPMAN, L. and TYRELL, G. (1973) 'Electricity Demand in the United States: An Econometric Analysis', Oak Ridge National Laboratories, ORNL-NSF-EP-49.

NEUBERG, L. G. (1977) 'Two Issues in the Municipal Ownership of Electric Power Distribution Systems', *Bell Journal of Economics*, vol. 8, no. 1, pp. 303–23.

PESCATRICE, Donn R. and TRAPANI, John M. (1980) 'The Performance and Objectives of Public and Private Utilities Operating in the United States', *Journal of Public Economics*, vol. 13, no. 2, pp. 259–76.

ROSS, T. W. (1984) 'Uncovering Regulators' Social Welfare Rights', *Rand Journal of Economics*, vol. 15, no. 1, pp. 152–5.

SHERMAN, Roger (1981) 'Pricing Inefficiency Under Profit Regulation', *Southern Economic Journal*, vol. 48, no. 2, October, pp. 475–89.

TAM, M. Y. S. (1985) 'Reward Structures in a Planned-Economy – Some Further Thoughts', *Quarterly Journal of Economics*, vol. 100, no. 1, pp. 279–89.

TAYLOR, Lester D. (1975) 'The Demand for Electricity: A Survey', *The Bell Journal of Economics*, vol. 6, no. 1, Spring, pp. 74–110.

# 9 Residential Electricity Demand Modelling with Secret Data

Christopher Garbacz

## 9.1 INTRODUCTION

Following the seminal work of McFadden, Puig and Kirschner (1977) and the general availability of national micro-data sets, residential energy demand studies have been conducted for electricity, natural gas, fuel oil, liquid petroleum gas and wood (see Garbacz, 1984, 1985). Employing the National Interim Energy Consumption Survey (NIECS) data, Garbacz (1984) developed a three-equation model (demand, price and appliance stock) to estimate national electricity demand via two-stages least squares for households by month. The study reported in this chapter builds on this previous work to estimate elasticities by month. It is hypothesised that elasticities vary substantially between the heating and cooling seasons. Previous work by Acton, Mitchell and Sohlberg (1980), Parti and Parti (1980), Archibald, Finifter and Moody (1982), Murray *et al.* (1978) and Garbacz (1984) supports this hypothesis.

The NIECS data base upon which this study, as well as a number of other studies, is based has a basic problem. There is no data for the actual prices that consumers face as a result of strict application of the confidentiality rule. If consumers faced an average price this would not be as much of a problem. However, since consumers face block pricing schemes that most often in the past have been declining block structures, if a simple average price is included in the model in lieu of a more complex price variable that takes account of the changing marginal price and the rate premium, the estimated elasticities may be inaccurate.

In earlier studies Garbacz (1984) constructed a marginal price and a rate premium from available data in NIECS. A criticism of this work is that the actual tariffs were not used to construct the price variables. This chapter re-estimates an earlier model and a new model with adjusted NIECS data. The data is adjusted with reference to the paper by Cowing, Dubin and McFadden (1982). With a high level of confidence, they were able to pinpoint the sample localities for almost all of the data from NIECS. This information has been matched with billing data from Typical Electric Bills and with climatic data from the National Oceanic and Atmospheric Administration (NOAA). The results obtained are quite different in some respects from the original model results, as might be expected. The implication for other work using NIECS without the above adjustments is clear. There may be inaccuracies in model estimates using unadjusted data. Furthermore, the fact that actual prices continue to be withheld by Department of Energy (DOE) in its Residential Energy-Consumption Service (RECS) public data tapes (1979-83) means that the data may be much less useful in modelling at least in the electricity and natural gas areas and possibly in other fuels as well.

## 9.2 MODEL

Given the nature of electric utility rate schedules (for the data base used in this study) residential electricity sales reflect decreasing marginal rates. (Material in this section draws heavily on Garbacz (1984).) Decreasing block rates result in a marginal price paid by households that is negatively related to the quantity purchased. Therefore, to ensure identification of the demand relationship, a price equation is included.

Residential demand for electricity may be looked upon as a derived demand, which is determined by the primary demand for the services of appliances and other electrical devices in the household. Generally, consumption depends upon the stock of electrical appliances, the size of the residence and the intensity with which the appliance stock and residence are used.

Short-run changes in income and price affect electricity consumption by changing the intensity of use of the current appliance stock and residence, whereas, in the long run, households have the opportunity to make adjustments to the appliance stock and residence size as well, mainly in response to changes in income.

The electricity demand equation, the price equation, and the appliance stock equation are:

$$\text{KWH} = a_0\, Y^{a_1} P^{a_2} A^{a_3} X^{a_4} C^{a_5} e^{a_6 U} u_1 \tag{9.1}$$

$$P = b_0\, \text{KWH}^{b_1} e^{b_2 R1} e^{b_3 R3} e^{b_4 R4} e^{b_5 SMSA} u_2 \tag{9.2}$$

$$X = c_0 Y^{c_1} P^{c_2} A^{c_3} C^{c_4} NA^{c_5} e^{c_6 U} u_3 \qquad (9.3)$$

where $e$ is the base of the natural logarithm and $u_n$ is an error term.

Equations (9.1), (9.2) and (9.3) are estimated simultaneously with a two-stage least squares (2SLS) technique. The estimating equations are in log-linear form. Table 9.1 contains the definitions of the variables. This basic model has been used by Garbacz (1984) to estimate seasonal demand. The model is re-estimated with a data base that includes a price variable related to each city in the sample. Also a model employing space conditioning and water heat fuel variables is estimated. The model above is modified to be so estimated with Equation (9.3) dropped and then with Equations (9.2) and (9.3) dropped. Appliance-price interaction terms are used to develop separate space conditioning, water heating and combined space conditioning-water heating price elasticities. These results are contrasted descriptively with previous results, Garbacz (1984), in part 1 of Section 9.4. Part 2 of Section 9.4 presents results of the three-equation model estimated with pooled cross-sectional data. Monthly interaction terms allow direct statistical tests for seasonality. Finally, in part 3 of Section 9.4, tests are constructed to determine if the new price data provides additional information over the old price data.

*Table* 9.1 Variable definitions

| *Variable* | *Definition* |
|---|---|
| KWH | Use per month per household (KWh) |
| *P* | Marginal price ($ per KWh) per survey area |
| *X* | Appliance stock index of the household |
| *Y* | Gross family income in $ for 1977 (divided by 12) plus or minus the rate premium |
| *A* | Average price ($ per 1000 Btu) of the fuels most used other than electricity within the survey area |
| *CDD* | Cooling degree days (65°F base). If *CDD* =0, then *CDD* = 0.001 |
| *HDD* | Heating degree days (65°F base). If *HDD* = 0, then *HDD* = 0.001 |
| *C* | Either *CDD* or *HDD* or both |
| *SMSA* | Dummy variable for urbanisation. 1 = other; 0 = *SMSA* |

*Table* 9.1 Variable definitions *cont'd*

| | |
|---|---|
| *R*1 | Dummy variable for location. 1 = Census Region North East; 0 = other. |
| *R*2 | Dummy variable for location. 1 = Census Region North Central; 0 = other. Held as the comparison variable. |
| *R*3 | Dummy variable for location. 1 = Census Region South; 0 = other. |
| *R*4 | Dummy variable for location. 1 = Census Region West; 0 = other. |
| *U* | Dummy variable for intensity of use of appliance stock. 1 = households with 3 or more members and the household head aged 29–59; 0 = other. |
| *NA* | Age of the household head |
| *AC* | Dummy variable. 1 = electricity used as main fuel for space cooling. 0 = other. |
| *EL* | Dummy variable. 1 = electricity used as main fuel for space heating. 0 = other. |
| *HW* | Dummy variable. 1 = electric water heater. 0 = other. |
| *B* | Dummy variable. 1 = both *AC* and *HW* or *EL* and *HW* in place. 0 = other. |
| *ACP* | $AC \cdot P$ |
| *ELP* | $EL \cdot P$ |
| *HWP* | $HW \cdot P$ |
| *BP* | $B \cdot P$ |

An application of the Nordin (1976) adjustment is used in the estimating equations. Since there is a premium paid by the consumer to gain access to the last consumption block (to which the marginal price is applied if the last block is accessed) Nordin has argued convincingly that this premium should be treated as an income effect and that it should carry a negative sign. To properly estimate the equations, then it is necessary to subtract this premium from income. The income variable, *Y*, therefore, is different by this amount (less in the case of declining block structure, more in the case of increasing block structure, and without effect for level pricing) than gross family income. The price variable will be marginal price as calculated from Typical Electric Bills using the 250, 500 and 1000 kWh blocks and matching the correct block to the level of consumption.

Equation (9.1), the demand equation, is a key equation since it generates the elasticity estimates. Marginal price appears as an independent, endogenous variable. Exogenous variables in Equation (9.1) are 'Nordin adjusted' gross family income, average price of alternative fuels, and climate variables.

Equation (9.2), the price equation, relates marginal price per kWh to kWh demanded per month, to a dummy variable for urbanization, and to dummy variables for region. An urbanisation variable is included to reflect the effects of population density on transmission and distribution costs. This variable might also capture part of the rate subsidy for rural electric cooperatives. The dummy variables for region are designed to reflect the differences in prices between regions. Three regional variables are used with the fourth region, North Central, held as the comparison variable.

Equation (9.3), the appliance stock equation, relates an index of appliances (estimates of typical usage) to marginal price per kWh, to income, to average price of alternative fuels, to climate, to age of the household head and to an intensity of use dummy variable. While the inclusion of estimates for room conditioning and hot water heat incorporate some lumpiness into the index, this approach is a viable and simple method for treating appliance stock.

Potential usages are estimated by category by regressing yearly Btu usage on dummy variables for room conditioning and water heater appliances for various residence sizes as defined by number of rooms (1–4, 5–6, 7 or more). The data is divided into three parts, one for each group of residence size, and each OLS regression is computed. The assumption is that residence size and room and water conditioning equipment decisions are joint decisions. The basic concept of the index of appliances is as an alternative to several (or joint) endogenous dummy variables for appliance stock (see McFadden *et al.*, (1977)).

The index of appliance is the result of the author's estimates and estimates by Response Analysis Corporation (US Department of Energy, 1981). The estimates seem to be reasonable in comparison with estimates of usage for major appliances from data for 1978–79 (US Department of Energy (1980)).

The estimated coefficients for income and price in Equation (9.1) are partial elasticities. Total elasticities of demand may be generated directly by reduced form equations or may be derived from the structural equations. Total elasticity estimates may approximate the long-run concept, in that differences in electricity demand across households are due to differences in intensity of use, residence size and appliance stock.

## 9.3 DATA

The United States Department of Energy's National Interim Energy Consumption Survey (NIECS) is the data base. The NIECS data contain 4081 household observation units surveyed for 1978–79. About 95 per cent of the surveys are the result of personal interviews. The remainder were carried out by mail.

The sample is a representative area probability sample of the contiguous United States. A unique feature of the survey is that utilities cooperated in providing detailed use and price data for almost all (95 per cent) of the respondents.

Subsets of respondents are developed to test the previously described model. Respondents who lived in single family detached homes, single family attached homes, apartments, and mobile homes are included.

## 9.4 RESULTS

### 1. Monthly Cross-Sectional Results

Table 9.2 shows the old results and Table 9.3 has the new results for the basic model. A comparison of the coefficients obtained with the adjusted data to the results with unadjusted data is in order.

The new results have price elasticities that are generally higher, though not in all cases. All of the coefficients are statistically significant at the 0.001 level except for June and July which are significant at the 0.05 level. The old results had three months (June, July and October) that did not have significant results at the 0.10 level or much higher levels. Finally, the new results are at very similar magnitudes for all months except June, July and December. Therefore, the seasonal effects are not as prominent though they still appear since June and July exhibit low elasticities and winter months have much higher elasticities. However, if we did not have these low elasticities in June and July, the obvious seasonal variation in elasticity would almost disappear. This is perhaps an intuitively appealing result if we have truly accounted for all the seasonal factors that would cause elasticity to diverge. Presumably, the reason that June and July cannot be shaken from their low levels is that there is no good fuel substitute for electric air-conditioning.

*Table* 9.2 Direct elasticities – demand equation*

| *Variable* | *April* | *May* | *June* | *July* | *August* | *September* | *October* | *November* | *December* | *January* | *February* | *March* |
|---|---|---|---|---|---|---|---|---|---|---|---|---|
| Constant | 2.396[a] | 1.182[b] | 0.0706[d] | 0.760[d] | 0.491 | 0.726[d] | 1.229[b] | 1.643[a] | 1.961[a] | 2.546[a] | 2.541[a] | 2.819[a] |
| | (0.377) | (0.378) | (0.419) | (0.418) | (0.486) | (0.407) | (0.409) | (0.311) | (0.372) | (0.421) | (0.362) | (0.447) |
| *P* | –0.593[a] | –298[a] | –0.075 | 0.036 | –0.171[c] | –0.127[c] | 0.045 | –0.395[a] | –0.312[a] | –0.395[a] | –0.488[a] | –261[b] |
| | (0.091) | (0.081) | (0.081) | (0.088) | (1.101) | (0.073) | (0.074) | (0.078) | (0.084) | (0.104) | (0.086) | (0.092) |
| *Y* | 0.155[a] | 0.037 | 0.082[b] | 0.071[c] | 0.088[c] | 0.062[c] | –0.052 | 0.023 | 0.018 | 0.051[c] | 0.084[a] | 0.022 |
| | (0.033) | (0.027) | (0.031) | (0.032) | (0.035) | (0.030) | (0.028) | (0.023) | (0.025) | (0.029) | (0.024) | (0.029) |
| *A* | 0.162[a] | 0.002 | –0.163 | –0.143 | –0.124 | –0.085 | –0.050 | 0.049 | 0.094[d] | 0.230[a] | 0.284[a] | 0.222[a] |
| | (0.047) | (0.048) | (0.056) | (0.056) | (0.066) | (0.054) | (0.054) | (0.041) | (0.049) | (0.055) | (0.048) | (0.058) |
| *X* | 0.408[b] | 0.938[a] | 0.922[a] | 1.050[a] | 0.922[a] | 1.011[a] | 1.295[a] | 0.832[a] | 0.930[a] | 0.830[a] | 0.801[a] | 0.922[a] |
| | (0.132) | (0.108) | (0.118) | (0.125) | (0.136) | (0.115) | (0.108) | (0.094) | (0.101) | (0.117) | (0.100) | (0.111) |
| *U* | 0.181[a] | 0.221[a] | 0.201[a] | 0.311[a] | 0.252[a] | 0.301[a] | 0.217[a] | 0.255[a] | 0.226[a] | 0.182[a] | 0.212[a] | 0.180[a] |
| | (0.026) | (0.027) | (0.029) | (0.029) | (0.033) | (0.027) | (0.029) | (0.023) | (0.026) | (0.030) | (0.026) | (0.030) |
| *HDD* | –0.005 | –0.003 | –0.049 | –0.046 | –0.045 | –0.030 | –0.000 | –0.007 | –0.004 | –0.009 | –0.011 | –0.024 |
| | (0.002) | (0.003) | (0.003) | (0.003) | (0.003) | (0.003) | (0.003) | (0.002) | (0.003) | (0.004) | (0.002) | (0.004) |
| *CDD* | 0.013[a] | 0.015[a] | 0.044[a] | 0.030[a] | 0.020[a] | 0.020[a] | –0.002 | –0.008 | 0.001 | –0.022 | –0.004 | –0.001 |
| | (0.003) | (0.003) | (0.004) | (0.003) | (0.004) | (0.003) | (0.003) | (0.002) | (0.003) | (0.005) | (0.007) | (0.006) |
| *N* | 2355 | 2346 | 2338 | 2419 | 2459 | 2608 | 2627 | 2664 | 2616 | 2458 | 2635 | 2581 |
| *F* | 173.3 | 165.7 | 143.0 | 188.9 | 130.5 | 194.2 | 118.0 | 231.6 | 161.4 | 137.8 | 216.6 | 124.0 |
| $R^2$ | 0.341 | 0.332 | 0.301 | 0.354 | 0.272 | 0.343 | 0.240 | 0.379 | 0.302 | 0.283 | 0.366 | 0.252 |

*Notes*: *Standard errors in parentheses.
[a] Significant at 0.001 level.
[b] Significant at 0.01 level.
[c] Significant at 0.05 level.
[d] Significant at 0.10 level.

*Table* 9.3 Direct elasticities – demand equation: new results

| *Variables* | *April* | *May* | *June* | *July* | *August* | *September* | *October* | *November* | *December* | *January* | *February* | *March* |
|---|---|---|---|---|---|---|---|---|---|---|---|---|
| Constant | 6.060[a] | 4.723[a] | 1.617[d] | 0.439 | 1.311[d] | 5.258[a] | 6.451[a] | 6.738[a] | 7.247[a] | 6.992[a] | 6.187[a] | 6.660[a] |
| *P* | −0.508[a] | −0.573[a] | −0.223[c] | −0.158[c] | −0.533[a] | −0.628[a] | −0.635[a] | −0.627[a] | −0.722[a] | −0.599[a] | −0.477[a] | −0.449[a] |
| *Y* | 0.138[a] | 0.075[b] | 0.092[b] | 0.084[c] | 0.097[b] | 0.071[b] | 0.115[a] | 0.092[a] | 0.120[a] | 0.089[a] | 0.040[c] | 0.143[a] |
| *A* | 0.246[a] | 0.106[b] | −0.145 | −0.103 | −0.158 | 0.196[a] | 0.215[a] | 0.237[a] | 0.284[a] | 0.365[a] | 0.325[a] | 0.387[a] |
| *X* | 0.236[c] | 0.492[a] | 0.819[a] | 1.002[a] | 0.652[a] | 0.467[a] | 0.194[d] | 0.235[c] | 0.129 | 0.373[b] | 0.653[a] | 0.225[d] |
| *U* | 0.171[a] | 0.145[a] | 0.165[a] | 0.229[a] | 0.177[a] | 0.195[a] | 0.183[a] | 0.189[a] | 0.163[a] | 0.139[a] | 0.167[a] | 0.195[a] |
| *CDD* | 0.015[a] | 0.055[a] | 0.028[b] | 0.153[a] | 0.235[a] | 0.084[a] | 0.012[a] | −0.003 | 0.008[a] | −0.014 | −0.018 | 0.012[b] |
| *HDD* | 0.020[a] | −0.018 | −0.036 | −0.028 | −0.0233 | −0.006 | −0.002 | −0.030 | 0.003 | −0.030 | −0.083 | 0.039[d] |
| *N* | 2198 | 2265 | 2293 | 2419 | 2395 | 2108 | 2499 | 2523 | 2571 | 2492 | 2541 | 2462 |
| *F* | 252.3 | 329.6 | 200.8 | 223.2 | 279.9 | 317.44 | 310.4 | 346.4 | 271.7 | 222.8 | 302.87 | 165.40 |
| $R^2$ | 0.446 | 0.506 | 0.381 | 0.393 | 0.451 | 0.514 | 0.466 | 0.491 | 0.426 | 0.386 | 0.456 | 0.321 |

*Notes*: [a] Significant at 0.001 level.
[b] Significant at 0.01 level.
[c] Significant at 0.05 level.
[d] Significant at 0.10 level.

Nordin adjusted income shows a much stronger statistical significance over the twelve months than previously. The order of magnitude, however, is not very much higher than before.

The coefficients for substitute fuel price are much more powerful statistically and in terms of supporting a seasonal elasticity trend. As before the elasticities are quite small and statistically not significant for June, July and August. But for every other month but one, the results are significant at the 0.001 level (May at 0.01 level). Also, there is a generally sustained rise in elasticity from months in which fuel substitution is difficult from months in which substitution is more reasonable (summer to winter).

The appliance stock index is much reduced in magnitude with the exception of June and July. Apparently *X* was picking up some of the price or climatic effect in the unadjusted data for ten of the months. This is the only coefficient that has such a drastic reduction in magnitude.

In general, the use coefficient is reduced in size from the previous estimates. However, the magnitude was already relatively small. It is difficult to spot any trend here.

The old results showed little climatic impact. This is found again with the new results, but there are some differences. Five more months have statistically significant results. The magnitudes are generally little different from zero, except for CDD in July, August and September, which appear to be reasonable values.

Now turn to Table 9.4 for a review of the results of appliance specific seasonal elasticities. OLS and 2SLS models are estimated for July and January. The results of the OLS models are not unexpected. Appliance specific elasticities are calculated by adding the coefficient on *ACP*, which represents the difference between *ACP* and *P*, to the coefficient on *P* (other electricity use elasticity) to obtain the elasticity for air conditioning use. Other appliance-specific elasticities are derived in like fashion. In general, the appliance-specific elasticities seem too high. The elasticities for combined appliances in each month seem to be the most reasonable, though these may still be too high. All other results seem reasonable. The $R^2$, of course, is quite high when there is no adjustment for the simultaneity problem.

When 2SLS is used to develop a demand and a price equation to take account of simultaneity in a declining block regime the appliance specific elasticities are substantially reduced. The interaction terms are created in an intermediate step between the first stage and second stage equation estimates. The elasticity for combined appliances in July is not unlike other results obtained using the unadjusted data. However, space conditioning elasticities are much higher than those reported using unadjusted NIECS data or WMCS data.

*Table* 9.4 Elasticity estimates – new models (adjusted data)

| *Variables* | *OLS* | | *2SLS* | |
|---|---|---|---|---|
| | *July* | *January* | *July* | *January* |
| Constant | 4.362[a] | 8.204[a] | 4.150[a] | 5.468[a] |
| *P* | −0.891[a] | −0.989[a] | −0.947[a] | −0.698[a] |
| *ACP* | 0.124[a] | – | 0.412[a] | – |
| *ELP* | – | 0.089 | – | 0.341[b] |
| *HWP* | 0.098[b] | 0.111[a] | 0.445[a] | 0.564[a] |
| *BP* | 0.377[a] | 0.564[a] | 0.807[a] | 1.597[a] |
| *Y* | 0.204[a] | 0.112[a] | 0.182[a] | 0.163[a] |
| *A* | −0.040 | 0.310[a] | −0.106 | 0.090[d] |
| *U* | 0.183[a] | 0.107[a] | 0.246[a] | 0.253[a] |
| *HDD* | – | −0.001 | – | 0.086[b] |
| *CDD* | 0.192[a] | – | 0.155[a] | – |
| *N* | 2419 | 2493 | 2419 | 2493 |
| *F* | 618.4 | 730.0 | 186.6 | 190.8 |
| $R^2$ | 0.672 | 0.702 | 0.383 | 0.381 |

*Notes*: [a] Significant at 0.001 level.
[b] Significant at 0.01 level.
[c] Significant at 0.05 level.
[d] Significant at 0.10 level.

Table 9.5 contains the results for the OLS and 2SLS models with unadjusted data. Comparing the $R^2$ values of Table 9.4 with those of Table 9.3, we find that the unadjusted data yields a much lower explanatory power. Also, in Table 9.4, results of OLS and 2SLS models appear to yield results that are much closer to one another for appliance specific elasticities than in the case of the models using adjusted data. This might lead the unwary researcher to conclude that simultaneity was not too much of a problem and need not be adjusted for. Finally, the results for 2SLS models with unadjusted data are similar in some respects and dissimilar in other respects to results with adjusted data. The fact that the two models generate price elasticities for air conditioning and water heater that are similar for July is somewhat remarkable. However, the price elasticities for both appliances (*BP*) and for *P* are quite different for July.

*Table* 9.5 Elasticity estimates – new models (unadjusted data)

| *Variables* | *OLS* | | *2SLS* | |
|---|---|---|---|---|
| | *July* | *January* | *July* | *January* |
| Constant | 3.910[a] | 2.735[a] | 2.904[a] | 3.349[a] |
| *P* | −0.320[a] | −0.522[a] | −0.390[a] | −0.189[c] |
| *ACP* | −0.186[a] | - | −0.199[a] | - |
| *ELP* | - | −0.068 | - | −0.093[c] |
| *HWP* | −0.108[a] | −0.118[a] | −0.187[a] | −0.177[a] |
| *BP* | −0.261[a] | −0.335[a] | −0.308[a] | −0.437[a] |
| *Y* | 0.203 | 0.228[a] | 0.194[a] | 0.231[a] |
| *A* | 0.121[c] | 0.011 | −0.016 | −0.057 |
| *U* | 0.346[a] | 0.269[a] | 0.332[a] | 0.305[a] |
| *HDD* | - | −0.008 | - | −0.012 |
| *CDD* | 0.002 | - | 0.001 | - |
| *N* | 1969 | 2011 | 1969 | 2011 |
| *F* | 151.3 | 179.4 | 121.7 | 114.4 |
| $R^2$ | 0.382 | 0.418 | 0.332 | 0.314 |

*Notes:* [a] Significant at 0.001 level.
[b] Significant at 0.01 level.
[c] Significant at 0.05 level.
[d] Significant at 0.10 level.

For January, the results are similar also for space heat and water heat for the two models, but not for both appliances (*BP*) or *P*. In both months, climate has a statistically significant impact on the model with adjusted data.

## 2. A Seasonality Test With Pooled Cross-sectional Data

In earlier work, Garbacz (1986) developed a simple test for seasonality. This involved estimating the basic three-equation model discussed here with a pooled cross-sectional data base using an unadjusted price variable. Equations for each month were then estimated. An F-test was then applied that rejected the hypothesis of equal coefficients with a high level of statistical significance.

The present section goes a step beyond this earlier work. A model is estimated for pooled cross-sectional data (with adjusted prices) that includes interaction variables for each of eleven months with the twelfth month held as the comparison variable. This allows for a specific *t*-test on each variable in each month. The results are contained in Table 9.6.

As in the case of the monthly equations of the previous section in Table 9.3, the price elasticities for June and July are much lower than in other months. All other months have the same price elasticity except for October and November which have elasticities in the −0.72 range.

Income and use elasticities are the same for each month. The climate variables are stable and of low values. These results are similar to the results in Table 9.3.

The elasticity for substitute prices, *A*, is the same for all months except September, January, February and March. In September, the coefficient approaches zero. However, in the other three months the elasticity goes up substantially. This reflects the increased possibility of substitution in winter months as opposed to other months. Similar results appear in Table 9.3, but the results of Table 9.6 are higher.

Finally, the appliance stock variable has an elasticity that is the same for all months except for June, July and August, where the elasticity rises sharply. Apparently, the appliance stock variable is much more sensitive to cooling needs. The results from Table 9.3 show much more variability than those of Table 9.6, though the summer elasticities are similar.

### 3. The Appropriate Price Variable

It is argued in Section 9.1 that data including actual prices is better than data for which prices are constructed after the fact. This is an argument that most economists will generally agree with. However, not everyone may be convinced by what appears to be obvious. There is good reason to be cautious as the economic literature has taught us on numerous occasions.

In this section two formal tests of the appropriate price variable are constructed. The first test requires the construction of a new variable. This is a dummy variable that represents 1 when the difference between the unadjusted price variable and the actual price variable is equal to some minimum difference. There is no way to determine what the 'correct'

*Table* 9.6 Direct elasticities – demand: pooled cross-section results

| *Variables* | *April* | *May* | *June* | *July* | *August* | *September* | *October* | *November* | *December* | *January* | *February* | *March* |
|---|---|---|---|---|---|---|---|---|---|---|---|---|
| Constant | 3.351[a] | 3.351[a] | 0.303[a] | 0.135[a] | 0.410[a] | 1.397[b] | 3.351[a] | 3.351[a] | 3.351[a] | 5.059[b] | 3.351[a] | 4.927[b] |
| *P* | −0.462[a] | −0.462[a] | −0.166[c] | −0.082[b] | −0.462[a] | −0.462[a] | −0.712[c] | −0.737[c] | −0.462[a] | −0.462[a] | −0.462[a] | −0.462[a] |
| *Y* | 0.079[a] | 0.079[a] | 0.079[a] | 0.079[a] | 0.079[a] | 0.079[a] | 0.079[a] | 0.079[a] | 0.079[a] | 0.079[a] | 0.079[a] | 0.079[a] |
| *A* | 0.250[a] | 0.250[a] | 0.250[a] | 0.250[a] | 0.250[a] | 0.017[a] | 0.250[a] | 0.250[a] | 0.250[a] | 0.511[a] | 0.398[d] | 0.449[b] |
| *X* | 0.479[a] | 0.479[a] | 0.897[b] | 1.080[a] | 0.791[c] | 0.479[a] | 0.479[a] | 0.479[a] | 0.479[a] | 0.479[a] | 0.479[a] | 0.479[a] |
| *U* | 0.178[a] | 0.178[a] | 0.178[a] | 0.178[a] | 0.178[a] | 0.178[a] | 0.178[a] | 0.178[a] | 0.178[a] | 0.178[a] | 0.178[a] | 0.178[a] |
| *CDD* | 0.005[b] | 0.020[b] | 0.052[b] | 0.043[b] | 0.027[b] | 0.020[b] | 0.005[b] | 0.005[b] | 0.005[b] | 0.005[b] | 0.005[b] | 0.005[b] |
| *HDD* | 0.006[b] | 0.006[b] | 0.006[b] | 0.006[b] | 0.006[b] | 0.006[b] | 0.012[d] | 0.006[b] | 0.012[d] | 0.006[b] | 0.006[b] | 0.006[b] |

$F = 141.1$
$R^2 = 0.261$
$N = 29196$

*Notes*: [a] Significant at 0.001 level.
[b] Significant at 0.01 level.
[c] Significant at 0.05 level.
[d] Significant at 0.10 level.

difference should be because we do not know the sensitivity of the model to varying levels of difference. Some threshold value might be required. Therefore, a grid search is undertaken. Dummy variables are defined through a range of possible differences. The levels selected were \$0.001, \$0.005, \$0.01, \$0.02, and \$0.03 per kWh of difference between the calculated price and the actual price.

The full model with unadjusted data was then estimated separately with each dummy variable included. Table 9.7 shows the results for all three equations. Table 9.8 reports the results for each dummy variable and each old price. In every case $D$ is found to be statistically significant at the 0.001 level. Note the remarkable stability of the coefficients for $D$ as well as $P$.

It is concluded from this test that the differences in price provide important information to the model. Without this information it appears that the model will tend to underestimate the price elasticity of demand.

A second test is conducted that is the same as the first test except now the model is restricted. The model is estimated as in Table 9.7 with $D$ excluded. Then the coefficients of the model are restricted to these estimates, the dummy variables are added one at a time and the model is estimated five separate times. The result is a grid search as in the first test, except now the dummy variable is the only variable in the model that is allowed to contribute additional explanatory power. There is no interaction between the variables that might mask the true effect of the dummy variable.

These results are reported under part B of Table 9.8. All of the dummies measuring differences of \$0.005 or more are highly significant. Only in the case of the \$0.001 difference is the dummy variable not significant. Since almost 93 per cent of the differences are \$0.005 or more, this 'threshold effect' is of little importance for this particular case. However, if the magnitude of the difference in prices is important, this may have bearing on other data sets or other years of this series.

## 9.5 CONCLUSIONS

It has been shown that a model using an adjusted data base (accounting for 'secret' or confidential block price data) leads to substantially different results than a model using unadjusted data. This result has important implications for research in the residential energy area – most notably in regard to electricity and natural gas. By now, much work has been published in this area and much is in progress. Without having available the actual tariffs and climate data, models using the RECS data are in jeopardy.

*Table* 9.7 The model without restrictions

| *Variable* | *Demand equation* | *Price equation* | *Appliance stock equation* |
|---|---|---|---|
| Constant | 1.640[a] | 1.990[a] | 0.904[a] |
| *KWH* | | −0.169[a] | |
| *P* | −0.223[a] | | −0.687[a] |
| *D* | −0.285[a] | | −0.135[a] |
| *Y* | −0.014 | | 0.270[a] |
| *A* | 0.092[a] | | 0.298[a] |
| *R*1 | | 0.120[a] | |
| *R*3 | | −0.102[a] | |
| *R*4 | | −0.291[a] | |
| *SMSA* | | −0.151[a] | |
| *X* | 1.221[a] | | |
| *U* | 0.193[a] | | 0.074[a] |
| *NA* | | | 0.196[a] |
| *CDD* | 0.002[c] | | 0.003[a] |
| *HDD* | −0.016 | | 0.001[a] |
| *F* | 1136.7 | 591.8 | 1189.8 |
| $R^2$ | 0.251 | 0.098 | 0.259 |

*Notes*: [a] Significant at 0.001 level.
[b] Significant at 0.01 level.
[c] Significant at 0.05 level.
[d] Significant at 0.10 level.

Variable estimates and policy implications must be used with extreme caution.

In order to correct the current situation, the Department of Energy (DOE) should make available the actual tariff schedules, TEB schedules, their own error innoculated block marginal prices and actual climatic data to determine which set of data allows the best model development. Confidentiality and cost efficiency can be protected by allowing researchers to submit preprogrammed models to be run against the various data sets. A small amount of funds could be set aside by DOE or individual researchers could contract for the services of the DOE.

*Table* 9.8 Test of the appropriate price variable

| | | | | | |
|---|---|---|---|---|---|
| A. Grid search without restrictions | | | | | |
| Variable/$ per KWH difference | 0.001 | 0.005 | 0.01 | 0.02 | 0.03 |
| *D* | −0.380[a] | −0.285[a] | −0.229[a] | −0.257[a] | −0.238[a] |
| Standard error | (0.040) | (0.018) | (0.013) | (0.009) | (0.010) |
| *P* | −0.241[a] | −0.223[a] | −0.197[a] | −0.148[a] | −0.219[a] |
| Standard error | (0.043) | (0.043) | (0.043) | (0.043) | (0.043) |
| B. Grid search with restrictions | | | | | |
| Variable/$ per KWH difference | 0.001 | 0.005 | 0.01 | 0.02 | 0.03 |
| *D* | −0.0039 | −0.018[a] | −0.035[a] | −0.039[a] | −0.043[a] |
| Standard error | (0.0046) | (0.005) | (0.005) | (0.004) | (0.005) |
| C. Distribution of the dummy variable | | | | | |
| Descriptive statistics/$ per KWH difference | 0.001 | 0.005 | 0.01 | 0.02 | 0.03 |
| Mean | 0.986 | 0.928 | 0.836 | 0.543 | 0.292 |
| Standard deviation | 0.117 | 0.258 | 0.370 | 0.498 | 0.455 |

*Note*: [a]Significant at the 0.001 level.

This chapter is the only model available that makes use of the actual price data as developed by Cowing, Dubin and McFadden (1981). Model results are quite different than previous results with the same model and data (minus correct prices). A formal statistical test is developed to test for seasonality. The basic finding is that seasonality of elasticities still exists in the case of price, substitute price and appliance stock, but the degree of seasonality is substantially moderated.

## Notes

I have been attempting to gain access to the actual electricity tariffs through the Residential Energy Consumption Survey (RECS) for some time. It seemed preferable to me to use the latest data (now available for 1982–83 with a longitudinal set) for estimation. My proposal was to run several models against the RECS data in blind runs administered by DOE. This would protect confidentiality as well as allow the best model estimation. Of course, it would also provide a controlled test of whether the actual tariff data made any difference in comparison to calculated marginal prices or marginal prices made available on the tape but error innoculated. I had known about the Cowing, Dubin and McFadden (1982) paper for some time, but when it was suggested to me in comments at the 1984 American Economic Association Meetings on another paper of mine (see revised paper under new title, Garbacz (1986) by Paul Joskow and Daniel McFadden) that actual tariffs should be used with the NIECS data, it jogged my memory. Later, after negotiation to acquire access to confidential data at the DOE bogged down, I decided that the adjusted NIECS might be a way to show that access to the confidential data was essential. John Trapani, Jeremy Bloom, Michael Crew, Ali Parhizgari and Erick Erickson provided valuable comments and suggestions on several versions of this paper. The author, of course, is responsible for what remains.

## References

ACTON, Jan Paul, MITCHELL, B. M. and SOHLBERG, R. (1980) 'Estimating Residential Electricity Demand Under Declining-Block Tariffs: An Econometric Study Using Micro-Data', *Applied Economics*, vol. 13, no. 1, April, pp. 145–61.

ARCHIBALD, Robert B., FINIFTER, D. H. and MOODY, C. E. Jr. (1982) 'Seasonal Variation in Residential Electricity Demand: Evidence from Survey Data', *Applied Economics*, vol. 14, no. 2, April, pp. 167–81.

BEIERLEIN, James G., DUNN, J. W. and McCONNON, J. C. Jr., (1981) 'The Demand for Electricity and Natural Gas in the Northeastern United Stated', *Review of Economics and Statistics*, vol. 63, no. 3, August, pp. 403–8.

COWING, T., DUBIN, J. and McFADDEN, D. (1982) 'The NIECS Data Base and Its Use In Residential Energy Demand Modelling', Discussion Paper No. 24, MIT-EL 82–041NP, June.

GARBACZ, Christopher (1983) 'A Model of Residential Demand for Electricity Using a National Household Sample', *Energy Economics*, vol. 5, no. 2, April, pp. 124–28.

GARBACZ, Christopher (1984) 'A National Micro-Data Based Model of Residential Electricity Demand: New Evidence on Seasonal Variation', *Southern Economic Journal*, vol. 51, no. 1, pp. 235–49.

GARBACZ, Christopher (1985) 'Residential Demand for Fuelwood', *Energy Economics*, vol. 7, no. 3, July, pp. 191–3.

GARBACZ, Christopher (1986) 'Seasonal and Regional Residential Electricity Demand', *The Energy Journal* (forthcoming).

McFADDEN, Daniel, PUIG, C. and KIRSCHNER, D. (1977) 'Determinants of the Long-Run Demand for Electricity', in *American Statistical Association, 1977 Proceedings of the Business and Economics Statistics Section (Part 2)*, pp. 109–14.

MURRAY, Michael P., SPANN, R., PULLEY, L. and Beauvais, E. (1978) 'The Demand for Electricity in Virginia', *Review of Economics and Statistics*, vol. 60, no. 4, November, pp. 585–600.

NORDIN, John (1976) 'A Proposed Modification of Taylor's Demand Analysis: Comment', *The Bell Journal of Economics*, vol. 7, no. 2, Autumn, pp. 719–21.

PARTI, Michael and PARTI, C. (1980) 'The Total and Appliance-Specific Conditional Demand for Electricity in the Household Sector', *The Bell Journal of Economics*, vol. 11, no. 1, Spring, pp. 309–21.

US DEPARTMENT OF ENERGY (1980) *Residential Energy Consumption Survey: Consumption and Expenditures. April 1978 through March 1979* (Appendices A,B,C,D) DOE/EA-0207/5. (Washington, DC.: Department of Energy).

US DEPARTMENT OF ENERGY (1981) *National Interim Energy Consumption Survey: Report on Methodology, Part III, Household and Utility Company Surveys.* Appendices B-G (Prepared by Response Analysis Corporation, Princeton.) Office of the Consumption Data System, EIA (Washington, DC: Department of Energy).

# 10 A Life-cycle Study of Commercial Cogeneration/Cooling: a State-of-the-art of Gas Technology

Richard L. Itteilag
and Christina A. Swanson

## 10.1 INTRODUCTION

The prospects for commercial gas cooling have improved dramatically over the last few years. There are four basic reasons for this change: (1) gas prices have declined; (2) the gas supply outlook is now very positive; (3) electricity prices continue to increase - particularly the price of electricity during peak usage periods; and, (4) a new generation of high-efficiency gas cooling systems is available in the domestic market, including heat recovery absorption units that can be coupled with gas cogeneration systems.

The increased use of commercial gas cooling could offer significant benefits to both the natural gas and electric utility industries and to their customers. For the gas and electric industries, gas cooling provides a means of more closely balancing their summer and winter loads, thereby permitting more efficient system operation. This might be especially important to the electric utilities, since summertime cooling energy demands contribute heavily to the need for costly new generation capacity. For commercial cooling customers, the switch to gas cooling could substantially reduce the summertime electricity price premiums imposed in many electric rate schedules in the form of summer/winter rate differentials, time-of-day rates, and peak demand charges.

The purpose of this chapter is to examine the economic competitiveness of direct gas-fired double-effect absorption chiller/heaters against electric chillers/gas boilers in the commercial market. The analysis evaluates the annualised energy and life-cycle costs of the two types of systems across three size categories in five areas of the United States that have different cooling loads and relative gas versus electricity prices. In addition, the analysis examines the energy cost benefits of including absorption cooling in gas cogeneration systems for relatively large commercial applications.

## 10.2 BACKGROUND

### 1. The Commercial Cooling Market

Commercial energy demand for space cooling can be expected to grow significantly in the future as the commercial sector itself expands. An American Gas Association (AGA) analysis has projected that real output in the commercial sector will grow at an average annual rate of three per cent through the end of this decade.[1] Because the commercial sector is highly labour-intensive, this level of projected economic growth implies continued expansion of commercial employment and, in turn, of commercial building space. The addition of new commercial floor-space should significantly augment existing cooling energy demand.

While the demand for commercial space cooling is increasing, the price differential between gas and electricity for cooling energy usage is steadily becoming more favourable to gas. In contrast to the recent decline in gas prices, a number of factors have created upward pressure on electricity prices and especially on prices applicable to peak usage periods. In general, the costs of constructing new base-load electric generation plants have soared over the last decade and these costs are being passed through to rate-payers.

In addition, demand management has become a key strategy at some electric utilities for balancing their loads and minimising peak requirements which, in most areas, occur during the summer months when cooling demand is high. Some utilities are attempting to discourage peak usage by implementing rate structures that include provisions such as summer/winter rate differentials, time-of-day rates, and demand 'ratchet' clauses. These innovative electric rate structures can greatly enhance the economic attractiveness of gas cooling.

A summer-peaking utility that imposes a summer/winter rate differential will charge a premium price for summertime electricity usage in at least one block of the demand or energy rate schedule. The customer, therefore, can counteract this price penalty only by reducing electricity usage throughout the summer months. In a time-of-day rate schedule, the customer is charged different rates for electricity used at times that the utility designates as 'on-peak' and 'off-peak' (and, in some cases, 'mid-peak'), with the highest rate accruing to the on-peak hours. Under this type of rate structure, the customer can mitigate the price penalty only by reducing electricity usage during the on-peak hours of each day, either by lowering his overall electricity needs or shifting the consumption pattern to the off-peak hours.

It is the demand charge, however, that may have the greatest impact on the commercial customer's electricity bill during the cooling season, since the demand charge is a basic component of most commercial electric rate schedules. The monthly demand charge is based on a building's maximum period of electrical demand (measured in kilowatts) recorded over a 'demand interval' established by the utility. The most commonly used demand interval is 15 minutes. Thus, in most cases, the highest 15 minute period of electrical demand recorded for a given month will set the demand charge for that month. In many parts of the country, the peak demand level increases dramatically due to the cooling load, thereby greatly increasing the demand charges assessed. Under current electric rate schedules, the demand charge can account for as much as half or more of the commercial customer's monthly electricity bill.

The impact of the demand charge is especially significant when the rate schedule contains a ratchet clause. Such a clause basically stipulates that the level of demand for which a customer will be billed in *any* month will be based on the maximum demand recorded at any time over a specified period, which is frequently the preceding year. Since in most areas maximum demand occurs during the summer when electric cooling equipment is in use, this means that the customer's demand charge during the non-cooling months will be based on some percentage of his summer demand level. In essence, then, the customer is charged over the entire year for a level of electrical demand that actually occurs only during the summer months and is largely attributable to electric space cooling.

## 2. Natural Gas Cooling Systems

During the last few years, a new generation of gas-fired commercial cooling equipment has been introduced into the United States market. Direct-fired double-effect absorption chiller/heaters, which are manufactured in Japan, began to be imported to this country in 1979. Although absorption technology has been in use for many years, the combination of direct gas firing and double-effect absorption technology represents an innovation in the domestic market and offers much greater efficiency in natural gas cooling. Furthermore, the direct gas-fired absorption equipment currently being marketed provides not only space cooling but also space heating. Manufacturers of the direct-fired, double-effect gas absorption systems include Hitachi, which manufactures chiller/heaters for the domestic market in the 100- to 1500-ton range, American Yazaki Corporation, which is marketing 7.5-ton to 100-ton chiller/heaters, and Sanyo Incorporated which is marketing chiller/heaters through Bohn Heat Transfer. At present, some United States manufacturers are also considering offering a gas absorption equipment line in the United States.

Absorption cooling is one of two types of cooling systems used in commercial buildings, the other being mechanical compression systems. The majority of the systems currently in use are mechanical compression systems with electric motors to drive the compressor. Any cooling system consists essentially of a refrigerant circulating in a closed circuit, in which the refrigerant undergoes pressure changes to permit the transfer of heat. The basic difference between the two types of cooling systems is that one utilises a compressor unit and the other an absorber-generator for producing the necessary pressure differences. A double-effect absorption system utilises two generators. In such systems, heat derived from refrigerant vapour boiled from solution in the first-stage generator is used to boil out additional refrigerant in the second generator. This reduces energy use per ton of cooling by about 30–40 per cent compared to single-effect units.[2]

## 3. Natural Gas Cogeneration Systems

Cogeneration is the sequential production of electrical or mechanical energy and useful thermal energy from a single fuel source, such as gas, oil or coal. The fundamental advantage of cogeneration is that such systems capture and use some of the energy that is wasted by conventional systems. Consequently, cogeneration systems require 10 to 30 per cent less fuel than conventional systems that produce electrical and thermal energy separately.[3]

In small gas cogeneration systems (less than 500 kW), internal combustion engines serve as the prime mover. Larger systems can also use gas or steam turbines, the latter coupled with gas boilers. Heat is recovered as a by-product from gas turbines, steam turbines or internal combustion engines, and the recovered heat can then be utilised for absorption air conditioning, for space heating and domestic hot water, or for industrial heating processes.

Although cogeneration systems have been in use since the early 1900s, cogeneration for industrial applications has grown significantly since the mid-1970s. This is especially true in industries with large process heat requirements, such as the chemical, petroleum refining, and paper industries. Furthermore, many economically attractive applications are being identified for commercial buildings.

According to AGA estimates, there are approximately 24.7 gigawatts of cogeneration capacity in operation, in the design/construction phase, or on order. About 44 per cent of the total cogeneration capacity is believed to be gas-fueled, resulting in annual gas demand of approximately 711 billion cubic feet (Bcf). Thus, cogeneration represents one of the most promising emerging markets for commercial buildings.

## 10.3 METHODOLOGY

This analysis compares the annualised costs of gas-fired and electric space cooling systems in hypothetical commercial applications. Specifically, the annualised energy costs (for cooling usage) and the annualised life-cycle costs of direct gas-fired, double-effect absorption chiller/heaters are compared to those of electric chillers (see Appendix A for the formulas used to calculate the annualised costs). Since the gas-fired units are capable of providing both space cooling and heating, the life-cycle cost calculations for electric chillers include the equipment cost for a gas boiler to incorporate the cost of comparable heating capability for the electric systems.

The cost comparisons are made for three different cooling capacities, in five geographical areas of the United States, under three scenarios. The cooling capacities are:

1. 30 tons (or 360 000 Btu per hour of heat removed from the conditioned space), which might typically be required in a building of about 10 500 square feet, such as a small retail store;[4]
2. 250 tons (or 3 000 000 Btu per hour), as might be required in a building of about 87 500 square feet, such as a five- or six-storey office building;
3. 500 tons (or 6 000 000 Btu per hour), which might be required in a building of 175 000 square feet, such as a ten- to twelve-storey office building.

For the 30-ton application, a gas-fired absorption chiller/heater is evaluated against an electric reciprocating chiller, since that type of electric unit is frequently used in small commercial buildings. For the 250- and 500-ton applications, the gas units are compared to electric centrifugal chillers, which are most commonly used in the larger commercial size ranges.

The geographic areas represented in this analysis are the Southwest, Northeast, Mid-Atlantic, Midwest, and Southeast. These areas were chosen to reflect a broad range of climates and cooling requirements which, in conjunction with different relative energy price trends, should indicate the competitive posture of gas chiller/heaters in many potential applications.

To perform the cost calculations, the following data inputs were necessary:

1. estimated equivalent rated full-load hours of operation (EFLH) for each area, which provides an approximation of the number of hours a cooling system would be in use over the cooling season if it were always operating under full-load conditions;
2. expected system lifetime of each type of unit;
3. estimated equipment costs and annual maintenance costs for each system; and
4. operating costs for each unit.

The operating costs are determined by the size (cooling tonnage) and hours of operation of each system in each location and by the following performance characteristics and cost data:

1. for the gas units, gas and electrical requirements per hour of operation, where electrical requirements include auxiliaries, the condenser water pump, and the cooling tower fan;
2. for the electric chillers, electrical requirements per hour of operation for the compressor, condenser water pump, and cooling tower fan;
3. for both types of systems, the make-up water requirement, which in turn depends on the condenser water flow rate and the rates of evaporation and bleed-off;
4. water and sewer costs for each area; and
5. projected gas and electricity prices.

Two of the data inputs – the equivalent full-load hours of operation and the water/sewer costs – had to be based on data specific to particular cities in each area. These cities were chosen to maintain a wide range of climates and cooling requirements. Accordingly, data for Dallas were used in the calculations for the Southwest, for New York in the Northeast, for Washington, DC in the Mid-Atlantic, for Chicago in the Midwest, and for Tampa/St Petersburg in the Southeast.

The estimated equivalent full-load hours of operation were taken from the *1981 Fundamentals Handbook* (Chapter 28: 'Energy Estimating Methods'), published by the American Society of Heating Refrigeration and Air Conditioning Engineers (ASHRAE). That publication contains a range of estimated full-load cooling hours for each city under consideration here. As suggested in the *Handbook*, however, the upper end of each range was used in this analysis since it pertains to commercial rather than residential applications. Although operating costs for both the gas and electric systems were based on full-load performance, actual operating conditions would create varying load factors. Under part-load operating conditions, gas systems would generally show better part-load performance characteristics than electric systems. The operating hours adopted for each area are: 1000 EFLH in New York (the Northeast) and Chicago (the Midwest); 1200 in Washington, DC (the Mid-Atlantic); 1600 in Dallas (The Southwest); and 2700 in Tampa/St Petersburg (the Southeast).

The remaining performance and cost parameters are summarised in Table 10.1. The data provided in that table were obtained from a number of sources, including manufacturer's specifications for different types of cooling systems, trade periodicals, and gas industry personnel with expertise in cooling systems. Formulas were obtained from AGA's *Marketing Manual: Natural Gas Cooling* (see note 3) for calculating the electric requirements for the condenser water pump and cooling tower fan for both the electric and gas units. Additional formulas were taken from the same source for calculating the make-up water requirements, although the condenser water flow rates were taken directly from manufacturers' literature. (The exception in both sets of calculations is the 30-ton gas chiller/heater, for which data were obtained from a gas utility that is currently marketing that type of unit.)

Special note should be taken of some of the cost and performance data used in this analysis. First, a twenty-year system lifetime has been assumed for all of the cooling systems under study. Although actual system lifetimes can vary rather widely depending upon operating conditions, twenty years appears to be consistent, on average, with experience with commercial cooling units. Second, the annual maintenance costs are assumed to be equal for the gas and electric units in each of the three tonnages. Maintenance costs are difficult to estimate in absolute terms. However, the consensus of informed opinion held that, in relative terms, annual preventive maintenance costs should be similar for both types of systems.

*Table* 10.1 Performance and cost parameters for gas-fired chiller/heaters and electric chillers

| | *30-ton units* | | *250-ton units)* | | *500-ton units* | |
|---|---|---|---|---|---|---|
| | *Gas chiller/heater* | *Electric chiller* | *Gas chiller/heater* | *Electric chiller* | *Gas chiller/heater* | *Electric chiller* |
| System life (years) | 20 | 20 | 20 | 20 | 20 | 20 |
| Equipment cost[a] | \$26 000 | \$13 000 | \$104 000 | \$67 500 | \$173 000 | \$107 000 |
| Annual maintenance cost | \$1 000 | \$1 000 | \$1 200 | \$1 200 | \$1 200 | \$1 200 |
| Gas consumption (Btu per hour) | 379 000 | NA | 3 255 560 | NA | 6 520 000 | NA |
| Electrical requirement (kW) | 4.2 | 34.0 | 46.3 | 195.3 | 84.6 | 380.9 |
| compressor | NA | 31.2 | NA | 175.0 | NA | 345.0 |
| other components[b] | 4.2 | 2.8 | 46.3 | 20.3 | 84.6 | 35.9 |
| Make-up water (gallons per hour) | 177 | 106 | 1241 | 810 | 2473 | 1620 |
| Condenser water flow rate (gallons per minute) | 107 | 93 | 1149 | 750 | 2290 | 1500 |

*Notes*: [a]The equipment costs for the electric chillers include the cost of a companion gas boiler for heating as follows: for the 30-ton chiller, the cost of a boiler is \$3300; for the 250-ton chiller, the cost of a boiler is \$14 500; for the 500-ton chiller, the cost of a boiler is \$24 000.

[b]For the gas units, 'other components' include auxiliaries (that is pumps within the unit and controls), the cooling tower fan, and the condenser water pump. For the electric units, other components include the cooling tower fan and the condenser water pump, since cooling capacities for the electric units were listed in the manufacturer's specifications net of auxiliary requirements. Note that with a modestly priced special option which sizes the gas unit's water pump comparably to the electric unit's, the difference in the gas unit's electric requirement for other components over the electric unit's could be offset.

NA = not applicable. See text for a discussion of data sources.

The equipment cost estimates are a more significant component of the cooling systems' life-cycle costs. It therefore must be emphasised that this analysis incorporates *only* the *equipment* costs for the gas and electric units. This was done because of the wide variation that characterises the non-equipment components of installed system costs, which makes it extremely difficult to develop 'representative' installed costs as opposed to site-specific costs. The equipment costs for the gas chiller/heaters, electric chillers, and gas boilers were obtained from gas utility companies located in the South Atlantic, West North Central, West South Central, East South Central, and Pacific Census divisions. The utilities, in turn, obtained the cost data from local equipment distributors and manufacturers' representatives. The equipment cost data presented in Table 10.1 are based on averages of the information submitted by the gas utilities. It is noteworthy that, in most instances, the range of the cost data collected for particular unit types and sizes was quite narrow.

The gas and electricity price projections were taken from the AGA-TERA Base Case 1986-I, which provides projections for each of the nine divisions of the United States defined by the United States Census Bureau.[5] The divisional price projections used were those applicable to each city on which cooling load data were based.

The three scenarios on which the analysis is based are: the Worst Case; the Business-as-Usual (BAU) Case; and the Best Case. These three scenarios differ only with respect to revisions in the energy price projections employed. All other performance and cost parameters are the same across the three cases.

The Worst Case employs the AGA-TERA energy price projections without revision. This implies that gas distribution companies do not offer special commercial rates to encourage greater use of gas cooling. It further implies that the demand charges contained in commercial electric rate schedules are so low that they have little effect on the overall average cost of electricity for commercial cooling (that is the average cost per KWH once both the energy charge per KWH of energy consumption and the demand charge per KW of power demand have been assessed). Given the implication concerning the demand charges, this scenario represents not only the most difficult competitive situation for gas but also the least representative since, as noted earlier, demand charges can account for as much as half of the commercial customer's electricity bill.

The Business-As-Usual Case attempts to construct a more realistic scenario by adjusting the electricity prices upward by 30 per cent in order to account for the impacts of demand charges on the average electricity price. It must be noted that the increased electricity prices were applied only to the electric cooling systems in this scenario. The unrevised AGA-TERA Base Case electricity prices were applied to the electricity usage attributable to the gas chiller/heaters, since the amount of electricity used by the gas units is much lower than that used by the electric chillers, and therefore, is unlikely to have much effect on the demand charge assessed to a commercial customer.

The Best Case incorporates not only the higher electricity prices, but also gas prices that were reduced by 20 per cent to represent the discounted off-peak gas rates that are offered by some utilities to promote commercial gas cooling. In fact, according to an AGA survey, some twenty-five gas distribution companies have special cooling rates in effect for commercial customers.[6] In addition, the respondents to another AGA survey indicated that the average discount currently offered is about 20 per cent below the average firm commercial rate.[7] Thus, from the perspective of the gas industry, this case represents the most promising competitive environment for gas cooling.

This analysis also compares the annualised cooling energy costs calculated for the 500-ton electric centrifugal chiller to those of a 500-ton heat recovery absorption chiller/heater coupled with an 800 KW gas turbine cogeneration system. This comparison was made for each of the three scenarios described above, using the same gas and electricity price projections and with no revisions to the input data or results for the electric chiller.

In many instances, economic evaluations of cogeneration deal with cooling energy costs by estimating the offset electricity costs produced by substituting absorption cooling for conventional electric cooling and including these savings in the total net annual savings (if any) accruing to the use of the cogeneration system. This permits the calculation of measures such as the payback on the cogeneration system's installed cost. This analysis differs in that it attempts to specifically estimate the gas energy costs incurred in operating an absorption cooling unit via a gas cogeneration system over the life-cycle of the system. These costs are then compared, on an annualised basis, to the costs of using a conventional electric chiller for cooling.

As indicated above, the analysis focuses exclusively on the annualised cooling energy costs of the cogeneration/absorption cooling systems rather than on the total annualised life-cycle costs, which include equipment costs, maintenance costs and make-up water costs. This was done due to the difficulty inherent in comparing these additional costs for a 'total energy system' to those which provide cooling and heating but not electricity. Furthermore, the comparison of energy costs should provide an indication of the potential energy cost benefits of including absorption cooling in a cogeneration system, in addition to the fact that absorption cooling provides a means of using the recoverable heat from a cogeneration system as fully as possible.

For the cogeneration configuration, the analysis assumes that an 800 KW gas turbine serves as the prime mover and that cooling is produced by a high-efficiency 500-ton heat recovery chiller/heater. The overall efficiency of the cogeneration system was assumed to be 70 per cent, while the cooling coefficient of performance for the chiller/heater was set at 1.08 (after accounting for electrical energy requirements). These efficiency estimates were obtained through a review of manufacturers' specifications for the relevant systems, especially those published by Solar Turbines Incorporated (a subsidiary of Caterpillar) for the Saturn gas turbine and by Gas Energy Incorporated for the Hitachi PARAFLOW Heat Recovery chiller/heater.

The performance data obtained from these sources results in a gas input estimate of about 7.93 MMBtu per hour to the cogeneration system to produce the energy required to operate the chiller/heater. This is significantly lower than *total* input per hour required to operate the cogeneration system, since the estimate is intended to reflect only that portion of the gas input that will ultimately result in production of cooling energy. Although the hourly gas input for this configuration is considerably higher than that for the direct-fired absorption chiller/heater, the difference in total energy costs between the two systems can be mitigated by the fact that the chiller/heater's electrical requirements can be met by the cogeneration system itself, while the direct-fired unit must draw on the electric utility for necessary electricity inputs.

## 10.4 RESULTS

For the Worst Case, the BAU Case, and the Best Case, Table 10.2 provides the ratio of the annualised energy costs of gas cooling to electric cooling under each scenario, while Table 10.3 indicates the ratio of the annualised life-cycle costs of gas cooling to electric cooling for the three cases.

With respect to relative annualised energy costs, the gas absorption chiller/heaters show strong competitive potential in most cases. Under the Worst Case, the annualised energy costs of the 30-ton gas units range from only 61 per cent of the electric chiller's energy cost in the Northeast to 69 per cent in the Southwest. This gap narrows in the Worst Case for the 250- and 500-ton units, due to the fact that the cooling efficiency differential between the gas chiller/heater and the electric centrifugal chiller is larger than that between the gas chiller/heater and the electric reciprocating chiller (as indicated by the data presented in Table 10.1). For the 250-ton units, the energy costs of the gas system are slightly lower than the electric chiller's costs in the Northeast, while the energy costs of the gas unit exceed those of the electric chiller by 7 per cent in the Southeast and Mid-Atlantic and by 8 per cent in the Southwest. Very similar results are obtained under the Worst Case for the 500-ton units.

*Table* 10.2 Ratio of the annualised energy costs of gas cooling to electric cooling

| | *Southwest* | *Northeast* | *Mid-Atlantic* | *Midwest* | *Southeast* |
|---|---|---|---|---|---|
| *30-ton units* | | | | | |
| Worst case | 0.69 | 0.61 | 0.68 | 0.64 | 0.68 |
| BAU case | 0.53 | 0.47 | 0.52 | 0.49 | 0.52 |
| Best case | 0.44 | 0.40 | 0.44 | 0.41 | 0.44 |
| *250-ton units* | | | | | |
| Worst case | 1.08 | 0.97 | 1.07 | 1.00 | 1.07 |
| BAU case | 0.83 | 0.75 | 0.82 | 0.77 | 0.82 |
| Best case | 0.70 | 0.63 | 0.69 | 0.65 | 0.69 |
| *500-ton units* | | | | | |
| Worst case | 1.08 | 0.97 | 1.07 | 1.01 | 1.07 |
| BAU case | 0.83 | 0.75 | 0.83 | 0.78 | 0.83 |
| Best case | 0.70 | 0.63 | 0.70 | 0.65 | 0.69 |

*Table* 10.3 Ratio of the annualised life-cycle costs of gas cooling to electric cooling

| | *Southwest* | *Northeast* | *Mid-Atlantic* | *Midwest* | *Southeast* |
|---|---|---|---|---|---|
| *30-ton units* | | | | | |
| Worst case | 1.04 | 1.02 | 1.10 | 1.08 | 0.93 |
| BAU case | 0.88 | 0.87 | 0.94 | 0.93 | 0.76 |
| Best case | 0.82 | 0.82 | 0.89 | 0.88 | 0.70 |
| *250-ton units* | | | | | |
| Worst case | 1.20 | 1.13 | 1.22 | 1.17 | 1.16 |
| BAU case | 0.99 | 0.94 | 1.03 | 0.98 | 0.95 |
| Best case | 0.89 | 0.86 | 0.94 | 0.90 | 0.84 |
| *500-ton units* | | | | | |
| Worst case | 1.21 | 1.13 | 1.23 | 1.18 | 1.17 |
| BAU case | 0.99 | 0.93 | 1.03 | 0.97 | 0.94 |
| Best case | 0.88 | 0.84 | 0.93 | 0.88 | 0.83 |

The energy cost comparisons also demonstrate that the imposition of electric demand charges enhances the competitive position of gas cooling. It is particularly noteworthy that, under the pricing assumptions of the BAU Case, the annualised energy costs of the gas chiller/heaters do not exceed those of the electric chillers in any area or for any of the three application sizes. In fact, under this scenario, the annualised energy costs of the gas unit are at least 17 per cent lower than the competing systems' cots. Thus, the results of the BAU Case imply that substantial energy cost savings can accrue to the use of gas rather than electric cooling. Furthermore, this applies to a range of cooling tonnages and climatic conditions.

Under the Best Case, large energy savings accrue to the use of gas cooling compared to electric cooling in all areas. In fact, for the 30-ton units, the annualised energy cost of the gas chiller/heater is less than half of the electric chiller's in all five regions. For the remaining applications, the energy costs of the gas system range from 63 per cent of the electric chiller's costs for the 250- and 500-ton units in the Northeast to 70 per cent for the 250- and 500-ton units in the Southwest and the 500-ton unit in the Mid-Atlantic.

With respect to annualised life-cycle costs, which include the annualised energy costs plus the annualised costs of the unit, condenser make-up water, and maintenance, the gas chiller/heaters still exhibit competitive potential against the electric chillers/gas boilers. Under the Worst Case, the annualised life-cycle costs of the gas units range from 7 per cent below the costs of the electric chiller for 30-ton application in the Southeast to 23 per cent above the electric chiller's cost for 500-ton units in the Mid-Atlantic.

Under the BAU Case, the cost gap again narrows. In fact, the gas chiller/heater is either the lower-cost option or about equal to the electric unit in all regions across all unit sizes. In fact, it is only in the Mid-Atlantic region for the 250 and 500-ton units that the gas units' costs exceed those of the electric unit, and then only by about 3 per cent.

In the Best Case, the gas chiller/heater is the lower annualised life-cycle cost option in all applications across all regions of the country. Thus, when reduced gas rates are offered and high peak electric demand rates are in effect, commercial gas cooling shows very strong market potential against the prevailing electric cooling systems.

The annualised energy cost ratios of the gas cogeneration/500 ton absorption cooling system and the 500-ton electric centrifugal chiller are summarised in Table 10.4. As shown in the table, even in the Worst Case the energy costs of the gas system do not exceed those of the electric chiller by more than five per cent, as is the case in the Southwest, and are as much as nine per cent lower in the Northeast. In the BAU Case, the potential impact of peak electric demand charges becomes apparent in that the cogeneration gas cooling system yields substantial energy savings of 29 to 19 per cent compared to the electric chiller.

*Table* 10.4 Ratio of the annualised energy costs of gas cogeneration/cooling to electric cooling: 500-ton units

| | *Southwest* | *Northeast* | *Mid-Atlantic* | *Midwest* | *Southeast* |
|---|---|---|---|---|---|
| Worst case | 1.05 | 0.91 | 1.04 | 0.96 | 1.04 |
| BAU case | 0.81 | 0.71 | 0.80 | 0.74 | 0.80 |
| Best case | 0.64 | 0.56 | 0.64 | 0.59 | 0.64 |

Under the Best Case assumptions, the annualised cooling energy costs of the cogeneration/absorption cooling system are much lower than those of the electric chiller, ranging from 36 to 44 per cent below the electric system's energy costs. These results demonstrate the substantial improvement in the competitive environment that can occur with special off-peak gas rates or, in this case, special cogeneration rates, which are now offered by 20 gas utilities. The results further reflect the energy savings attributable to the fact that the electricity for the heat recovery chiller/heater is provided by the cogeneration system itself. In genral, moreover, the energy cost savings obtained here illustrate that in addition to the other benefits offered by gas cogeneration, this technology can also provide commercial buildings with a cost-effective alternative to electric space cooling.

## 10.5 CONCLUSIONS

The results of this analysis give clear indication that the direct gas-fired, double-effect absorption chiller/heaters can pose strong competition to the electric chillers that are now in widespread use in the commercial sectors. The results indicate that under a wide range of assumptions concerning cooling loads and relative energy prices, commercial cooling customers could enjoy substantial energy cost savings by switching to natural gas cooling. With respect to total annualised life-cycle costs, offering off-peak gas air conditioning rates creates a favourable market environment for gas versus electricity. As discussed above, the assumption of off-peak gas rates reduces the differences in annualised life-cycle costs to the point where the gas units are either the lower-cost option or exceed the costs of the electric chillers by only a narrow margin. Overall, these results imply that with aggressive marketing and off-peak gas pricing, the outlook for commercial gas cooling is quite positive. It should be noted that recent regulatory trends at both the federal and state levels have and will continue to reduce the cost of gas during the off-peak summer months while increasing the price of electricity during peak periods.

## Notes

1. American Gas Association (1984) *Five Year Economic Outlook* (Arlington, VA), 21 December.
2. For an extensive discussion of air conditioning operating principles and of different types of cooling systems, see AGA Marketing Services Group (1982) *AGA Marketing Manual: Natural Gas Cooling, 1982* (Arlington, VA).
3. ARS Group, Inc. for the Gas Research Institute (1985) *Economic Screening Guidebook for Cogeneration in Buildings* (Chicago, Ill.) September.
4. Cooling loads and, therefore, required cooling capacities are highly dependent on factors such as the design features, orientation, location, occupancy rate, and business activity of individual buildings. Consequently, the size and type of building cited in connection with each level of cooling tonnage are *strictly* illustrative. Building sizes are based on a general rule-of-thumb that about one ton of cooling capacity is required for every 350 square feet of building space.
5. American Gas Association (1986) *AGA-Tera Base Case 1986-I*, (Arlington, VA).
6. American Gas Association (1986) *Gas Distribution Industry Pricing Strategies* (Arlington, VA) April.
7. American Gas Association (1986) *Fact Sheet: Natural Gas Cooling* (Arlington, VA) 2 May.

## Appendix: Life-Cycle Cost (LCC) Formulas for Gas Cooling Systems

$$\text{Total LCC} = \text{Installed cost} + \sum_{n=0}^{N-1} \frac{\text{Energy cost} + \text{Make-up water cost} + \text{Maintenance cost}}{(1+i)^n}$$

where:

$N$ = expected system life (years)

$i$ = discount rate

Installed cost = Equipment cost + Installation cost

$$\text{Energy cost} = \left[\begin{pmatrix}\text{Gas input}\\ \text{per hour}\end{pmatrix}\begin{pmatrix}\text{Equivalent full-}\\ \text{load hours}\end{pmatrix}\begin{pmatrix}\text{Commercial}\\ \text{gas price}\\ \text{in year } n\end{pmatrix} + \begin{pmatrix}\text{Electrical power}\\ \text{requirement}\end{pmatrix}\begin{pmatrix}\text{Equivalent full-}\\ \text{load hours}\end{pmatrix}\begin{pmatrix}\text{Commercial}\\ \text{electricity price}\\ \text{in year } n\end{pmatrix}\right]$$

$$\text{Make-up water cost} = \begin{pmatrix}\text{Make-up water}\\ \text{req't per hour}\end{pmatrix}\begin{pmatrix}\text{Equivalent full-}\\ \text{load hours}\end{pmatrix}\begin{pmatrix}\text{Water + sewer}\\ \text{rate in year } n\end{pmatrix}$$

Annualised LCC = (Capital recovery factor) (Total LCC)

where:

$$\text{Capital recovery factor} = \frac{i(1+i)^N}{(1+i)^N - 1}$$

*Note*: In this analysis, the discount rate ($i$) was set at 12 per cent in all calculations.

# 11 Estimation and Linking of Ecomomic and Financial Costs in Telecommunications

James H. Alleman and Veena Gupta

## 11.1 INTRODUCTION

Many corporate structures have pro forma financial models which are used to develop their plans and policy scenarios. GTE Service Corporation is no exception in this regard. GTE has had for some time a detailed planning model which computed all the entries in pro forma financial statements. The model required extensive inputs from the thirteen operating companies, since it virtually mirrored the financial reporting structures of the firm rather than model the key elements.

From the point of view of analysing today's telecommunications environment, this model was difficult to use and could not fully account for the changing price structure and competitive inroads or capture the role of changing depreciation policies as an incentive for investment. The costs determined in this model were 'separations'-based accounting costs, not economic cost.[1]

Recognising the need for an analytical economic model for policy analysis, econometric models of cost and demand were developed (Alleman and Goetz, 1985). The services were divided into subscriber access, exchange usage, intrastate and interstate toll messages. The estimated input demand equations were the basis for analysis of technology and costs at the aggregate GTE level. Subsequently, these models have been disaggregated to the telephone company level and respecified to take account of the dynamics of capital adjustment.

Our purpose here is not to describe these models in detail but to discuss the difficulties associated with policy applications of this type of modelling. Economists have a special jargon which includes concepts such as marginal costs, user cost of capital, economies of scale and scope. These cannot be readily translated into the language of management policy decision-making which is based on line items of income statements, balance sheets and flow of fund statements. The economic models are recognised as valuable in analysing the current issues such as alternative access charge scenarios or depreciation practices. Nevertheless, the full implications of the analysis and recommendations are not always intuitively obvious. This led to the realisation that it is necessary to link the econometric models with a financial model in order to achieve a better understanding of policy decisions.

Moreover, in the literature on the dynamic theory of the firm, we are now seeing attempts to synthesise two strands of research which have developed independently of one another. The issue of real investment decisions has been studied by micro and macroeconomists using simplifying assumptions about the firm's financial structure. Conversely, financial economists have addressed the issue of financing choices, taking the levels of investment expenditures as predetermined. Recently, the interrelationship of investment and financial choices has been analysed by Boadway and Bruce, 1980; Bernstein, 1983; Bernstein and Nadiri, 1985; Chirinko, 1985; Hayashi, 1984 and Steigum, 1983. In these studies, investment and financial behaviour are determined under different sets of constraints and assumptions about the nature of capital markets. So far none of these models was found empirically implementable for GTE, although it is generally recognised that the decisions regarding investment levels and financing aspects are intimately related.

This chapter summarises the effort undertaken at GTE to relate the econometric models of demand and cost based on neo-classical theory to the financial outcomes as represented in the various line items of the financial statements. The result of this exercise is a telecommunication financial model (TFM) which explicitly links together these models in simulation mode.[2] An added benefit is that the financial model can endogenise cost of funds and depreciation which were treated as totally exogenous in the econometric models. Policy evaluations based on the integrated model should therefore be more complete than when either model is simulated by itself.

Section 11.2 describes the strategic planning model and the system of econometric models of cost and demand linked by a pricing module. Section 11.3 describes the methodology of integrating these two sets of models into a simulation system. The most important points of linkage, that is effective tax rates, deferred taxes, investment tax credits and short-term financing are described in detail. Section 11.4 illustrates the interrelated nature of simulations in this system. Section 11.5 is a brief summary.

## 11.2 STRATEGIC PLANNING MODEL AND ECONOMETRIC MODELS

### Strategic Planning Model

The strategic planning model, or 'strat plan', produces a detailed five-year financial plan encompassing all lines of business, regulated and non-regulated, for each of the GTE telephone companies. Its output represents the combined projections of individual operating companies.

The standard financial reports are: income statement; balance sheet; a sources and uses of funds statement. These three reports are presented in Tables 11.1 to 11.3.

The strat plan effort consolidates data submitted by the telephone operating companies and utilises additional planning inputs to produce preliminary strat plan outputs. The database for the strat plan consists of the most recent actual financial data as well as current planning information for a five-year planning horizon. In addition to the basic financial statements, the strat plan also produces statistics on operations and consolidated reports by strategic business unit on a yearly basis.

Special modelling features of the strat plan include:

1. rate-base module
2. debt module
3. finance module

The rate-base module is equipped to develop the rate base for both interstate and intrastate services under given Separations factors.

The debt module calculates interest on long-term debt, preferred stock under differing scenarios of interst rates, new stock issues, retirements/buybacks and maintains the beginning and ending balances for these accounts on a rolling five-year basis.

The finance module deals with the need for borrowing of short-term debt to finance the operations of the company from year-to-year within this five-year plan. In order to properly account for interest payments on short-term borrowing, the model solves for the exact amount of short-

*Table* 11.1 Contribution format of the income statement

| *Heading description* | *Variable position* |
|---|---|
| **Revenues:** | |
| Regulated Revenues | ** |
| Unregulated Revenues | |
| Total Revenue | |
| **Variable costs of services:** | |
| Equipment Sales | ** |
| Maintenance | ** |
| Traffic | ** |
| Commercial | ** |
| Customer Accounting | ** |
| Miscellaneous | ** |
| Total Variable | |
| Gross Margin | |
| **Fixed factors of cost of service:** | |
| Operating Depreciation | ** |
| Property Taxes and Rents | |
| Total Cost of Services | |
| Operating Margin | |
| **Period expenses:** | |
| Marketing | ** |
| Sales | ** |
| Advertising | ** |
| Total Sales Expense | |
| Contribution before general and administrative and other | |
| Depr., Rent and Prop. Tax | ** |
| General and Admin. | ** |
| Other Period Expenses | |
| Less G. & A. and Other CAP | |
| Cost transferred | |
| Total Period Expense | |
| Earnings before interest and taxes | |
| Interest | |
| Preferred | |
| Less IDC | |
| Net Financing Cost | |
| Other | |
| Earnings before taxes | |
| Income Taxes | |
| Net income to common | |

Table 11.2 Balance sheet

| *Heading description* | *Variable position* |
|---|---|
| ASSETS: | |
| Customer Premise Equipment | ** |
| Switching Equipment | ** |
| Transmission Equipment | ** |
| Other (Buildings, Land) | ** |
| Organisation, Franchises and Patent Rights | |
| Total 100.1 Telephone Plant | |
| Total 100.2 Telephone Plant | |
| Total All Other Telephone Plant | |
| Total Telephone Plant | |
| Accumulated Depreciation | ** |
| Amort Reserve | ** |
| Total Telephone Plant Less Reserve | |
| Sinking Funds | |
| Other Funds | |
| Investments | |
| Direct Sale of Plant | |
| Reserve Direct Sale | |
| Total Investments and Funds | |
| Cash | |
| Accounts Receivable | |
| Accounts Receivable - NECA | |
| Uncollected A/R | |
| Uncollected A/R - NECA | |
| Unbilled - IXC Messages | |
| Other Receivables | |
| Notes Receivable Affiliates | |
| Total Materials and Supplies | |
| Materials and Supplies - Sales | |
| Materials and Supplies - BT | |
| Other Current Assets | |
| Total Current Assets | |
| Prepaid Expenses | |
| Discounts Outstanding LTD | |
| Expenses Outstanding LTD | |
| Other Deferred Charges | |
| Total PPD and Deferred Changes | |
| *Total Assets* | |

*Table* 11.2 (continued)

| | |
|---|---|
| LIABILITIES | |
| Accounts Payable - Other | |
| Accounts Payable - Inter-exchange carrier | |
| Accounts Payable - Affiliates | |
| Matured Long Term Debt | |
| Tax Accrued - Other | |
| Tax Accrued Fed Income Tax | ** |
| Interest Accrued - Carrier deposits | |
| Interest Accrued | |
| Dividends Accrued | |
| All Other Current and Liabilities | |
| *Total Current and Accrued Liabilities* | |
| Unamortised Investment Credits | ** |
| Deferred Income Taxes | ** |
| Other Deferred Income Taxes | |
| BTL Unamortised ITC Balance | |
| BTL Deferred Tax Balance | |
| Total Deferred Credits and Operating Reserves | |
| Total Retained Earnings | |
| Total Common Stock | ** |
| Other Capital | |
| Preferred Stock | |
| Total Equity | |
| Total Long-Term and Intermediate-Term Debt | |
| Total Short-Term Debt | ** |
| Total Debt | |
| *Total Liabilities* | |

*Table* 11.3 Funds statement

| *Heading description* | | *Variable position* |
|---|---|---|
| Capital requirements: | | |
| ATL Capital Adds (net removal and salvage) less Interest During Construction | | ** |
| Materials and Supplies | | |
| BTL Capital Adds (net removal and salvage) | | |
| Other Capital Additions | | |
| Other Requirements | | |
| Inventory | Increase/(Decrease) | |
| Accounts Receivable | Increase/(Decrease) | |
| Other Current Assets | Increase/(Decrease) | |
| Accounts Payable | Decrease/(Increase) | |
| Other Current Assets | Decrease/(Increase) | |
| *Net Working Capital* | | |
| Other Funds Required | | |
| *TOTAL USES* | | |
| Sources: | | |
| Net Income | | ** |
| Dividends | | |
| Depreciation and Amortisation | | ** |
| ITC Credits | | ** |
| Deferred Taxes | | ** |
| Interest During Construction | | |
| Other Sources | | |
| *Net Internal Sources* | | |
| Preferred Stock | | |
| Common Stock | | |
| Other Equity | | |
| Long-term Debt | | |
| Short-Term Debt | | |
| *Net External Sources* | | |
| *Total Sources* | | |

term debt necessary given the balance-sheet changes, taxes, controllable expenses and related items.

Typical exercises conducted within the framework of the strategic plan involve analysis of the impact of the following:

1. a dollar reduction in expenses on net income and revenues,
2. a dollar reduction in capital programme on net income, expenses, revenues, and internally generated funds (IGF),
3. an increase in equity on net income,
4. a change in interest rate assumptions on financials,
5. a change in capital recovery policies, that is depreciation rates on income, expense, and IGF,
6. a change in the interstate settlement ratio on net income and revenues.

## Econometric Cost and Demand Models

The econometric cost and demand models were developed as part of an overall system which integrates demand, cost, separations and pricing models for GTE via a comprehensive policy simulator. We will briefly describe the four models and how the simulator integrates them. A flow-chart of the system is presented in Figure 11.1.

The demand model is an econometric model with five endogenous variables: exchange switched access (ESA), non-switched access (NSA), exchange usage, intrastate toll usage and interstate toll usage. The exogenous variables are output prices and demographic and industry variables.

The cost model is a disaggregate short-run econometric model for each of GTE's domestic telephone companies. Output quantities and input prices are used to generate total economic cost and the demand for each of the inputs. The cost model generates total variable cost, which is broken down into seven expense categories, as well as the quarterly investment levels and fixed costs for four categories of capital assets.

The seven expense categories are:

1. official, managerial, professional and semiprofessional compensation,
2. business office, sales and clerical employees' compensation,
3. operators' compensation,
4. maintenance employees' compensation (station),
5. maintenance employees' compensation (non-station),
6. building supply and motor vehicle employees' compensation,
7. non-wage expense.

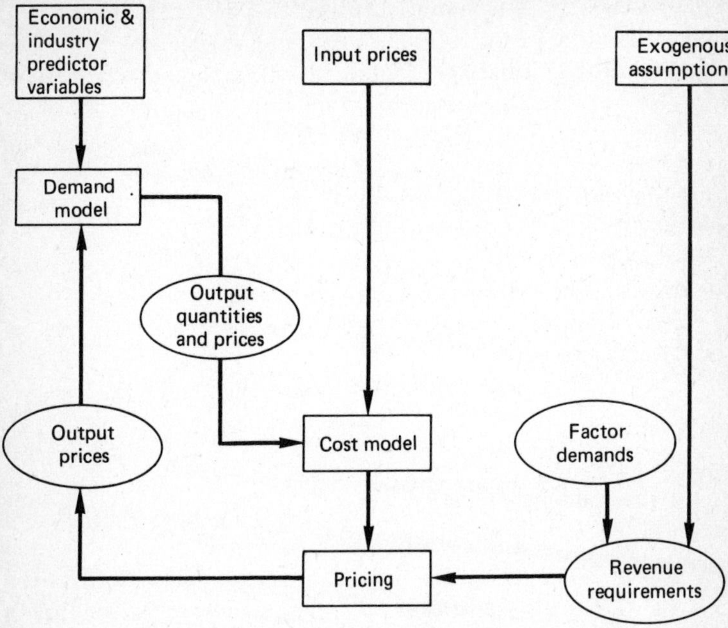


*Figure* 11.1 Econometric cost models without financial models

The four capital asset categories are:

1. customer premise equipment,
2. switching equipment,
3. transmission equipment and outside plant,
4. other (land, buildings, vehicles, and so on).

Input demand equations are derived based on the application of duality theory in a multi-output framework. The following assumptions are made:

1. The firm minimises the present value of its entire future stream of total costs subject to a production function, that is minimise $C = w\mathbf{L} + q\mathbf{K}$ subject to $Y = f(\mathbf{L}, \mathbf{K})$ where $Y$ is the vector of outputs, **L** and **K** are vectors of variable and quasi-fixed inputs, $w$ and $q$ are the corresponding input prices, that is wage rates and user costs of capital.
2. Input markets are competitive, that is prices of inputs are given to the firm.
3. Capital stocks adjust to their desired levels in a systematic manner; in this case a flexible accelerator was assumed.[3]

The predetermined variables in this econometric model consist of output quantities which are modified by hedonic variables, user costs for the four capital categories, and prices for each of the seven expense categories.

The four output categories are:

1. exchange switched access,
2. non-switched access,
3. exchange calls,
4. toll calls (state + interstate).

These outputs are adjusted for qualitative differences by using hedonic modifiers. The hedonics include:

1. distance,
2. trouble report rates,
3. inward/outward movement rates,
4. exchange call duration,
5. toll call duration,
6. operator handled ratio.

The prices of labour inputs are the average hourly wage rates. The prices of capital inputs are defined as 'user costs', which capture the effects of corporate income tax rate, the rate of investment tax credit, depreciation rates, indirect tax rates, present value of depreciation allowances, and the real cost of funds, as well as the assets' purchase prices. The concept of user cost of capital is discussed at some length in the following subsection since its various components are the main points of linkage between the real and financial aspects of investment.

Sep/Sim (GTE's model to simulate the Separations process) calculates expenses, book values of plant and taxes by jurisdiction based on allocations of the fixed costs and expense levels from the cost model. The financial data are used to generate revenue requirements reflecting part 67 separations rules, part 69 access charge rules, and subscriber CALC regulaions. Several options are available within Sep/Sim, such as changing authorised rates of return, tax rates, and various separations and access charge rules.

Although a variety of pricing options are available, the base case pricing mechanism is separations based, or revenue requirement pricing. After the revenue requirements by jurisdiction are generated by Sep/Sim, the pricing module computes prices for each of the services.[4] Other pricing options include marginal cost, fully-distributed cost and Ramsey pricing.

The four models described above are linked by the model simulator represented in Figure 11.1. For a base case simulation, no exogenous variables are changed, and no pricing or separation options are selected.

The base case begins with the demand model, which produces output quantities given demographic and industry variables and output prices. These output quantities, and exogenous input prices enter the cost module, which yields economic cost measures and input levels. These variables feed into Sep/Sim, which, based on a set of allocation factors, produces financial expenses, plant accounts and revenue requirements by service. Given the revenue requirements and a pricing option, prices for each service are generated by the pricing module. The completed cycle represents one iteration of the simulator.

If we wish to analyse the total effect of an exogenous shock such as an increase in one of the wage rates, the simulation proceeds as follows. In the cost model, the new wage rate is used together with the other input prices and the output quantities, which remain unchanged. The higher wage rate results in new values for the levels of all endogenous variables, that is expenses and investment levels and hence prices of output categories. A second iteration of the demand and cost models is based on new output prices and the higher wage rate. The ultimate effect is observed when the system has reached convergence.

## The User Cost of Capital

The user cost of capital is a key variable in determining the firm's incentives to invest. It incorporates several variables which capture the interactions between the economic and financial aspects of investment. Consequently, it is important that we explain the role of each of its components before proceeding to Section 11.3.

The concept of user cost of capital was introduced by Jorgenson (1963) as the main element of the neo-classical theory of investment. This defines the total cost of using capital in production. It is more than the 'cost of funds' since it includes a component for asset depreciation. It is a particularly useful tool for analysing the effects of a broad range of tax schemes on the incentives to invest.

The user cost of capital is derived from two optimisation conditions. For capital purchased at time $t$, the imputed rental or shadow price $q_t$ must equal the marginal product value per unit of capital services, that is the sum of economic depreciation and interest cost adjusted for inflation. Secondly, the price of new capital goods $P_k$ must equal the present value of future rentals. Taking account of the investment tax credit and deductibility of depreciation for tax purposes results in downward adjustments to $P_k$.[5]

The rental price of capital is defined as

$$q = P_k \frac{(r + \delta)(1 - k - uZ)}{1 - u}$$

where $P_k$ = price index for specific equipment
$r$ = after-tax real rate of return
$\delta$ = economic depreciation rate
$k$ = rate of investment tax credit (ITC)
$u$ = effective corporate income tax rate
$Z$ = present value of depreciation deductions over tax life of the asset.

This formula has a straightforward common sense interpretation in terms of current tax rules if broken down into the following steps (Mohr, 1984):

1. After tax rental price of capital can be defined as
   $(1 - u) q = P_k (r + \delta) (1 - uZ - K)$
2. If tax credit = 0 and depreciation is not allowed to be deducted as an expense, then
   $(1 - u)q = P_k (r + \delta)$
   where
   $P_k r$ = real after-tax opportunity cost expense of investing in vintage $t$ capital
   $P_k \delta$ = economic depreciation, that is the loss in market value due to wear and tear, fire, theft, accident and obsolescence.
3. If we introduce investment tax credit $k$ per dollar of new investment, the after tax investment price is reduced from $P_k$ to $(1 - k)P_k$. This in turn reduces the true opportunity cost of funds and the depreciation cost.

$$(1 - u)q = (1 - k)(r + \delta)P_k$$
$$= [P_k(1 - k)r] + [P_k(1 - k)\delta]$$

4. Next we allow deduction of depreciation over the tax service life of the asset. Since these tax savings accrue only over a period of years, these future savings must be represented by their expected present value per dollar of investment, that is $uZ$. The after-tax new investment price $P_k$

is further reduced from $P_k$ $(1 - k)$ to $P_k$ $(1 - k - uZ)$, yielding the formula as stated in step 1.

**Definition of Capital Stock**

The stock of capital in each asset category at time $t$ is defined as the sum of all vintages of previous net additions to capital adjusted for inflation. This requires deflating current period gross additions by current prices and current period retirements by the price prevailing when the assets were acquired. Although depreciation is parametrised in specifying the user cost, for the purpose of defining capital stock it is more appropriate to use historical data on retirement dollars since this represents the actual plant removed from service.[6]

## 11.3 METHODOLOGY OF THE FINANCIAL MODEL

The TFM model which integrates the various models is designed for the analysis of policy issues on a five-year time horizon. Results are presented in the form of three standard financial statements. While the separate models have 'stood alone', the purpose of this modelling exercise is to show how each can be linked in a meaningful manner. We will first describe the key variables of the models and then, more importantly, discuss how they can be linked to give a robust and more meaningful analysis of various policy alternatives than previously possible. The model specifications are based upon application of appropriate accounting principles. An overview flow-chart of the integrated system with the TFM model is presented in Figure 11.2.

**Overall Methodology**

The three major sources of information for compiling the financial statements are:

1. econometric cost and demand models,
2. GTE telephone operations strategic plan (strat plan),
3. TFM exogenous policy variables.

The effort to integrate information from these disjoint sources involved several steps. For the econometric cost and demand models all endogenous variables and the exogenous variables required to produce them were

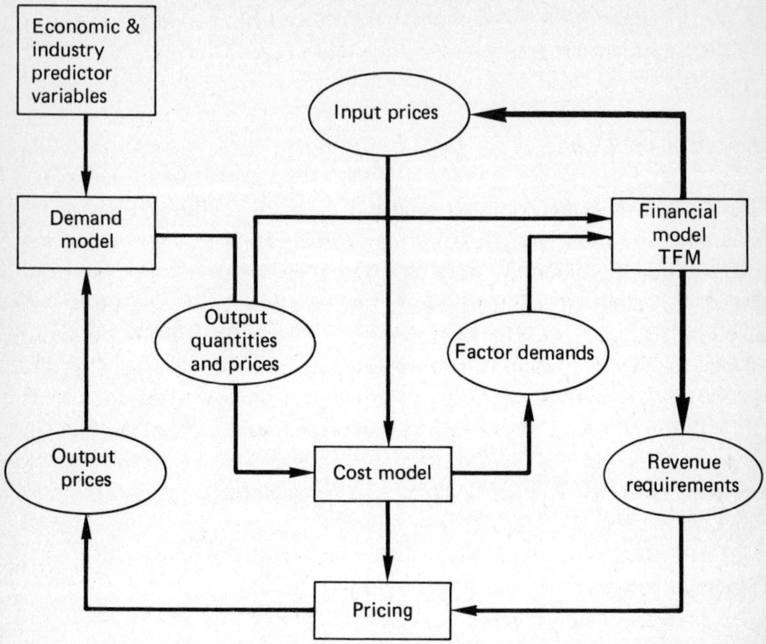


*Figure* 11.2 Economic cost models integrated with financial models

identified. The strategic plan modules, reports and database were reviewed and the key points of linkage to the econometric cost and demand models were established. The algorithms to generate all the line items in the financial statements were defined to incorporate results from the econometric models as well as the strat plan.

The econometric demand model produces regulated services output and price projections. These are combined to derive total regulated services revenues. The econometric cost model produces regulated services results for expenses and investment in plant assets and hence the beginning and ending balances of plant in service. The line items directly determined by econometric models are identified by ** in Tables 11.1 to 11.3 in the Appendix and corresponding subtotals are identified by *.

The major strat plan variables utilised by the TFM model are non-regulated income statement items and balance sheet items not captured by the cost model, debt balances and long-term debt and equity fixed charges.

The telecommunications financial model also requires some exogenous variables in order to allocate the projections from econometric models into the proper definitions of income statement and balance sheet items, and some corporate policy variables pertaining to the choice of financing methods.

**Key Points of Linkage**

The key to the development of TFM is in matching up the common variables. The most important points of linkage are expenses, investment, plant-in-service, deferred taxes and investment tax credit. The vintage based derivation of capital stock in the econometric model presented in Section 11.2 matched up in principle with the definition of plant-in-service in the strat plan. However, significant further effort was required in the development of expenses, deferred taxes and investment tax credits. In addition, the two most important reverse flows, that is from the financial model to the real investment model are based on the effective tax rate and the need for short-term debt. The methodology for each of these is discussed in turn.

**Expenses**

While the econometric models view occupationally defined labour categories as distinct factors of production, from the planning and budgeting point of view, the decision variables are expenses incurred for different activities. The functional categories of expenses defined in the strat plan income statement include maintenance, traffic, commercial, customer billing, marketing, advertising, general and administrative. A 6 × 11 translation matrix was prepared by each telephone company representing the percentage allocation of each of the six occupational labour classes into each of the eleven activities. These matrices were then used to convert simulation results of input demand equations into activity-based classification.

**Deferred Taxes**

The major cause of deferred taxes is that depreciation is taken on an accelerated basis for tax purposes but on a straight-line basis for accounting. This is significant since the cash flow generated from the excess of accelerated depreciation over straight-line basis can be a major source of funds for future capital expansion plans.

While the internal revenue service (IRS) allows the use of accelerated depreciation when computing taxable income, regulatory proceedings, annual reports to stockholders and internal reports utilise straight-line methods of depreciation. Therefore, income tax payments are lower in the early years of the useful life of the asset and higher in the later years under IRS rulings. For growing firms, the deferred income tax accounts accumulate to large amounts that diminish only if the firm reduces its level of investment. On the balance sheet the liability account of deferred taxes continues to grow and it is also a source of funds in the funds statement. The amount of deferred taxes as a percentage of net additions to plant varies across plant categories, since some are allowed greater accelerated depreciation rates than others.

The amortisation schedule for the accelerated depreciation on plant acquisitions and disposals is developed for each simulation year, for each plant category $K_j$. The total accelerated depreciation for any simulation period consists of two components: accelerated depreciation based on plant decisions during the simulation period and accelerated depreciation from past decisions reflected in the embedded plant, taking account of both (ACRS) depreciation and pre-ACRS depreciation.[7] The straight-line depreciation adjusted in accordance with the Tax Equity and Fiscal Responsibility Act of 1982 (TEFRA)[8] is subtracted from the accelerated (tax basis) depreciation to derive the deferred income tax generated by the timing difference of the two methods. Therefore it is clear that this important source of funds is sensitive to changes in tax rates, depreciation rules as well as the level and mix of gross additions of current and previous years.

At this point we should recall that in the derivation of user cost (Section 11.2) the variable $Z$ was defined as the present value of depreciation deductions and hence $uZ$ as the tax savings per dollar invested. What we have shown in this section is the step-by-step computation of $uZ$ in dollar terms from the financial statements. The tax saving effect of the deductibility of depreciation is distinguished from the tax deferment effect of accelerated depreciation. Thus, in simulation mode this linkage ensures that the tax incentive to invest due to accelerated depreciation is accurately reflected in user cost variations.

### Investment Tax Credits Plus Unamortised Investment Credits

Investment tax credits (ITC) are used as direct reductions of income taxes. Gross additions to plant that qualify are allowed ITC equal to various percentages of the original costs of the depreciable assets. Thus investment tax credits generate tax savings based on the level and mix of investment.

The anticipated savings are an incentive for capital spending captured in the user cost of capital by the parameter $k$.

In computing the magnitude of tax savings for regulatory purposes, the model recognises GTE's normalisation method in comparison with the flow-through method. The flow-through method claims the investment credit in the year in which taxes otherwise payable are reduced by the credit. The deferral method requires that the investment credit should be reflected in net income over the productive life of the asset.

The ITC claimed in any year for the $j$th category of capital is determined by the ITC rate (usually 10 per cent) based on life of asset and the dollar value of gross investment ($GA_j$) adjusted down for:

1. percentage of $GA_j$ that is capitalised for book purposes but expensed for tax purposes (usually between 0.0 and 0.15),
2. the percentage of $GA_j$ that is not eligible for investment tax credit treatment.[9]

Amortisation tables are developed for the ITC credits on a straight-line basis over the book-life of the ITC property. The total amortisation for a period (AITC) is the sum of ITC amortisation developed from simulated plant additions and the amortisation of ITC on previous years' embedded plant. For any given period, the total amortisation (embedded and simulated) is subtracted from the total ITC claimed to determine the net balance of unamortised ITC credits, one of the major liabilities in the balance sheet. It should also be noted that ITC is an important source of funds.

**Effective Federal Income Tax Rate**

The effective federal income tax rate often differs from the statutory rate stated in the federal regulations. The effective tax rate ($u$) is derived from the statutory tax rate (SFIT) as follows:

$$u = \text{SFIT-STAX-IDC-PCT-YAITC-BKTX}$$

where

STAX = state taxes, net of federal income tax benefit
YAITC = amortisation of deferred investment tax credits
IDC = interest during construction, that is allowance for funds used during construction
PCT = plant construction costs deducted for tax purposes

BKTX = book depreciation versus tax depreciation adjustments (exclusive of accelerated depreciation).

All values are stated as percentages of earnings before taxes.

The general methodology requires both direct inputs (TFM exogenous) and internally computed (TFM endogenous) variables.

The direct input variables are of two types: those that are truly exogenous (SFIT) and those that should be endogenous but cannot be modelled at the present time (IDC and PCT) or whose relative magnitude is too small to justify an extensive modelling effort (STAX).

The internally computed variables are amortisation of deferred investment tax credits (YAITC) and book depreciation versus tax depreciation adjustments (BKTX). These variables warrant special modelling because they are directly influenced by investment decisions and are also of significant magnitude.

As explained above, since GTE uses the deferral method, YAITC is the sum of simulation period amortisations and embedded plant amortisations of deferred investment tax credits stated as a percentage of earnings before taxes. YAITC is determined by IRS rules and the level and mix of gross additions. For firms with large capital spending plans this is often the main difference between the statutory and the effective tax rate.

The ratio of book to tax depreciation adjustment (exclusive of accelerated depreciation) is the sum of total tax savings due to book to tax adjustments for all plant categories as a percentage of earnings before taxes. It is determined by the statutory federal income tax rate, gross additions of plant in each category and the corresponding ratio of plant that was capitalised for book purposes but expensed for tax purposes.

**Debt to Equity Ratio**

The requirement for additional short-term and long-term borrowing and common stock issuance is determined by the imbalance of total sources and uses of funds in combination with the corporation's policy regarding its financial structure. This is a crucial element in the feedback from financial policy variables to the real investment decision through the average cost of funds and the effective tax rate. The most significant use of funds for a telecommunications utility is investment in capital assets. The major sources of funds are depreciation and amortisation, net income, deferred taxes due to accumulated depreciation and ITC, in that order. In our integrated system, each of these major components of the sources and uses of funds are determined by the econometric cost and demand models.

The corporation's policy regarding its financial structure is reflected in several control variables: long-term debt, short-term debt and common stock issuance. We take long-term debt and preferred stock as determined by the debt module of the strat plan. The amount of short-term debt is determined endogenously in TFM. The control variable we focus on is the ratio of additional short-term debt to common stock issued, defined as

$$F = \frac{\text{STDCH}}{\text{STDCH} + \text{CS}} \tag{11.1}$$

where

$STDCH$ = current year's required additional short term debt
$CS$ = current year's common stock issuance

The choice among alternative policy options regarding the target value of $F$ operates through the sources and uses of funds. The interdependence of interest paid on short-term debt (an income-statement quantity) with the levels of short-term debt and common stock (balance-sheet quantities) is reflected on different sides of the sources and uses of funds statement. The change in short-term borrowing plus the common stock issued in any year must equal the difference between total uses and total sources other than short-term borrowing. This identity is represented by:

$$\begin{aligned} &\text{CS} + \text{STDCH} = \text{TOTUSE} - \text{NETFLW}_x - \\ &(\text{EBIT} - \text{OTHDBT} - (\text{STDCH*RSTD}))^*\,(1 - ub) \end{aligned} \tag{11.2}$$

where

TOTUSE = total uses of funds
$\text{NETFLW}_x$ = sources other than net income, short-term borrowing and common stock issuance
EBIT = earnings before short term interest and taxes
OTHDBT = interest payments on debt other than short-term debt
$ub$ = the effective corporate tax rate for the level of earnings before interest and taxes (EBIT).
RSTD = interest rate on short-term debt.

The levels of STDCH and CS are determined by the policy option regarding F. If F is taken as a fixed percentage applying to the current year's increments of debt and equity, without regard to previous years ratios, then substituting CS = STDCH*(1 – F)/F from Equation 11.1 into Equation 11.2 yields.

$$\text{STDCH} = \frac{\text{F(TOTUSE} - \text{NETFLW}_x - (\text{EBIT} - \text{OTHDBT})^*(1 - ub))}{1 - \text{F*RSTD*}(1 - ub)} \tag{11.3}$$

It should be noted that STDCH is sensitive to capital spending since that is the major use of funds. It is also sensitive to depreciation, earnings before taxes and the effective tax rate. EBIT incorporates the impact of investment through (straight-line) depreciation and of expenses, output prices and quantities. Thus all the key variables from the econometric models have an impact on STDCH through TOTUSE, EBIT, $\text{NETFLW}_x$ and *ub*.

Common stock issuance is derived as CS = STDCH * (1 – *F*)/*F* if the calculated value of STDCH is positive. If the calculated value of STDCH is negative it means additional short term borrowing or stock issuances are unnecessary and excess funds are used to reduce short-term borrowing.[10]

An alternative method for determining the mix of STDCH and CS (and therefore *F*) is to set a target value for the ratio of total debt to the sum of debt plus common stock. Each year's additions are then designed to achieve the target ratio or move towards it as much as possible. In this case *F* becomes conditional on starting values of debt and equity relative to the target.

Thus the financial policy can be integrated with the decisions regarding gross investment levels by evaluating the impact of proposed investment on the need for funds *vis-à-vis* the availability of funds (from accumulated depreciation, earnings before taxes, tax benefits, deferred taxes) and the cost of borrowing the additional funds.

## 11.4 SIMULATIONS OF THE SYSTEM INCORPORATING TFM

As described in Section 11.3, TFM consists of deterministic algorithms which link revenue and cost variables with the assets and liabilities as well as the sources and uses of funds for the firm. These algorithms were extracted from the strat plan model and embedded into TFM. The various amortisation schedules are appropriately set up and information for any specific period is extracted as needed. This ensures appropriate accounting of the stock and flow aspects of capital assets, depreciation and debt balances over a five-year horizon.

The behavioural aspects of cost and demand come from the econometric models. Investment decisions are based on levels of output, relative prices of capital services and costs of adjustment of capital stock to its optimum level. Similarly, expenses are related to output levels, relative prices of labour and existing capital stock. These systems of multi-variate equations overwrite the strat plan algorithms where gross additions are defined as fixed ratios of output at highly disaggregated levels and expenses are fixed ratios of plant-in-service. The econometric models also specify demand as a function of environmental variables and price of output in contrast to the strat plan where demand forecasts are generated independently of the revenue-requirement based pricing.

Policy analysis using simulations of the integrated system are designed to be more complete than if either model is simulated in isolation. Figure 11.3 depicts the flows among the various models. The flow of variables endogenous to TFM which play a role in the cost model and in Sep/Sim have been highlighted using heavier arrows. Without these flows, TFM would merely be a reporting system presenting a combination of data from disjoint sources.

In a system of this type, simulations can begin with any of the models, provided the changes to exogenous variables in that model are appropriately represented. Exogenous variables such as wage rates, price of materials and separations factors are relatively straightforward. We illustrate the workings of the system in terms of output and user cost of capital, since each of these variables consists of both exogenous and endogenous elements.

**Output**

Both investment and expenses are influenced by the macroeconomic outlook through the levels of demand for access lines, local and toll messages. In our multi-output framework it is possible to trace the impact of the changing mix of output which may be the result of by-pass or the firm's marketing strategies. Moreover, in the econometric models variations in output attributes or qualities also need to be supported by changes in the mix of investment and of expenses. The key attributes whose impact can be simulated in this system are changes in certain characteristics of the network, trouble reports and completion ratios. The output impact now has several additional dimensions which could easily be associated with different marketing or network planning strategies of the firm.

The levels of demand themselves depend upon prices of services which are at the present time determined by revenue requirements. Alternative

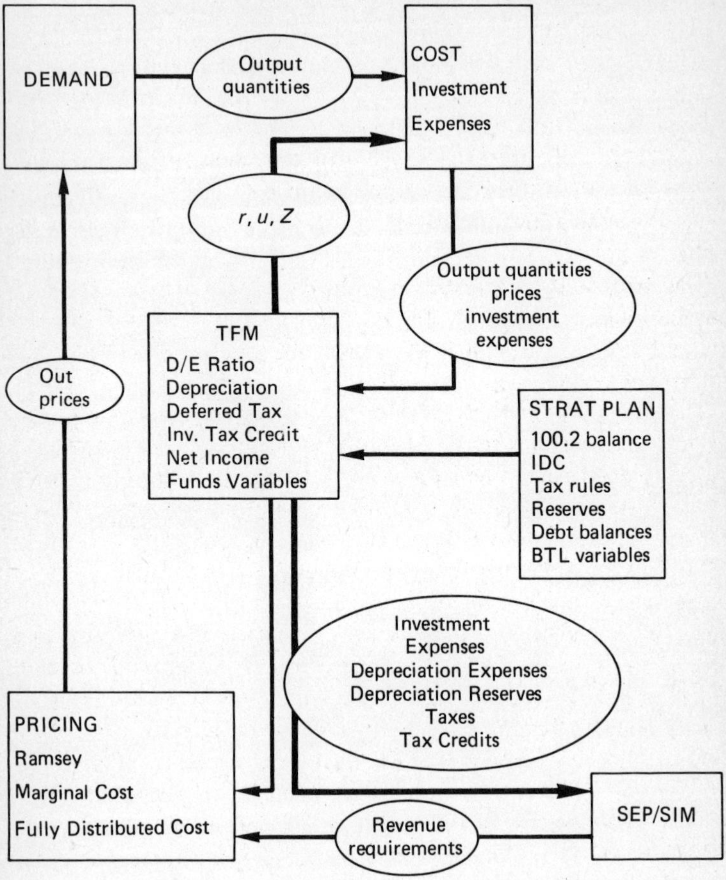


BTL = below the line variables.

*Figure* 11.3 Structure for TFM integration

pricing options such as marginal cost pricing and Ramsey pricing are incorporated into the system (as before) through demand elasticities and marginal costs. Most of the revenue requirement components are now derived in TFM and related to economic costs. The revenue requirement and therefore, prices of services are more sensitive to variations in investment and expenses.

**User Cost of Capital**

The user cost of capital determines investment and capital stock. Besides its direct effect on investment, it also influences the levels of expenses through the stock of capital and through relative prices. As described in Section 11.2, it incorporates several variables. Some of them are entirely exogenous while others can be influenced by the firm's own choice of policies regarding investments and the method of financing these investments.

The exogenous components include the price index for capital assets, prevailing interest rates on different instruments, statutory income tax rate and IRS rules regarding investment tax credit, depreciation methods and lives of assets.

The firm does, however, choose its level of aggregate investment and the mix of assets purchased. As shown in Section 11.3, these choices are critical in determining the current and future levels of the (accrued) effective tax rate through depreciation deductions and investment tax credits and also the taxes deferred due to accelerated depreciation.

The choices regarding financial structure also determine the effective average cost of funds to the firm in conjunction with the prevailing interest rates. This is a significant improvement in the use of econometric models, since $r$, one of the key components of user cost is endogenised. The indirect effects of policy initiatives such as long-term debt or equity infusion can now be analysed in terms of their effect on gross additions.

Another area of improvement is the impact of depreciation policy. In defining user cost, both $\delta$ and $Z$ were taken as exogenous to the firm. On the other hand, the direct impact of possible depreciation policy changes on costs, net income and IGF are analysed in great detail in the strat plan framework. For example, shorter lives of capital assets would not only increase annual (straight-line) depreciation and total cost, but also tax deductions for the firm. There would also be an increase in revenue requirements based prices in the short run. The integrated model will capture all of the above and some additional effects:

1. the role of higher output prices in reducing demand depending upon the demand elasticities,
2. the role of increased annual depreciation in increasing the user cost of capital and negative incentive for future investment depending upon the price elasticity of investment,
3. second round effects of decreased demand on expenses, investment and the consequent reduction of tax benefits.

The net changes will depend upon the relative magnitudes of parameters of output and prices in the equations for demand, investment and expenses. It is only after the system has iterated through all the models and converged that the total effect of an exogenous 'shock' can be evaluated.

In practice, policy simulation exercises with this system usually involve a package of policy changes, rather than one change in isolation. The integrated system of econometric and financial models enables the user to trace the direct and indirect effects of each exogenous shock individually as well as in combination with other policy initiatives.

## 11.5 SUMMARY

The main thrust of this chapter is that it is necessary to relate the economics of demand, cost and finance. TFM is a first step in the direction of fully integrating stochastic econometric models of cost and demand with financial models.

The ultimate quality of the results will depend, as before, on the reliability of the estimated parameters in the econometric models. Nevertheless, by incorporating the impact of financial variables into the user cost of capital and into revenue requirements, the interactions of cost and demand are captured more accurately. The integrated system has enabled us to conduct more comprehensive analysis of a richer set of alternative scenarios, in the hope of generating realistic and useful policy recommendations.

### Notes

Of necessity we had to eliminate some of the discussion which would not be of interest to all readers. However, additional details are available from the authors.

1. 'Separations' is a cost allocation scheme used by the telephone industry which arbitrarily divides investment cost between exchange and inter-exchange plant.
2. The original econometric models were developed with the support of PNR & Associates. The work linking econometric models with financial models has been developed with the support of Peat Marwick Mitchell & Co. and PNR & Associates.
3. The resulting estimating equations for capital and labour are:

$$K_t = K(Y_t, q_t, w_t, K_t - 1)$$
$$L_t = L(Y_t, w_t, K_t - 1, \Delta K_t)$$

The level of $L_t$ is conditional in the short run on the level of capital stock and the level of investment.

4. State and interstate prices are appropriately based on the inter-exchange industry revenue requirements.
5. Two key assumptions are employed. First, that capital goods depreciate exponentially. This means the economic depreciation rate is invariant with respect to the interest rate and depreciation becomes a technological parameter. Secondly, the assumption of a constant marginal cost of capital makes the price of new capital $P_k$ exogenous. The simple adjustment for indirect business taxes is ignored in order to focus on the most important components.
6. $K_t = K_{t-1} + \Delta K_t$

$$= \frac{V_i}{P_{ki}} + \frac{GA_t}{P_{kt}} - \frac{R_t}{P_{kh}}$$

where

$V_i$ = gross additions of vintage $i$
$GA_t$ = gross additions in current period
$R_t$ = retirements in period $t$ of vintage $h$
$P_{kh}$ = price index of appropriate category of capital. It is based upon estimates of the average life of capital assets retired.

7. ACRS stands for the accelerated cost recovery depreciation instituted by the Economic Recovery Act of 1981.
8. Prior to 1982, the amount of investment tax credit generally did not reduce the basis of property with respect to which credits were allowed, either for purposes of determining depreciation or determining gain or loss at a taxable disposition of property. Since the enactment of TEFRA, a taxpayer must reduce the basis by one half of the amount of the credit.
9. This is partially offset to the extent that some proportion of current years' retirements may be subject to ITC recapture.
10. The model at present does not permit the investment of surplus cash balance, that is cash balances do not generate any interest income.

## References


ALLEMAN, J. H. and GOETZ, M. (1985) 'Economics of Scale and Scope in Telecommunications. Results from GTE' presented in Advanced Workshop in Public Utility Economics and Regulation, Rutgers University, February.

BERNSTEIN, J. I. (1983) 'Taxes, Financing and Investment for a Regulated Firm', in Courville, L. A. de Fontenay, and R. Dobell (eds), *Economic Analysis of Telecommunications: Theory and Applications*, New York: North-Holland.

BERNSTEIN, J. I. and NADIRI, M. I. (1985) 'Financing and Investment in Plant and Equipment and Research and Development', CV Starr Center Research Report 82–27, New York University.

BOADWAY, R. and BRUCE, N. (1980) 'Alternative Approaches to the Financial and Investment Decisions of the Firm: A Synthesis', Kingston, Queen's University.

CHIRINKO, R. (1985) 'Tobin's Q and Financial Policy', Cornell University Working Paper 332.

HAYASHI, F. (1985) 'Corporate Finance Side of the Q Theory of Investment', *Journal of Public Economics*, vol. 27, no. 3, pp. 261–280.

JORGENSON, D. (1963) 'Capital Theory and Investment Behavior', *American Economic Review*, vol. 53, May, pp. 247–59.

MOHR, M. (1984) 'The Theory and Measurement of the Rental Price of Capital in Industry – Specific Productivity Analysis. A Vintage Rental Price of Capital Model', US Department of Commerce, Bureau of Industrial Economics, BIE-SP84-1, January.

STEIGUM, E. 'A Financial Theory of Investment Behavior', *Econometrica*, vol. 51, no. 3, pp. 637–45.

# Index


access
  cost and demand 178–81
  pricing 79, 81
Acton, J. P. 137
Aigner, D. J. 105n
Alchian, A. A. 45
Alleman, J. H. xi, 2, 4, 171–94
allocative efficiency 8–9, 43
alternative governance structures 9
American Gas Association (AGA) 156, 159, 161
American Telephone and Telegraph Company 1
Archibald, R. B. 137
Atkinson, S. E. 112
Averch, H. 2, 7, 25, 39
Averch–Johnson (A–J) model 25–6, 39
Aumann-Shapley prices 82
automatic fuel adjustment clause (AFC) 11
Axelrod, R. 51–2

Bailey, E. E. 104n, 106n, 130
Baron, D. P. 22n
Baumol, W. J. 85–6, 104n, 133n
Bawa, V. S. 26
Bernstein, J. I. 172
Bhagat, S. 67, 71, 75n
Bidwell, M. O. xi
Bloom, J. A. xi
Boadway, R. 172
Bohi, D. R. 134n
Bowring, J. xi
Boyer, E. xi
Bradford, D. F. 85–6, 104n, 133n
Braeutigam, R. 104n
Brealey, R. 63
Brennan, M. J. 27–8, 39
Brown, D. J. xi, 2–3, 77–82
Brown, R. 105n
Brown, S. 82
Bruce, N. 172

Camfield, R. J. xi
capital
  cost determination 2, 25–40
  user cost of 181–3, 193–4
Cataldo, L. xi
Caves, D. 105n
Chapman, L. 93, 134n
Chirinko, R. 172
Christensen, L. R. 92, 105n
cogeneration/cooling, gas, commercial 4, 155–69
  market for 156–7
  natural gas cogeneration systems 158–9
  natural gas cooling systems 157–8
  study 159–68
commissions, regulatory 1–2, 9–10, 46–7
comparative institutional assessment 7
competition, and price regulation 1–2
costs
  of capital 2, 25–40; user 181–3, 193–4
  economic and financial, telecommunications 4, 171–94
  governance, efficiency 9
  production and transaction 43–4
  of regulation, water 43–61
Cowing, T. 138, 152, 153n
Cox, J. C. 28, 39
Crain, M. xi
Crawford, R. G. 45
cream-skimming 77–8, 80–1

Crew, M. A. xi
governance costs of regulation, water 43–61
productivity incentives and RoR regulation 7–21
regulating utilities in an era of deregulation 1–4
transactions costs of regulation 104
Cross, J. G. 10
Curran, B. xi

Dann, L. Y. 68
De Alessi, T. 112–13
deferred taxes 185–6
demand
charge 157
econometric models 178–81
residential, electricity 137–52
Denny, M. 16–17
Dhatt, M. 75n
Diewert, W. E. 15–16
Dubin, J. 138, 152, 153n
dynamic efficiency 9

Eckels, C. M. 86, 103, 104n
econometric models
electricity, pricing 86–91
telecommunications 171–83
Edgemon, D. L. xi
efficiency
allocative 8–9, 43
dynamic 9
governance cost 9
pricing 111–13, 124–8
production 111–12, 128–30
static 111
X- 9, 43
electricity 1
demand, residential 137–52; model 138–42
and gas cooling 155–6, 159–68
ownership mode 111–33
peak-load pricing 156–7
Ramsey pricing 85–104; econometric model 86–91; estimation 91–9; welfare gains 99–103
equity financing practices 63–75
market efficiency 71–4
rights issues 63–4, 66–8; theory of 65–8
underwritten public issues 63–4, 66–8
utility survey 68–71
Erickson, C. 81

Fare, R. 112
Faulhaber, G. 77–8, 82n
Feldstein, M. 104n
Finifter, D. H. 137
financial and economic costs, telecommunications 171–94
econometric cost and demand models 178–81
methodology of financial model (TFM) 183–90; debt to equity ratio 188–9; taxes 185–8
simulations incorporating TFM 190–4; output 191–2; user cost of capital 193–4
strategic planning model 173–8, 183, 192
user cost of capital 181–3
financing *see* equity financing
Friedlaender, A. F. 106n
Funkhouser, R. 113
Fuss, M. 16–17, 105n

Garbacz, C. xi, 2, 137–52
gas 1
commercial cogeneration/cooling 155–69
George, A. 104n
Goetz, M. 171
Goldberg, V. P. 45
Gollop, F. M. 105n
Gordon, M. J. 76n
governance cost efficiency 9
governance costs of regulation, water 43–61
Greenberg, E. 26
Greene, W. H. 105n
Grosskopf, S. 112
GTE Service Corporation 4, 171–94

Guido, Hon. R. N. xi
Gupta, V. xi, 2, 4, 171-94

Hackensack Water Companies 44
Halvorsen, R. 112, 133n
Hamilton, W. D. 51
Hansen, R. 67, 75n
Hawk, S. L. 65
Hayashi, P. M. xi
pricing efficiency and mode of ownership 2-4, 111-33
Ramsey pricing, electricity 86, 103, 104n, 106n; investment 172
Heal, G. M. xi, 2-3, 77-82
Heinkel, R. 67
Heuer, M. xi

incentive schemes, and RoR regulation 3, 7-21
industry benchmarks 12
Ingersoll, J. E. 28, 39
institutional economics, new 43-4
investment tax credits (ITC) 186-7
Itteilag, R. L. xi, 2, 4, 155-69

Jensen, M. C. 63
Johnson, L. L. 2, 7, 25, 39
Jorgenson, D. W. 92, 181
Joskow, P. 104n, 153n

Karlin, S. 30
Kirschner, D. 137
Klein, B. 45
Kleindorfer, P. R. xii
governance costs of regulation, water 43-61
productivity incentives and RoR regulation 7-21
transactions costs of regulation 104
Klevorick, A. K. 26
Kuh, C. xii

lawyers 53, 55
Le, C. D. 15, 22n
Leibenstein, H. 2, 9, 43
Leland, H. E. 26, 86, 103, 104n, 112
Leventhal, H. 39
Loeb, M. 10
Logan, J. 112
Lusztig, P. 75n

MacAvoy, P. W. 104n, 113
McFadden, D. 137-8, 141, 152, 153n
Magat, W. A. 10
Marino, A. M. 112
Marsh, P. 75n
Marshall W. J. 26
Mashaw, J. 47, 61
Mastrangelo, C. xii
Meyer, R. A. 86, 103, 104n, 112
Mikkelson, W. K. 68
Mirman, L. 82
Mitchell, B. M. 137
Moody, C. E., Jr 137
Moran, E. A. xii
Mount, T. 93, 134n
Mulligan, J. G. xii
Munk, K. J. 104n
Murray, M. P. 137
Myers, S. 63

Nadiri, M. I. 172
National Association of Water Companies (NAWC) 44
National Interim Energy Consumption Survey (NIECS) 137-8, 142, 144
natural monopoly 43, 45
Nelson, J. P. xii, 2, 4, 85-104
Nelson, R. A. 86, 103, 104n, 105n
Neuberg, L. C. 112
Nordin, J. 140, 145
Norgaard, R. xii

Olley, R. E. 15, 22n
ownership, mode of, and pricing efficiency 3-4, 111-33
cost equation 119-23
demand elasticities 124
empirical model 116-19

evaluation of pricing efficiency 124–8
evaluation of production efficiency 128–30
welfare maximising 113–16

Panzar, J. C. 106n
Parsons, J. 67
Parti, M. and C. 137
Patterson, C. S. xii, 2–3, 63–75
peak-load pricing 156–7
Peltzman, S. 104
Perrakis, S. 26
Pescatrice, D. R. 112
Pinkerton, J. M. 67, 75n
policy, regulatory 1
asymmetric 2
under uncertainty (*q. v.*) 25–40
Posner, R. 104
pricing
access 79, 81
Aumann–Shapley 82
efficiency 111–13, 124–8
marginal cost 91
monopoly 91
and ownership mode 3–4, 111–33
peak-load 156–7
regulation of 1–2; *see also* commissions
*see also* Ramsey pricing
Prisoner's Dilemma 50–3
private and public firms *see under* ownership
production costs 43–4
production efficiency, relative 111–12, 128–30
productivity incentives 11–19
application of 19–21
and RoR regulation 3, 7–21
total factory 12
public and private firms *see under* ownership
Public Utility Regulatory Policies Act (1978) 1
Puig, C. 137
Pusateri, T. xii

Ramsey pricing 3
efficiency 111–13, 124–8
electricity 85–104, 111–33
telecommunications 77–82
rate-of-return (RoR) regulation 45–6
opportunities for improving 8–12
and productivity incentives (*q. v.*) 7–21
transactions costs of 47–60
under uncertainty (*q. v.*) 25–40
Raviv, A. 67
regulation 45–7
*see also* utilities
relative production efficiency 111–12, 128–30
rent-seeking 45, 47, 52–3
residential electricity demand 137–52
model 138–42
Residential Energy Consumption Survey (RECS) 138, 150, 152n
rights issues 63–75
theory 65–6
Roberts, M. J. xii, 2, 4, 85–104, 105n
Rodgers, J. D. xii
Ross, S. A. 28, 39
Ross, T. W. 113–15
Rowley, C. K. 7, 44

Sappington, D. 15
Schlenger, D. L. xii, 2, 9, 43–61
Schwartz, E. S. 27–8, 39, 67
Scott, F. A. 22n
'secret' data 137–8, 142, 150–1
Sep/Sim model 180–1
Sevier, M. xii
pricing efficiency and mode of ownership 2–4, 111–33
Ramsey pricing, electricity 86, 103, 104n, 106n
Sharkey, W. 78, 80
Sherman, R. 104n, 112
Shleifer, A. 12, 15
Sibley, D. 15, 82
Sibley, D. S. 26
Smith, C. W. 63, 67, 71, 75n

Smith, P. B. xii
Smith, R. L. 74n
social welfare function 25, 30, 39–40
  *see also* Ramsey pricing
Sohlberg, R. 137
Spier, K. 82n
static efficiency 111
Steigum, E. 172
Stevenson, R. E. 105n
Stigler, G. J. 104
stochastic models
  econometric 171–83
  equilibrium 28, 39
strategic planning model (strat plan) 173–8, 183, 192
Sudit, E. F. 13
Swanson, C. A. xii, 2, 4, 155–69

Taggart, R. A. 22n
Tam, M. S. 16, 19, 133n
Tauman, Y. 82
Tax Equity and Fiscal Responsibility Act (1982) 186, 195n
taxes
  deferred 185–6
  effective federal income tax rate 187–8
  investment tax credits 186–7
Taylor, H. M. 30
Taylor, L. D. 106n, 133–4n
telecommunication financial model (TFM) 172, 183–4, 190–4
telecommunications 1
  economic and financial costs (*q. v.*) 4, 171–94
  Ramsey pricing 3, 77–82
Telser, L. 78, 80
Thatcher, L. W. 65
Thompson, H. E. xii, 2, 25–40
tit-for-tat 51–2
transactions costs of governance, water 2, 43–61
Trapani, J. M. xii
  pricing efficiency and mode of ownership 2–4, 111–33
  Ramsey pricing, electricity 86, 103, 104n, 106n
Tromp, E. P. xii, 2, 4, 85–104
Tullock, G. 44–5, 53
Tyrell, G. 93, 134n

uncertainty, regulatory policy under 25–40
  effect of regulatory controls 31–9
  social welfare function 30, 39–40
  valuation equation 27–9
underwritten issues 63–75
Ursel, N. D. xii, 2–3, 63–75
user cost of capital 181–3, 193–4
utilities
  control of earned RoR 25–40
  demand modelling, residential, electricity 137–52
  equity financing 63–75
  financial and economic costs, telecommunications 171–94
  gas cogeneration/cooling 155–69
  governance costs, water 43–61
  ownership, electricity 111–33
  productivity incentives 7–21
  Ramsey pricing: electricity 85–104; telecommunications 77–82
  regulation of 1–4, 45–7
  under uncertainty 25–40

Vogelsang, I. 15, 19

water supply 1
  governance costs of regulation 43–61
Waverman, L. 105n
Weitzman, M. 16
welfare, social 25, 30, 39–40
  *see also* Ramsey pricing
White, R. 75n
Williamson, O. E. 7, 10, 43, 45
Willig, R. D. 104n, 106–7n

X-efficiency 9, 43

Yawitz, J. B. 26

Zang, I. 82